CONTEMPORARY ART

FROM CRESCENT MOON PUBLISHING

The Art of Andy Goldsworthy: Complete Works: Special Edition
by William Malpas

The Art of Andy Goldsworthy
by William Malpas

Andy Goldsworthy: Touching Nature
by William Malpas

Andy Goldsworthy In Close-Up
by William Malpas

Richard Long: The Art of Walking
by William Malpas

The Art of Richard Long: Complete Works: Special Edition
by William Malpas

Constantin Brancusi: Sculpting the Essence of Things
by James Pearson

Alison Wilding: The Embrace of Sculpture
by Susan Quinnell

Eric Gill: Nuptials of God
by Anthony Hoyland

*The Erotic Object: Sexuality in Sculpture
From Prehistory to the Present Day*
by Susan Quinnell

Minimal Art and Artists in the 1960s and After
by Laura Garrard

Land Art, Earthworks, Installations, Environments, Sculpture
by William Malpas

*Land Art: A Complete Guide to Landscape, Environmental,
Earthworks, Nature, Sculpture and Installation Art*
by William Malpas

Richard Long In Close-Up
by William Malpas

Land Art In Close-Up
by William Malpas

*Colourfield Painting: Minimal, Cool, Hard Edge, Serial
and Post-Painterly Abstract Art From the Sixties to the Present*
by Laura Garrard

Mark Rothko: The Art of Transcendence
by Julia Davis

Jasper Johns: Painting By Numbers
by L.M. Poole

William Malpas has written books on land art (including land art in the U.K. and land art in the U.S.A.), Richard Long, and three books on Andy Goldsworthy (his first study of Goldsworthy, *Andy Goldsworthy: Touching Nature,* was published in 1994).

Andy Goldsworthy
In America

ANDY GOLDSWORTHY

IN AMERICA

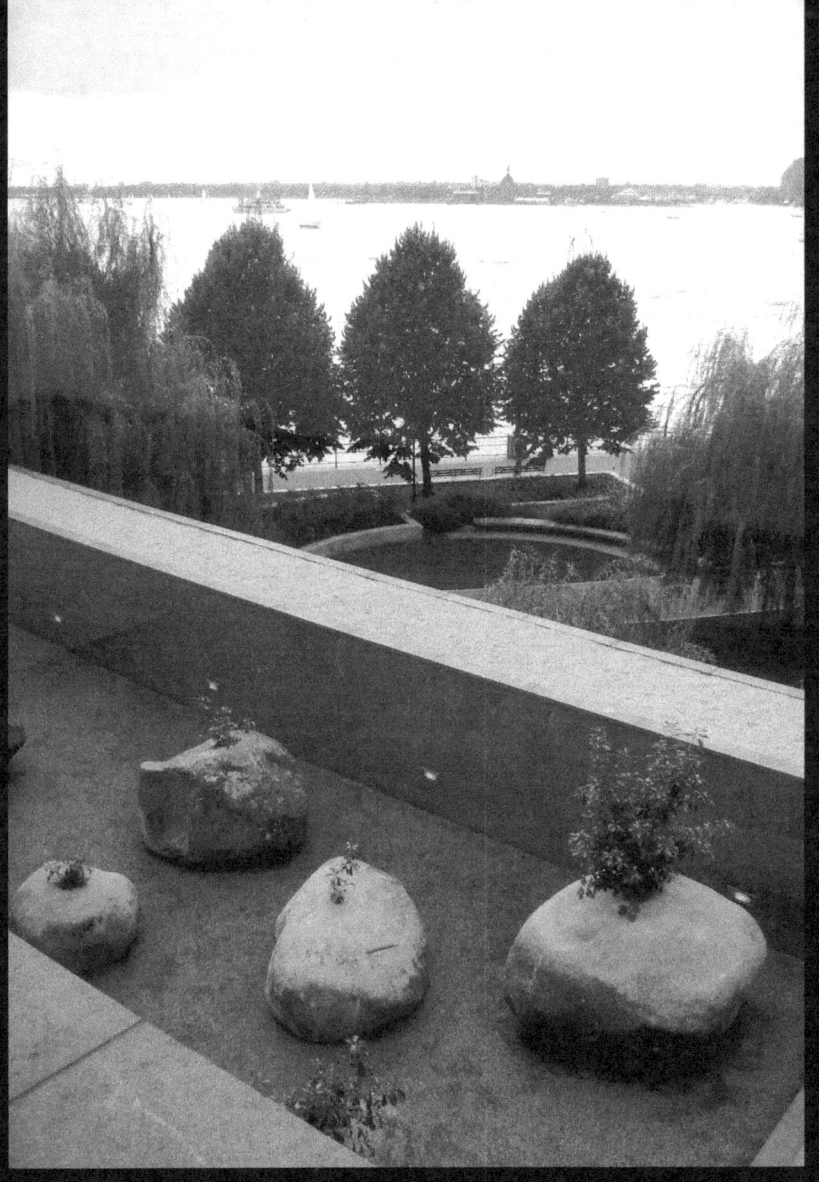

WILLIAM MALPAS

CRESCENT MOON

CRESCENT MOON PUBLISHING
P.O. Box 393
Maidstone
Kent, ME14 5XU
United Kingdom

First published 2011.
© William Malpas 2011.

Printed and bound in the U.S.A.
Set in Rotis Serif 10 on 14pt.
Designed by Radiance Graphics.

British Library Cataloguing in Publication data

Malpas, William
Andy Goldsworthy In America – 1st ed. – (Sculptors Series)
1. Goldsworthy, Andy, 1956 – Criticism and interpretation
2. Outdoor sculpture – United States
I. Title

730. 9'2

ISBN-13 9781861713049

Contents

Acknowledgements

Thanks to Andy Goldsworthy; Ellie Hall; Viking Press, London; Penguin, London; Thames & Hudson, London; Cameron Books, Moffat; Harry N. Abrams, New York; Michael Hue-Williams Gallery/ Albion, London; Henry Moore Centre for Sculpture, Leeds; Storm King Art Center, New York; Fabian Carlsson, London; Galerie Lelong, New York; Galerie S65, Aalst; Galerie Aline Vidal, Paris; Haines Gallery, San Francisco; the British Museum, London.

Thanks to the authors quoted and their publishers.

Illustrations by Andy Goldsworthy © Andy Goldsworthy.

Thanks to the copyright holders of the illustrations:
Musée d'Art Moderne de la Ville de Paris. Tate Modern, London. John Weber Gallery, New York. Chinati Foundation, Texas. Lisson Gallery, London. Howard Lipman, Connecticut. Richard Long. Hamish Fulton. Chris Drury. Carl Andre. James Turrell. Christo. Walter de Maria. Michael Heizer.

Andy Goldsworthy's art dealers: Fabian Carlsson, London; Galerie Lelong, New York; Galerie S65, Aalst; Haines Gallery, San Francisco; Springer und Winckler, Berlin; and Michael Hue-Williams Gallery, London.

Abbreviations

ANDY GOLDSWORTHY

S	*Andy Goldsworthy: Stone*
AG	*Andy Goldsworthy,* 1990
HE	*Hand to Earth: Andy Goldsworthy, Sculpture, 1976-1990*
SS	*Snowballs in Summer Installation*
RSS	*Rain sun snow hail mist calm*
WH	*Winter Harvest*
MC	*Mountains and Coast, Autumn into Winter*
Sh	*Sheepfolds*
W	*Wood*
BS	*Black Stones*
TM	*Time Machine*
Wall	*Wall*
A	*Arch*
MS	*Midsummer Snowballs*
T	*Time*
RA	*Réfuges d'Art*
P	*Passage*

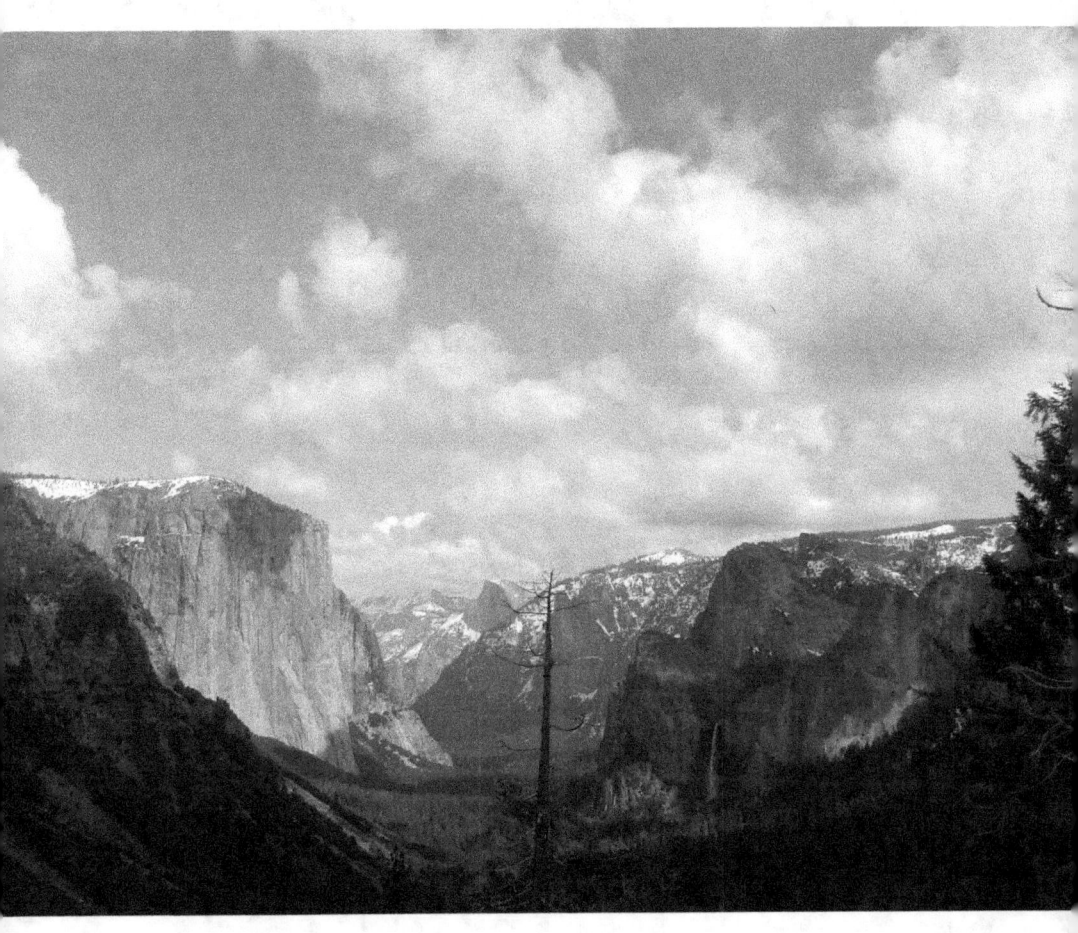

Andy Goldsworthy is working in a country famous
for its extraordinary landscapes.

On the following pages are some images of America
which I took in 2008 and 2009, beginning with Yosemite Valley in California

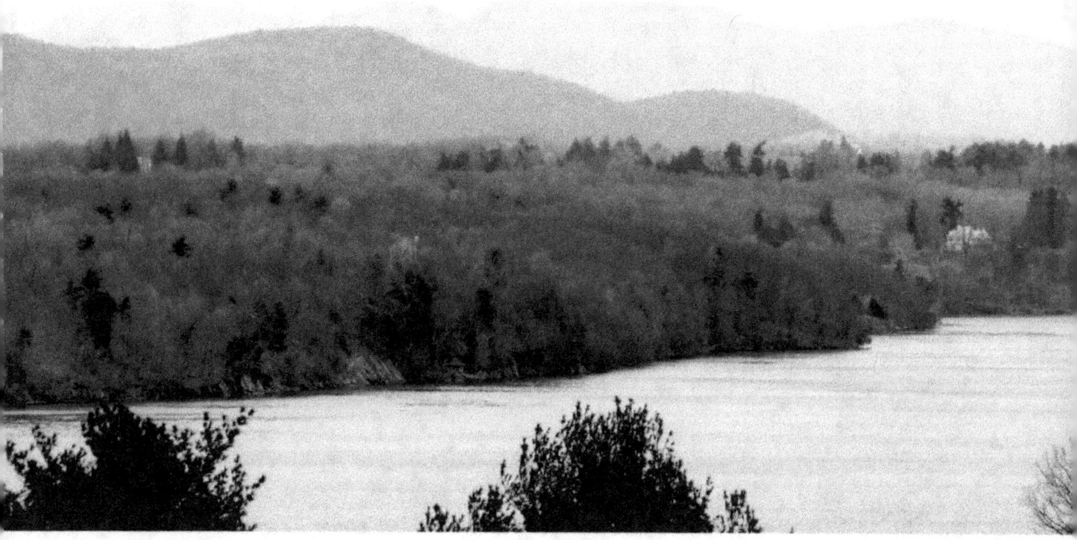

The Hudson River Valley, above.
Niagara Falls, below.

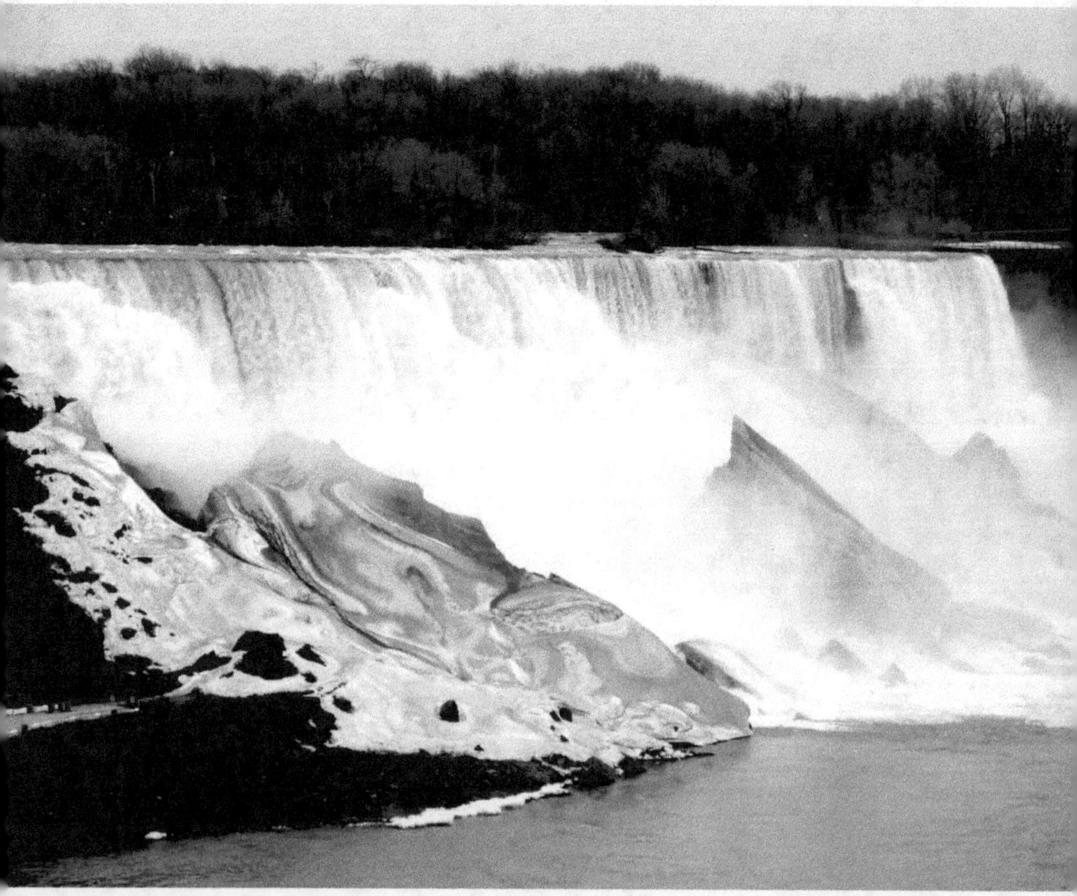

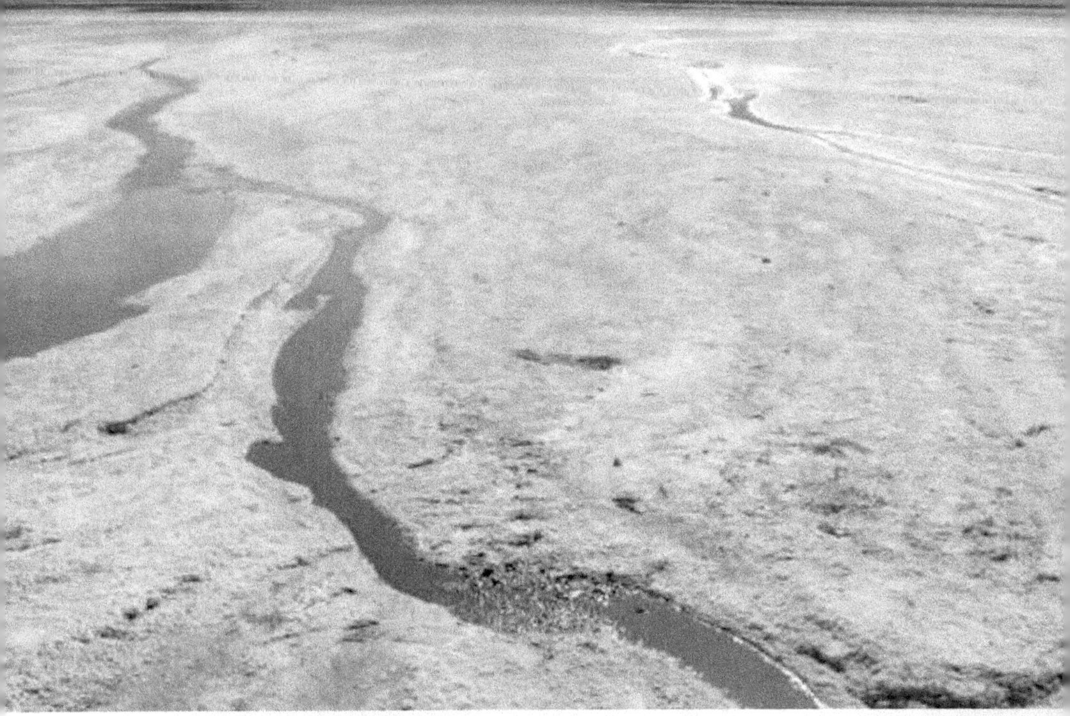

The Californian desert: Zabriskie Point (below),
and salt flats at Death Valley (above).

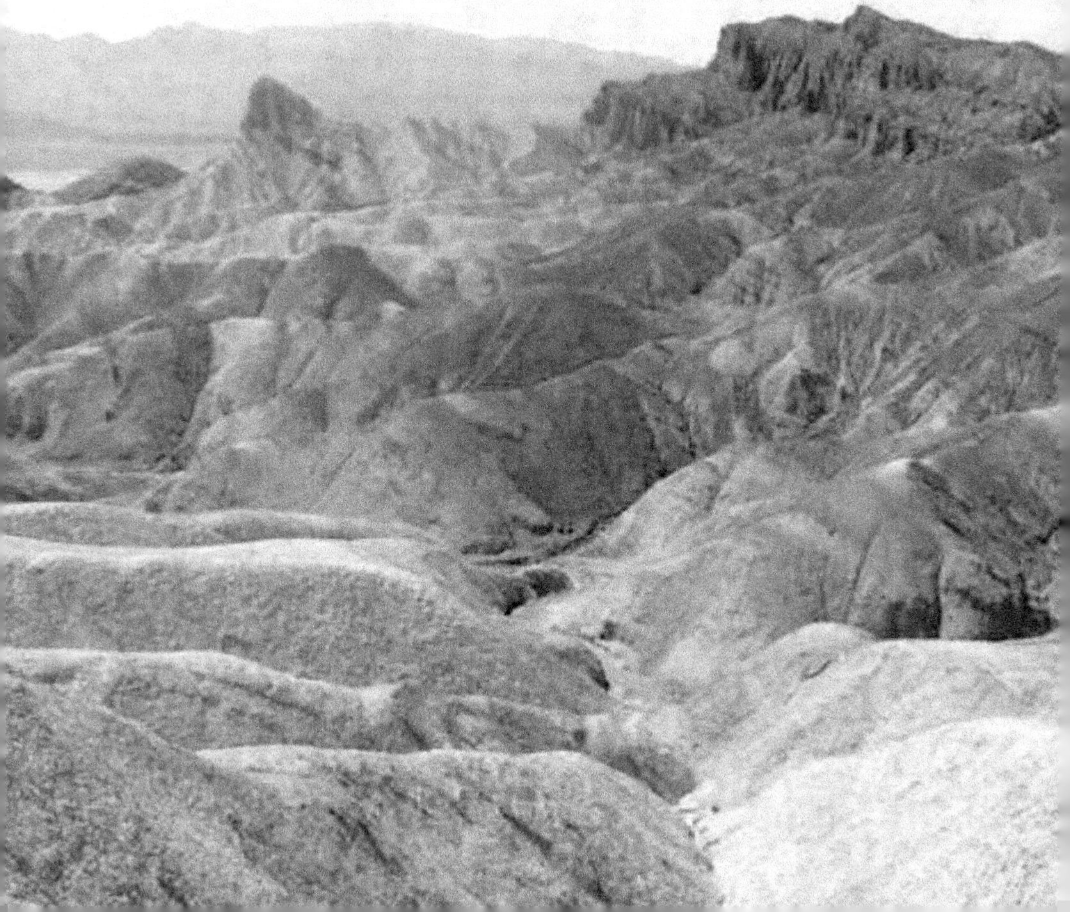

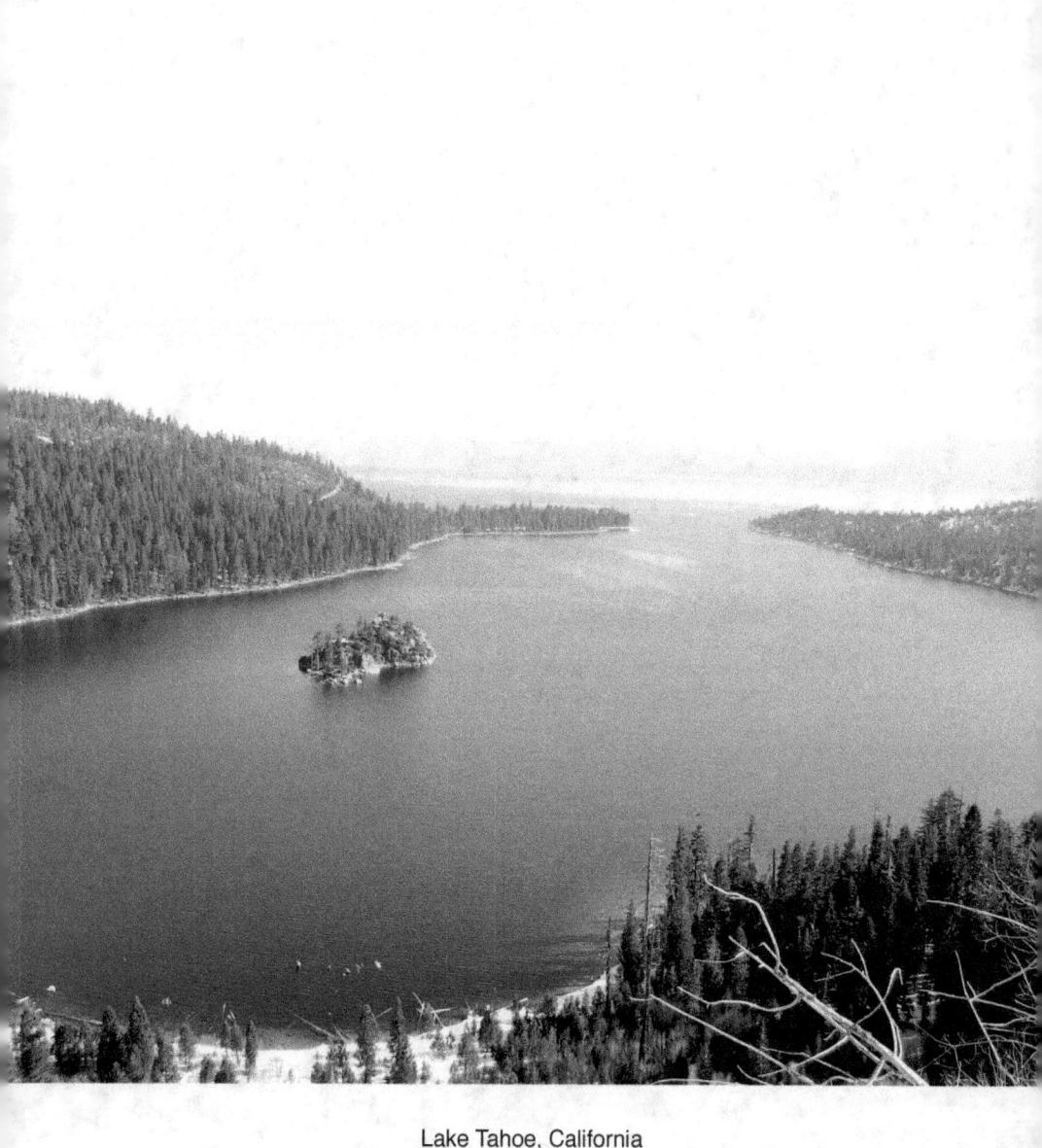

Lake Tahoe, California

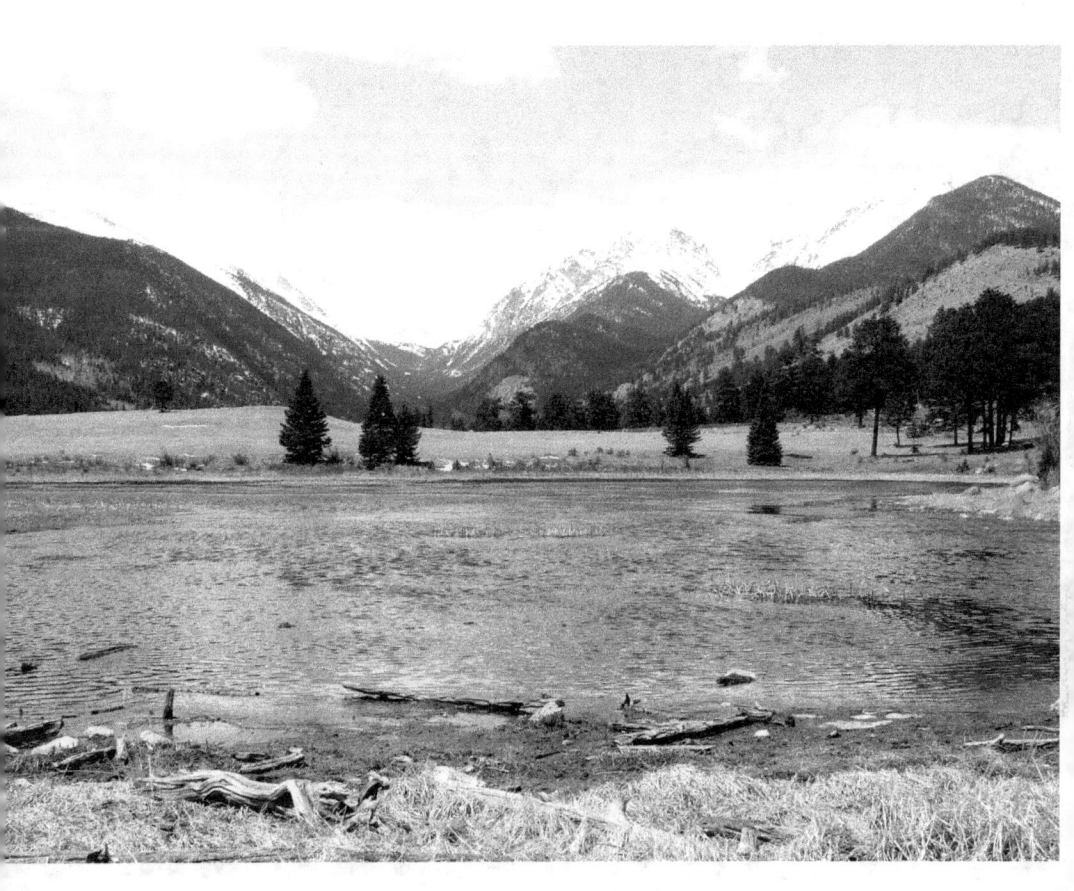

The Rockies, Colorado

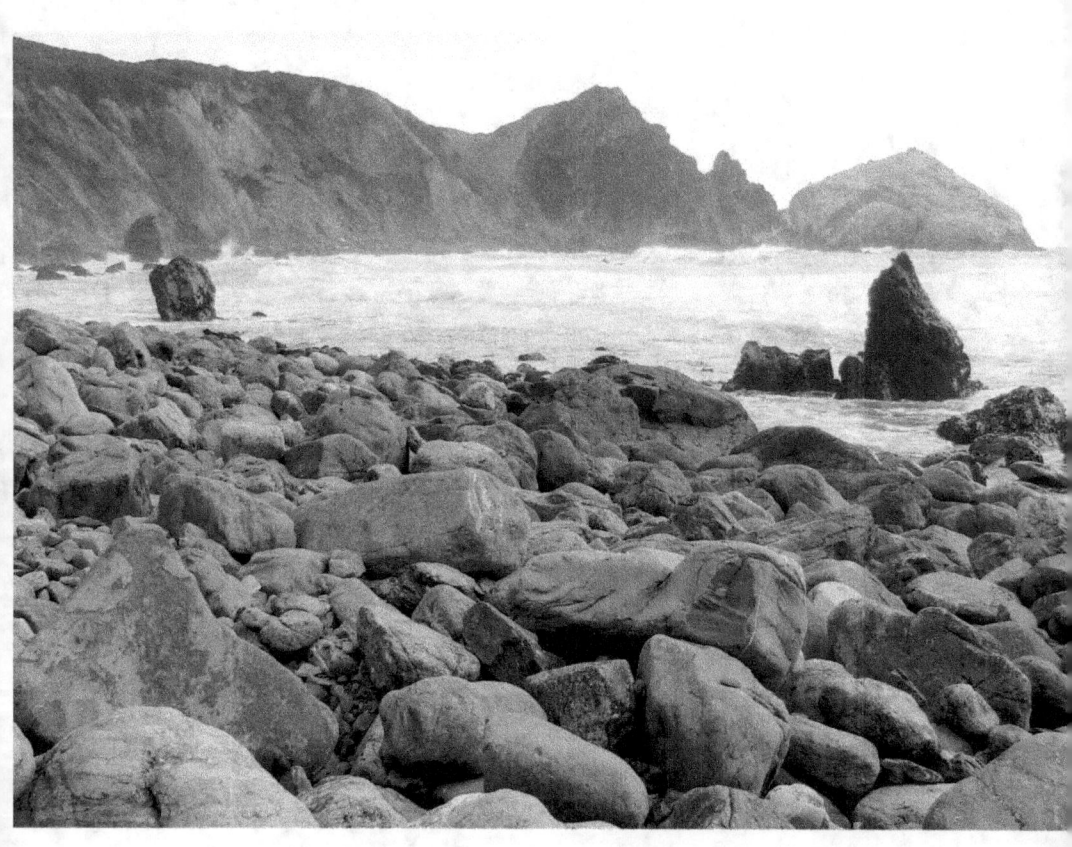

The Pacific coast near San Simeon, California

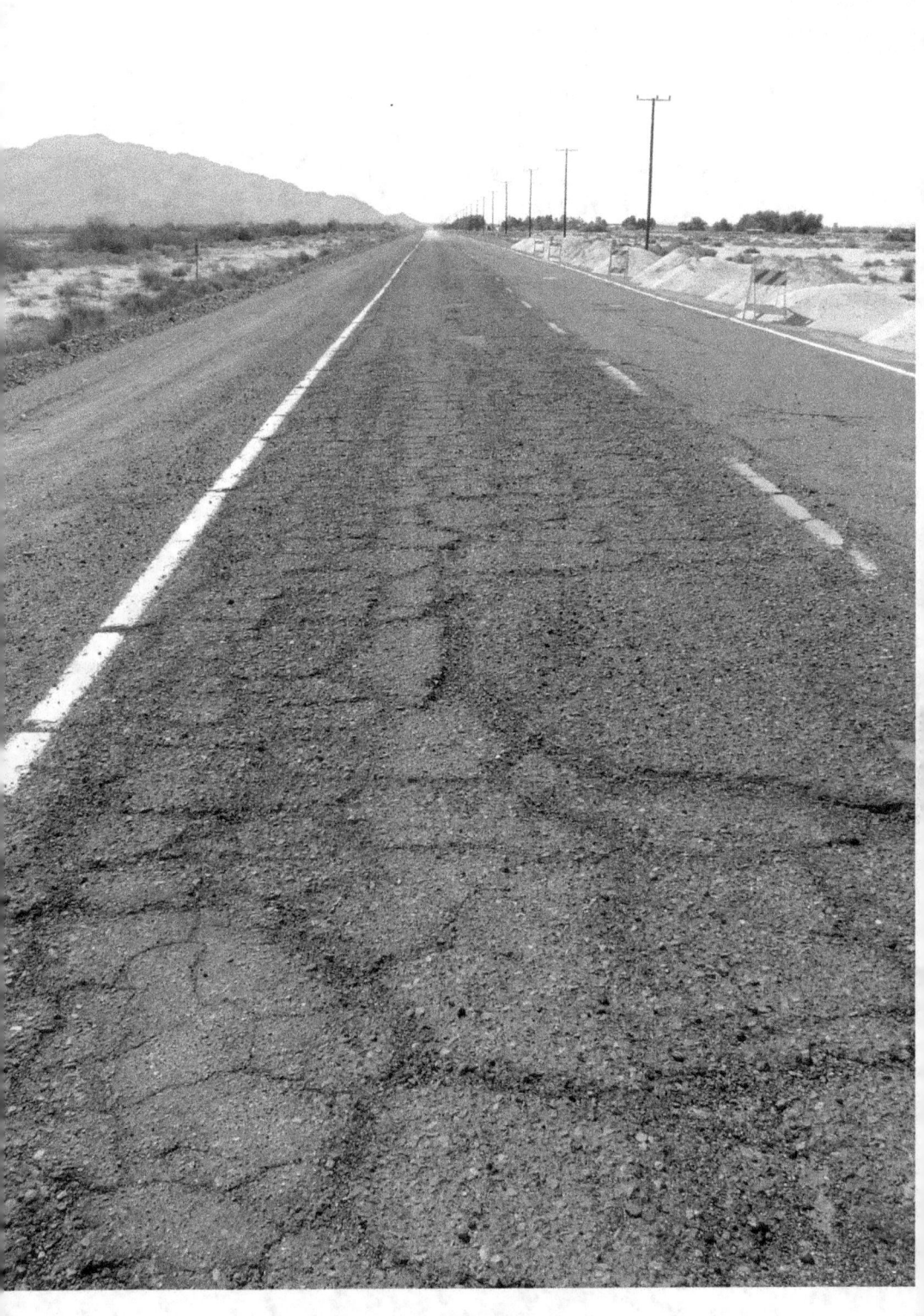

The 'Mother Road', Route 66 in California

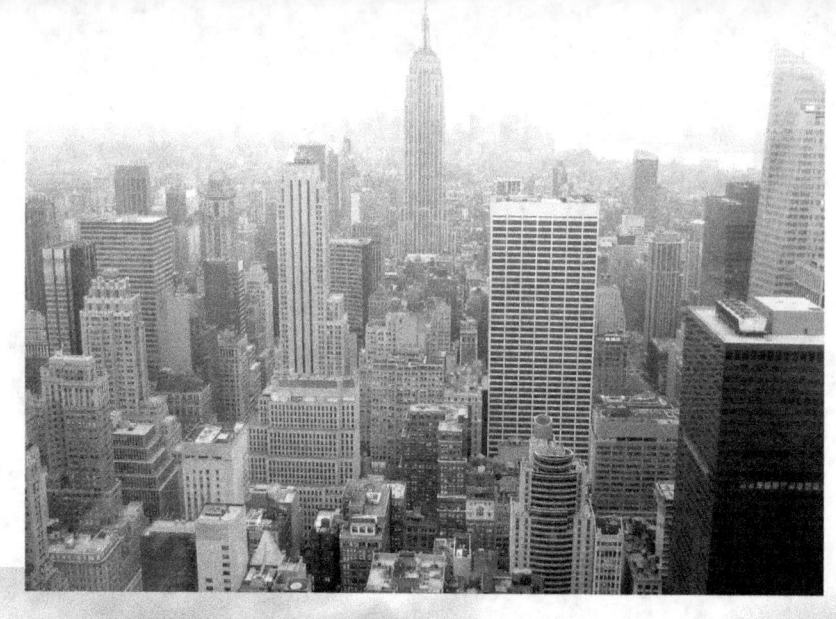

Some of America's spectacular cities:
Gotham (above), L.A. (bottom), and Chicago (below).

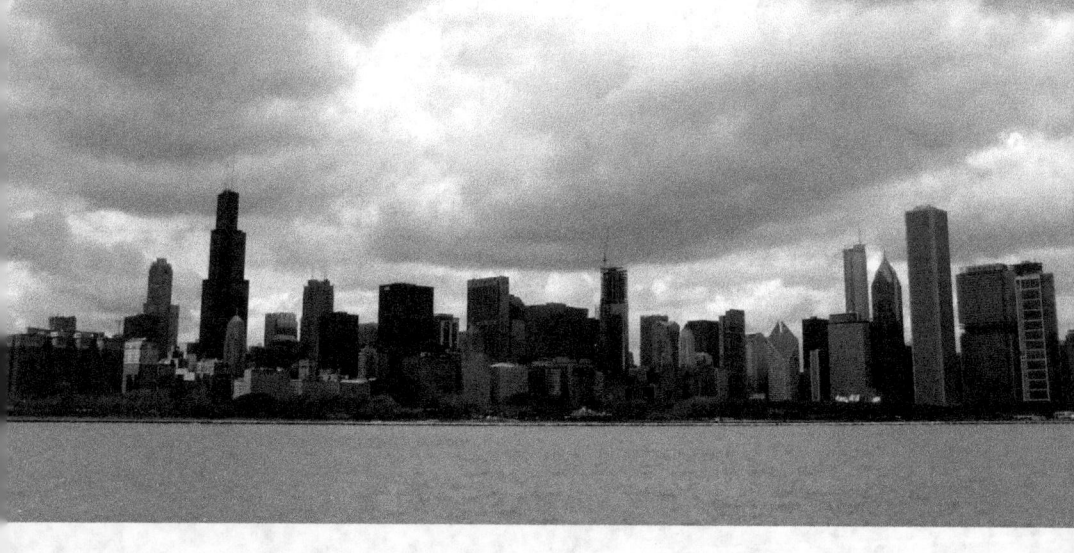

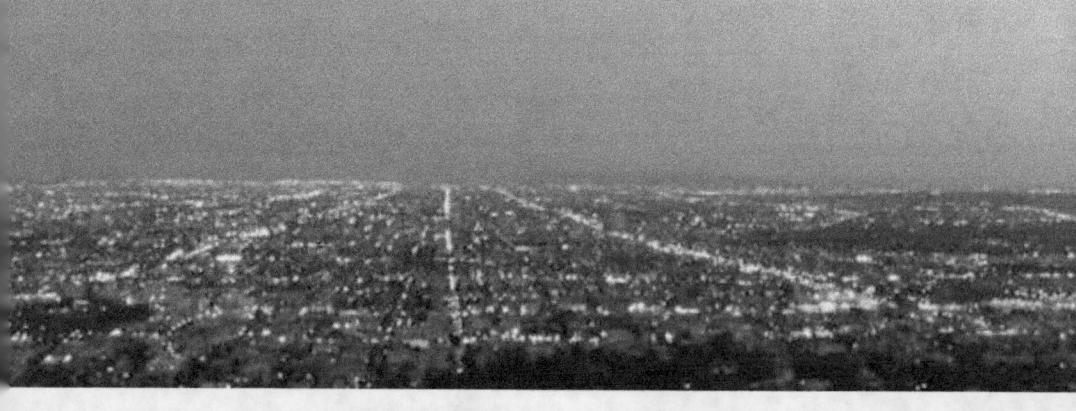

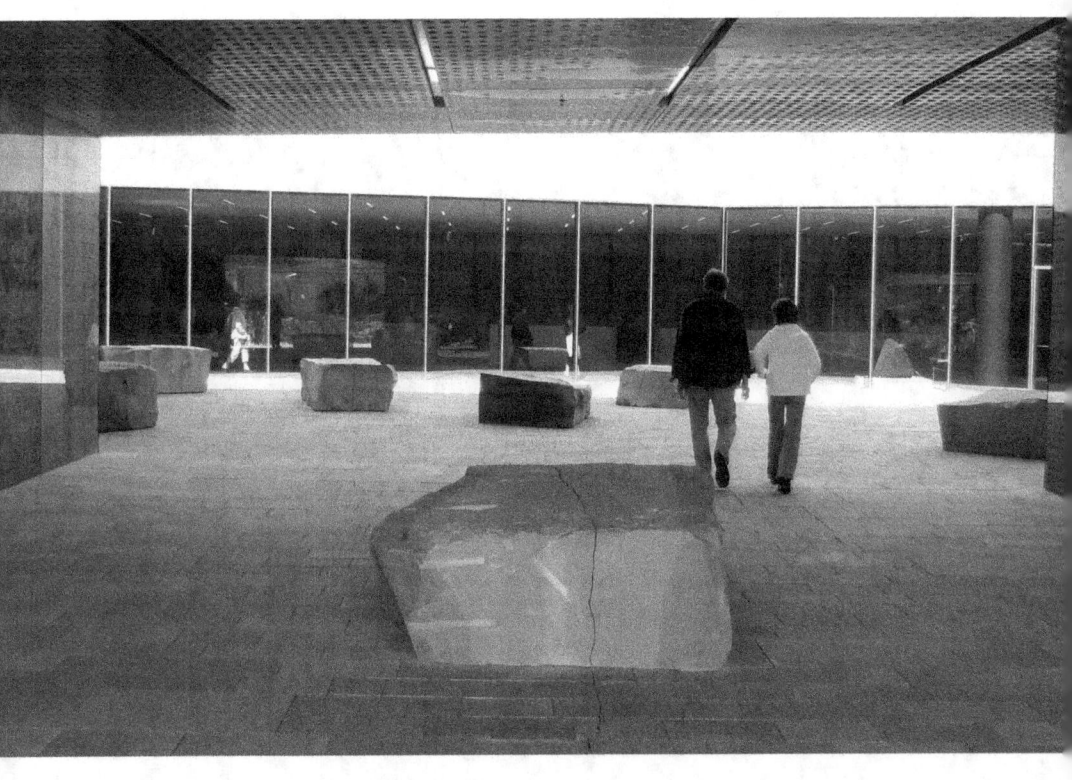

Some of Andy Goldsworthy's recent works in the United States of America
are shown on this page and the followng pages.

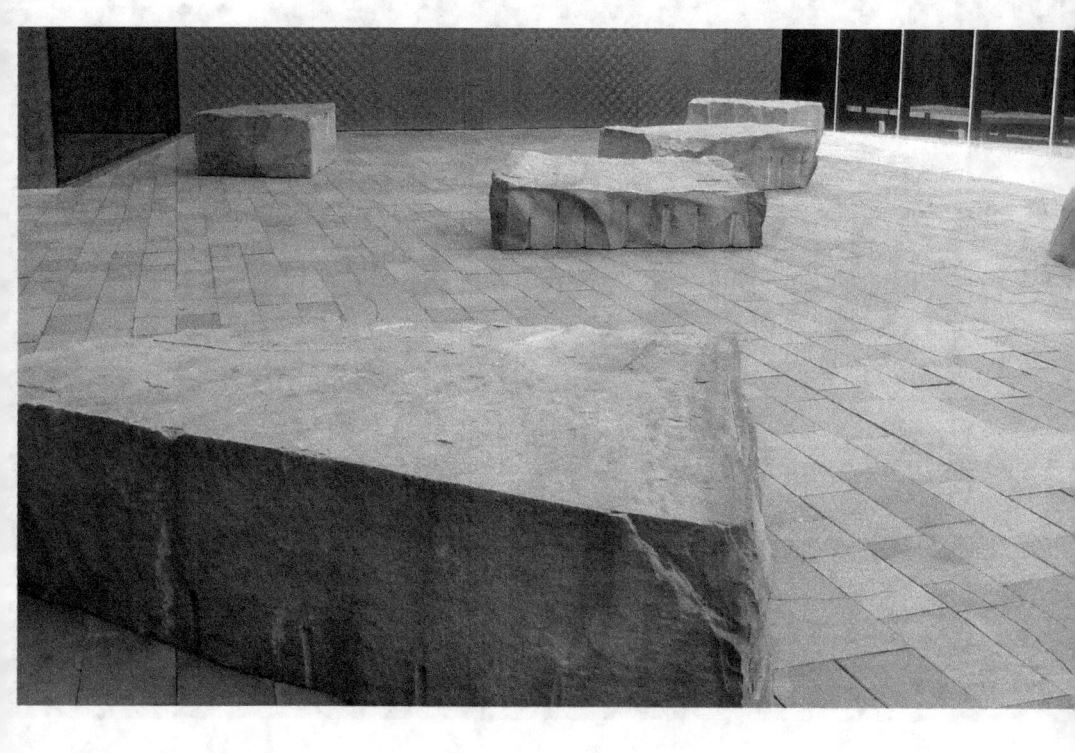

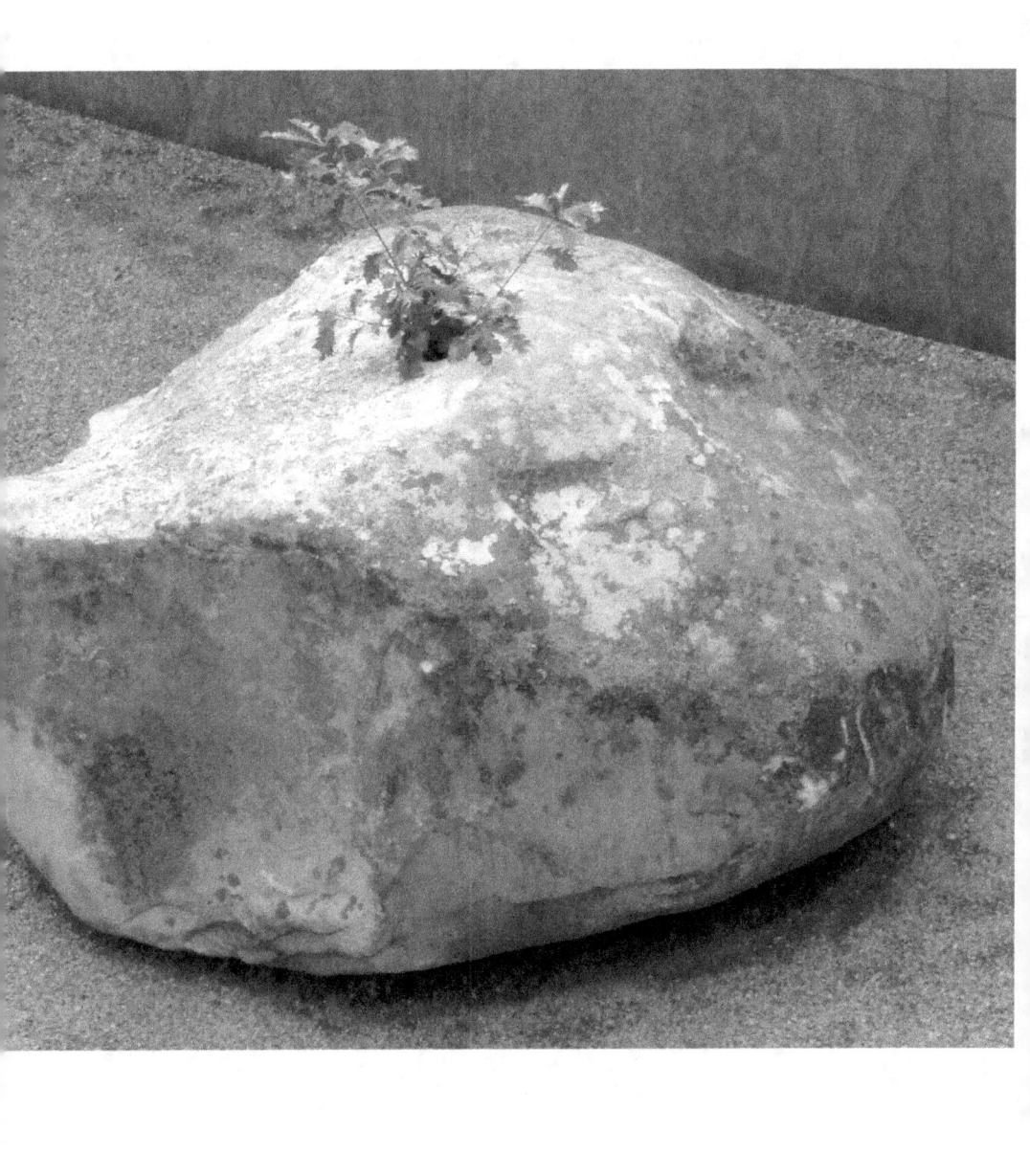

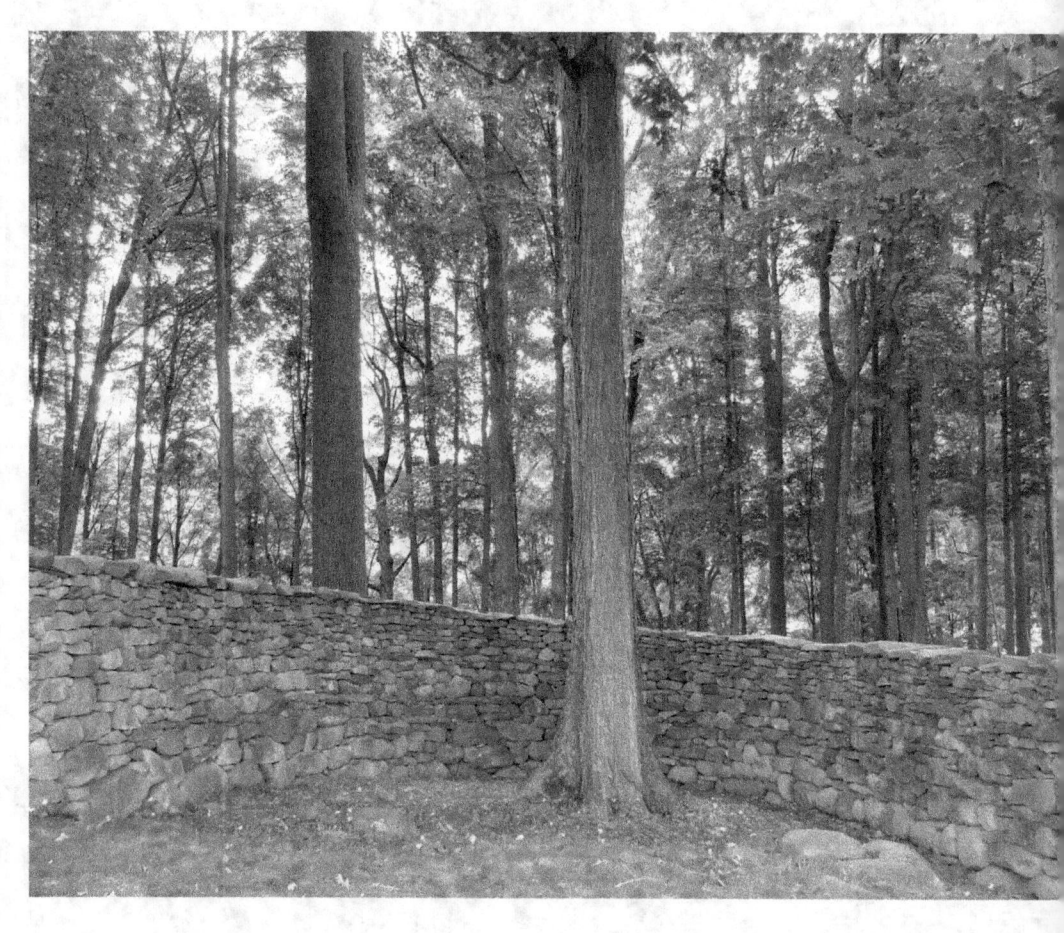

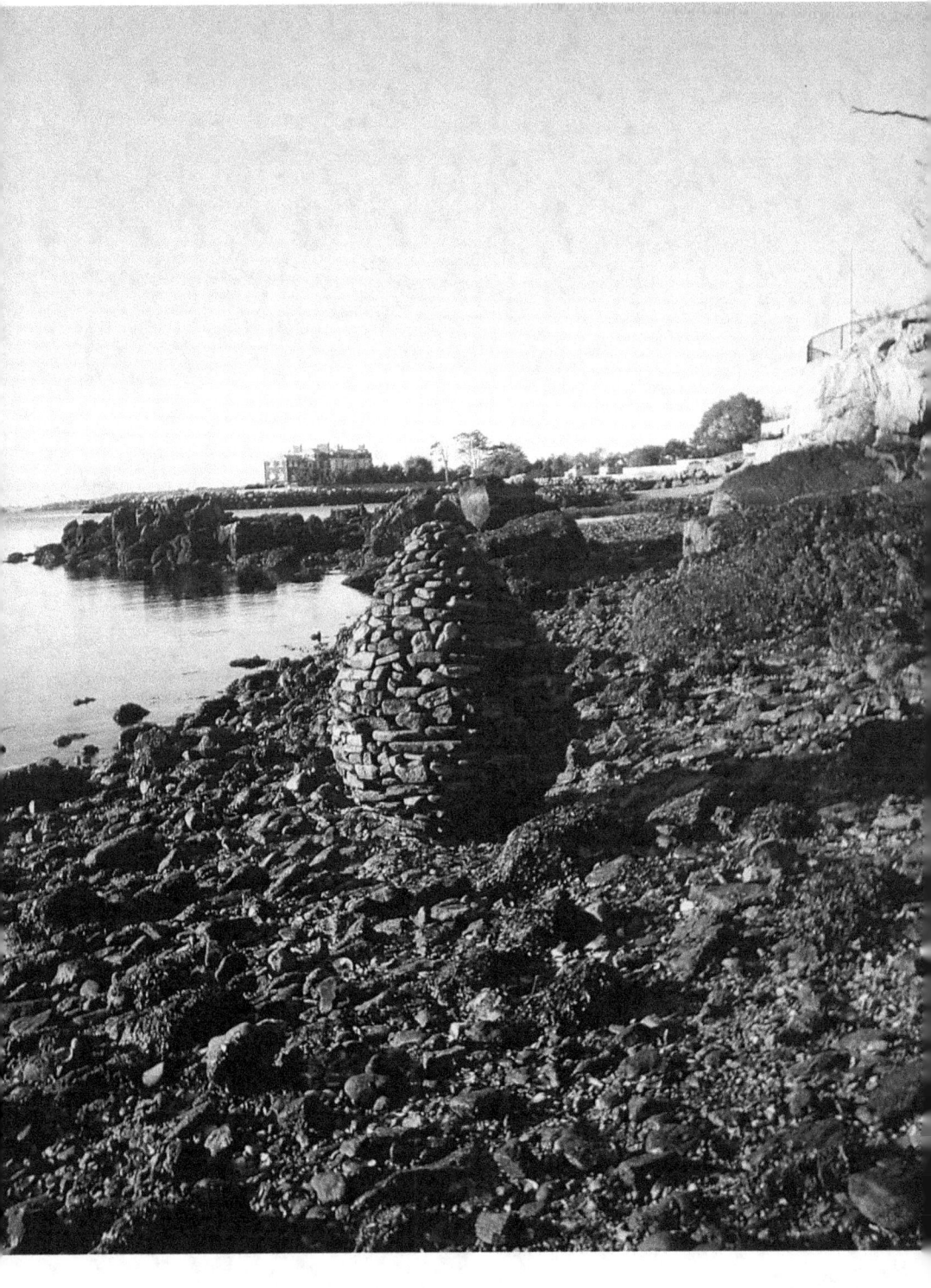

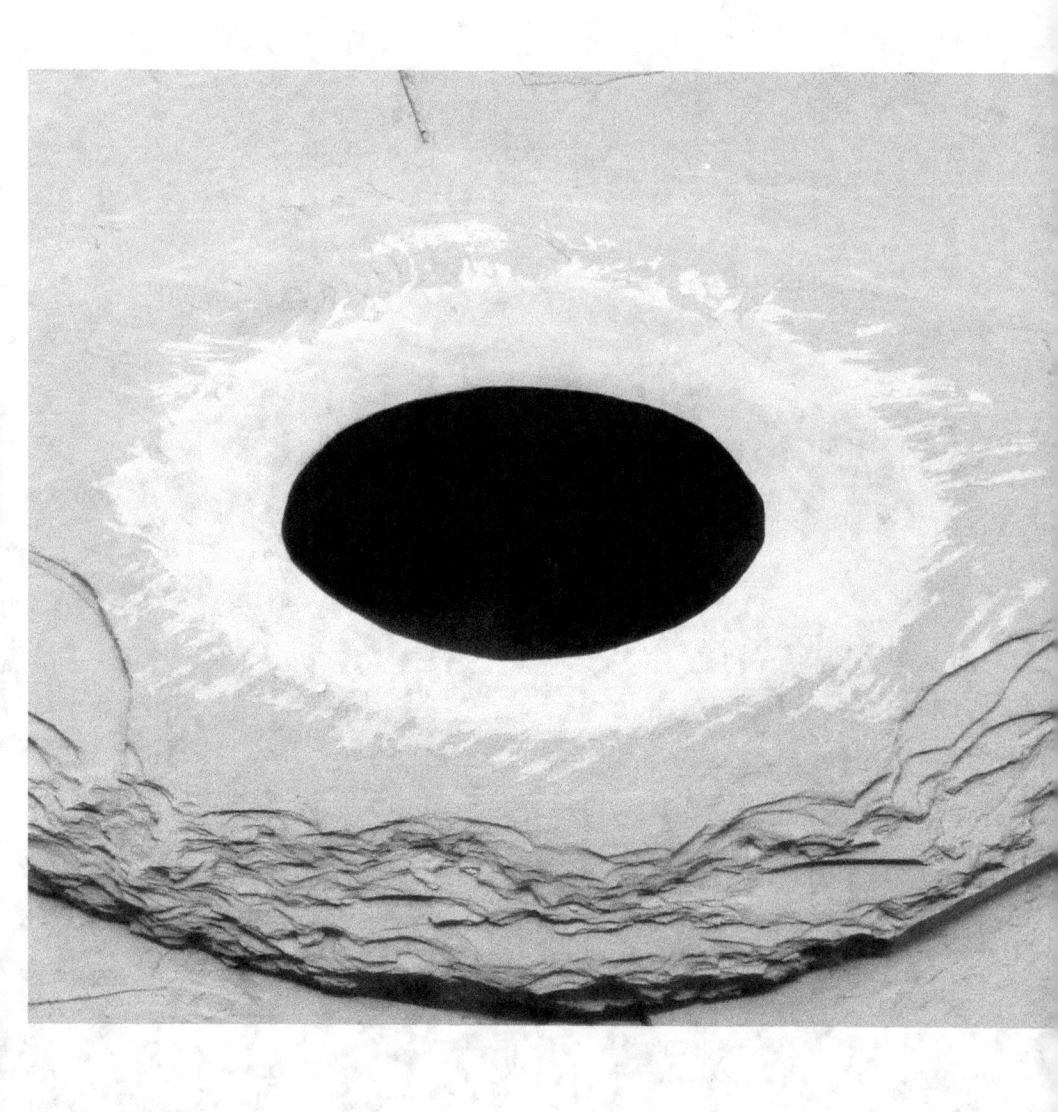

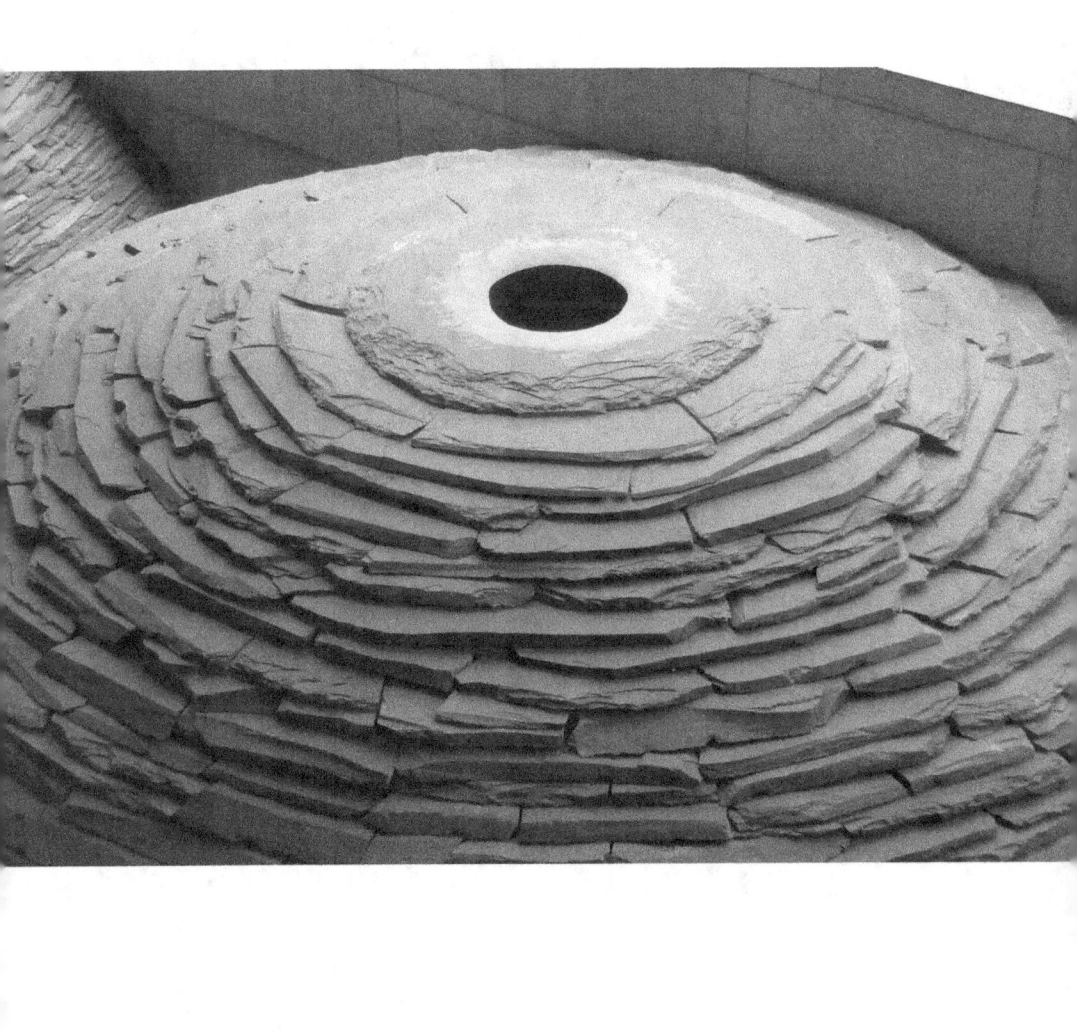

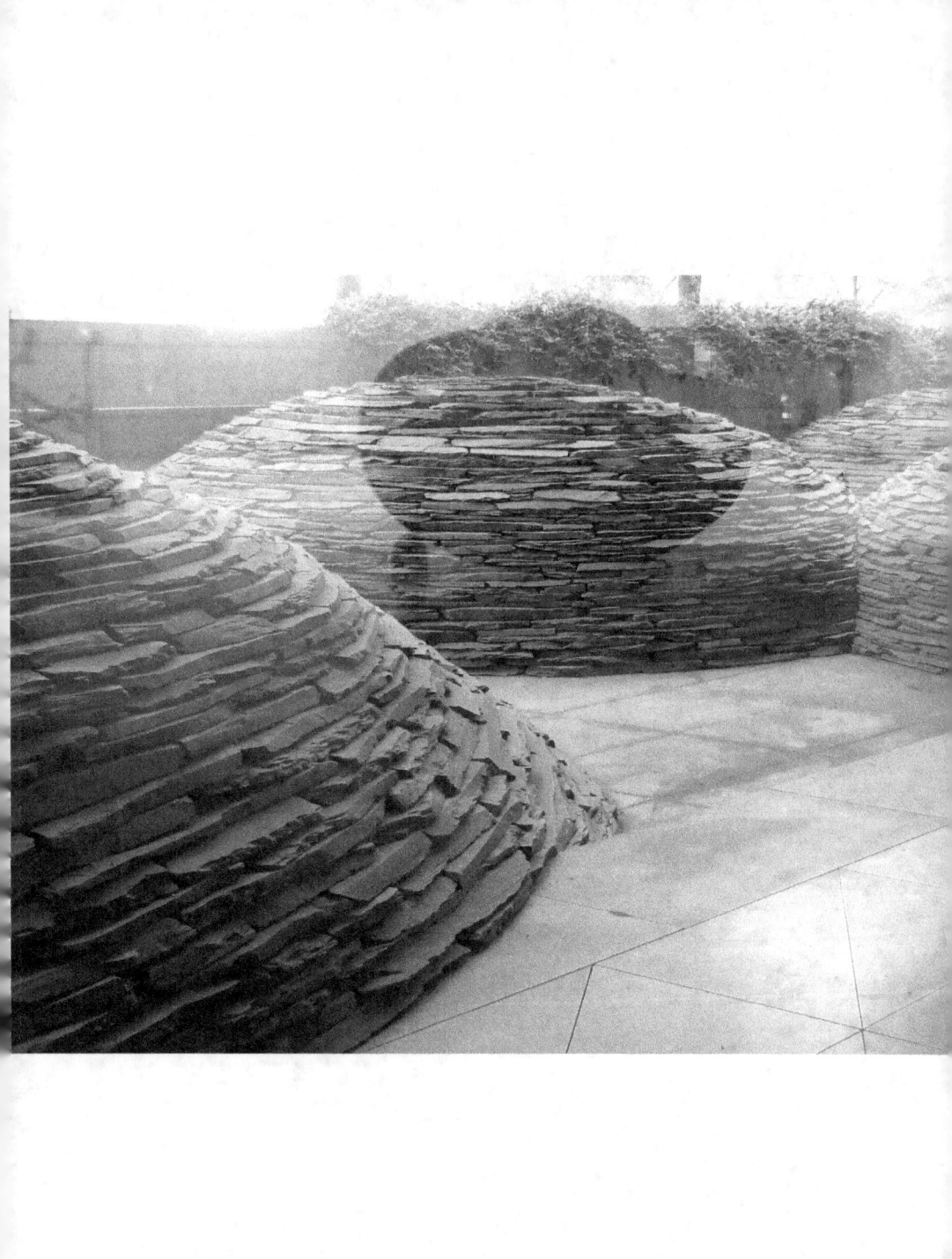

INTRODUCTION

This study looks at the contemporary British artist, Andy Goldsworthy, and his work in the United States of America. Goldsworthy's presence in America grew steadily with a series of exhibitions beginning in the late Nineties with the *Storm King Wall* and show. This was followed by: Cornell University in 2000; the *Three Cairns* show and installations in 2002-03; Austin Museum in 2003; the *Garden of Stone* and *Stone Houses* in New York City in 2003-04; and *Roof* in Washington in 2005.

There are a number of essential sites to visit for Andy Goldsworthy in America: (1) the mounds in Washington's National Gallery of Art; (2) *Garden of Stones* in New York's Museum of Jewish Heritage; (3) the cracked stones at the de Young Museum and *Spire* in San Francisco; (4) the *Storm King Wall* in New York; and (5) *Three Cairns* in Des Moines, Iowa.

Andy Goldsworthy's sculpture grew out of modernism and, in particular, 1960s art, the era of late Henry Moore, Robert Morris, Robert Smithson, Yves Klein, Michael Heizer, Anthony Caro, William Tucker, Tony Smith and Phillip King. It was the 1960s-70s era of what Rosalind Krauss called 'expanded field' sculpture, the High Renaissance of land art. The whole planet became a site for art.[1] Krauss's 'expanded field' sculptors included Robert Irwin, Michael Heizer, Richard Serra, Walter de Maria, Sol LeWitt, Bruce Nauman, Alice Aycock, Mary Miss, Dennis Oppenheim, Nancy Holt, George Trakis, Richard Long, Hamish Fulton, Christo and Joel Shapiro. The artists that impressed Goldsworthy at art college included Gordon Matta-Clark, Mark Boyle, Ben Nicholson, Yves Klein and land artist Christo. In his *Sheepfolds* book (1996) some of the artists that Goldsworthy cited as important included Ben Nicholson, Paul Nash, Joseph Beuys, David Nash and Constantin Brancusi (Hokusai is also noted). Goldsworthy attended lectures by Richard Long and David Nash at Preston Polytechnic when they visited in 1978 (both Long and Goldsworthy have noted that it was more common in the mid-1970s to hear about new art and artists from Europe and the States rather than from Britain).

Goldsworthy admired Henry Moore and Barbara Hepworth, two of the biggest names in 20th century British sculpture (and both, like Goldsworthy, were associated with the North of England). Goldsworthy exhibited at the Yorkshire Sculpture Park and the Henry Moore Centre. In *Passage* Goldsworthy describes visiting Hepworth's wonderful gallery and sculpture garden in St Ives, Cornwall, in 2003, and taking some friends to see Moore's *King and Queen* sculpture (1952-53), which's situated at Glenkiln in Scotland (P, 68).

Among the artists who are very close to Goldsworthy's art in their works are Richard Long, Chris Drury, David Nash, Giuseppe Penone and Nils Udo. Some of those artists have fashioned sculptures that are so close to Goldsworthy's own, they can easily be mistaken for Goldsworthy's (Nash, Long and Udo). Some of Giuliano Mauri's woven sculptures, hanging from trees or sited in pools, recall Goldsworthy's art.

---

1 R. Krauss, 1979.

This book includes material from my previous books, *Andy Goldsworthy: Touching Nature* (Crescent Moon, 2007) and *The Art of Andy Goldsworthy* (2007).

I have included some photographs that I've taken of Andy Goldsworthy's works in America, including in Washington, DC, San Francisco, New York state and Iowa.

Some of the artworks cited in the text are listed in the "List of Works".

William Malpas
London

PART ONE

ANDY GOLDSWORTHY'S ART

1

ANDY GOLDSWORTHY: LIFE AND WORK

LIFE

Andrew Charles Goldsworthy was born in Sale Moor (10, Delamere Avenue), Cheshire, on July 25, 1956. Goldsworthy and his three siblings grew up in Cheshire (at 10, Delamere Avenue, Sale Moor and, from 1961, Bowden Vale in Altrincham), and on a housing estate on the edge of Leeds (in Alwoodley, where his family moved in 1963, when he was 7). Goldsworthy worked on a farm part-time (Grove House Farm, Alwoodley) from age thirteen. Goldsworthy later said (in 2000) that working on the farm had been as important as attending art college. 'The farm and farming were to be as significant to my development as art school, especially as far as response to the land and the working of materials were concerned' (T, 180). Goldsworthy remained fond of farming and farmers throughout his life, often referring to that way of life and work. 'I like being amongst people who farm', he said in 2003 (P, 66), and in 2002 commented: '[m]any of my responses to sculpture have been formed by my experience of working on farms' (P, 118). 'I am not making sculptures directly about farming, but about a landscape that has been farmed,' Goldsworthy wrote in 1997 (E, 94).

Goldsworthy failed the 11-plus exam, for the grammar school system, and went to Harrogate High School instead. Goldsworthy would subsequently fail to gain entrance to his chosen foundation and degree colleges. (Ironic, perhaps, because his father was Professor of Applied Mathematics at Leeds University). The Goldsworthy family moved to Ilkley (Yorkshire) in 1975 (while Goldsworthy, now 19, remained in Alwoodley, living in a caravan with his brother at Grove House Farm and working part-time on the farm).

Goldsworthy studied at Wigton Moor County Primary School, Wheatlands Secondary Modern and Harrogate High School (up to 1974). He attended Bradford College of Art (after being rejected from the Jacob Kramer College of Art, Leeds, his first choice) and Preston Polytechnic (based in Lancaster, not Preston), where he studied on the BA Fine Art course, graduating in 1978 (Preston Poly was tried at the last minute, because Goldsworthy hadn't got into Leeds, Nottingham and Hull Polytechnics, his preferences). The archetypal British art school ethics of liberalism, experimentation, art history discussions and the embrace of *avant garde* art prevailed at Bradford and Preston.[2]

As a young art student, Andy Goldsworthy spent much of his time outside college, working on the beaches at Morecambe and Heysham. Goldsworthy preferred to learn by direct experience, finding out about leaves, mud, stone, rivers and tides by living amongst them. Goldsworthy would go into college for one or two days a week, for the art history classes. This was not enough for the lecturers, who suggested

---

2 For an excellent exploration of the influence of the art school system on British popular culture, see S. Frith & H. Horne, *Art into Pop*, Methuen, London, 1987.

that he spend more time in college, including attending life drawing classes. Little did Goldsworthy's lecturers know – that their truant student, who spent hours clambering around the muddy reaches of Heysham Head and Morecambe Bay instead of dutifully attending college classes, would one day become an artist of international renown, with exhibitions and commissions around the world. At the time (*circa* late-1970s), Goldsworthy must have seemed just another crazy art student, pursuing his own wacky ideas (British art schools still contain plenty of kooky folk – not all of them students). Hearing of his beach-mud-stone-tide antics, Goldsworthy's tutors must have sighed heavily and put another stroke through the 'absent' column on his attendance record. Amazing to think that this artist-in-the-making would one day be exhibiting at the most prestigious museums in the world (the British Museum and the Metropolitan Museum of Art), designing Royal Mail stamps, and making a Holocaust memorial in New York.

For Goldsworthy, the time spent working at Grove House Farm and the Lancashire beaches was as critical as his art education: '[t]he energy and unpredictability of art outside the studio and gallery were important to me. Going outside art college felt so much more raw, and that's what interested me' (T, 180). However, Goldsworthy did use some of his art school education – the artist's journal and workbook, for instance – the centrepiece of art training in the UK – has remained a significant tool for Goldsworthy (indeed, the accounts in his published books such as *Wood* and *Passage* derive from his notebooks).

There's not a lot of anger, or angst, or suffering, or self-doubt, or lust, or violence, or propaganda, or neurosis, or disturbance in Andy Goldsworthy's art. He's definitely not a haunted, tormented artist like Vincent van Gogh, or an aggressive, flamboyant self-publicist like Salvador Dali or Andy Warhol, or an ironic, fey commentator on the postmodern condition, like Jeff Koons or Robert Rauschenberg, or a stridently ideological combatant like Ana Mendieta or Karen Finley, or an in-your-face performance artist like Stuart Brisley or Annie Sprinkle, or a darling of the *avant garde* scene, like Yoko Ono or Matthew Barney. Goldsworthy is a much more modest artist, at least in his public persona, which may be one reason why he hasn't been fêted by the popular media in Britain like the YBAs (although he's had plenty of media exposure: there are now hundreds of articles and reviews of his work).

Andy Goldsworthy's wife, Judith Gregson, was a ceramics teacher (she studied at Ilkley Teacher Training College in Yorkshire, and later taught at St Aidan's, Carlisle, Cumbria. Her father, Barry Gregson, ran the Lunesdale Pottery, which Goldsworthy used to make art). Judith Gregson's influence on Goldsworthy's art would probably include his use of ceramics (such as working with clay), and various collaborations. You can see Judith Gregson and Goldsworthy's children in the 2001 documentary *Rivers and Tides*. Later, Goldsworthy lived with Tina Fiske, an art historian who came to Goldsworthy's studio to help catalogue his work. Goldsworthy's wife moved out with the children in 2004, and a divorce followed.

Apart from his family, important people in Andy Goldsworthy's life include land artist David Nash, Steve Chettle (Public Arts Officer for Cumbria County Council), stone wallers Joe Smith and Steve Allen, the Earl of Dalkeith (Scottish land-owner), gallery owners Fabian Carlsson and Michael Hue-Williams, filmmaker Thomas Riedelsheimer, dance director Régina Chopinot, Simon Cutts (Coracle Press), photographer Julian Calder, assistants Ellie Hall and Andrew McKinna, Nadine Gomez (Digne museum), Guy Martini (director of Réserve Géologique in Haute-Provence), Jacob Ehrenberg (in the US) and art critics Terry Friedman, Kenneth Baker, Clare Henry and Andrew Causey (one-time Chair of North West Arts).

'My art', Andy Goldsworthy noted in *Time*, 'is rooted in the British landscape, and this is the source to which I must return' (T, 7). Goldsworthy has lived mainly in the North of the UK: Cheshire, Leeds, Bentham and Ilkley (Yorkshire), Brough (Cumbria) and Penpont (Dumfriesshire). In Ilkley Goldsworthy created works in the River Wharfe valley and nearby woods. 'I understand best the places where I have worked most often. I have a large well to draw on when realising works in Britain and consequently most of my permanent sculpture has been made there' (*Wall*, 22).

In 1986 Goldsworthy moved from Yorkshire and Cumbria, where he'd spent most of his life, to Fernside, Penpont in Dumfriesshire, where he has remained ever since. This's where Goldsworthy produces most of his work. Pretty much most of Goldsworthy's exhibitions (and books) feature something made around Penpont. A nearby 2 1/2 acre piece of land (dubbed Stone Wood by the artist) was leased from the Bucclech estate in the late 1980s. The River Scaur, one of Goldsworthy's most beloved spots, is on one side. Goldsworthy's first *Wall,* and many other works, were made at Stone Wood.

WORKS

Andy Goldsworthy has created land art in Grise Fiord, the North Pole, in Japan, upstate New York, California, the U.S. Mid-West, Castres, Digne, La Rochelle and Sidobre in France, the Australian outback, and in Haarlem, Holland. The first work that Andy Goldsworthy sold was a bunch of photographs to the Arts Council (via Andrew Causey at North West Arts). He has had one-man shows in France, Japan, Holland, the U.S. and the UK, and participated in groups shows in Italy, Germany, and the U.S.

Among his one-man exhibitions in the U.S. and Canada are *Sand Leaves* (Chicago Arts Club, 1991); *California Project* (San Francisco, 1992); *Wood Land* (Galerie Lelong, New York, 1993); *Stone* (London, Paris, Cardiff, St Louis, San Francisco); *Breath of Earth* (San Jose Museum of Art, 1995); *Black Stones, Red Pools* (New York, 1995); *Wood* (London, New York, San Francisco, 1996); *Arche* (Montréal, 1998); *Two Rivers* (Santa Fe, New Mexico, 2000); an important show at Storm King in upstate New York and Galerie Lelong (2000); *Fall Creek* (Cornell University, 2000); Austin Museum of Art (2003); *Stone Houses* (New York, 2004); *Roof* (National Gallery of Art, Washington, DC, 2005); *Stone Light Drawings* (Haines Gallery, San Francisco); *Arches* at the Frederick Meijer Sculpture Garden, Grand Rapids (MI); *Two Creeks – Andy Goldsworthy: Ephemeral Works in the Roaring Fork Valley* and *Stone River* in Aspen, Colorado (2006); *White Walls*, Galerie Lelong, New York (2007), and *Spire* (San Francisco, 2008-09).

A major retrospective, *Hand to Earth: Andy Goldsworthy: Sculpture: 1976-1990*, was held at the Henry Moore Centre for the Study of Sculpture, Leeds City Art Gallery: the show also travelled to the Royal Botanic Gardens in Edinburgh, Stedelijke Musea, Gouda and Centre Regional d'Art Contemporain Midi-Pyrénées in Toulouse. This show also produced the most useful and detailed publication to date on Goldsworthy's art (*Hand to Earth*, later reprinted – see bibliography). 2000's *Time* is a handy update.

Official websites are few on Andy Goldsworthy. There is the Sheep-folds site: <www.sheepfolds.org>, and the *Rivers and Tides* DVD info at:

<www.skyline.uk.com/riversandtides>

Also worth looking at are: The Artists: <www.the-artists.org>

Sculpture at Goodwood, CASS: <www.sculpture.org.uk>

and Crescent Moon Publishing: <www.crescentmoon.org.uk>.

One of Goldsworthy's first appearances in the U.S.A. was in the 1984 book *Earthworks and Beyond*, John Beardsley's excellent survey of land art (one of the standard texts on the subject). Goldsworthy's first one-man show in the land of the free was in Chicago in 1991, at the Arts Club.

In the 1990s, Andy Goldsworthy's art began to rise in popularity: the glossy coffee table book *Stone* became a bestseller (bear in mind it was priced at 35 pounds or about 55 U.S. dollars. 'Bestseller' in art book or hardback terms is not the same as trade paperback fiction. We're not talking about millions of copies sold.) Thames & Hudson, Golds-worthy's British publishers, announced that over 30,000 copies of *Time* had been sold by late 2004 (healthy sales for a hardback art book).

Other Goldsworthy shows and projects of the 1990s and after in America included various wall commissions (such as in New York, 1993, 1996 and 1997); various *Cones* (New York and Oxford, 1995);

Fieldgate (New York, 1993); clay holes and throws at Runnymede Sculpture Farm, California (1992); a clay installation (a hole) in L.A. (at the Getty Center For the Arts, 1997; later destroyed by a burst pipe); 'ice houses' and stick lines made in Alaska (1995); the new *Wall* at Storm King (1998); another wall at Storm King (*Folded Wall,* 1999); a large stone arch in Montréal (1998); a *Stone River* at Stanford University (2001); *Three Cairns* (Des Moines Art Center, Iowa, 2002); *Garden of Stone*, a memorial for victims and survivors of the Holocaust, sited in Manhattan (2003); the *Stones House*s exhibited at Gotham's Met in 2004; the slate domes (*Roof*) in the U.S. capital in 2005; a *Stone River* in Aspen, Colorado (2006); and *Spire* in the Presidio in San Francisco (2008).

Andy Goldsworthy's private commission clients tend to opt for stone cairns/ cones, stone walls and stone arches. Goldsworthy has undertaken private commissions for clients such as British Airways, Royal Mail, Cirque du Soleil, Parnham Trust, Greenpeace, Coracle Press, and many private houses and collectors (many of the commissions are for outdoor works – in the U.S.A. in New York state and California).

Deborah Solomon wrote in the *New York Times* about America embracing Andy Goldsworthy:

> Curiously enough, these days, Goldsworthy is more valued in America than he is in his native England, perhaps because the London art world tends to disparage the notion of landscape as too gentlemanly and old-fashioned, too English. (The Tate, with its canonical holdings of British art, has yet to acquire one of his works.) But here in America, where we romanticize nature as an escape from our civilized selves, Goldsworthy is revered as a figure of Thoreau-like purity, and lately he has been inundated with requests for large-scale commissions. Compared with Christo, who is also having a show at the Met now – and is planning on installing 7,500 gates in Central Park next winter – Goldsworthy doesn't turn his sculptures into community projects involving everyone from city councilmen to Boy Scouts. Instead, he wanders around by himself, and most of the time you don't even know he is there.

While many public museums and galleries around the globe have bought and exhibited Andy Goldsworthy's work, in his home country, the premier public art gallery, the Tate Gallery, has tended to avoid it (up until 2009). While many Young British Artists have exhibited at the Tate, as well as most of Goldsworthy's contemporaries (Nash, Long, Cragg, Gormley, Flanagan, Fulton *et al*), Goldsworthy has not. (However, Goldsworthy has had exhibitions at prestigious public sites such as the British Museum, the Barbican, the Victoria & Albert Museum, the Yorkshire Sculpture Park, and the Henry Moore Centre).[1]

It's an intriguing coincidence, perhaps, that Goldsworthy's art has become increasingly popular in the United States at the same time that it's become increasingly ignored in Britain. There are numerous reasons for this; one is that the Tate Gallery and other public contemporary art spaces have since the 1980s or perhaps before then aligned themselves with Conceptual art, with postmodern art, and with art that some critics deem to be 'cutting edge' or 'avant garde'. Needless to say, Goldsworthy's art does *not* fit into that trendy, fashion-conscious mold of Conceptual or post-Conceptual art. Another reason may be that Goldsworthy's art is thought too lightweight, too romantic, and too beautiful, and not addressing weighty or political issues. Among the general public, though, Goldsworthy's art is *very* popular.

Goldsworthy artist residencies include Yorkshire Sculpture Park (1987-88), the Lake District National Park (1988), St Louis Arts Festival (1986), Quay Arts Centre, Isle of Wight (1987) and Hampstead Heath (1985-86). In June, 2000, he was appointed Visiting Professor at the University of Glasgow, and in July Andrew D. White Professor-at-Large at Cornell University.

Goldsworthy has had many proposals which haven't been realized. One of Goldsworthy's proposals, which has been submitted a number of times, was for five hills along a road, twenty metres tall and planted with trees, which would change with the seasons and the light (T, 192). This work's concerns would have been 'travel, time and distance' (HE, 140). The Autumnal colours of the trees would be a central feature of the piece, and two of the hills would be positioned to catch the sun at dawn and twilight (ibid.).

Another proposal was for a line of rocks and a stone enclosure (S, 113) on a cliff in Toronto, Canada (1992), which would collapse as the cliff eroded. A row of trees growing out of circular openings in stone structures (1994) was unrealized. Many of the *Réfuges d'Art* (Digne) proposals were unrealized. In 1997 Goldsworthy proposed siting a group of fired boulders on the roof of the National Museum of Scotland in Edinburgh (abandoned because of technical problems [T, 199]). The *Snowballs In Summer* project had an American counterpart, which Goldsworthy proposed in Chicago in 1998 (this U.S. snowball project will probably resurface some time). Many of the *Sheepfolds* ideas have yet to be realized. A recurring Goldsworthy proposal is for a group of cones, in close formation: cones made from branches in *Woodland Cones* (1990), proposed for Vassivière in France; steel cones for Gateshead (1991); wooden cones for Grizedale; and stone cairns for Penpont and Grizedale (1987).

Andy Goldsworthy's publications often favour stark (one-word) titles: *Rain sun snow hail mist calm, Hand to Earth, Wood, Stone, Arch, Time, Passage, Leaves, Garden Mountain* and *Sheepfolds. Wood* is divided into chapters with single-word titles: "Earth", "Seed", "Leaf" and so on. These titles came from *Végétal*, the dance performance that Goldsworthy collaborated on in 1995. The title, *Wood*, continued Goldsworthy's preference for single-word titles, begun in *Stone* (and continued in *Arch, Wall, Time* and *Passage*). However, *Wood* might as easily be called *Snow* or *Ice* or, again, *Stone,* because there are many works based mainly on those elements.

Goldsworthy continues to work in countries such as Japan, Australia, Canada, North America and France, but his home ground of Dumfriesshire in Scotland remains (at) the heart of his work. (From the mid-Nineties, Goldsworthy worked increasingly frequently at Digne in South France; it became one of the most valuable places for the sculptor outside of his home in Scotland, and was the site of a major commission, *Réfuges d'Art* [T, 82]). Digne became the site of the biggest concentration of Goldsworthy art in the world.

It's significant, I think, that Goldsworthy worked as a gardener (for the first half of the Eighties). Goldsworthy's art parallels developments and trends in gardening in Britain and elsewhere. For instance, the use of stones and pebbles in the gardens as ornaments or sculptures (paralleling the increased interest in other garden forms, including oriental gardens, as with *feng shui* in New Age culture). The popularity of Goldsworthy's art, I would argue, is in tune with events such as: (1) the rise in gardening shows on TV (and those shows' links with house, food and interior design programmes); (2) the spread of DIY stores and gardening centres; (3) more gardens being open to the public (including many more private gardens in the *Yellow Book* scheme in the UK); (4) the interest in ecological and environmental politics, anti-pollution and recycling drives; (5) and the increase of New Age and mind/ body/ spirit pursuits (such as *feng shui* and American Indian religion).

Some of the things that fuel this revived (or new) interest in gardens, art and the environment include: (1) an increase in leisure time (and money for entertainment); (2) an ageing population (which also lives longer); (3) new technologies; and (4) new distribution and consumption networks.

Andy Goldsworthy has not created art everywhere. There are plenty of places Goldsworthy has not visited for making art. Even in the British Isles, Goldsworthy has not made much art in Cornwall or Devon or the South-West, or the East (Norfolk, Suffolk, the fens), not much in the English Midlands, only a few works in Wales, and hardly any in Ireland. If Goldsworthy makes work in the UK, it's usually Scotland, Northern Britain (Cumbria and Yorkshire, but not so much the North-East), or London. (Sussex has been the site of one or two works, such as the *Night Path* and *Chalk Stones Trial*, or the sculptures at Goodwood).

It's partly to do with the distribution of the major cultural centres in Britain: most art is exhibited in London and the South-East, and in some regional centres such as Liverpool, Bath, St Ives, Edinburgh and so on. But it's also Goldsworthy's preference for Northern Britain. Given the choice between making art in, say, Cumbria or Hampshire, Goldsworthy will plump for the former.

Around the world, Goldsworthy has concentrated on Westernized territories: on America, of course (it's the centre of land art, and the international art market), Western Europe, Australia and Japan (with the odd excursion to exotic spots, such as the North Pole). Goldsworthy has not made much art in Eastern Europe, in Russia, in mainland China, in India, in Africa or South America. (Goldsworthy did visit Russia in 1991, but 'administration difficulties' prevented the intended work in Siberia [T, 193]). Visits to India, Africa, China and so on will probably come.

CRITICS OF ANDY GOLDSWORTHY'S ART

Andy Goldsworthy's art has been discussed widely in the popular and scholarly media, including most of the major art journals (though an appearance in *Farmer's Weekly* – in 1988 – probably pleased Goldsworthy more than articles in *Art in America* or *Modern Painters*). Goldsworthy's supporters include Terry Friedman, Simon Schama, Andrew Causey, Kenneth Baker, Neil Hedges, Michael Hue-Williams, David Nash, Paul Oakes, Mary Beaumont, Paul Nesbitt, John Beardsley, Neil Sinden, and curators such as Hans Vogels, Susan Lubowsky Talbott, Nadine Gomez, Guy Martini, Stephanie Hanor and Chris Gilbert.

Andy Goldsworthy's art has been criticized on a number of levels. For example, its avoidance of political or 'important' or problematic issues, such as AIDS, poverty, 'Third World' debt, globalization, colonialism, war, terrorism, and so on. Its romanticizing of the natural world. Its conservatism. Its nostalgia (such as for a vanished agricultural, working-class past that never existed in the first place). Its escapism. Its self-indulgence. Its élitism. Its repetition and lack of imagination. Its lack of formal experimentation. Its over-simplification of its subjects.

Goldsworthy insists that his art is not about nostalgia:

> I am not interested in nostalgia. My touch is of the present. I want my work to resonate with, rather than merely repeat, what was there – using the

language that is already inscribed in a place but in a way that speaks of today. (92)

For the nay-sayers, Goldsworthy's art is a romantic retreat into escapist, nostalgic fantasies about nature, with nothing to say about the anxieties, problems and challenges of living in the contemporary, 21st century world. For the critics who deride Goldsworthy, he's a bearded hippy in jeans who panders to the middle class's nostalgia for nature, seen from the perspective of neurotic city dwellers who hanker for the peace and quiet of the countryside. It's also an art that flatters and assuages the bourgeoisie's liberal guilt over wrecking the natural world with its ceaseless, massive consumption and pollution. For detractors, Goldsworthy's art doesn't seem to say much about the particular world they valorize – a late capitalist world, a technological, post-industrial, consumer society.

Tim Richardson wrote in 2007:

> Yet, although sometimes painfully sentimental or symbolically heavy-handed, at its best Goldsworthy's work explores a mystical connection between artist and nature that possesses a powerful emotional charge.

A critic who dislikes Goldsworthy's art, Jonathan Jones, is typical. In a newspaper article on Grizedale, where the director of the sculpture park, Adam Sutherland, was shifting the Grizedale Society and the park away from Goldsworthyan land art, Jones complained that 'Goldsworthy's art says nothing about the violence, hypocrisy and waste of our relationship to nature and is about as radical as the Body Shop'. While the U.S.A. had big, romantic works of (land) art, such as Robert Smithson's *Spiral Jetty* or Walter de Maria's *Lightning Field*, that were authentic attempts to grapple with the sublime in the natural world, Britain had tree huggers and Goldsworthy's 'twee arrangements of twigs and stones'.[3]

Goldsworthy said that when he was working outside sometimes it was difficult to explain to the general public what he was doing there. Occasionally, he had 'to deal with the anger and bitterness that is

---

3 J. Jones, "Something nasty in the woods", *The Guardian*, Mch 4, 2000.

sometimes shown towards contemporary art' (A, 74). There is a suspicion and distrust of contemporary art among parts of the population of the UK (*viz.*, the hostile reactions to 'Young British Art' or the Turner Prize). Americans, Goldsworthy remarked, were more sympathetic and welcoming (*Wall*, 12). In Digne in 2002 Goldsworthy encountered some resistance to his *Réfuges d'Art* sculptures (the cairns and monuments) – 'the usual dislike of contemporary art' – with some talk of locals sabotaging them. Goldsworthy attended a public meeting (as he has done from time to time) to defend his art (RA, 59). Goldsworthy's sculptures have occasionally been vandalized: for instance, the snowballs (which some folk can't resist kicking over), and the Gateshead *Cone* – the top part was stolen. Maybe some of the opposers of Goldsworthy's installations and sculptures grow to like them eventually. Some of the people who tried to block Christo's *Running Fence* in California in 1976 got to appreciate it (and some missed it when it was taken down).

Goldsworthy wasn't so sure about encouraging the general public to make their own sculptures, or add to his sculptures: of an idea to invite walkers to add to one of his sculptures on the Digne walking route in 2002, Goldsworthy had second thoughts: 'I'd feel uncomfortable if art released a frenzy of cairn, or sculpture-building' (RA, 97). That's unlikely. It would be more along the lines of some of the works of Richard Long: he has added one stone to an existing pile of stones or a cairn beside a route (cairns being way-markers for walkers).

On this page and the following pages are the works of some of Andy Goldsworthy's contemporaries in America

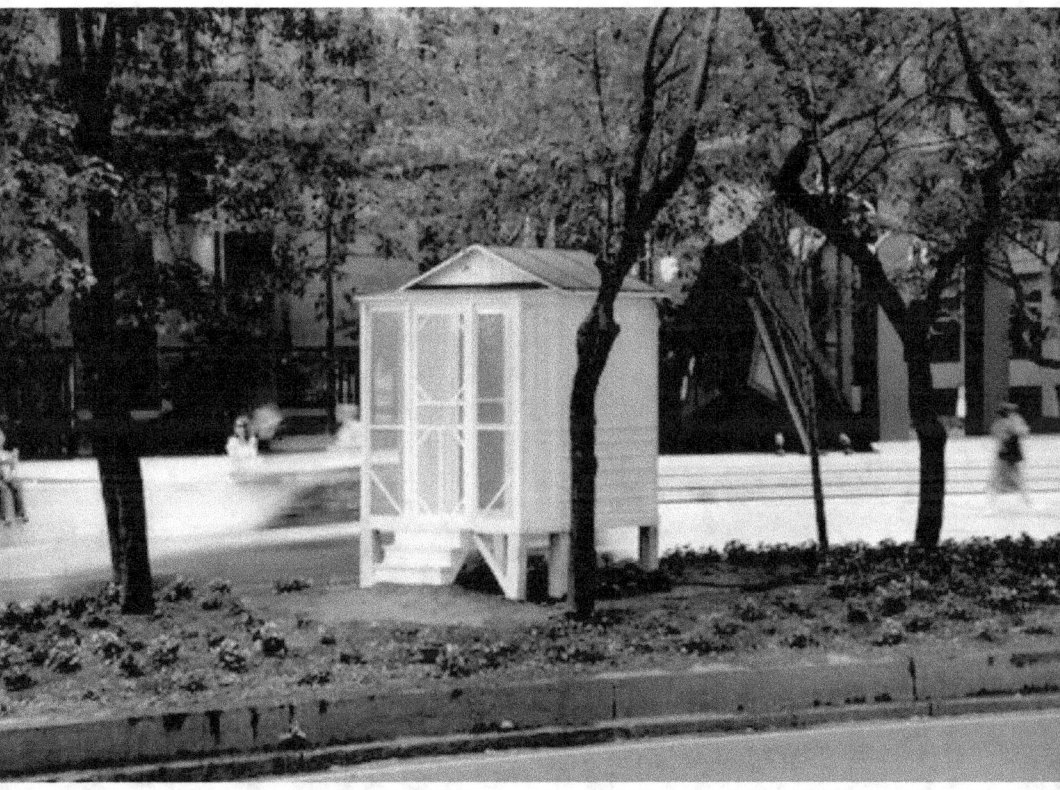

Donna Dennis, Tourist Cabins On Park Avenue, 2007

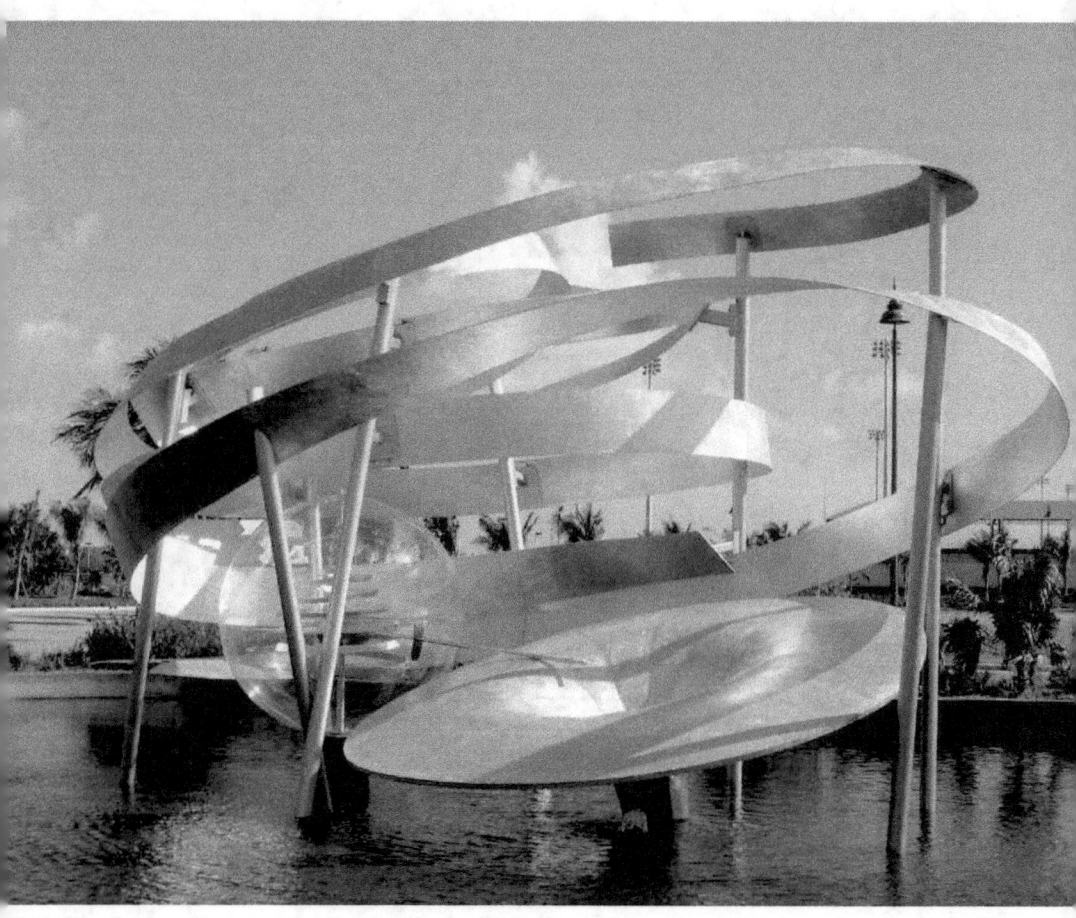

Alice Aycock, Waterworks Sculpture Proposal
for the Central Broward Regional Park, Broward County, Florida, 2004

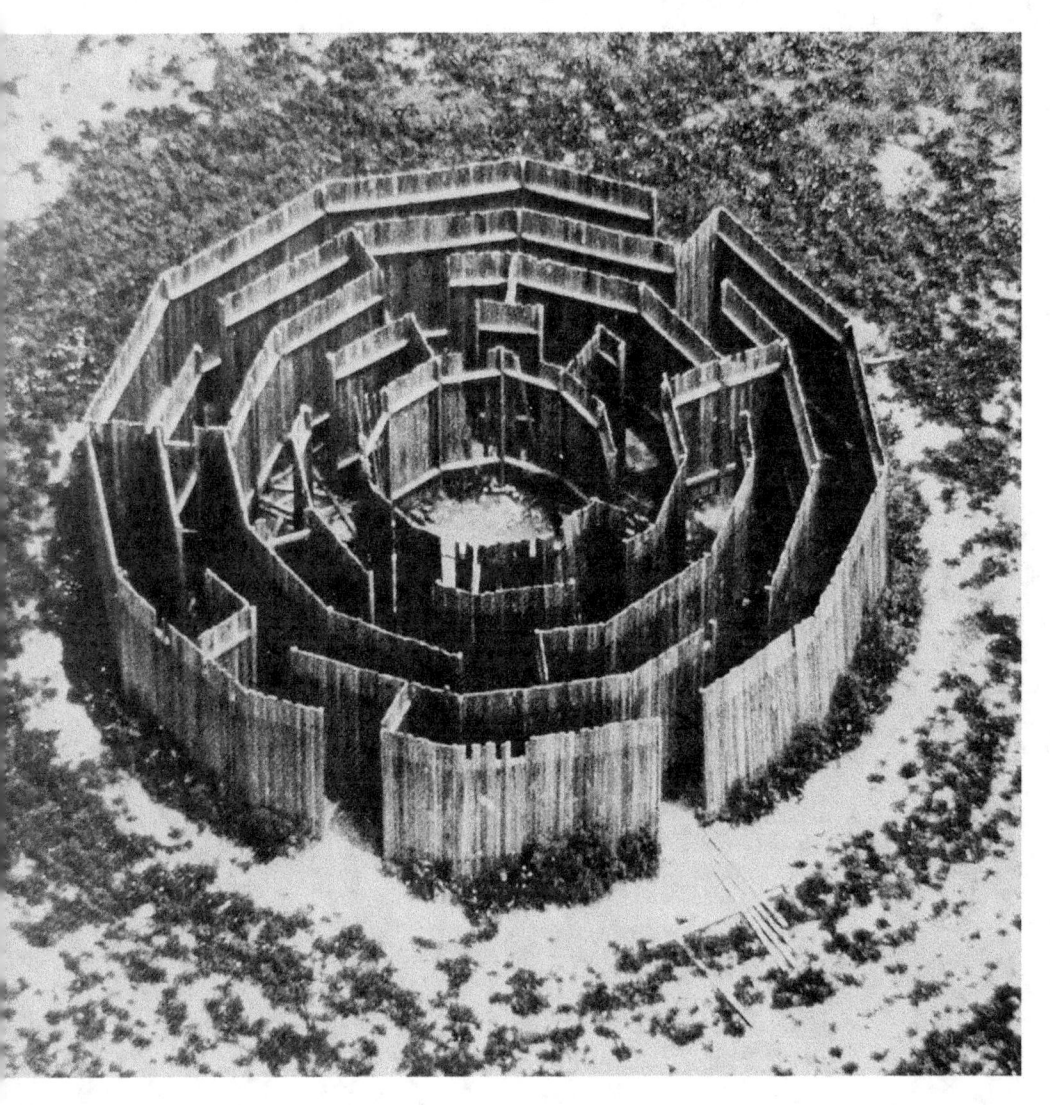

Alive Aycock, Maze, 1972

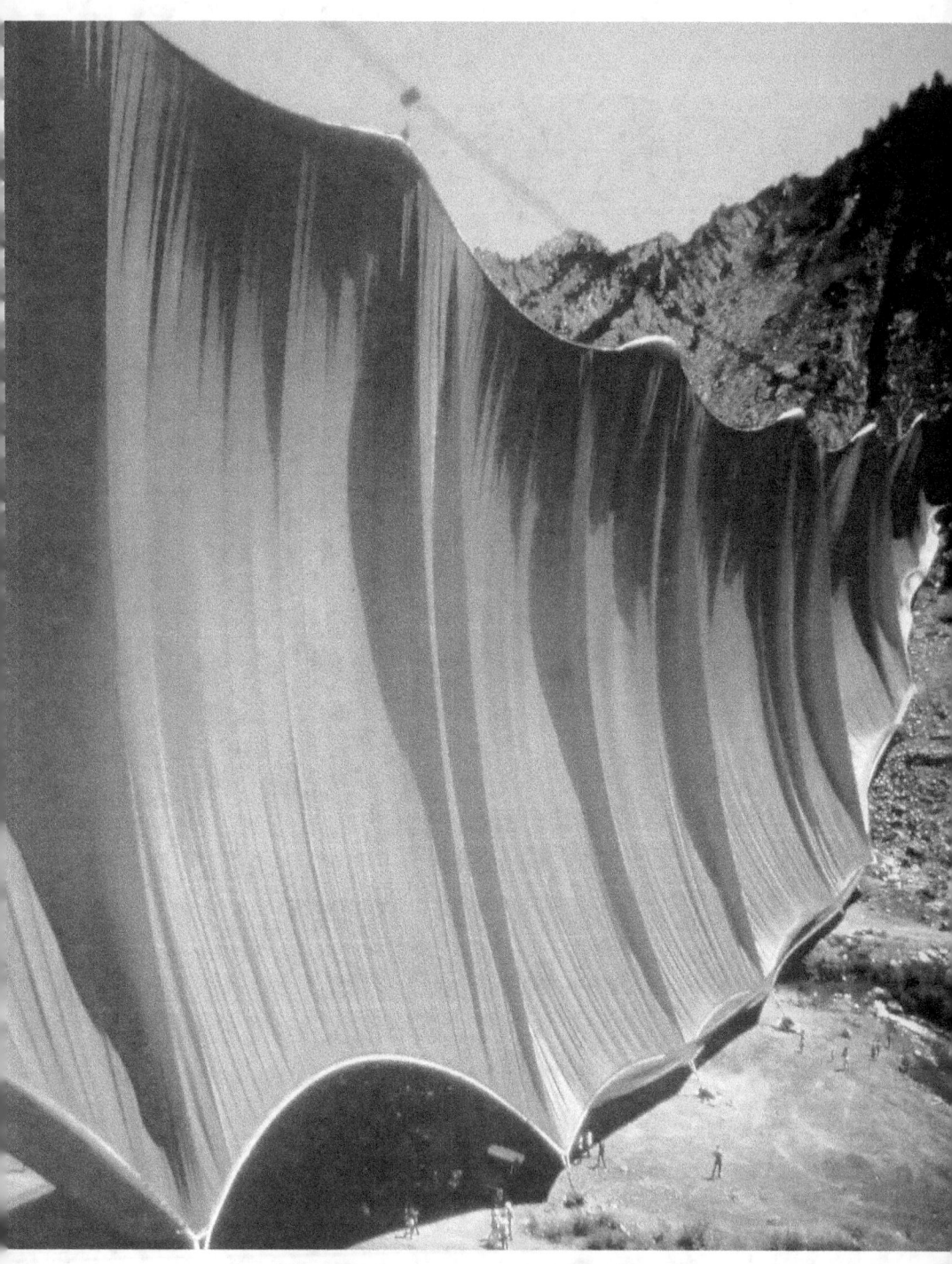

Christo, Valley Curtain, Colorado, 1972

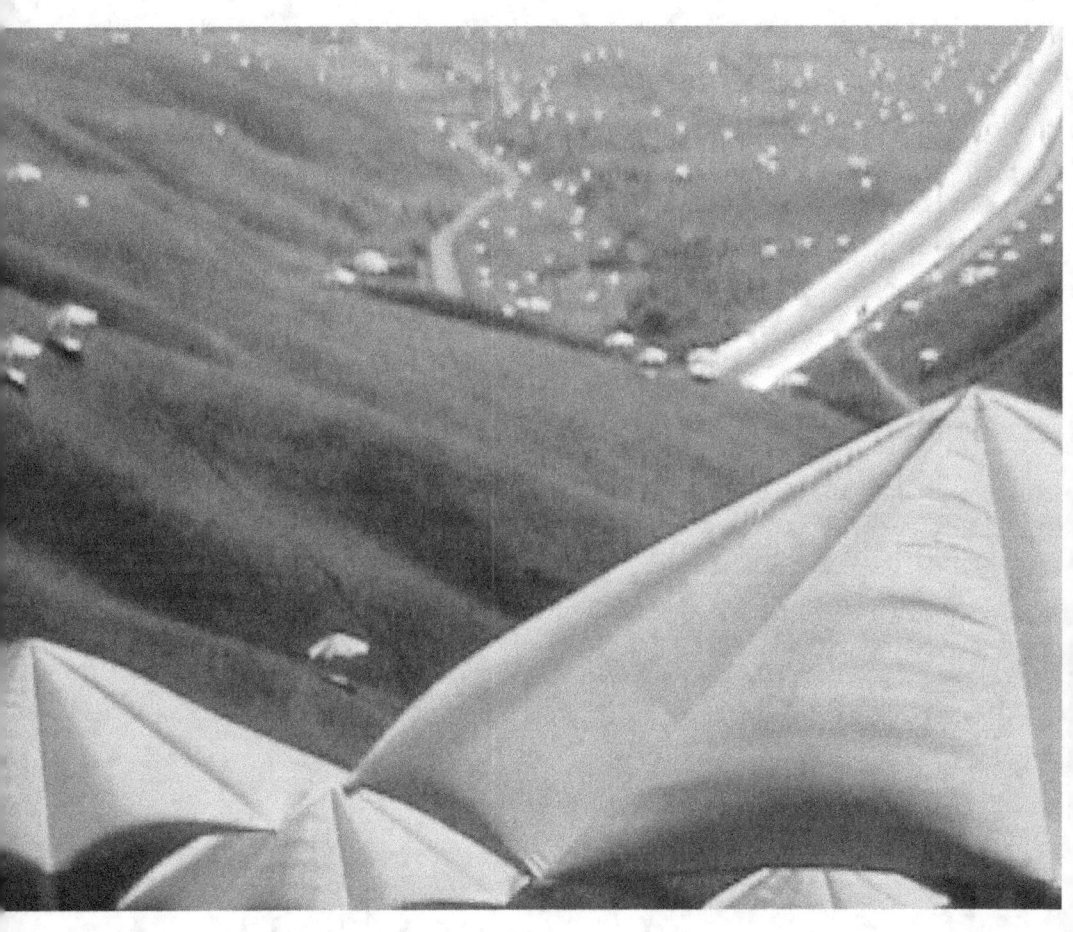

Christo, Umbrellas, 1976

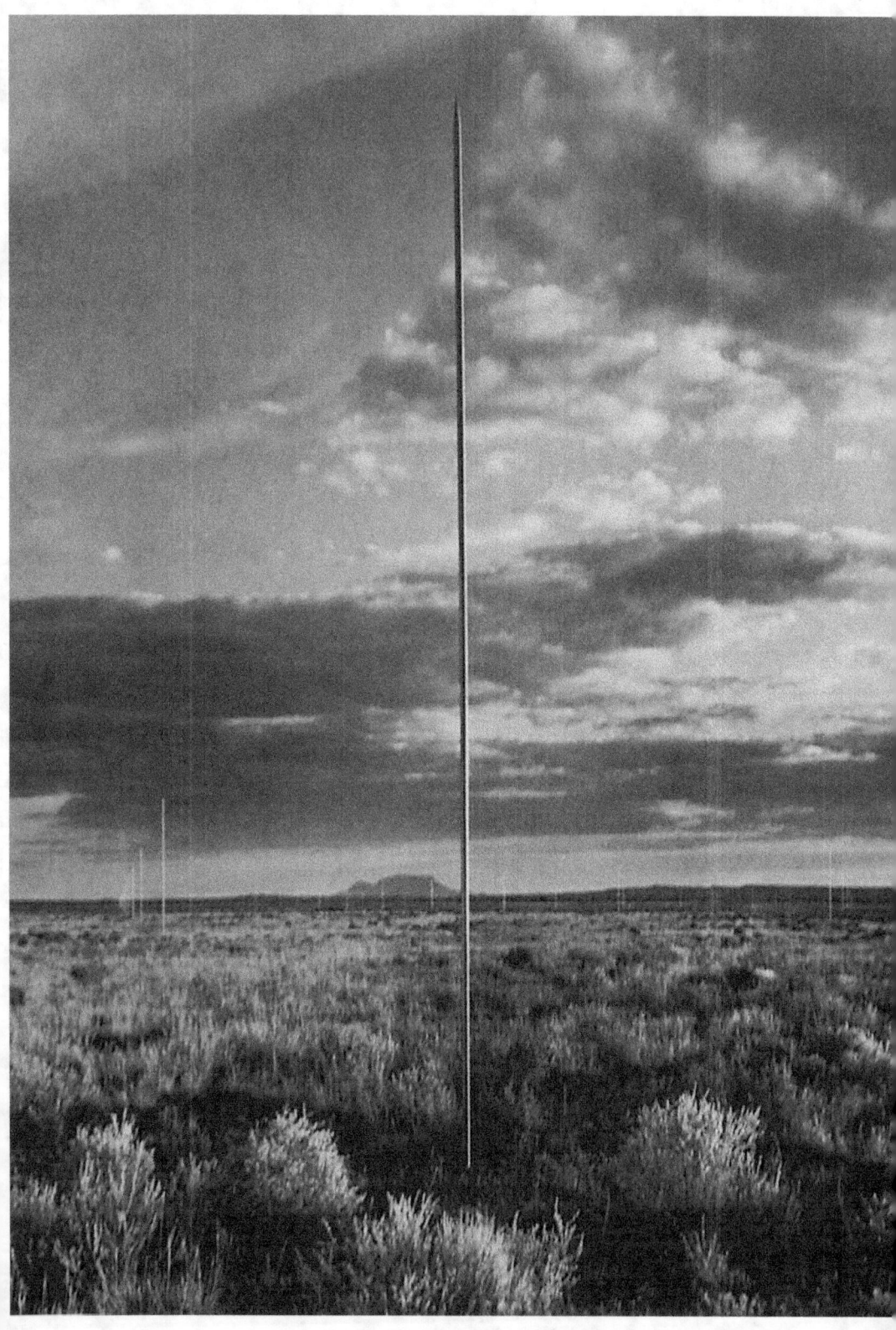

Walter de Maria, Lightning Field, 1977

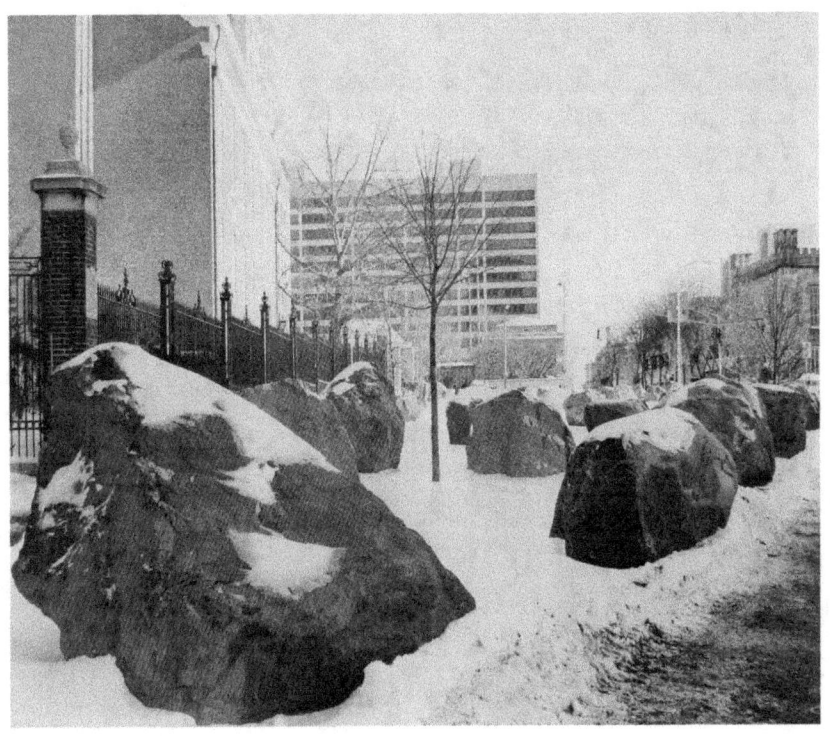

Carl Andre, Stone Field, 1977

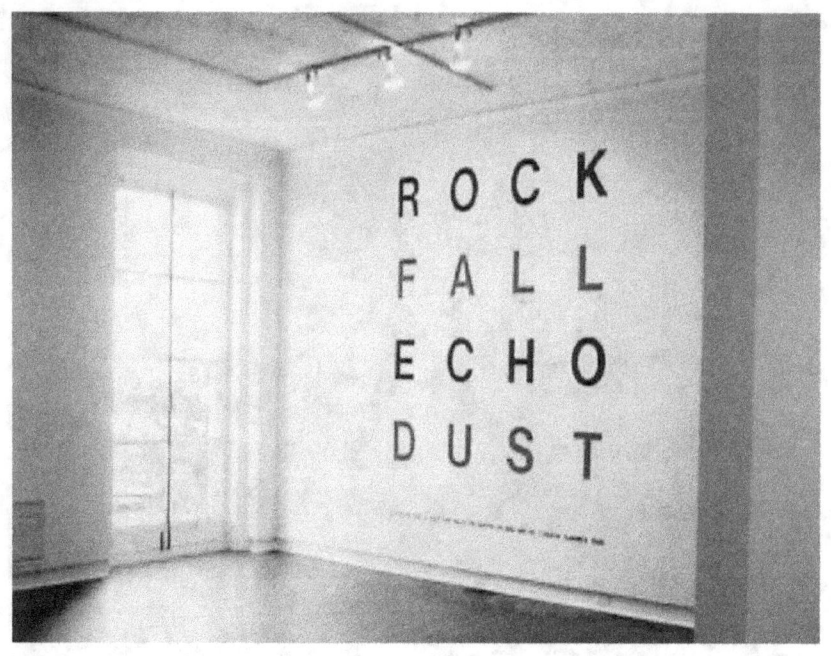

Hamish Fulton, Rock Fall Echo Dust, 1988

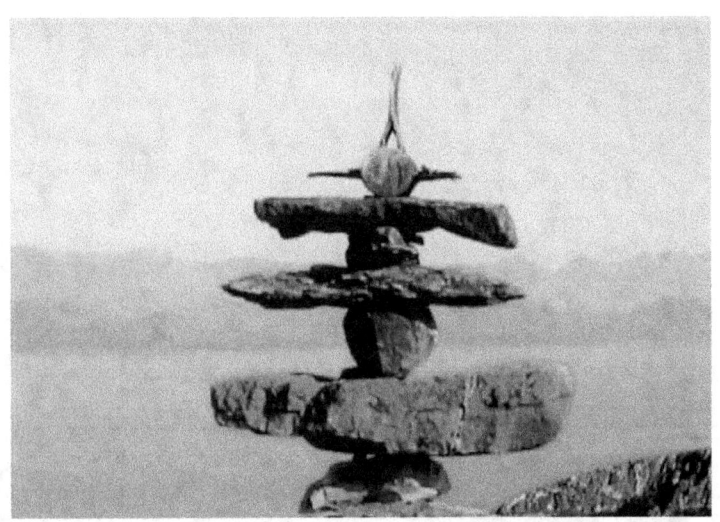

Chris Drury, Whale Bone Cairn, 1993

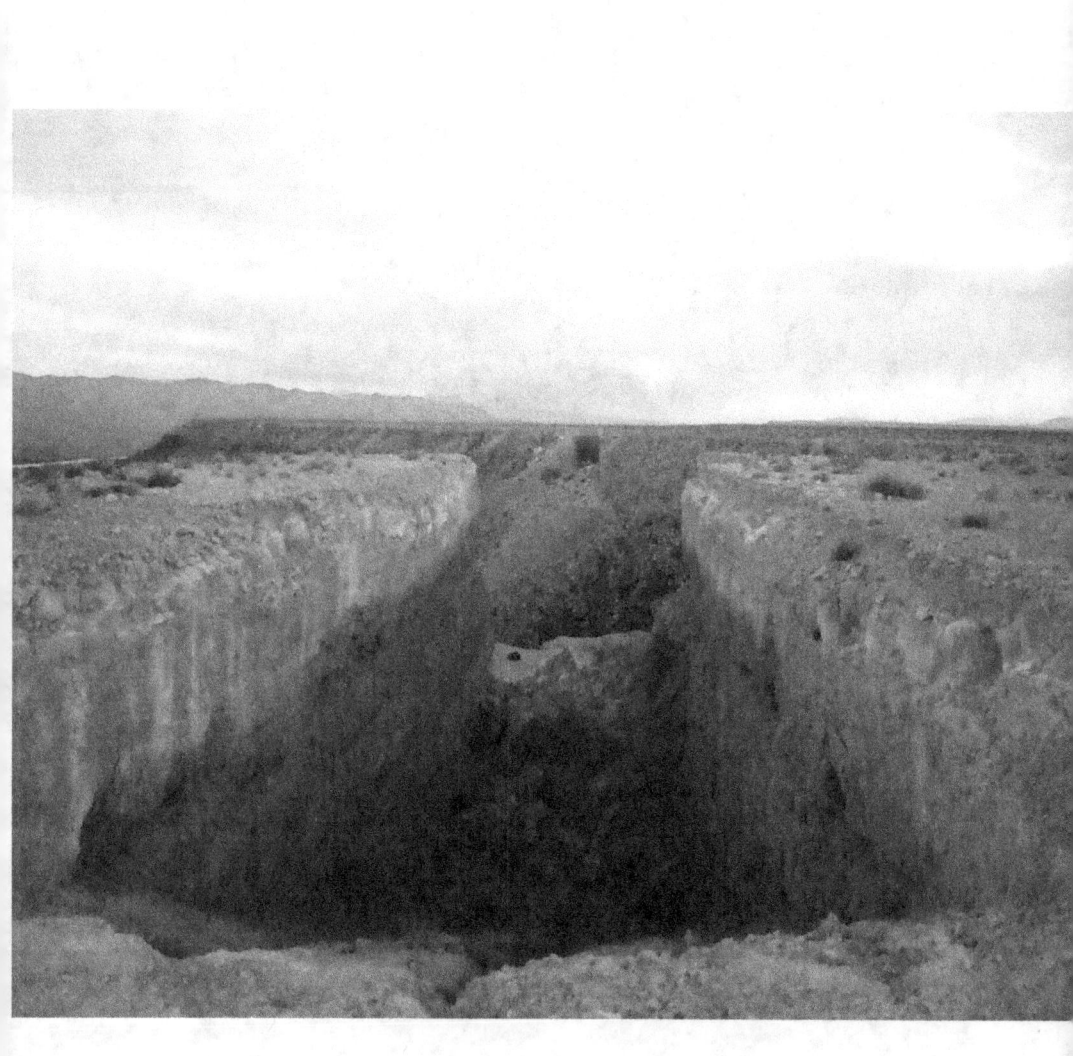

Michael Heizer, Double Negative, 1970

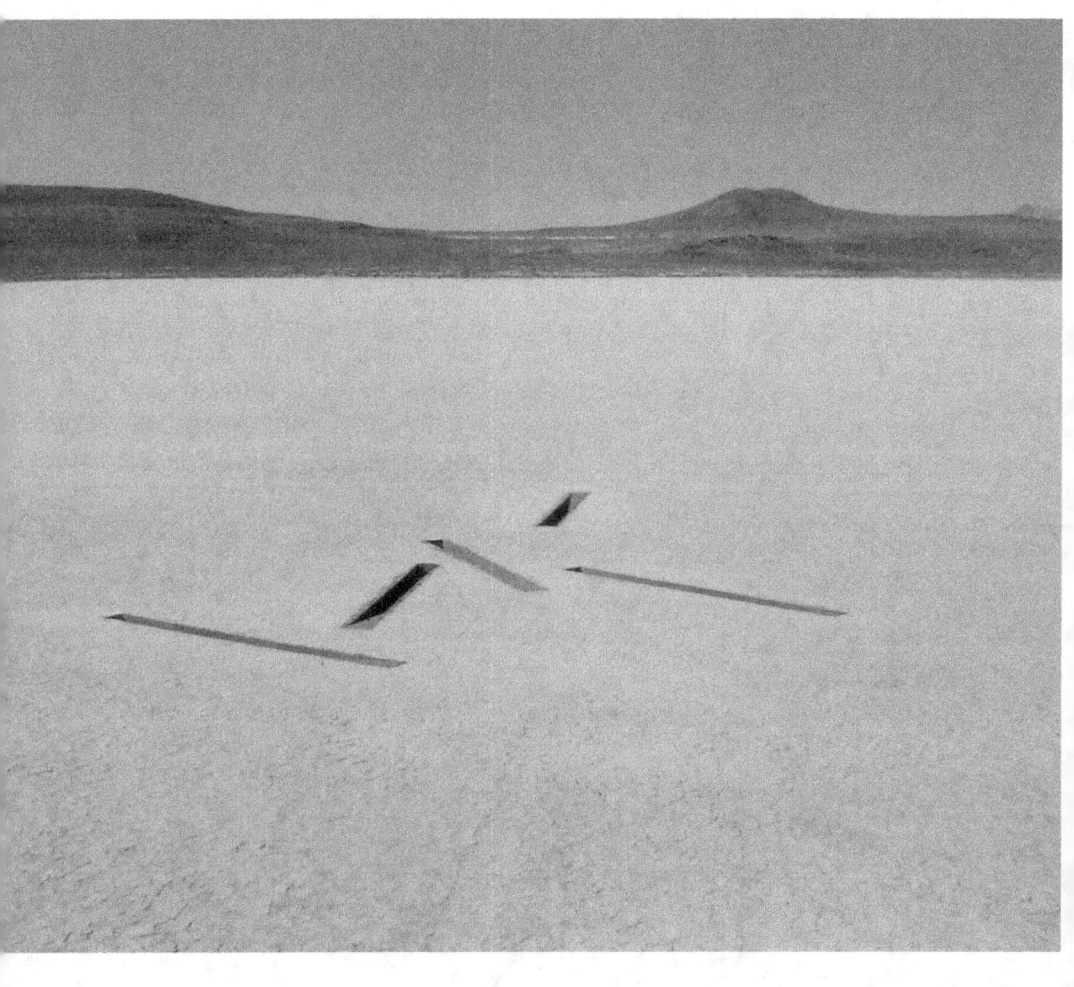

Michael Heizer, Nine Nevada Depressions, #8, 1968

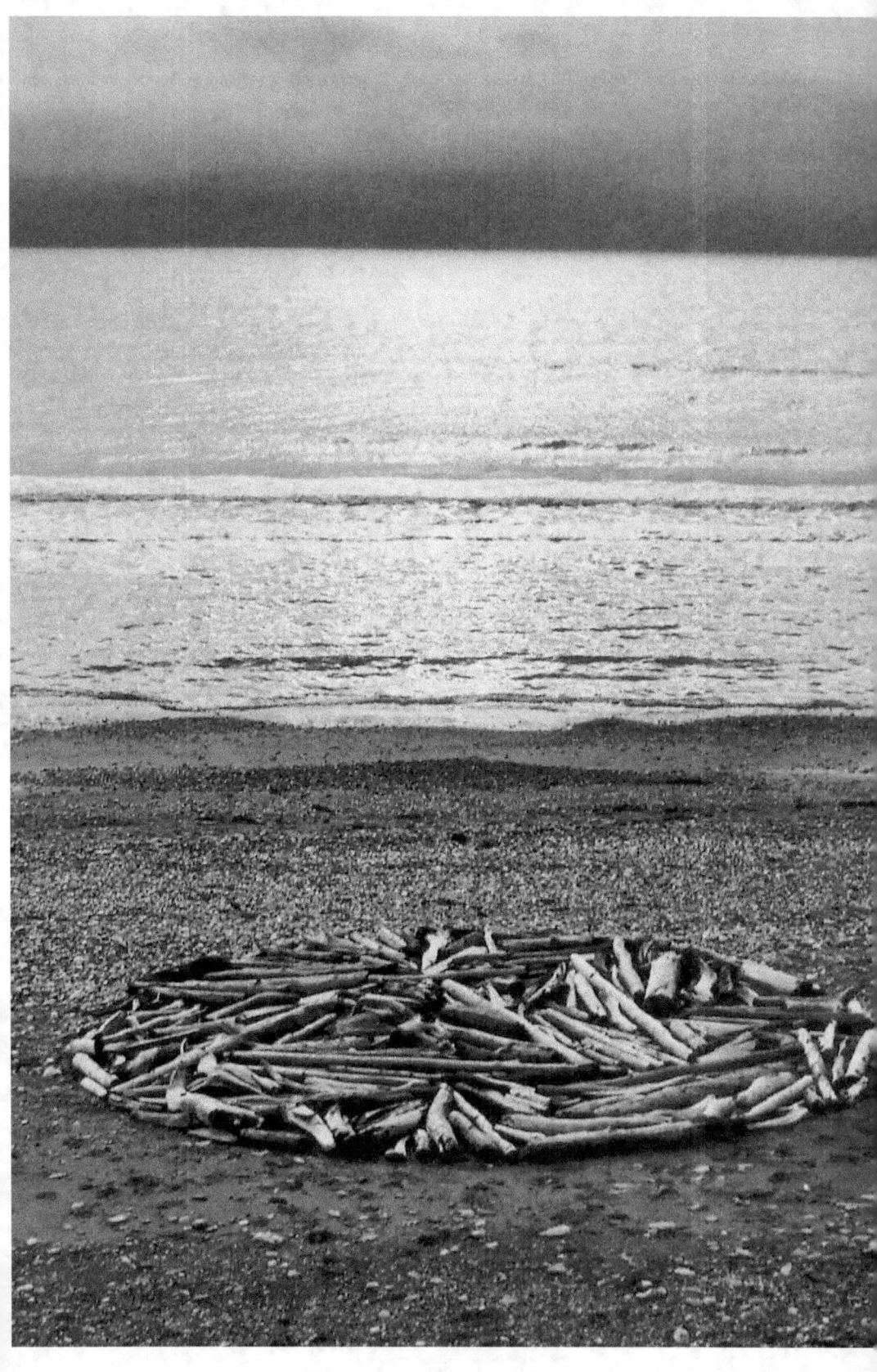

Richard Long, A Circle In Alaska, 1977

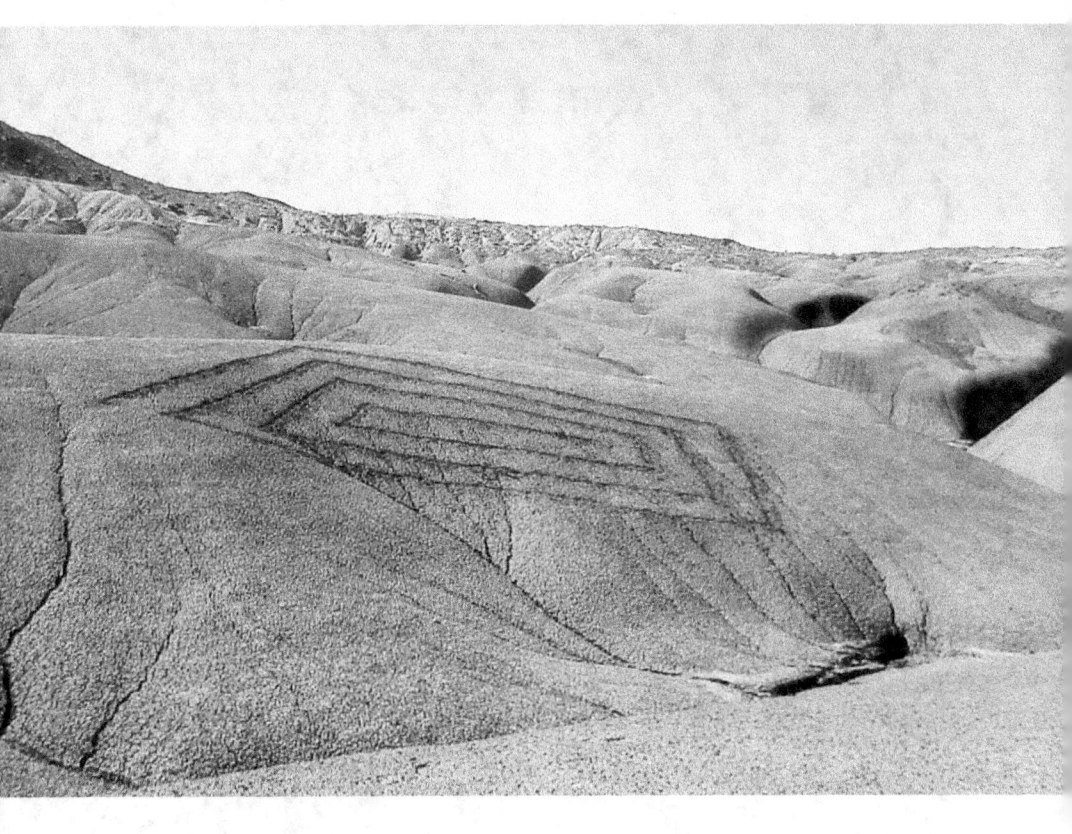

Richard Long, Arizona, 1970

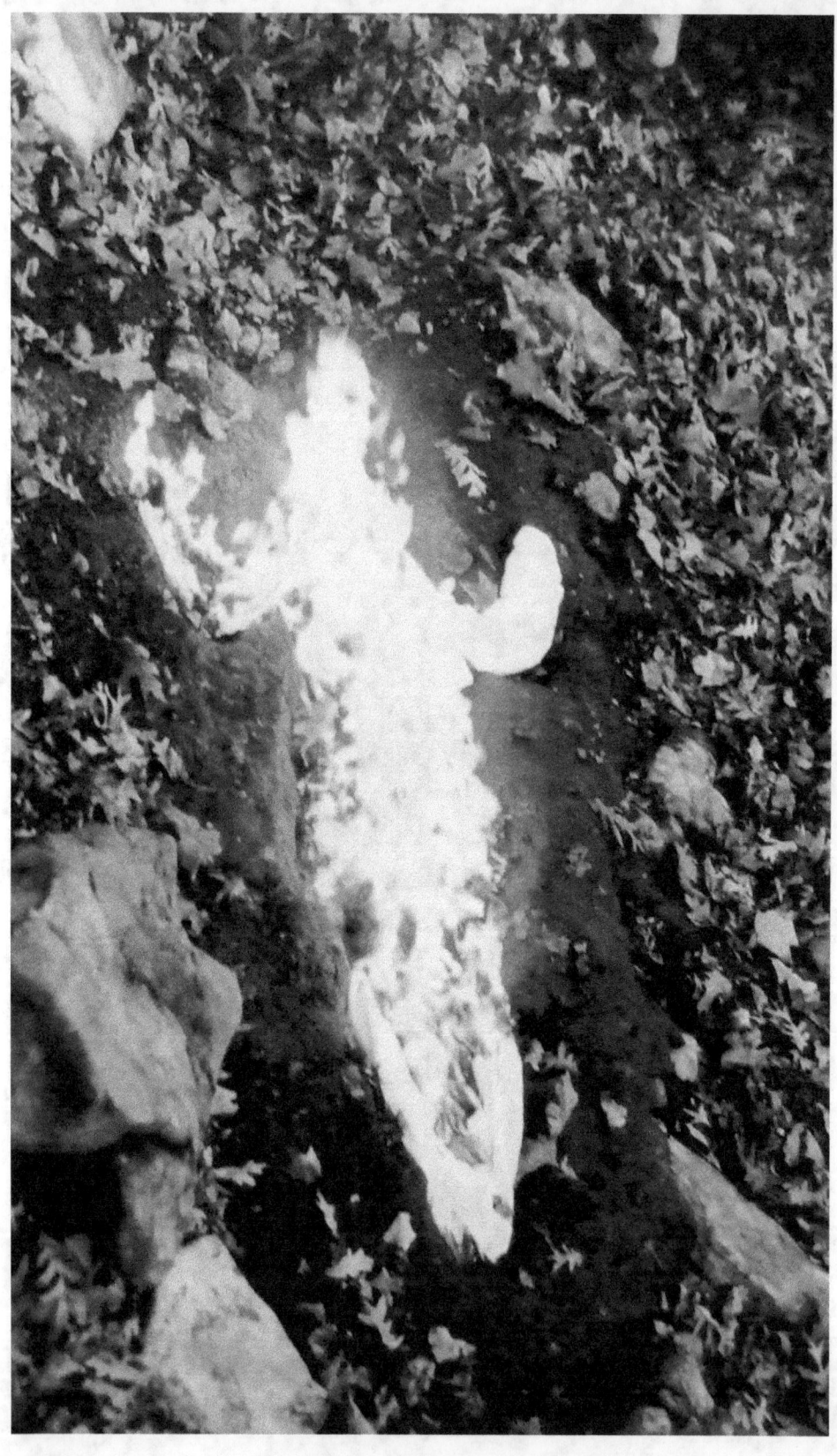

Ana Mendieta, Soul Silhouette On Fire, 1975

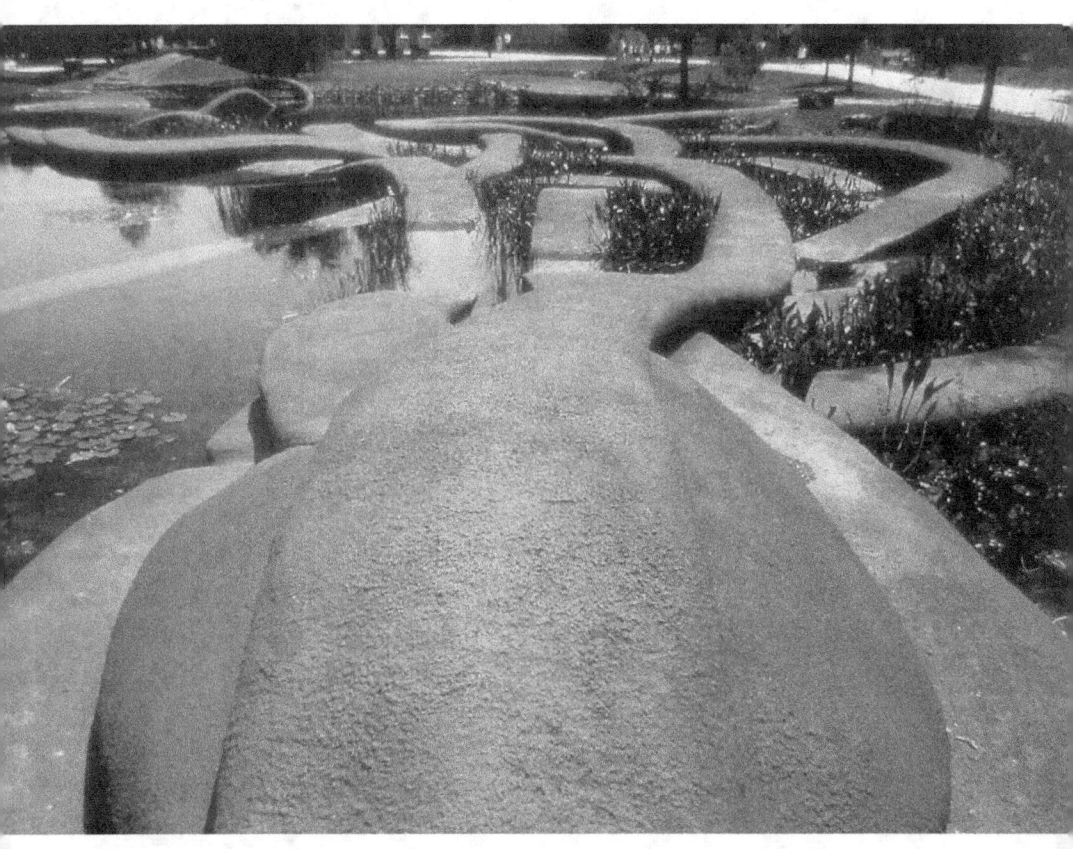

Patricia Johanson, Fair Park Lagoon, 1981-86

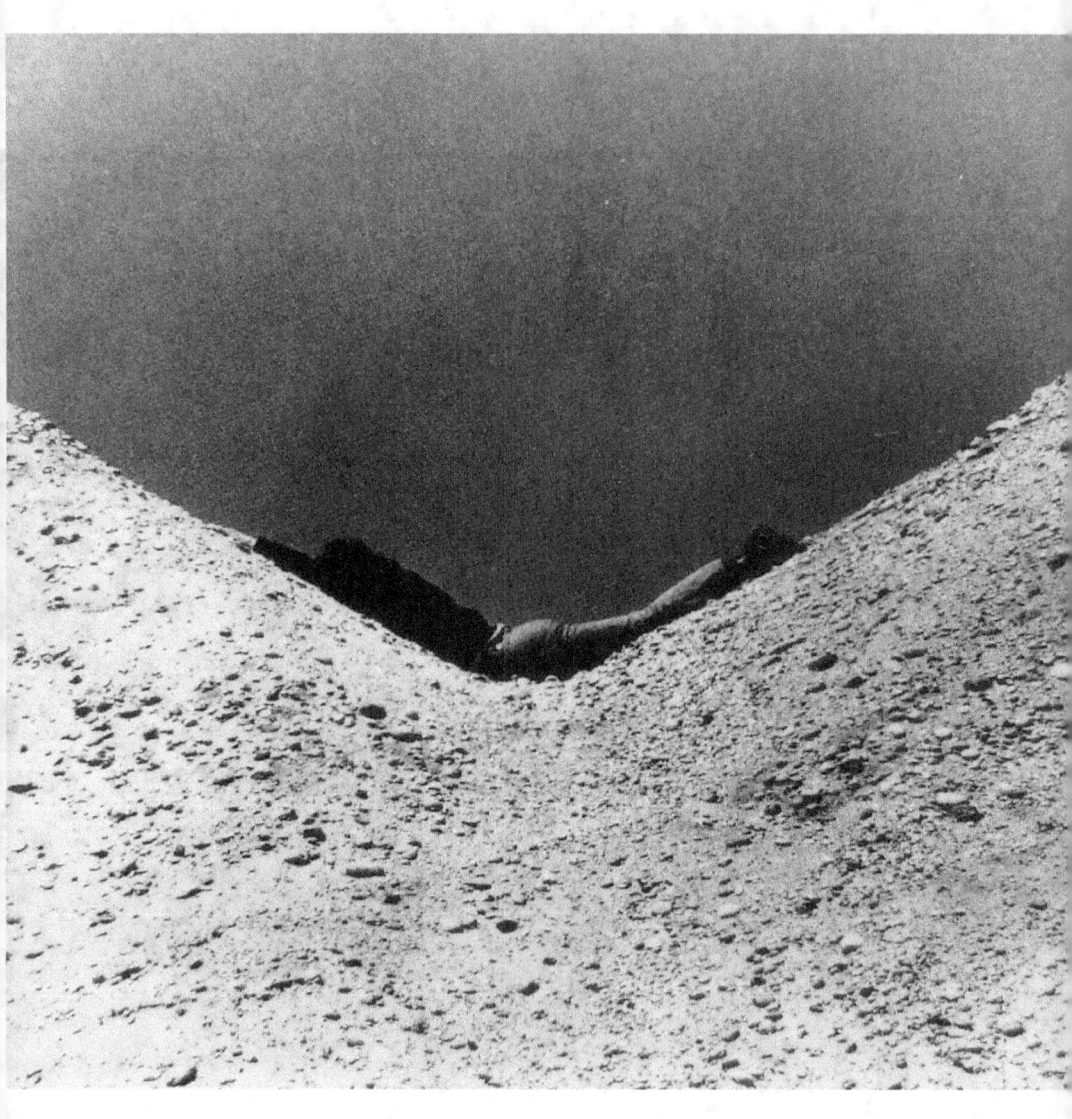

Dennis Oppenheim, Parallel Stress, 1970

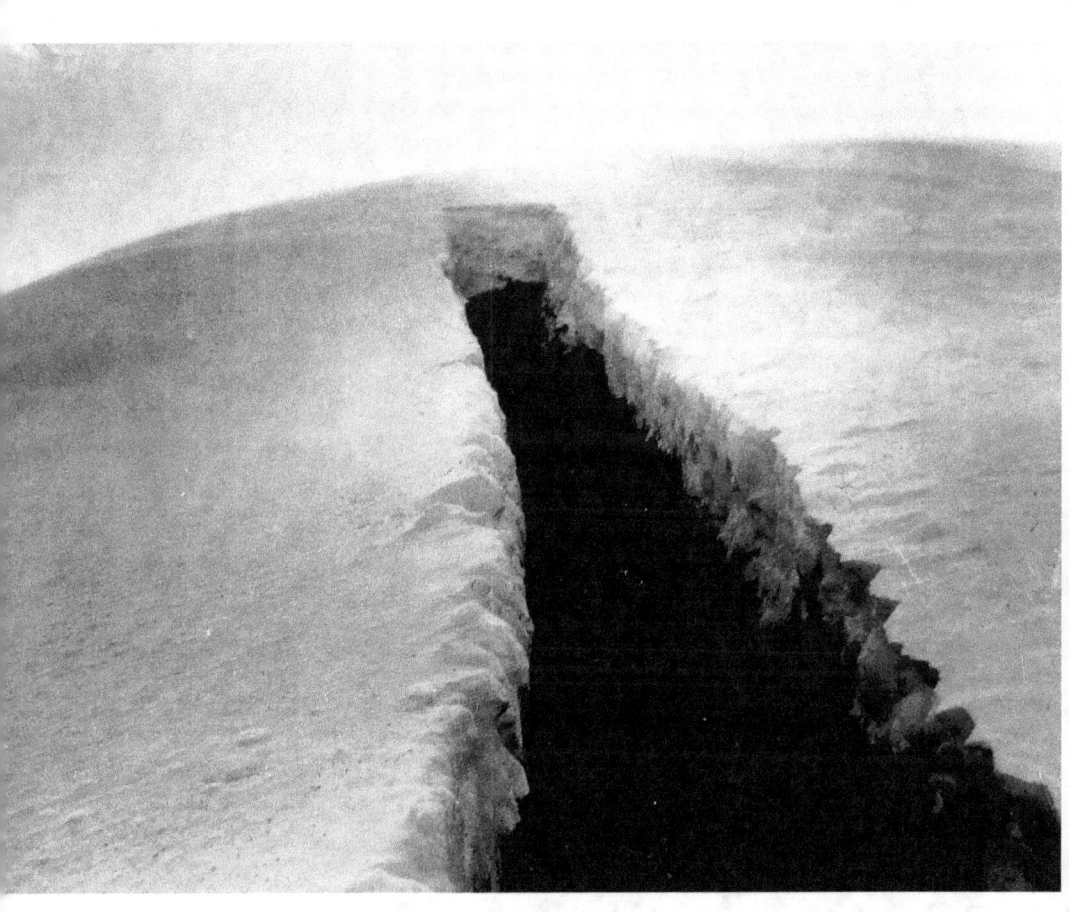

Dennis Oppenheim, Negative Board, 1968

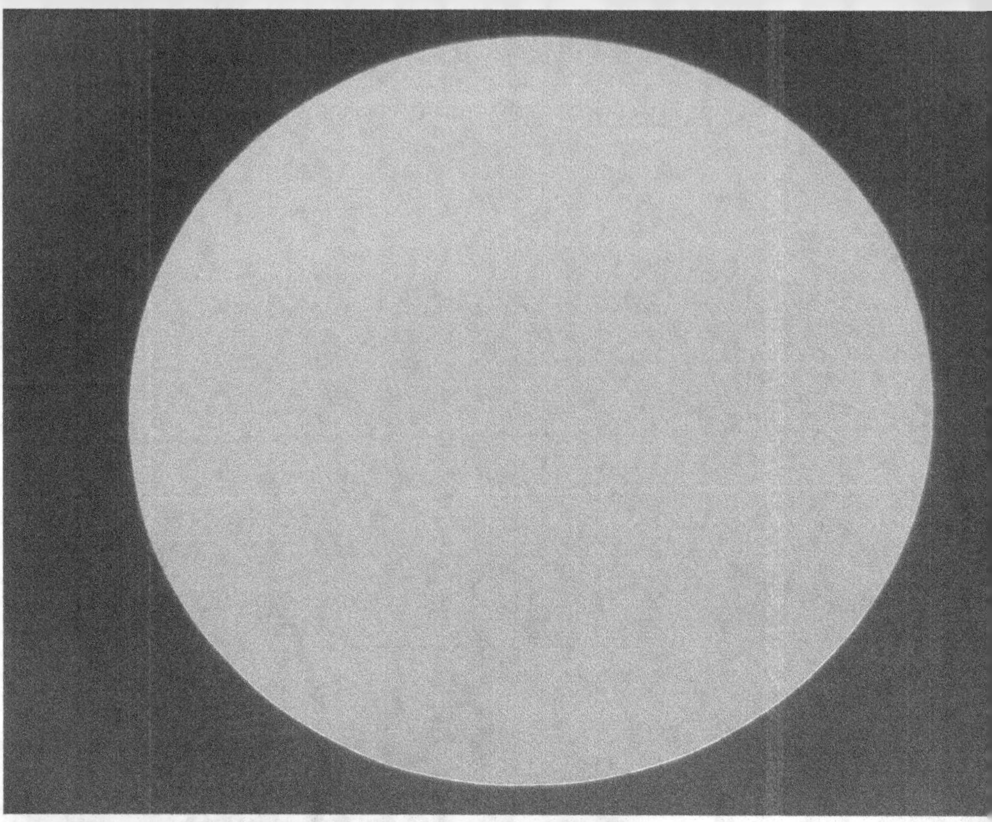

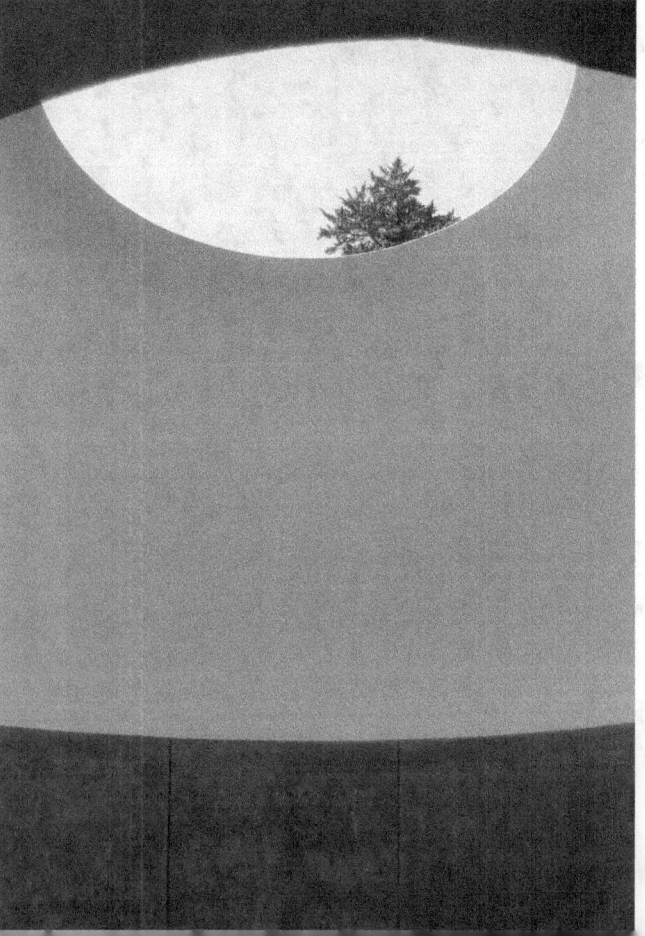

James Turrell's skyspace
at the de Young Museum
in San Francisco

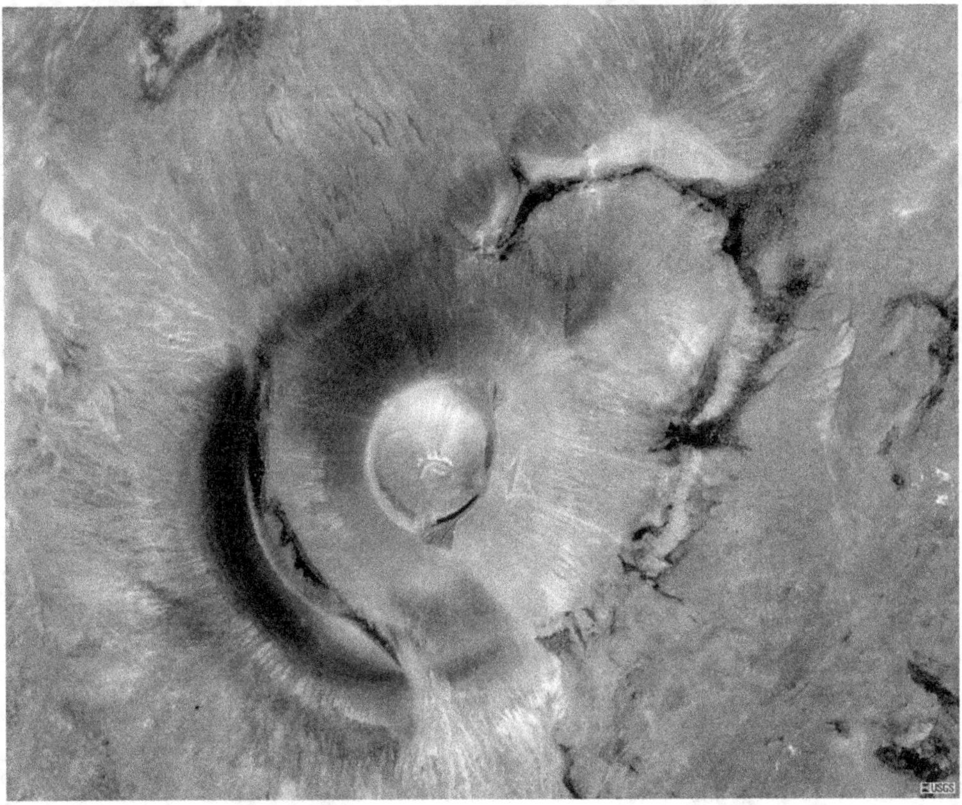

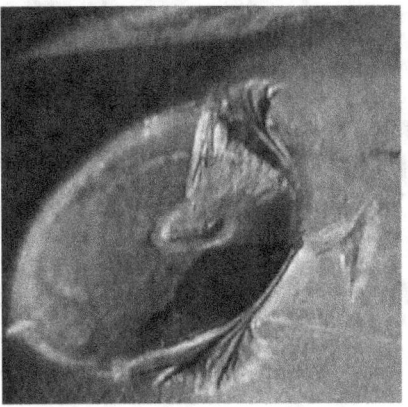

James Turrell's Roden Crater seen from above

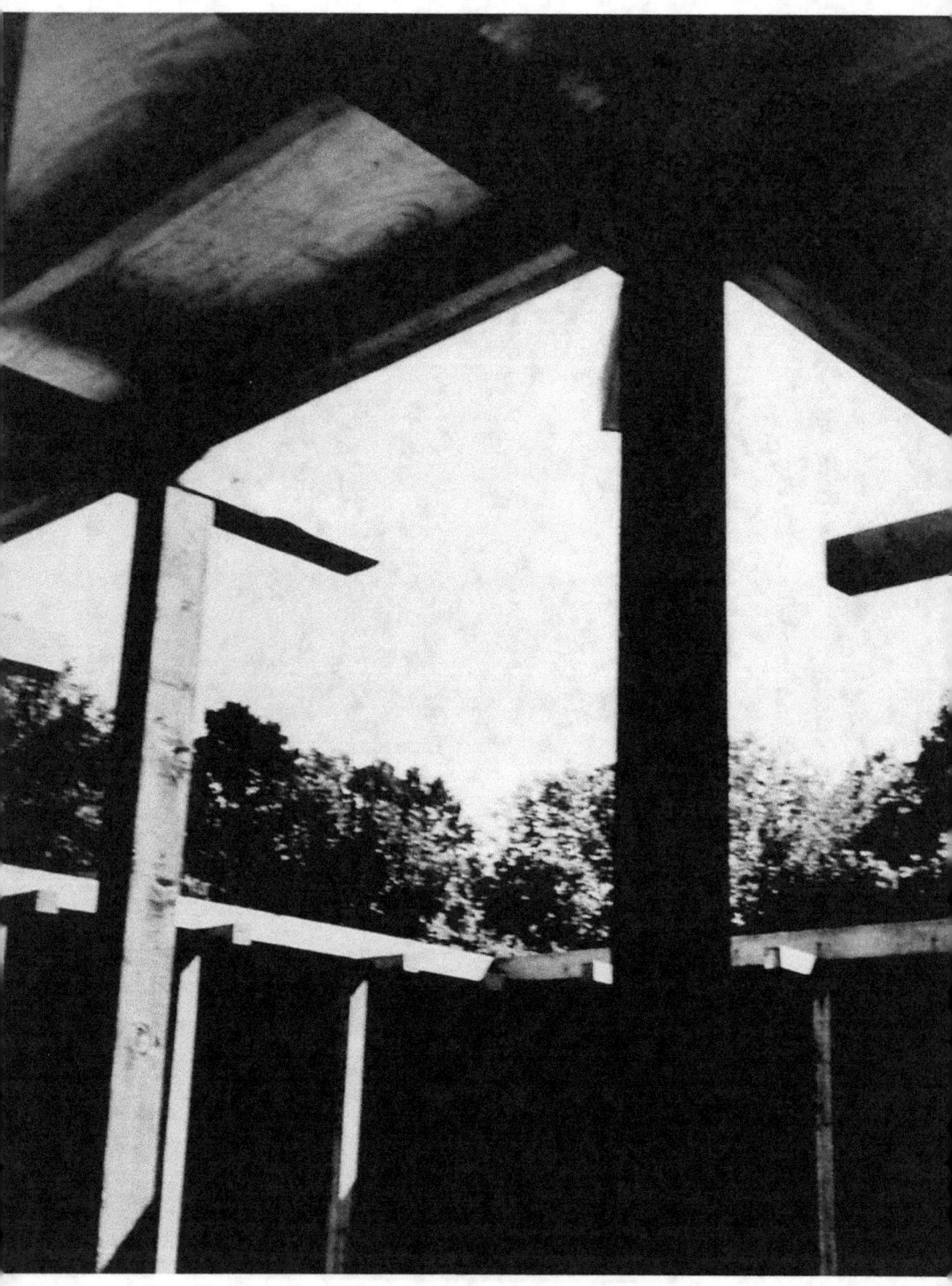

Mary Miss, Perimeters/ Pavilion/ Decoys, 1978

2

ANDY GOLDSWORTHY
AND LAND ART

SPIRIT OF PLACE: LAND ART

...it is an intensely spiritual affair I have with nature: a relationship.

Andy Goldsworthy[1]

For the land artist, the whole planet can be an artist's studio. The land artist ranges over the whole globe. A desert, a beach, a field, a forest can become a studio, a place of creative activity. The landscape itself is crucial in land art: every aspect of a landscape. The weather. The light. The wind. The very texture and colour and shape and dampness and

---

1 A. Goldsworthy, in N. Hedges, 69.

springiness and strength and size of moss, for instance. Or a stone. Or a crevice in a rock formation. The way the light falls on a patch of grass, with little bits of dead, yellowish grass on top of newer, green grass. Pine cones, closed-up. Icicles forming on a wall. Flowers turning sunward in the late afternoon. The sound of water.

> I have always paid great attention to natural forms, such as bones, shells, and pebbles, etc [wrote Henry Moore in the 1930s]. Sometimes for several years running I have been to the same part of the seashore – but each year a new shape of pebble has caught my eye, which the year before, though it was there in hundreds, I never saw. Out of the millions of pebbles passed in walking along the shore, I choose out to see with excitement only those which fit in with my existing form-interest at the time.[2]

These are the things land artists deal with in making art. These are the actualities that artists employ when they create artworks. To fully appreciate land art, then, the spectator has to look really closely, to grasp the details, as well as the overall conception and the distant view. This is true of Andy Goldsworthy's sculptures, as well as the larger American earthworks.

Environmental or land or garden art can include American earthworks (such as those by James Turrell and Mel Chin); ephemeral interventions in the environment (such as those by Andy Goldsworthy, Hans Haacke and Michael Singer); architectural installations (such as those by Mary Miss, Alice Aycock, and Nancy Holt); land art as performance art (Richard Long, Hamish Fulton, Christo), even if the artist is the only audience; land art that involves landscaping and garden art (such as Alan Sonfist, Patricia Johanson, Robert Irwin and Ian Hamilton Finlay); and sculpture or art parks. There are 'video gardens', too, such as Matthew McCaslin's *Bloomer* installation: 12 TV monitors played tapes of flowers blooming in time-lapse. The TV sets were arranged in groups like plants, with the cables tangled on the floor (St Louis Art Museum).

Key land art shows include *Earth Art* (Andrew Dickson White

---

2 H. Moore, "The Sculptor Speaks" in *The Listener*, Aug, 1937, quoted in H. Chipp, 595.

Museum of Art, Cornell University, 1969), which showed Dibbets, Long, Smithson, Oppenheim and Morris, *Land Art* (Hanover, 1970), *Earthworks* (Dwan Gallery, 1968), *The New Sculpture, 1965-75* (Whitney, 1990), *Qu'est-ce que la sculpture moderne?* (Paris, 1986), *Virginia Dwan, Art Minimal, Art Conceptuel, Earthworks* (Paris, 1991), *Earthworks* (Seattle, 1979), *Conceptual Art, Arte Povera, Land Art* (Turin, 1971), and many of the Documenta exhibitions at Kassel. At *Earth, Air, Fire, Water* (Boston, 1971), Haacke, Christo, Smithson, Oppenheim, Long, Sonfist, Huebler, Hutchinson, Warhol and Heizer showed works. Some of the key writers on land art include Rosalind Krauss, Lucy Lippard, Michael Fried, Kenneth Baker, John Beardsley, Lawrence Alloway, John Coplans, Diane Waldman, Harold Rosenberg, Stephanie Ross, Robert Hobbs, David Bourdon, Mel Gooding, Germano Celant, Alan Sonfist, Baile Oakes, Jeffrey Kastner, Andrew Causey and Gilles Tiberghien.

THE POLLEN PATH: ART AND LIFE

Land artists, like nature poets and nature mystics, are inspired by particular places. Nature poets, like religious mystics or land artists (or all artists) can be described as 'following their bliss' (Joseph Campbell's term). When you follow your bliss 'you come to bliss'.[3] Campbell used the model or metaphor of following the 'pollen path' of the Navaho Indians. As Campbell defined it:

> The Navaho have that wonderful image of what they call the pollen path. Pollen is the life source. The pollen path is the path to the centre. The Navaho say, "Oh, beauty before me, beauty behind me, beauty to the right of me, beauty to the left of me, beauty above me, beauty below me, I'm on the pollen path".[4]

---

3 J. Campbell, *Power*, 118.
4 J. Campbell, ib., 230.

This is one way of imagining the creative journey – towards the centre, the life source. Paradise, the Golden Age, Eden, was not back there then, but it is now. 'Eden *is...*this is it, this is Eden' (ib.). It's *now*, and can only be 'now'. There is no other time it could possibly be. The journey, whether physical, psychic, spiritual or imaginary, is along the *feng shui,* the 'dragon lines', or along the 'lines of song' or 'dream tracks' of the Australian aborigines, or the 'pollen paths' of the Navaho Indians.[5]

THE ALCHEMY OF MATTER

> *There is no habitation between our road and the Schroon river four miles cross country. I enjoy the phenomenon of nature, the sounds, the Northern lights, stars, animal calls, as I did the harbor lights, tugboat whistles, buoy clanks, the yelling of men on barges around the T.I.W. in Brooklyn. I sit up there and dream of the city as I used to dream of the mountains when I sat on the dock in Brooklyn. I like my solitude, black coffee, and daydreams. I like the changes of nature; no two days or nights are the same.*

David Smith (1951)[6]

R.W. Emerson wrote of the ecstasy of being alone in nature:

> The lover of nature is he whose inward and outward senses are still truly adjusted to each other... His intercourse with heaven and earth becomes part of his daily food. In the presence of nature a wild delight runs through the man in spite of real sorrows.[7]

Land art in its grander moments echoes the gestures of High Romanticism (the Blakean, Hölderlinian, Goethean, Turnerian

---

5 On the 'pollen path', see J. Campbell, *The Power of Myth,* 230; on Australian 'dreamtime', see P. Devereux, *The Dreamtime Earth and Avebury's Open Secrets,* Gothic Image, Glastonbury, 1992, 7-12.
6 "David Smith Makes a Sculpture", 1951, in D. Smith, 149.
7 R.W. Emerson, *Nature,* 1836, in H. Hugo, 386-7.

gestures) which have become so familiar in Western art. One of the apotheoses of High Romanticism is Johann Wolfgang von Goethe's novel *The Sorrows of Young Werther,* where the soul alone actualizes the myriad aspects of nature. In this passage from Goethe one can see similarities with the more opulent (sublime) moments in the art of Andy Goldsworthy, Robert Smithson and James Turrell:

> Ah, to view this vast landscape from there! Oh, distance is like the future: before our souls lies an entire and dusky vastness which overwhelms our feelings as it overwhelms our eyes, and ah! we long to surrender the whole of our being, and be filled with all the joy of one single, immense, magnificent emotion.[8]

The 'Land Art Sublime' (*pace* Robert Rosenblum's coining of the term 'Abstract Sublime' to describe Barnett Newman's and Mark Rothko's paintings) might include the snow and stone circles made in the wildernesses of Scotland, Ladakh and Peru of Richard Long; the stone circles of Nancy Holt; Christo's islands surrounded with pink polypropylene; and of course Smithson's *Spiral Jetty.* The 'Goldsworthy Sublime' would include works such as *Touching North* at the North Pole, the Durham maze, *Montréal Arch, Garden of Stones* and the stone walls (such as the *Storm King Wall*).

THE ECONOMICS OF LAND ART

Not all but much of land art is very expensive. That is, it is expensive moving tons of earth around. Taking a motorbike out into the desert and drawing lines with it is one thing (as Michael Heizer had done in *Circular Surface Displacement* [1968], North of Las Vegas), but making a 40 mile 18 foot high fence (Christo) is another. Much of land art requires patrons, sponsors, co-ordination with galleries, lawyers,

---

8 Wolfgang Goethe, *The Sorrows of Young Werther,* tr. M. Hulse, Penguin, London, 1989, 44.

public administrators, helpers and industry. (The costliness of land art may explain why much of it is American).9 Land art requires investment with no immediate return. Patrons are crucial to land art. In heyday of American earthworks the key patrons were the Dia Art Foundation, Robert C. Scull and Virginia Dwan, director of the Dwan Gallery between 1966 and 1971.

If he'd been American, Andy Goldsworthy mused, his art would have probably developed differently. American earth art for Goldsworthy tended towards conflict, division, and the pioneering spirit (W, 11). It's easy to view Christo's wrapped buildings or Walter de Maria's $500,000 *Vertical Earth Kilometer* as expensive, pointless art. This sort of land art may be 'true capitalist art', an art of excessive cost and excessive waste, but then, art has been full of silly amounts of money for ages.

What about Christo's wrappings? They cost a bomb, for sure, but, as Christo says, he pays for it himself, with money made from selling smaller works. Christo's *Running Fence* cost $2.5 million; *The Umbrellas* in Japan and California cost $26, 000,000. Christo says his art 'has to do with things that are very simple'.10 This definition can also apply to other land artists, including Goldsworthy: they, too, transform ordinary things.

---

9 1. A. Henri, *Total Art*, 81-82.
10 In A. Haden-Guest, 40.

LAND ART AND CONCEPTUAL ART

Land art is related to, and a part of, Conceptual art. Much of land art exists only in photographs, memories, words, and various cultural texts which are not the land art itself. Works that can be seen and those that are hidden or 'invisible' have the same importance for the artist. One of the hallmarks of the 'ideal Conceptual work', as Mel Bochner pointed out, is 'an exact linguistic correlative, that is, it could be described and experienced in its data and it could be infinitely repeatable'.[11] Land art is often Conceptual art: Dennis Oppenheim's *Whirlpool Eye of Storm* (a jet trail in the sky), Hans Haacke's balloons floating over Central Park, Robert Morris's steam pieces, and many of Andy Goldsworthy's leaf, stone, snow, mud and clay sculptures exist now only as photographs, memories and criticism.

By contrast, James Turrell wanted to place the viewer right in the midst of his artworks, so they could experience directly the subject of his art (light, the sky, celestial events) for themselves. It was important for Turrell that his art wasn't a record or a photograph of something that happened elsewhere, that the viewer hadn't seen or couldn't see for themselves. Thus, at Roden Crater in Arizona, Turrell constructed spaces that the spectator could enter physically, to experience light and the sky directly.

The pictorial or visual aspect of land art was over-emphasized by critics and viewers, Dennis Oppenheim argued in 1992. It was 'basically the *idea* of earthworks, the idea of the salt flats' that was important, not the visual element; '[t]he visual quotient is not as strenuous as you think'. Many land artworks were conceptual, mental, not visual or even physical. 'In other words,' said Oppenheim, talking about Smithson's *Spiral Jetty*, 'it's about the salt, submersions, the jetty, what is around the salt flats. In the end it's about mental configurations' (1992). This presents a problem, because most land artworks are known primarily in a visual form – in photographs. It'd be great if all land artworks were visited or directly experienced, as Oppenheim and others intended, but they aren't. For Richard Serra, the 'focus of art for

11 "Mel Bochner on Malevich", interview with J. Coplans, *Artforum*, June, 1974, 62.

me is the experience of living through the pieces', but the actual work itself, the physical object, was not the whole point, or the whole pleasure, of making art: 'that experience may have very little to do with the physical facts of the work of art'.12

LAND ART AND PHOTOGRAPHY

In land art photographs, the spectator is often not offered a *range* of viewpoints of a work, although land artists clearly take more than one shot of each work they make. No artist takes just *one* photo out of a 36 exposure 35mm film, or one frame out of a twelve shot 120mm format film, or one digital shot out of hundreds on a digital still camera. No, an artist, like an photographer, takes a range of shots, at different, bracketed exposures (as Andy Goldsworthy does [P, 95, 101]), from different viewpoints. Even with bracketing exposures, though, still meant that only one or two shots might be properly exposed (this made Goldsworthy anxious when he used his panoramic camera, because it only had four shots per roll of film).

Goldsworthy also spoke of not being able to capture the collapse of a sculpture (such as a *Sea Cairn*) because he was re-loading the camera, or winding on the film, or taking another light reading. Of the California *Sea Cairn* (2001), for instance, Goldsworthy remarked: 'changing film was a nervous business, and I always held a finger on the shutter release, just in case' (P, 106). Goldsworthy said he could have a photographic assistant, or more cameras, but he didn't want to get too deeply involved with the photographic side of his art (P, 101). At the same time, of course, Goldsworthy is always very reliant on photography, and photography is absolutely central to his art.

Andy Goldsworthy, for example, typically takes two viewpoints or

12 R. Serra, in *Richard Serra, Interviews,* Hudson River Museum, New York, NY, 1980, 37.

shots: a close-up, which is about the artist's subjective relationship with his work – taken from just a few feet away. Then there is a second, more 'objective' view, showing the sculpture as the independent observer might see it. This second photograph shows the work in its environment, which is crucial. Goldsworthy's photos are a mix of these two viewpoints, the subjective and the objective, close-up and distance: often the most powerful shots are not the near-side images, showing the detail in the sculpture, but the distant views.

LAND ART AND RELIGION

It's no surprise that the American form of earth art should be sympathetic to Oriental mysticism, as Zen Buddhism, Hinduism, Shinto, Confucianism and Taoism were particularly popular in 1960s culture (in the Beats and 'dharma bums', or the West Coast hippies, or the graduates of Western universities, or rock musicians, for example). It was a logical cultural development, it seems, from Parisian Existentialism to Californian Zen Buddhism, from the Old World philosophies based on Classical ideals to the New World's appropriation of the even older Oriental philosophies. Many of the chief precepts of Taoism, Confucianism, Hinduism, Shinto and Zen Buddhism chime with those of land art, not only the American earthworks, but also the British form of land art of Goldsworthy, Long, Drury, Fulton, Nash and others. Matsuo Basho, an important Oriental poet, wrote:

> Go to the pine if you want to learn about the pine, or to the bamboo if you want to learn about the bamboo. And in doing so, you must leave your subjective preoccupation with yourself.[13]

13 M. Basho, *The Narrow Road to the Deep North and Other Travel Sketches*, tr. N. Yuasa, Penguin, London, 1966, 33.

And Makoto Ueda glossed Basho thus: '[f]or learn means to enter into the object, perceive its delicate life and feel its feelings.'[14] These notions of searching for the 'essence' are absolutely in tune with the æsthetics of Goldsworthy, Brancusi, Andre, and Judd. Goldsworthy spoke in exactly the same terms of trying to find the 'essence' of nature, of going out into the natural world in order to learn about it. Goldsworthy followed Basho's Taoist precepts of going to nature to study it to the letter.

In *Being and Circumstance,* Robert Irwin proposed four types of land art: 'site dominant', such as monuments and murals; 'site adjusted', in which some considerations are made towards the site, but it's still studio-made; 'site specific', in which steps are made towards integrating the work into the site; and 'site conditioned', work which responds to its surroundings. The 'site determined' category is the one Irwin preferred, and it's also the type of sculpture favoured by Andy Goldsworthy. Irwin defined 'site conditioned' work as an 'intimate, hands-on reading of the site', which results from 'sitting, watching, and walking through the site'; it means being aware of water, weather, sound, surface, movement, history, and so on. Such considerations determine whether the response 'should be monumental or ephemeral, aggressive or gentle, useful or useless, sculptural, architectural, or simply the planting of a tree, or maybe even doing nothing at all' (1985).

Andy Goldsworthy builds transience into many of his sculptures; indeed, the subject matter of some works is their ephemerality (with the form as secondary). They are about the fact that they won't last very long. In fact, the bulk of Goldsworthy's art is ephemeral, with 'permanent' works – such as the Storm King *Wall*, the Montréal *Arch*, the New York *Garden of Stones*, the Cumbrian *Sheepfolds* and the Digne *Water Cairns* – in the minority. Making permanent works was restrictive for Goldsworthy, because his art was an art founded on ephemerality (RA, 111).

---

14 M. Ueda, *Matsuo Basho*, Twayne, New York, NY, 1970, 167.

CIRCLES IN LAND ART

The circle motif, one of the primæval symbols of eternity, cycles, time, rebirth, and so on, is employed throughout the work of Andy Goldsworthy and much of land art (Goldsworthy realizes that it's virtually impossible to do away with the circle). Circles in land art are made from slate, timber, snow, salt, grass or by walking in a circle; they seem to be gentler, more eco-friendly kinds of sculpture. The circle shape itself speaks of organic forms, and, in some religions, evokes the 'feminine' and the Goddess. Not a few sculptors and land artists have made the circle crucial to their works: Alison Wilding, Richard Deacon, Stephen Cox, Mary Miss, Anish Kapoor, Peter Randall-Page, Robert Morris and Dennis Oppenheim.

Land art based on circles includes Vijali's *World Wheel* (1987), Alan Sonfist's *Circles of Life* (1987) and *Pool of Virgin Earth* (1975), Adam Purple's *The Garden of Eden* (1975), Charles Jencks' *Snail Mound* (1992-94), Michael Heizer's *Circular Surface Planar Displacement Drawing* (1970), Stan Herd's *The Circle* (1992), and Mel Chin's *Revival Field* (1993). Many of Nancy Holt's works are circular: *Annual Ring* (1981), *30 Below* (1980), and *Sun Tunnels* (1976).

Donald Judd produced two circular steel bands, 180 inches in diameter, as well as a concrete circular 'wall'. Robert Morris made gigantic circular works, such as his *Observatory* (1971), which was a huge earthwork recalling the megalithic structures of ancient times, such as Avebury stone circle. Morris's *Labyrinth* (1974) was a maze-size sculpture, the kind of maze one finds in theme parks and country houses, except that Morris's *Labyrinth* used the ancient pattern of the Cretan labyrinth, itself a motif some see as distinctly feminine, speaking of Goddess mysteries. Herbert Bayer's *Mill Creek Canyon Earthworks* (1979-82) was a series of earthworks recalling ancient monuments. Robert Smithson's *Closed Mirror Square* was like an Aztec ziggurat, while his *Amarillo Ramp* recalled the massive embankments found at Neolithic earthworks in Western Europe.[15]

Many land artists have made mounds which recall prehistoric burial

15 See M. Berger, 1989.

mounds (apart from the works cited above) including Charles Jencks (*Snail Mound*, 1992-94), Judy Varga's *Geometry of Echoes Converge* (1980), Maya Lin's *Wave Field* (1995), Peter Walker's *Turf Mountain* (1993) and James Pierce (*Burial Mound*). These (Minimal) sculptures are ambivalently related to ancient monuments, however, as Samuel Wagstaff remarked of Tony Smith's works: '[t]hey are related to early cultures intentionally or through sympathy – menhirs, earth mounds, cairns... [and] to this culture with equal sympathy – smokestacks, gas tanks, dump trucks, poured concrete ramps.'[16]

One of the most exciting developments of contemporary sculpture and art is the installation, the taking over of a whole space or environment – the floor, walls and ceiling of a gallery, as in Rebecca Horn's *Ballet of the Woodpecker* (1986-87), a room full of mirrors, or Sylvia Stone's *Crystal Palace*. Andy Goldsworthy's art, like many land artists' works, is clearly related to the art installation: it is an art of environments, where the relatively small addition of a stack of stones forming a cairn sets alive the surrounding landscape. One sees the landscape in a new way: context is all-important. (Sometimes, Goldsworthy has created installations, such as *Snowballs in Summer* on the streets of London in 2000. *Garden of Stones* (2003) and *Stone Houses* (2004) in Gotham can be regarded as installations).

---

16 Quoted in L. Lippard, 1967c, 26.

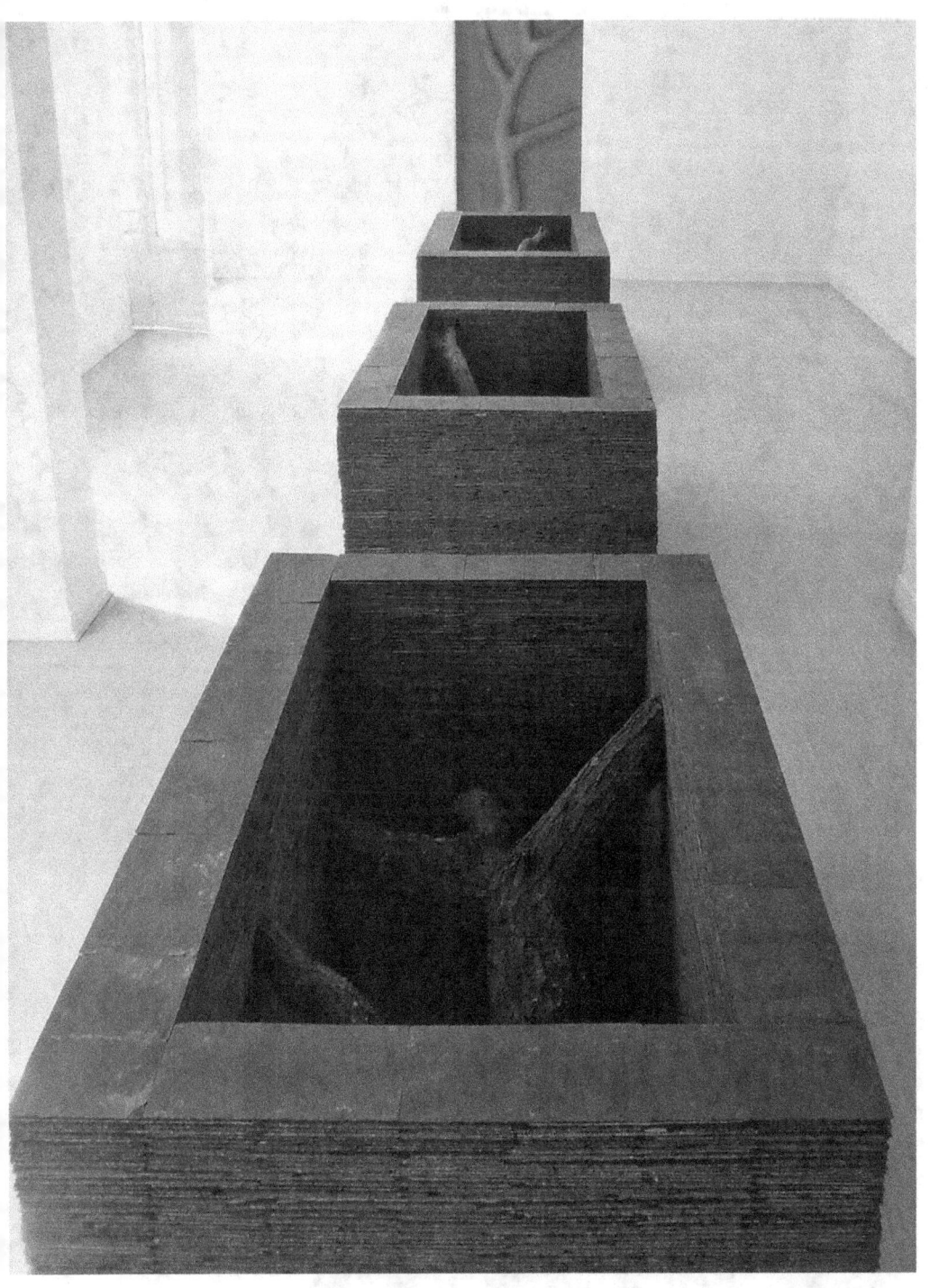

Andy Goldsworthy, installation, Paris, 2006

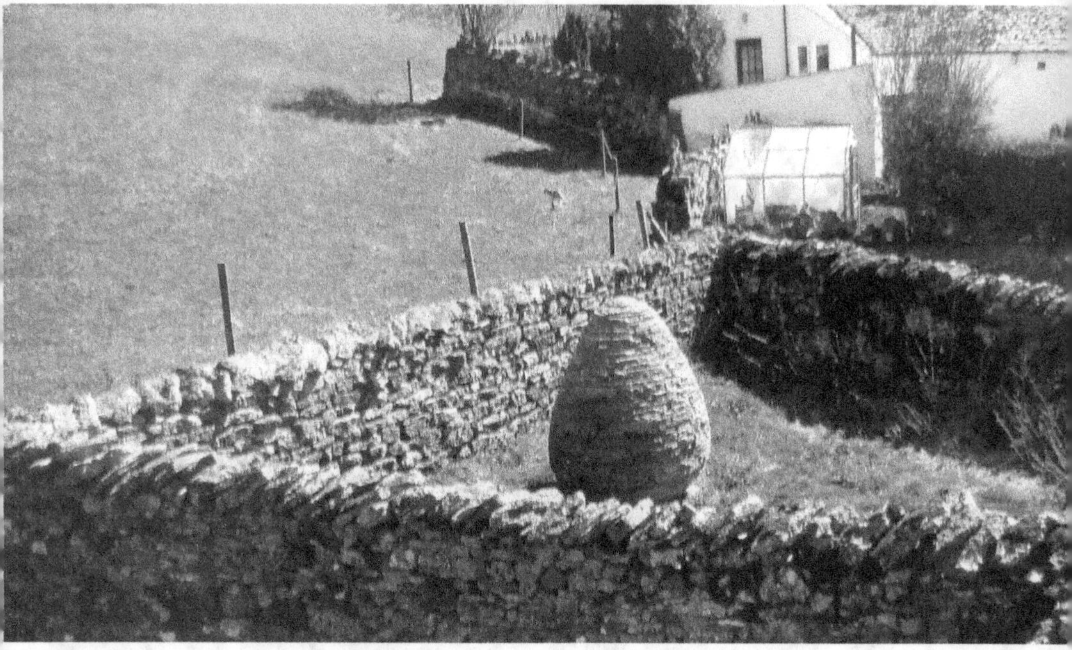

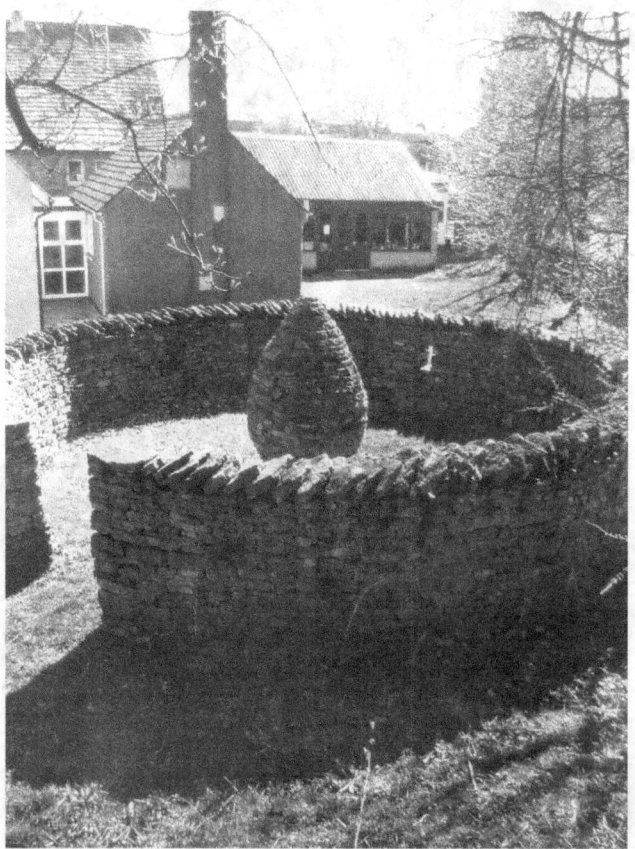

Andy Goldsworthy,
Brough Pinfold Cairn, 2001,
left.
Crosby Ravensworth
Pinfold Cairn, 2004,
above.

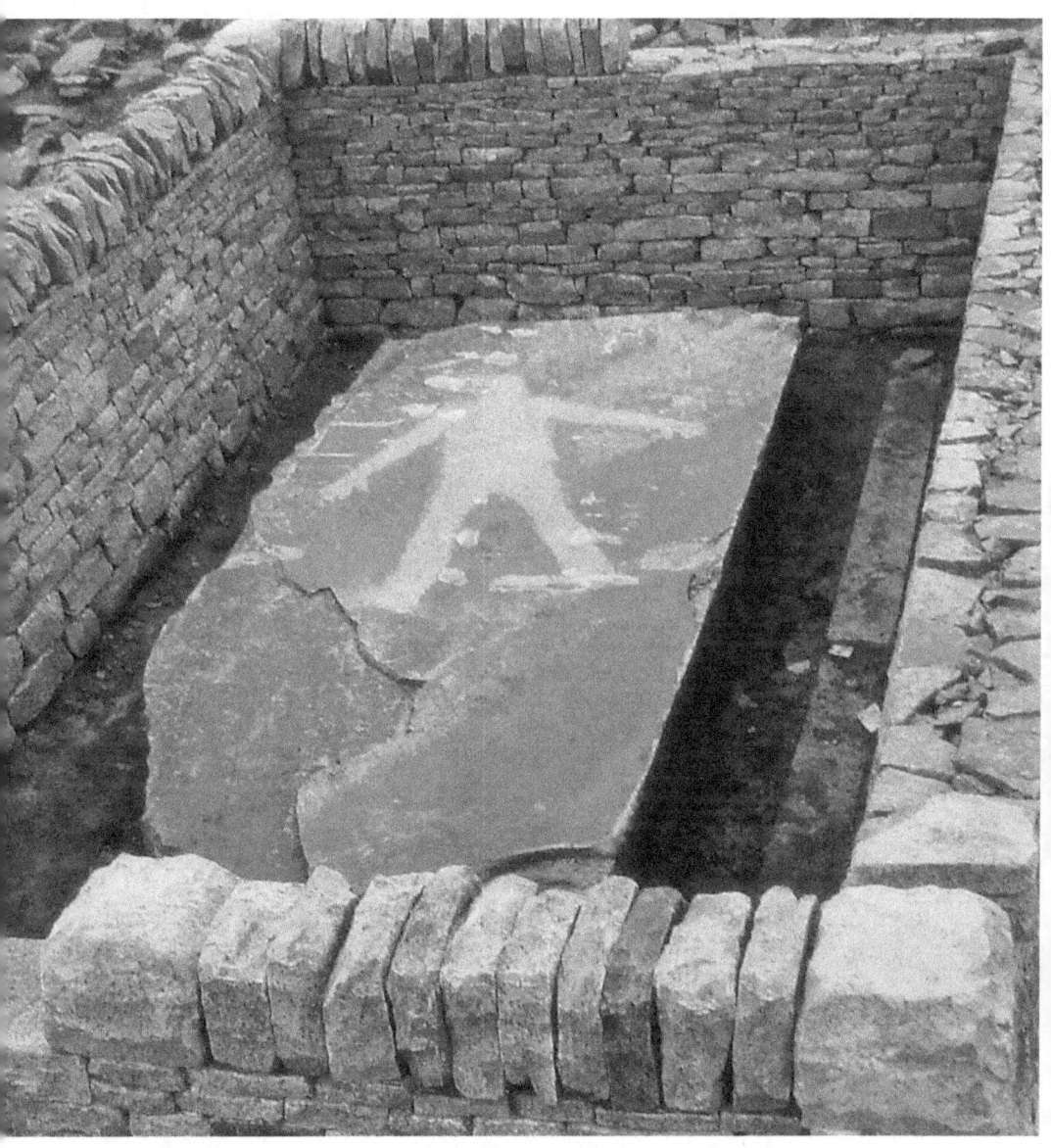

Andy Goldsworthy, Shadow Stone Fold, 2007

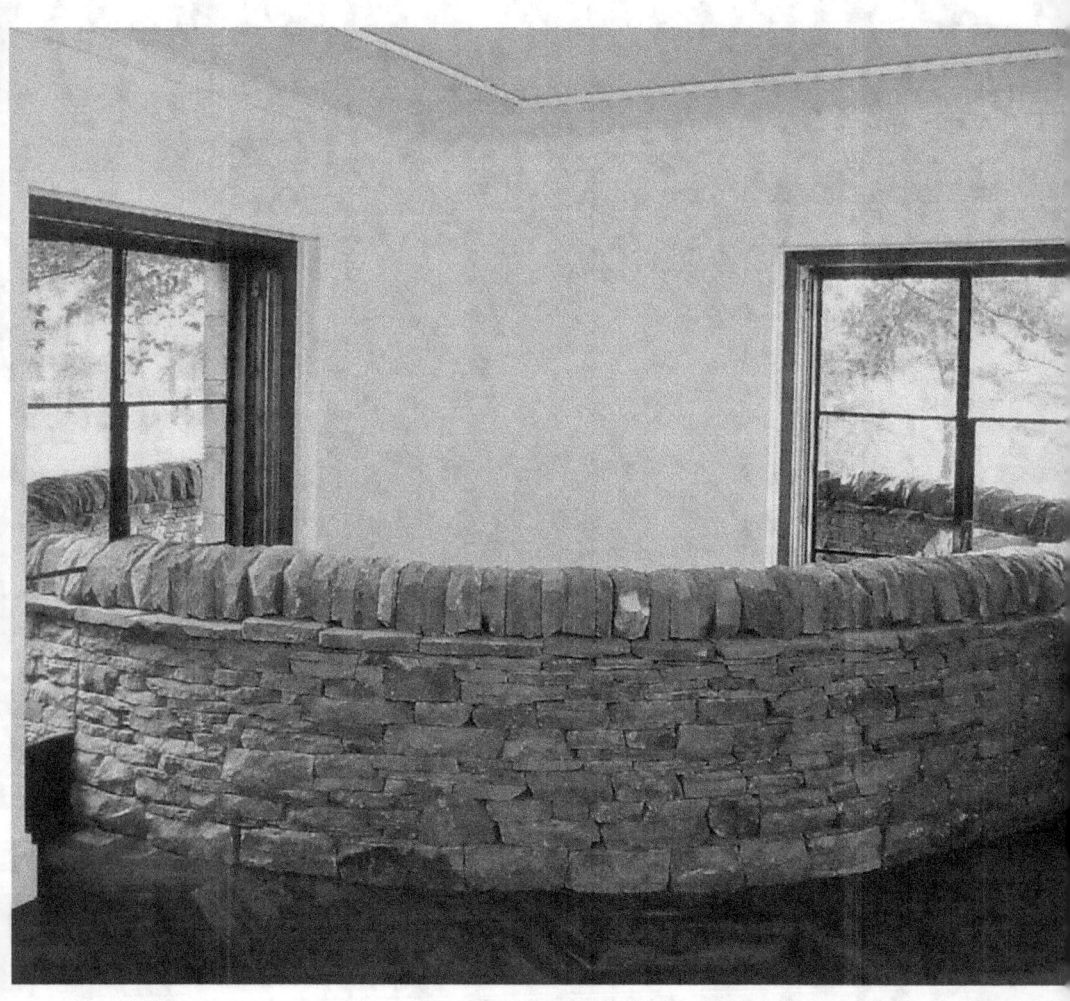

Andy Goldsworthy, Storm King Fold, New York, 2000

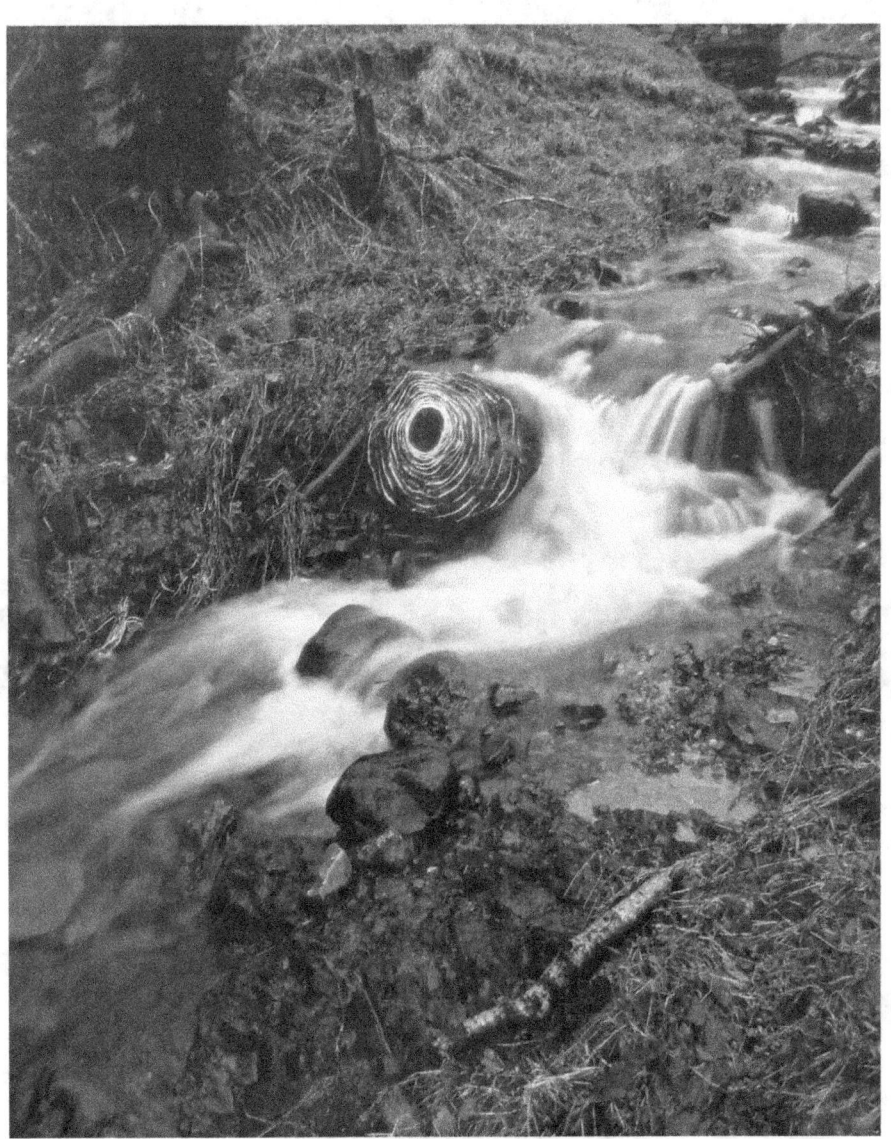

Andy Goldsworthy, Wet Wool, 2007

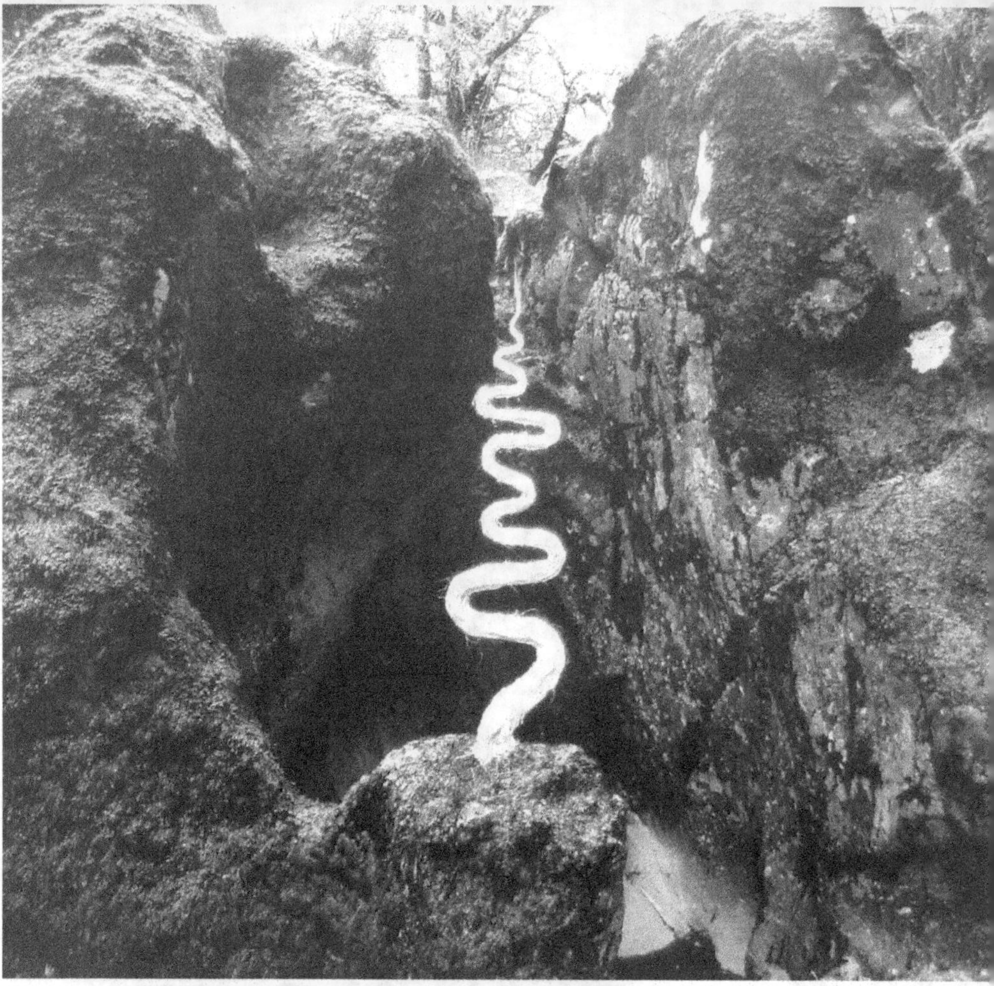

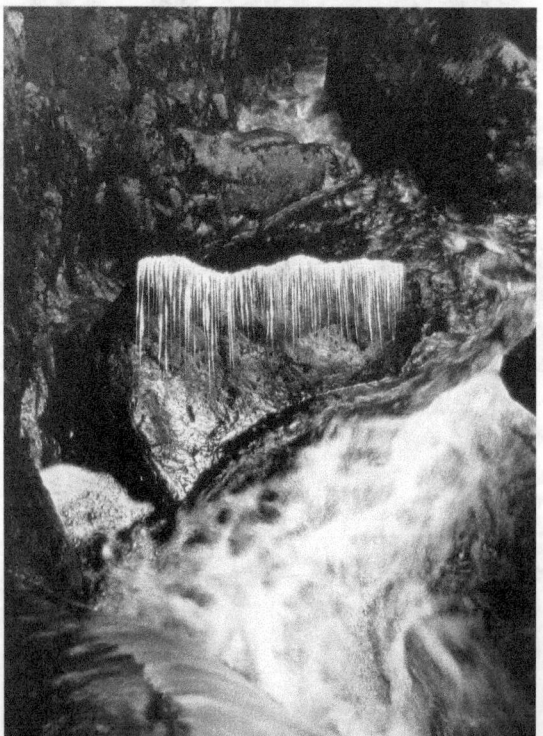

Andy Goldsworthy,
Wet Wool, 2005 (above)
Wet Wool, 2006 (left)

3

ANDY GOLDSWORTHY:
WHOLE EARTH ARTIST

Andy Goldsworthy works with the natural world, and within nature. He uses natural materials in natural shapes and forms set in natural contexts. Goldsworthy takes his cue from nature: as Jan Dibbets put it in 1969: 'I realized that if you want to use nature, you have to derive the appropriate structure from nature too'.[1] Nature may be the starting-point but, as we'll see, the end-point – art – is entirely cultural and not something you'll ever find in the natural world.

Andy Goldsworthy seems to be a particularly gentle and sensitive artist, compared to many sculptors and land artists: he stitches

---

1 J. Dibbets, in D. Ashton, ed. *20th Century Artists on Art,* Pantheon, New York, NY, 1985, 174.

together leaves to form lines (which're often placed in water, or over branches), or makes circular slabs of snow, or entwines twigs in an arc. He creates a delicate spiral of chestnut leaves, called *Autumn Horn* (1986); he pins bright yellow dandelions on willowherb stalks in a circle, on bluebells (1987); he makes lines and cairns of pebbles; a horizontal line of red sumach leaves was pinned to a willow (at Storm King in 1998); he rubs red stones to stain rockpools; he pins leaves to tree trunks; he fashions a zigzag line of hogweed stalks along a fallen elm tree (2002); he makes hollow, circular structures, recalling igloos, from slate, leaves, driftwood and bracken; he makes long wavy ridges in Arizonan and Australian desert sand; he throws sand and sticks in the air and photographs the moment; he makes arches, globes, hollow spheres, slabs, spires, spirals and star-shapes out of snow and ice. Very impressive it all is. The sculptures made of sticks, for instance, stuck together in an arch, or a line, reflected in the mirror-like water of Derwent Water in Cumbria in 1988, are indeed wonderful. The sculptures exude tranquillity, an early morning calm (quite the opposite of another water work, Klaus Rinke's *Water Sculpture*, where a water canon blasted water over visitors as they approached a gallery, or Jim Sanborn's 1995 *Coastline*, which employed a wave generator to simulate waves in a Maryland garden).

Then there's the globe Goldsworthy made from oak leaves in various states of autumnal decay, superb (Dumfriesshire, 1985). Or the sphere of sticks made in Fairfax, California (1995), set next to a sheltering tree. Or the sand serpent in the British Museum (1994). Or the globe made out of snow, and perched amidst some young trees (1980), or the slabs of snow, set up in a line with slits cut in them (1988).

Goldsworthy said: 'I want an intimate physical involvement with the earth. I must touch'.[2] Touching is 'deeply important' for Goldsworthy.[3] Only touching gives the artist the deep understanding of his materials and nature, he asserted.[4] Goldsworthy's *Forked branch and twig* is exactly that: a forked branch with a twig suspended between the two parts of the branch. The photograph of this 1978 work shows a space

2 A. Goldsworthy, in A. Causey, 1980.
3 3. A. Goldsworthy, in *Aspects*, 1986.
4 4. A. Goldsworthy, ib., HE, 165.

enclosed by the twig and branch, a rough circle of air and sky enclosed by the twig and branch. Goldsworthy rarely uses animals in his art; stones and vegetation are his usual materials. Some sculptures refer to animals (such as sheep and cows). One or two pieces were made from feathers (*Goose feathers* [1983], *Wood pigeon wing feathers* [1977], *Feathers plucked from a dead heron* [1982], and *Wet feathers wrapped around a stone* [1999]). And some from wool (*Wool line*, 1995). (Goldsworthy has increasingly used wool, particularly in the works related to the grand *Sheepfolds* project. For example, a line of shreds of wet wool hanging over a stream in *Wet wool* (2001) *Wool hung wet* (2006), and *Wet wool* (2006), concentric circular and linear patterns on boulders and branches (in *Wet wool*, 2007, *Wet wool*, 2006, *Line*, 1999, and *River bed rock,* 2001), which recall the ridges Goldsworthy's made with sand on beaches, *Wool throws* (1997), and the lines of leaves on rocks, dry wool set atop a wall (*Wall*, 1996), wool spread over grass in large rectangles (*Wool*, 1997), and wet wool that's frozen and been shaped into a standing sculpture, as in *Wet wool* (2005).)

Andy Goldsworthy has made more 'traditional' forms of art in galleries: his bracken, fern and horse chestnut stalk works, for instance, were created by pinning the materials onto white gallery walls. These works – *Bracken fronds* (Ecology Centre, London, 1985), *Reeds, bracken and horse chestnut stalks* (Centre d'Art Contemporain, Castres, and Galerie Aline Vidal, Paris, 1989) and *Reed line drawing* (Paris, 1990) – were essentially free, open wall drawings, often employing basic motifs such as the circle and open curve. Hanging screens of plants that Goldsworthy made in galleries include the *Susuki grass* and *Horse chestnut leaf stalks* (both made in Japan in 1993), *Horse chestnut leaf stalks* (1994, Japan), *Yucca blades* (New Mexico, 2000), and *Rushes thorns* (1992, San Francisco). *Rosebay willowherb* (1990) was crafted in Goldsworthy's studio.

In a 1992 Scaur Water sculpture, Goldsworthy took up rosebay willowherb stalks, one of his favourite media, and fashioned them into three curved, intertwining lines which moved down from a waterfall over mossy rocks. It was a variant of the many lines of leaves

Goldsworthy has constructed. Goldsworthy called it 'drawing a waterfall' (P, 38). *Rush Line Drawing* (1999) employed linked rush stalks in a continuous, serpentine line, looping across the front of a group of butterbur plants. The stalks were held in place by piercing the edges of the large leaves.

In the course of his work outdoors, Goldsworthy must have been bitten and stung by insects, stung, scratched and cut by plants, rained on millions of times, frozen by cold, burnt by the sun, blown about by the wind, deafened by thunder, snowed on, and bruised by rocks and branches. Interrupted by people (and animals) many times. Mud, freezing water, birds and traffic would be frequent problems. And one of the biggest challenges in working out of doors is invisible: the wind (Goldsworthy often mentions it).

Although he has carved stone from time to time, in the traditional sculptural manner, and also modelled clay, Goldsworthy disliked both processes. Although both methods have been central to sculpture for centuries, Goldsworthy rarely used them. 'I dislike the malleability of modelling and the imposition of carving as processes. Carving is a process that relies upon the integral strength of the block of stone' (RA, 105). Instead, Goldsworthy preferred to employ drawings or shaping with his hands, or weaving stalks or plants or leaves, or rubbing stone to make powder, or splitting stone to make walls or cairns, or piling up snow, or throwing stalks in the air, or balancing rocks.

Rather than modelling with clay, dabbing on a bit here and there, Goldsworthy preferred to add one layer after another, until the work was complete. The form emerged partly from the process, then – a notion very much in keeping with 1960s art practice, with its emphasis on process and the *experience* of making an artwork. Goldsworthy spoke of forms that were 'integral' or 'rooted internally' in the materials (RA, 105). Many other contemporary sculptors have emphasized following the dictates of the material, and the actualities of making the work. It's a sculptural process that incorporates spontaneity, accident, mistakes, and external forces such as weather.

In 1995 Goldsworthy was invited to have his art appear on British Royal Mail stamps, as part of their 'Springtime' Royal Mail Mint stamps (a stamp commission is one of the signs of becoming 'establishment'). Significantly, the Royal Mail chose Goldsworthy's leafworks for the stamps (some of his most approachable and appealing sculptures). The stamps comprised photographs of five leafworks, printed in landscape format, with the Queen's head and the price of the stamp printed in silver. The artist's name did not appear on the stamps: instead, the word 'Springtime' was printed in silver. The 19 pence stamp was an open circle of dandelions, with the ubiquitous black Goldsworthy hole at the centre. The first class (25 pence) stamp was a leaf horn made from sweet chestnut leaves.

Andy Goldsworthy's Royal Mail stamps were marketed as small, delicate but ecologically-friendly expressions of the pastoral sublime. In the information card that went with the presentation pack, the blurb, in a flamboyant green script, waxed lyrical about the changing of the seasons, the coming of Spring and Maypole dancing (clichés of Spring in British culture), before introducing Goldsworthy as an artist of the ephemeral and pastoral, a poet who catches the spirit of nature as it changes and grows. The sensitivity, fragility and empathy of Goldsworthy's art were emphasized. 'Andy has celebrated *springtime* in a language that is all his own', purred the Royal Mail brochure. Pull quotes were placed around the text, with colour photographs of Goldsworthy's sculptures.

The Royal Mail commission was another example of the widespread acceptance of Goldsworthy's art. Stamps are a prestigious assignment. Simply in terms of numbers, millions of Royal Mail stamps will be printed. Goldsworthy's sculptures appeared on all manner of letters and parcels. The 'transient' nature of Goldsworthy's art was made 'permanent' on a massive scale. A further set of stamps, featuring Goldsworthy's ice works, appeared in 2003.[5] The icework stamps appeared in Winter, making them suitably seasonal.

Andy Goldsworthy has always spoken of the significance of the surrounding environment in his works. His sculptures are as much

5 The Christmas 2003 stamps, valued at 20p, 38p, 53p, 68p and £1.12, comprised *Ice Spiral, Icicle Star, Wall of Frozen Snow, Ice Ball, Ice Hole, Snow Pyramids*. They were designed by Dick Davis from Goldsworthy's photographs. The stamps were also featured as Smilers™ stamps, personalized stamps in photobooths, and also part of the gamecard promotion with a first prize of £1 million.

about the surroundings in which they are situated, as they are about the sculptures themselves. An exhibition inside, under a roof, in a gallery, is always going to be a problem, then. The contemporary gallery, with its sparse settings, white-washed walls and trendy magazines and postcards, is a powerfully *cultural* environment (and commercial – a gallery is a store selling art). The contemporary gallery is not 'natural' at all, it is not 'nature', it is not a place of mist, wind, skies and soil. No wonder, then, that earth artists such as Walter de Maria wanted to fill a whole gallery with dark soil, to bring nature into the contemporary art gallery in a big way.

Andy Goldsworthy's shows are something of a disappointment, in one way, because the works have to breathe without their usual natural surroundings. Goldsworthy did emulate Walter de Maria in a direct way: in November, 1992, he covered the interior of the London gallery of his agent with clay (*Hard earth – Dorset clay smoothed out, left to dry*). The exhibit began as a smooth creamy-white expanse of wet clay/earth on the floor. It looked as if the gallery was empty, said Goldsworthy (S, 64), recalling Yves Klein's gallery showing nothingness, *Le Vide*, of 1958. *Hard earth* directly re-echoed de Maria's *New York Earth Room*: the natural world was present in the gallery in both works in force: in de Maria's *New York Earth Room* (1977) the dark soil had a solemn, weighty, fecund presence; in Goldsworthy's *Hard earth* time and transformation played a part: gradually, the clay dried and cracked, allowing the Goldsworthyan vision of the dark energies of nature to well up: nature was erupting in the gallery space.

Andy Goldsworthy tended to add a few pages of his own writing to his published art books, drawn from his artist's journals. The books mainly consisted of colour photographs of his artworks. In one or two books, such as *Time, Passage, Midsummer Snowballs* and *Arch*, Goldsworthy wrote considerably longer pieces. In *Time*, for instance, there are about 50 pages of writing by Goldsworthy.

Goldsworthy's writings are sometimes simple, sometimes blunt and always matter-of-fact – in an indomitable, Northern British fashion. Goldsworthy's persona in the texts is a rugged man of the wild, a 'whole earth man', ecologically sensitive, someone 'in touch' with nature, working with his bare hands, in boots, hat and an anorak, often in Winter. A modern-day Thoreau living off the land at Walden. There is a macho posturing to this (no doubt unintentional), in which the relationship with nature is 'fundamental', 'raw', 'violent', 'intense'. Goldsworthy sees working in the hard conditions of Winter a challenge, a 'test of my commitment to the landscape'.6 Goldsworthy has spoken about being 'shocked' by small-scale natural events, about work suddenly becoming 'intense', about the 'raw energy' of colours (he doesn't mean 'shock' in the usual sense, though). Goldsworthy's writings are marked by words such as 'powerful', 'wildness', 'deeper', 'rooted', 'flesh and bone', 'feeling', 'essential', 'sense', 'energy', 'touching' and 'essence' (these words are taken from a single page of Golds-worthyan philosophy, in *Stone* [6]).

All this talk of raw, powerful essence in nature suggests one British poet in particular – Ted Hughes, the stolid Yorkshireman and former Poet Laureate whose books (*River, Hawk in the Rain, Lupercal, Wodwo, Elmet*) are full of post-Gerard Manley Hopkinsian evocations of wild shingle beaches, desolate moorland, ancient forests and craggy heights. If ever there was a poetic equivalent of Goldsworthy's boulders, melting snowballs, slate cairns and red mud 'throws', it is Ted Hughes' verse. Another link is nature-man Mellors in *Lady Chatterley's Lover* (1928), the no-nonsense outdoor man who is in fact a New Man, painfully sensitive and alive (an amazing lover, too, and he lives alone in the woods; macho, self-sufficient, a 'man's man'). The D.H. Lawrence connection with Andy Goldsworthy has been emphasized by Goldsworthy himself: in *Stone* he quoted from Lawrence's *The Rainbow* (1915), one of those euphoric, ithyphallic passages about the ecstasy of consummation in an arch. Here's an extract from Nottinghamshire's greatest artist, from a scene where Will Brangwen visits Lincoln cathedral:

Here the stone leapt up from the plain earth, leapt up in a manifold, clustered desire each time, away from the horizontal earth, through twilight and dusk and the whole range of desire, through the swerving, the

6 Interview with T. Friedman, *Third Ear*, June, 1989 in HE, 166.

declination, ah, to the ecstasy, the touch, to the meeting and the consummation, the meeting, the clasp, the close embrace, the neutrality, the perfect swooning consummation, the timeless ecstasy. There his soul remained, at the apex of the arch, clinched in the timeless ecstasy, consummated.[7]

Hardly anyone writes like that these days; Goldsworthy can't be the only artist who'd love it if critics wrote about their art like that. Lawrence's intensely poetic novel about three generations of a Midlands family (his 'Brangwen-saga') is a strident inrush of energy into Goldsworthy's otherwise pedestrian prose in the book *Stone*. Goldsworthy's own pontifications can be banal, and the quotes from Locke and Lawrence (as in *Stone*) highlight that.

The arrogance which Goldsworthy occasionally voices is inescapable: for all his humble sensitivity, he is a proud and confident artist. For example, of a 12 foot high cairn sculpture made beside a river in Illinois, Goldsworthy said that the work 'gives a feeling of the weight, power and volume of a river in flood in a way that a marked pole never could' (S, 37). He was so sure of the effect his sculpture will have on the viewer. But this interpretation of the cairn only makes sense if the viewer is primed first about the 1954 flood, and regards a pile of stones as more powerful as a measurer of a river's flood than a marked pole. After all, the dumb punter might remark, one can stand right under a 12 foot pole (if it's in the same place) and see it towering over one's head. A pole may be just as impressive as a stone mound (it has measurements and dates painted on it, for instance, of the floods in, say, 1858, or 1916). Goldsworthy was cautious about appearing too self-confident. In an interview in *Sheepfolds* (1996) he said '[m]y monuments do not sit arrogantly on top of the hill, [but] that doesn't mean that they don't have a power' (Sh, 17). Of course: no artist wants their sculptures to be overwhelmed by the landscape; they have to assert themselves within the environment.

'At its most successful, my 'touch' looks into the heart of nature', Goldsworthy affirmed in the late Eighties (WH and AG). This is a pretty self-confident statement. It's like a Hollywood movie director

---

7 D.H. Lawrence, *The Rainbow*, Penguin, London, 1981, 244.

saying 'my films touch the heart of contemporary society • war-torn Vietnam • life on a Mid-West farm' or whatever. Goldsworthy does not say my art *tries* to look at or explore nature, but 'my 'touch' looks into the heart of nature'. It's a formidable æsthetic, one with a self-assurance right-wing philosophers like Friedrich Nietzsche or Plato would be proud of.

Of a cairn made out of scrap steel which was placed next to an old foundry, Goldsworthy claimed that the cairn 'touches the nature of an urban environment' (S, 35). Does it 'touch the nature' of the place? What is the nature of the place? How can a human 'touch the nature' of the place? What is the quality of this touching? What kind of touching is it? And what is the nature of 'the nature of an urban environment'? How does the artist know he's touched it? Simple: he believes wholeheartedly in his subjective, intuitive feelings. He just *knows*, like a mystic.

Of steel, for example, the artist stated: 'I can feel its source' (ibid.). Huh? What does this 'source' 'feel' like? And what is the 'source' of steel? The planet itself? The energies that formed it? The people that dug the original material out of the ground and shaped it? How, too, does the viewer know about this feeling for the source of a material? Is it expressed in the work? How can the audience test the authenticity of the artist's feelings? These are questions which one can (and should) fire at any artist. Goldsworthy's art is often unsure about the answers. It knows it is about nature, ecology, place, organic form, and so on, but its views on these matters, and its relation to them can be often confused, ambiguous, banal or simplistic.

A dandelion work such as *Dandelions* (1993 [S, 21]) highlights the recurring problems with Andy Goldsworthy's sculpture: it has instant appeal: brilliant yellow dandelions are set in a mossy, pitted rock next to a stream. The work seems to emphasize the relative beauty of both the flowers and the setting: the 'organic', individual shape of the rock pool (this shape, and no other), the contrasts in brightness and colour in the natural world (grey and green rock, yellow dandelions), the transience of nature (the dandelions' colour will fade; the flowers will be pummelled by the next rain, or wind, or swept away when the river rises). Yet the sceptical viewer might also say, well *anyone* could make that work (or many other Goldsworthy sculptures). There is little 'technique' (art) or skill (craft) involved: it seems that one simply places dandelions in a pool (or rocks on top of each other, or wraps boulders in clay, or rubs the bark off twigs, or cracks open pebbles, and so on).

Dandelions seems so simple, so easy, like so many of Goldsworthy's sculptures (*Beech leaves, Balanced stone, Balanced rocks, Two Scaur Water snowballs, Red river rock pools, River rock, Peat, Clay-covered rocks, Torn stones, Red sand thrown into a blue sky, Orange stones* and *Yellow elm leaves,* to cite some works from *Stone*). Hang on, the sceptic might claim, the fraud has simply stuck some flowers in a pool! That can't be 'art'! Easy to see how Goldsworthy's art can seem a sham, like Carl Andre's bricks, or Yves Klein's leap, or Andy Warhol's six hour film of someone sleeping. *Come on*, the sceptic'll say, this can't be *serious.*

Some artists make a virtue of simplicity and ease: Jan Dibbets said he liked projects that anyone could do. For example, he chose four sites at random on a Netherlands map and went to each place and took a photo. It was '[q]uite stupid. Anybody can do that', Dibbets admitted. But Dibbets said he enjoyed searching for the places and photographing what was there. It was also silly for people to buy such works: 'it's stupid for other people to do it, or to buy it from me. What matters is the feeling'. And the feeling of the artist was something that couldn't be bought (1970). Similarly with Goldsworthy's art: the audience with the best view, the deepest connection to the sculptures, and the richest experience of the artworks is the artist himself.

4

ANDY GOLDSWORTHY
AND PHOTOGRAPHY

Andy Goldsworthy sculptures such as *Yellow elm leaves, Red maple leaves, Beech leaves, Red river rock pools* and other riverside works seem so simple, so easily put together. But Constantin Brancusi's eggs and fish and heads are also very 'simple' shapes and forms: he reduced and rationalized natural forms until he reduced them to an 'essence' (the 'essence' of a fish, of a head, of a bird in flight). Yet Brancusi does not get accusations of superficially and banality thrown at him. Indeed, his sculpture is really powerful precisely because he radically simplified it. (What the viewer doesn't see in the gallery, of course, are the hundreds of failed attempts, the mistakes, and the years of research and refinement to get to that stage. Simplicity is achieved at great cost and after years of refinement).

With Goldsworthy's art, though, the simplicity is of a different order: is the confusion over and criticism of Goldsworthy's work because he is using the *actual* material of nature? An actual leaf, rock, petal or ice sheet, not an imitation or image of them? Is it that anti-Goldsworthy critics see a rock covered with real leaves, not a mock-up made in an artist's studio, or a bronze or marble interpretation? Is it that Goldsworthy is getting so 'close' to nature that he is using the very material of nature itself, without altering it much at all? Goldsworthy doesn't seem to *do* much with his materials: he wraps them round a rock, sticks them in a pool, builds a mini tower out of 'em, takes a photo, and then it's 'art'. Is it that his art does not do anything more than this?

Andy Goldsworthy does not, for example, spend hours painting flowers in a meticulous, painstaking fashion, like Leonardo da Vinci. Leonardo also thought of himself as investigating nature: he drew lilies and oak sprigs so beautifully, but the beauty was partly in the 'faithfulness' of Leonardo's recording of the plant; that is, the 'beauty' was in the plant (in nature) itself. Leonardo was perhaps revealing again to the viewer what was already there in the world (one of art's noblest and most important functions). Goldsworthy too does this: it is one of his aims. But Leonardo da Vinci made an *image* out of the flower, while Goldsworthy uses the flower itself: he puts the flower into a pool, or takes the petals and wraps them around a boulder. There isn't that same distance between subject and representation that there is in Leonardo's drawings: the traditional way is to draw, paint, sculpt, film, sing or act the thing. Goldsworthy uses the thing-in-itself, by itself.

This is how the art of postwar (postmodern) artists such as Goldsworthy, Yves Klein, Andy Warhol, Joseph Beuys and Carl Andre differs from traditional Western art. They use the *actual object*, a process begun by Marcel Duchamp with his *Urinal* and umbrella stand and developed by Kurt Schwitters. Schwitters' reasoning was along the lines of: why not stick some real objects into an artwork? Jasper Johns reasoned the same way: he preferred the real object itself to a representation of it. Instead of using a replica or an imitation or an image of a rock or an icicle or a leaf, Goldsworthy uses the rock and icicle and leaf themselves.

The confusions of this relationship between reality and illusion, object and image, life and art in Goldsworthy's art are compounded by his use of photography, which instantly renders everything an image, a mode of representation, a text, a simulation, a copy, subject to all the strictures and structures of art, politics and representation. Goldsworthy's photographs are plainly *not* the object in itself, but a *representation,* a simulation, an equivalent of it, which is very different, and much more complicated.

Andy Goldsworthy has written two short statements on the relation between photography and his art (both entitled "The Photograph" – in *Hand to Earth* [9], and *Stone* [120]). Both mini-essays reveal a confusion and ambiguity regarding photography and art. Firstly, Goldsworthy states that the photograph simply records the work, in a direct, clear, routine fashion. His idea is to 'capture' (document) the work of art, which may change at every minute or moment. The photograph, Goldsworthy said, is the *outcome* of his art, not the initial reason for it. He quoted Yves Klein, one of his gurus, discussing his monochrome pictures:

> They are the leftovers from the creative process, the ashes. My pictures, after all, are only the title deeds to my property which I have to produce when I am asked to prove that I am a proprietor. (HE, 9)

A photograph is necessary for Goldsworthy because it brings an outdoor experience into the context of the indoor gallery. The photograph, Goldsworthy says, is necessary to communicate something of the outdoor work in an indoor context, even though '[m]uch of the energy is lost' (HE, 9).

This is all very well, this view that Goldsworthy propounds of the photograph as a necessary record of the outdoor work. In *Stone*'s "The Photograph" essay, the urge to 'capture' the sculpture out of doors becomes much more anxious (it was published in 1994). For example, if the film goes wrong, Goldsworthy says he feels disappointed – the photograph is needed to 'confirm the success or failure' of the work. He's dismayed if he misses photographing the collapse of his sea cairns. Goldsworthy acknowledged in *Wood* that in making balanced columns of stones there were 'inevitably more failures than successes' (23). Throughout his career Goldsworthy must have known hundreds of failed artworks, and must have plenty of photographs of sculptures that didn't work. If the film doesn't come out, Goldsworthy continued, then the sculpture becomes 'dislocated – like a half-forgotten memory' (i.e, it becomes memory, memory being one of the most mysterious of all human phenomena).

These statements demonstrate just how important photography is for Goldsworthy. He is not only a sculptor or land artist: he is also very much a photographer. The photograph is needed by Goldsworthy to keep the work alive – for himself, in his memory: it 'completes' the work, rounds it off. And, crucially, photography shows the work to others. Photography is Goldsworthy's main means of displaying his outdoor work. Rarely are the general public invited to see Goldsworthy making a work of art: 'I am not a performer', he says (S, 120). The ephemeral, outdoor sculpture 'lies at the core of my art and its making must be kept private' (ib.).

Further confusions arise when Goldsworthy discusses the conceptual aspects of photography: it is appropriate, he says, to use a time-sensitive medium such as photography. Why not, then, move into video and film? Why not record the red mud splashes on film? Why not take out stills from the movie of a collapsing arch, and exhibit those? Why not employ time-lapse photography, over a period of a year, to record changes in season, hue, form? In fact, Goldsworthy already has done just that: he has returned to a stone over a year; he has taken motor-wind shots of collapsing stone sculptures; he has made works on the sites of former works. Video was part of the *Time* exhibition (2000) in London, where footage of the snowballs installation of June 21, 2000 was featured. The documentary *Rivers and Tides*, in which Goldsworthy collaborated with filmmaker Thomas Riedelsheimer, appeared in 2001 (and on DVD in 2004). Of Goldsworthy's show at Galerie Lelong in New York, Goldsworthy's U.S. representatives, Bridget Goodbody wrote:

'The video becomes a poignant meditation on the brevity of human life and the brutal eternity of nature's processes: One moment you're here, the next moment you're gone, but nature's inexorable cycles continue nonplussed'.

Future developments in Goldsworthy's art over the next decades will include, one imagines, more use of video and film technology. Instead of using large Cibachrome framed photographs, maybe slides will be projected onto gallery walls, *à la* installation art. Then 'the visual smell and detail of the work' might be even better expressed than in a Cibachrome print. Or maybe the artist will experiment with Quantel paintbox video technology, or Photoshop, or digital technology, like Peter Greenaway and David Hockney, and produce sequences of kinetic sculpture. Surely Yves Klein, Goldsworthy's guru, would have leapt into these new computer/ digital/ video/ film technologies just as vigorously as he 'leapt' into space in his faked *Leap Into the Void.*

Andy Goldsworthy's biggest confusion concerning photography, however, is about that age-old philosophical chestnut, the 'reality' of the image, photography's troubled relationship with 'the real'. Ever since photography was invented, in the early/ mid-19th century, critics have pondered on how 'real' photography is (famous explorations of the thorny subject include those by Roland Barthes, Susan Sontag and John Berger). Goldsworthy's confusion on this point is illustrated by his last words in *Stone*: '[i]f the photograph were to become so real that it overpowered and replaced the work outside, then it would have no purpose or meaning in my art' (S, 120). Aren't photographs already 'real' then? Or are they mere 'illusions'? Surely the photograph is 'real' already, because Goldsworthy admits it is a 'record' of the work, needed to confirm the work? What does he mean, about photography becoming 'so real'? Isn't photography or the image already 'so real', like film and television are 'so real'? Film/ TV/ photo images are 'so real', in fact, they are consumed as 'real', believed as 'true': the average Briton, for instance, spends over 40 hours a week watching TV. That's 85 continuous days per year of watching television. Or nearly three months of the year are spent continuously consuming TV. Is that not 'real' too, in Goldsworthy's æsthetics? What about other forms of technological recording; are these, too, not yet 'so real'? What about virtual reality, or the 'cyberspace' of the internet, or the 'hyperspace' of telephone conversations? Are these, too, still lodged in an archaic argument of being mere 'illusion'? No.

One way of estimating how far things have changed since before mass communication is to consider how people how consume art generally nowadays. Many people will have seen an Andy Goldsworthy artwork in person, but far, far more will have read about his work, seen it in newspapers and magazines, seen it in books, or on the internet, or in TV documentaries, or posters, or stamps.

Goldsworthy has to face up to the fact that most people know about his art (and love his art) from photographs. Most people who know of Goldsworthy have *not* seen a Goldsworthy exhibition; have *not* seen his art in its outdoor environment; have *not* seen Goldsworthy making a work. They have bought the books *Time* and *Wood,* or seen photos of his art in magazines and books. For the punter who consumes art in books and printed material (or on TV or radio or the web) the 'real' art object doesn't need to exist: what counts is the media representation or simulation of it. But this would upset a realist and sensualist (a modernist) like Goldsworthy, who so passionately needs 'to touch' ('I must touch' as he puts it), who needs the real object. A world of computerized virtual reality would be abhorrent to him, where experience is only simulations and images. Yet that is how his art is mainly consumed. Punters have bought the books, seen the photos in magazines and that, for them, is Andy Goldsworthy art. Thus, the *photographs* of Goldsworthy's sculptures are *already* 'so real' that they have, for the consumer, replaced his art.

Goldsworthy has said that it is important for the viewer of his art to fill in the gap between the photograph of the sculpture and the real sculpture that he made someplace else. The photographs are incomplete on their own, as artworks: they require the spectator to create the rest of the artwork by using their imagination and memory, by remembering what it was like to be cold or wet or in a wood. To recall what it was like to be a child, touching leaves or snow or ice (S, 120).

The viewer, then, supplies the 'reality', the 'real' experience, the effect, which the photographs suggest but cannot complete. This could be another reason for Goldsworthy's popularity: that his art leaves some part of the sculptures incomplete, and the viewer can supply the rest from their many memories of the real world. There's a space for the viewer included in the work. A kind of art of interactivity, fed by nature photography. It's also a not insignificant fact that by the time the photographs are published in books or on the net or exhibited in a gallery, most of Goldsworthy's sculptures have already ceased to exist (they've been blown away, collapsed, eroded, dissolved, etc).

Of course, art consumers would probably like to know that the stones *really were* balanced on top of each other on the Welsh coast, or the icicles *really were* stuck to a stone wall in Dumfriesshire. It's probably essential, in fact, for many spectators to think that Goldsworthy really made those works. But Yves Klein faked his *Leap*, and invited people to see an empty gallery. In the age of art impresarios and art gangsters (such as Yves Klein, Andy Warhol, Claes Oldenburg, Jeff Koons, Bruce Nauman, Piero Manzoni, Gilbert & George, the KLF), when artworks are only known through radio, TV, the web and the press, Goldsworthy could have faked everything. (There are numerous techniques to fake images – not just with modern computers, digital manipulation and Photoshop software, but older methods such as montage, airbrushing and printing separate negatives. Consider masters of photographic superimposition such as Oscar Rejlander, Henry Peach Robinson, Alexander Rodchenko, Max Ernst or John Heartfield).

5

COLOUR AND DECORATION
IN ANDY GOLDSWORTHY'S ART

ANDY GOLDSWORTHY'S ART AND DECORATIVE ART

For Richard Long, Andy Goldsworthy is a 'second generation' artist, and is 'decorative (!)' ('decorative' being a put-down).[8] Many (but not most) critics, though, have been extremely praiseworthy of Goldsworthy's art. Neil Hedges wrote: '[t]he artist always achieves his goal, establishing and stimulating our own senses to view or touch conversant shapes and materials with much delight' (73).

Andy Goldsworthy uses modes of art-making dubbed 'feminine': *weaving* stalks or *stitching* leaves together. Weaving, sewing and

---

8 R. Long, in W. Malpas, 1995.

stitching are regarded as 'feminine' means of production, linked with art and craft, and denigrated by masculinist criticism. Artist Miriam Schapiro took up materials branded 'feminine' by patriarchal culture (cotton, taffeta, burlap, wool, sequins, buttons, thread) and fashioned artworks (she calls them 'femmages') that dealt with notions of the home, feminist iconography, abstraction and the æsthetics of 'Pattern and Decoration'. Schapiro said: 'I wanted to explore and express a part of my life which I had always dismissed – my home-making, my nesting'.9 A number of male artists have explored traditionally 'feminine' notions of pattern, decoration and colour, among them Robert Zakanitch, Lucas Samaras, Robert Kushner, Rodney Ripps, Kim MacConnel, Frank Stella and Ned Smyth. But it is women artists who make the most flamboyant and intricate artworks in these areas, such as Joyce Kozloff or Valerie Jaudon.

The 'traditional' 'women's' arts and crafts of textiles, pattern, sewing, decoration, pottery, and so on, are bound up with the economies of labour, race, class, identity, patriarchy, politics and money. They are modes of production and art that are regarded as secondary by patriarchal culture, not as 'high art', such as painting or sculpture. The economics of artistic production are embedded with patriarchal slants, just as much as the images themselves. The piece of textiles, the decorative tile, the pot, are objects that in the patriarchal system speak of their second-rate mode of production. As Catherine King wrote, '[m]edia associated with 'malestream' codes, like bronze, marble, or oil, have been regarded with suspicion' by women artists.10 Although Goldsworthy uses impermanent materials such as leaves and snow, he also uses traditional, 'masculine' media such as stone. This helps his art to be regarded by the art establishment as 'high', 'serious' art.

The beech leaves Goldsworthy placed in a rock pool at Scaur Water in Dumfriesshire (in October, 1992) are certainly pretty and decorative. The next Spring, Goldsworthy put dandelions in the same pool. The two works were printed in the art book *Stone*, and look like a diptych of the seasons Autumn and Spring. They were an obvious exploration

9 In D. Wheeler, 1991, 285.
10 C. King, "Feminist Arts", in F. Bonner *et al*, eds. *Imagining Women Cultural Representations and Gender*, Polity Press, Cambridge, 1992, 185.

of time and seasons, a reading emphasized by the use of the same viewpoint for each photograph. Handfuls of more dandelions were set on top of a large rock in the midst of Scaur Water. A different yellow, of elm leaves, was the colour component in another Scaur Water rock work, *Yellow elm leaves* (1991). In a 2000 sculpture at Townhead Burn in Dumfriesshire Goldsworthy placed yellow elm leaves around a mossy boulder. And another waterbound boulder sculpture was covered with red Japanese maple leaves; the colours, yellow and red, stood out dramatically from the subdued greys and greens of the water and surrounding rocks of the rivers. These works were also about the fact that the intense colours will one day fade and die. 'The intensity and beauty of the yellow are heightened by the knowledge of the decay that will inevitably follow', Goldsworthy remarked in *Passage* (128).

Andy Goldsworthy's art is 'decorative', definitely, but the colours and patterns are taken from nature: the seemingly 'pretty' colours of bluebells and dandelions, of maple leaves and the Australian outback, are colours already present in the natural world: they've been there for millions of years. Rather than finding colour 'decorative', for Goldsworthy it is 'raw with energy' (S, 6). The published books might have contributed towards the impression of the artist as decorative, Goldsworthy admitted, but he would carry on using colour anyway, because it was part of the natural world (P, 61).

When Goldsworthy placed red Japanese maple leaves in water their colour 'becomes so intense' he said.[11] Many of his works are built on the 'patterns' found in nature. For example, there are many sculptures of Goldsworthy's which create patterns from leaves or stones which have changed colour. He makes lines of bramble leaves which have changed colour, becoming yellowed and browned (1985, AG). He aligns the coloured sections of the leaves together. There are lines made of cherry leaves, poplar leaves and rosebay willowherb leaves (1981-86, reproduced in *Andy Goldsworthy*). The colours of the cherry leaves (Cumbria, 1984) turn from green through yellow to red then brown. Some lines fuse different coloured pebbles together (*Line*, at St Abbs, 1985), going from grey through yellow to white to red. Red, yellow and

---

11 A. Goldsworthy, *Mountains and Coast, Autumn into Winter*, 1988, HE, 163.

green beech leaves were laid in a pool in 1999, their colours blended. These are Autumnal works, rejoicing in the incredible colours of the season. Even in clogged-up, noisome, foggy cities the changing colours of Autumnal leaves may be noticed. In the countryside settings of (most of) Goldsworthy's sculpture, the colours are really rich. They really stand out, when the visual clutter of the modern, technological city is left behind. The 'shield' of sycamore leaves made on Hallowe'en, 1986, in Glasgow, for instance, glowed bright gold. Goldsworthy was excited by the colours of this particular Autumn:

> I arrived during a week of the most intense autumn weather I have experienced and the most extraordinary range of colours in the leaves scattered everywhere – sycamore, elm, chestnut...12

The suspended leafshield turned out to be 'one of the best pieces I have ever made', as Goldsworthy put it. The hanging leafworks enable light to become a key element in the sculpture: the translucence of the leaves was highlighted (Goldsworthy usually photographed the leafsheilds back-lit, i.e. with the leafshield in between the artist and the sun). The sun completed the sculpture, making the leafwork as 'extraordinary as going to the Arctic' (HE, 167).

Light is one of the key formal elements that Andy Goldsworthy explores in his sculpture. Critics have spoken of Goldsworthy's 'stunning effects of light and atmosphere'.13 The two leafworks of October, 1997, at the Storm King Art Center in New York state (orange and yellow leaves stuck onto a rock), were made specifically to catch the morning sunlight.14 Another shield, *Horse chestnut leaves* (Yorkshire, 1987), was deliberately made for darkness, hanging in amongst some rhododendron bushes. The Getty Institute clay hole was positioned so that the sun would shine on it once a year, at Midsummer (using solstices or equinoxes or full moons or other celestial events is common in land art). Some of Goldsworthy's *Réfuges d'Art* were constructed to take advantage of certain lighting effects (such as the rising sun at certain times of the year [RA, 85]). *Pool of*

12 A. Goldsworthy, sketchbook no. 13, and in N. Sinden.
13 K. Carter, "*Stone*", *New Welsh Review*, 27, Winter, 1994-95, 100.
14 A. Goldsworthy, *Wall*, 68-69.

Light (2000) was a wooden installation in France built to reveal the changing light (but throughout each day, not over a year). One of the key decisions with regard to light is whether to photograph a sculpture against or with the sun – with the sun backlighting the work, or illuminating it frontally (the leafshields were often photographed from both sides, with Goldsworthy preferring the backlit side).

Another favourite Andy Goldsworthy motif was the rectangle of leaves pinned together (usually measuring a foot and a bit by a couple of feet, but sometimes much smaller, as in *Elm Leaves*, 2000 [P, 133]). Sometimes these leaf oblongs were shields hung from trees (Glasgow, 1986); sometimes they were leaves pressed into the bole of a tree (Dumfriesshire [1998], New York state [1998]), or a rock (New York state, 1997); and sometimes they were set afloat on rivers (*Leaf sheet*, Digne, 1998). Goldsworthy has also covered solitary branches with poppy petals and leaves in many locations, including Yorkshire (1981), TICKON (1993), Stonewood (1992) and Cornell (1999).

A form Goldsworthy has occasionally explored is the serpentine extension of the roots and base of trees, so the roots appear to spread across the ground outwards from the base of the tree in the form of snake-shaped tubes a few inches thick (at Drumlanrig, Dumfriesshire [1999], and Holland [1999]). These tree extensions are usually made from sand or mud (and sometimes snow). Goldsworthy has also carved humpbacked tubular forms, from ice and snow, the loops and humps recalling the Loch Ness monster (Holland, 1984).

Another favourite Goldsworthy sculpture is the serpentine hole (or 'river') carved out of sand, usually on a beach (Holland, 1999), but sometimes inland (Goldsworthy dug quite a few in New Mexico in 1999). Another snake form on the ground was *Woven windfallen ash* (1983), fashioned from branches. Goldsworthy has also made many upright drawings on tree trunks and walls in his customary serpentine form, out of sand, clay and water (in Holland [1999], and Digne [1998]).

Because place is so important,[15] light (and colour) becomes a

15 'My strongest work is so rooted in place that it cannot be separated from where it is made' Goldsworthy wrote in *Stone* (6).

primary tool. Some Goldsworthy works pivot very much on luminosity and opacity, not just the leafshields, but some of the snow walls, the holes in sand, and so on; so that without the right sort of lighting, they do not work properly. Some sculptures are created in response to certain lighting conditions – the stick sculpture in the Lake District (1988), made in the pale, liquid light of dawn, for example, or the red leaves on the tip of a rock in Government Island in 2003. 'When I work with the land I work with the sky. When I work with water I am working with the clouds' Goldsworthy stated (HE, 167). The branches from a mulga tree in Australia (in 1991) were edged with red sand in order to catch the light of the setting sun: set end to end, the red-edged branches looked like a snake (appropriate for the Australian outback). Some of Goldsworthy's weakest works were made in Australian in 1991: *Mulga branches* had the branches laid on the red sand in two directions; they changed colour as the light changed.

Other sculptures are seen in a variety of lighting conditions – stormlight, snowlight, misty skies (the snow wall of 1988 at Blencathra in Cumbria is an obvious instance). Some of the brightest of Goldsworthy's leafworks have been made in Japan, where the maple leaves are dazzling in October and November (in, for example, *Maple patch*, November 22, 1987, or *Japanese maple*, November 21-22, 1987).

Andy Goldsworthy's flower pieces are inevitably 'pretty'. It's difficult to use flowers, in poetry, sculpture, painting or performance, without appearing 'pretty' (Goldsworthy realizes this [S, 6]). Think of Rainer Maria Rilke's many flower poems (to roses, irises, lilies), or the beautiful, sonorous flower watercolours of the German Expressionist Emil Nolde. Like Nolde's radiant flowerpieces, like the flowerworks of 17th century Flemish and Dutch art, Goldsworthy's flower sculptures are luminous. The dandelion piece (April 28, 1987), which is a spread of flowers forming a hole in the middle, is striking not because of the shape the artist's made, but because of the vibrant yellow of the flowers.

Flowers are amazing, some of the most exquisite creations on Earth. All Goldsworthy seems to have to do is to arrange them in a simple structure and the beauty of the flowers does the rest. What's also noteworthy about *Dandelions newly flowered* is that the sculpture is set on 'a grass verge between dual carriageways', so the title informs the viewer. If this is so, then this sculpture and photograph is very noisy: there will be cars roaring up and down the roads on either side of the sculpture. Goldsworthy's art reveals, as good poetry does, the incredible beauty of nature, even amongst the horrible, smelly, grey environment of a busy highway. Even at the verges of roads, in hedges beside ugly freeways, on empty roundabouts, there are amazing things growing.

Sometimes Andy Goldsworthy goes too far in evoking the beauty of nature. In another dandelion piece, *Dandelion flowers pinned with thorns to wind-bent willowherb stalks laid in a ring held above bluebells with forked sticks* (May 1, 1987), Goldsworthy fashioned a large open circle of dandelions and ranges them above a field of bluebells (S, 11). But it's too much: the incandescent yellow of the dandelions set against the equally rich blue of the bluebells. Bluebells in a wood don't require anything to make them look beautiful. Thus, *Dandelion flowers* (May 1, 1987), is a powerful image, but does nothing to explore nature, Goldsworthy's avowed artistic aim. Other dandelion works include a line of dandelions laid on grass growing in a pool (Yorkshire, 1987), dandelion petals edging mud slits (Yorkshire, 1987), a line of dandelions following the outline a rock (Dumfriesshire, 1994), a line of dandelions pressed into the edge of a village lane (Cahors, France, 1996), and dandelions laid along the Capenoch tree (1994). (Note that Goldsworthy hasn't used dandelions so much since the 1990s, along with all other flowers).

It's noteworthy that Andy Goldsworthy has only used a very small selection of flowers in his sculptures: poppy, foxglove, dandelion. He's far more inclined to use leaves or grass or stalks (such as hogweed or willowherb). Also, when Goldsworthy does use flowers, he avoids the hugely symbolic flowers of the Western tradition, such as the rose, lily or iris. And the flowers of Britain are also sidestepped: the daffodil, the primrose, the snowdrop, the carnation, the gladioli, the tulip, the forget-me-not, and so on. In addition, Goldsworthy has not made many flowerpieces in his later work.

Notice also that Goldsworthy tends to produce work outdoors with a very small number of plants: he has his favourite materials, such as willowherb stalks, or yellow beech or elm leaves, or green sycamore leaves. He has not fashioned many sculptures from nettles or brambles (for obvious reasons, perhaps). Or thistles. Or ferns and bracken. Cowslips, gorse bushes, ivy, pine cones and mistletoe are other plants Goldsworthy doesn't use much (although he has put some of these elements in his snowballs). And among trees, Goldsworthy hasn't employed the following trees much: yew, pine, laurel, willow, hawthorn, holly, vine. Goldsworthy may avoid certain plants and flowers for all sorts of reasons, some practical, some æsthetic, some social, and some symbolic. Some of the plants noted above are loaded with thousands of years of symbolism: rose, lily, willow, laurel, hawthorn, mistletoe. Goldsworthy really likes the colour red, for instance, and it would be so easy for him to employ rose petals: instead, he opts for the poppy.

Some of the most popular flowers, like tulips, roses, irises and carnations, come in many different hues and types, and are cultivated on an industrial scale. That may be another reason (a social one) why Goldsworthy prefers not to use those flowers. Maybe they've lost their wildness, their individuality, their magic, and now they've become commercial, mass-produced products, just another part of the natural world that humans have 'tamed' and turned into commodities.

The attention to the minute, detailed qualities of nature that Goldsworthy's art rejoices in is mirrored in Romantic poetry and nature poetry. John Cowper Powys, for instance, could get excited by nothing more 'spectacular' than a patch of moss on a wall. Goldsworthy's sculpture has the same delight in the small, seemingly unimportant aspects of the natural world, stuff that would be overlooked by most all of contemporary culture. In his *Autobiography* (1934), John Cowper Powys wrote: 'I am looking at a patch of moss on a greenish marbly rock and I am aware of a deep sensual pleasure' (41). And in Cambridge, on one of his many walks around the outskirts of the city, Powys remarked that 'certain patches of grass and green moss transported me into a sort of Seventh Heaven' (199). (Like land artists such as Robert Smithson and Dennis Oppenheim, Powys liked the outer areas of towns, border zones and abandoned realms).

In his fiction (still criminally neglected by the literary establishment), John Cowper Powys described the ecstasies that (land) artists have when interacting with nature. Powys's characters, like those in the work of William Wordsworth, Johann Wolfgang von Goethe, George Seferis, or Maria Tsvetayeva, are nature mystics, just as land artists such as Goldsworthy, Nash, Randall-Page, Holt, Drury and Smithson are in part nature mystics. Sam Dekker, in Powys's massive nature mysticism novel *A Glastonbury Romance* (1932), experiences a *participation mystique* with the Earth: '[w]hat he felt was a strange and singular reciprocity between his soul and every little fragment of masonry, of stony ground, of mossy ground...'16 And Dud No-Man in the last of the Wessex quartet books, *Maiden Castle* (1936), when he comes to 'a patch of green moss on a grey wall' gets 'a sensation that's more important than what you call 'love', or anything else, nearer the secret of things too!'17

COLOUR IN ANDY GOLDSWORTHY'S ART

Colour is an expression of life.

Andy Goldsworthy (*Passage,* 127)

Andy Goldsworthy has spoken of the significance of using the colour red: in Japan, he remarked, he learnt about a 'deeply disturbing' red (W, 15), a 'heightened awareness of red. A bright red maple tree in the middle of a green forest, like an open wound' (in ib.). It is the *colour* of the 'red splashes' or 'throws' that contributes much in making them powerful. Goldsworthy often uses red in his art – in the boulders covered in red maple leaves (1991) or the poppy-leaved covered stones (1989), or poppy petal-covered branches (1992), or the ridged holes made on the beach at the Isle of Wight with red edges (1987, AG). Red

---

16 J.C. Powys, 1955, 926.
17 10. J.C. Powys, 1937, 353.

maple leaves climb up rocks or are layered on top of little rockpools (1993). Goldsworthy relates red to the iron in human blood.

The Harrlemmerhout, Holland work, *Poppy petals* (1984), was a seven-foot long line of poppy petals held together with spit which was hung from an elderberry. It was, a critic said, 'one of the most impressive and poetic works' Goldsworthy made during his time at Haarlem.[18] At Hampstead Heath (in London) an associated work, a line of beech leaves, was floated over a pool.[19] Red-tinted water spread like blood over the floor of the Barbican Centre in London, melted from inside a snowball (2000). In Australia the colour red did not arrive in Goldsworthy's work, as one might expect, from flower petals or red stones, but from red sand: Goldsworthy rubbed the sand into the bark of a mulga tree (1991). Gathering rain clouds and a brilliant, low sun created the right lighting conditions to bring out the red tree against the brooding grey sky (S, 54-55). Goldsworthy said that the red of the Australian outback was 'deeply moving spiritually'. 'I have tried to touch that colour not just with my hands, but also with light' he added (W, 15).

Andy Goldsworthy is using a standard observation of natural science: the colour red really stands out in a landscape. In the historical Japanese Zen garden, colours are carefully orchestrated, so that a single leaf can set off a vast acreage of predominantly green or ochre. In the Oriental garden, notions of *feng shui* and *yin* and *yang* control how a landscape is shaped by humans. In the system of *feng shui*, the elements of a garden or a building must be in harmony with the natural forces of air, water and earth. Get it wrong and one messes up the creation. The Zen or Taoist harmonizing approach is very much that of Goldsworthy's art. In the manner of the ecologically-friendly follower, Goldsworthy speaks of wanting to be in harmony with nature. Goldsworthy, like other artists, can be seen as an ecological

18 H. Voegls, "Haarlemmerhout", in HE, 54.
19 1985, HE, 59.

artist, artists committed to ecological issues.[20] (Although other artists foreground political concerns far more often. In fact, Goldsworthy does not define himself as an ecological artist, and is not trying to make political statements about the negative impact of humanity upon the world in his art).

Chinese gardens were designed by balancing the principles of *yin* (feminine) and *yang* (masculine), water and mountain. Goldsworthy's art, like other land art, can be seen as a kind of modern *feng shui*, a Westerner's (secular) way of harmonizing the *yin* and *yang* elements. Land artists reorganize the landscape, building mountains, digging holes, creating pools, as in *feng shui*.

Oriental gardens were asymmetrical – in that single æsthetic element they differ greatly from Western formal gardens with their patterns, squares, crosses, parallel paths, and mathematically exact *parterres*. Oriental gardens were founded on stone, sand, water, flowers, moss and trees, an elementalism that chimes with land art concerns (compare with the materials Goldsworthy favours: ice, water, petals, leaves, stone). If sand was used, it could evoke water by being raked into wave-like shapes. Stones could be mountains, but also, via abstraction, other natural forms. In the 'dry garden' of Zen Buddhism (the *karesanui*), stone could be water, or cascades. Stones were valued highly for gardens, and were bought and sold. Many kinds of stone were used in Oriental gardens, including schist, volcanic rock, granite, limestone, slate and jasper.

Perhaps the most famous of the Japanese Zen gardens is at Ryoanji, Kyoto (made in the 1480s). It is 30 by 70 feet with white gravel raked parallel to the longer side. There are 15 rocks placed in it, and a verandah surrounds it. The Ryoanji garden is garden design reduced to its simplest elements, an ultimate in reduction and purification. There

---

20 Robert Rosenblum wrote:

There's a German artist Wolfgang Laib who does something of this sort too. He spends a lot of time in the woods gathering such things as pollen and collecting it and forming minimal geometric patterns out of gossamer and natural materials such as honey or dust of various kinds. It is some kind of ecological last gasp of communion with some pure beautiful stuff of nature. I guess this attitude is expiring even though it may, as in the case of Richard Long, still produce some marvellous artists. (R. Rosenblum, 1988, 11)

are no trees, flowers or plants in the garden. In Goldsworthy's art there is a similar emphasis on asymmetry, on keeping forms as they appear in nature, on contemplation, on valuing objects such as stones as sacred in their own right, with nothing needing to be added to them.

Contemplation was clearly a key purpose of the Oriental garden. 'Contemplation gardens' were meant to be consumed from one viewpoint (from the noble's house, for example). The 'contemplation garden' was often a 'dry garden', with various islands in its midst having particular meanings. Some of Goldsworthy's sculptures recall the 'islands' in Oriental gardens; like contemplation gardens, Goldsworthy's works are usually designed to be viewed from one point (Goldsworthy endorses the single-viewpoint in his work in his use of photography, with its monoscopic vision. Artworks are built to be seen from one viewpoint – unless they are public sculptures, which visitors can explore from a variety of angles). Goldsworthy can thus be seen as creating Western versions of Oriental and Zen gardens, in which contemplation is the primary activity for the art consumer.

J.M.W. Turner also knew the impact and beauty of the colour red. Turner's artistic rival, John Constable, recounted an incident where he, Constable, had painted a famous river scene which he was sure would be the pride of the Royal Academy show. Not to be outdone, Turner came in when Constable was away and added a smudge of red to an otherwise grey seascape. The red blob was intended to be a buoy, and it lifted up Turner's painting a few notches. Constable was enraged. It's a nice story of a great artist knowing exactly how to wield colour.

In a similar way, Goldsworthy puts in a red object in amongst the soft, muted colours of green moss and grey, wet rocks of South-West Scotland. The colour red stands out even more on wintry, overcast days, when there is hardly any deep colour in the surroundings. In 1993 Goldsworthy fashioned a number of sculptures in small pools of water he found on the rocks at his beloved Scaur Water in Dumfriesshire. He stained the pools with the powder from some red stones. The manufacture of these sculptures consisted of nothing more elaborate than rubbing some stones together to stain some water (other, later pools had red maple leaves or poppy petals laid in them, as at Storm King in New York in 1995). The results, though (photographed in *Stone* and *Black Stones, Red Pools*), are dramatic: as Goldsworthy says, often a good sculpture needs only a delicate or small-scale touch in the right place to make it work (S, 95). In amongst the weather-worn and water-worn boulders of Scottish streams the mid-red stands out vividly. It reveals the contours of the surrounding rock; the relation between the pool of water in its isolation from the rest of the river (which formed it); and the elegant ovals and circular shapes of each pool. These are the landscapes of Goldsworthy's art, these bleak, grey, wintry scenes, beside a lake, or the sea, or a river, or halfway up a mountain. Next to a mound of grey slate, the colour red stands out, like 'a wound', as Goldsworthy says, emphasizing the flesh-and-blood nature of his art.

It is the leafworks that are the most colourful of Andy Goldsworthy's sculptures. What the leaf sculptures demonstrate is how beautiful the colours of nature can be: Goldsworthy shows the viewer these subtle colours by contrasting one leaf with another. *Maple patch* (1987, Japan) grouped the red/ orange/ yellow of Japanese maple leaves together; *Poppy leaves* (1984, Netherlands) set the red poppy leaves against the mid-green of an elderberry bush; a Stone Wood sculpture of 1992 (*Poppy petals*) consisted of poppy leaves wrapped around a hazel branch, the red contrasting vividly with the wet green leaves of late Summer; *Dock Leaves* (1978, Morecambe) interwove red leaves in green grass stalks. Two sycamore leafworks of 1980 and 1981 (in Yorkshire) were very simple: a leaf black from cow shit was placed against pale Autumn leaves; another leaf, bleached white, was set down on a bed of dark leaves. Goldsworthy pinned together two colours of sycamore leaves (sycamore is a favourite Goldsworthy medium) in *Sycamore leaf sections* (1988), and hung the line of leaves from a tree. Shot with the sun behind them, the photograph of the leaves showed them glowing green and gold, the two classic colours of poetry and alchemy. The Fall colours of course connote nostalgia, decadence, sensuality, Romanticism, time passing, the decay of the year, and so on, all those things John Keats wrote about in his 'Ode: To Autumn', and in a billion other poets in a billion poems about Autumn.

Other lines of leaves laid on water include Digne (1998), *Japanese maple* (Japan, 1987), *Horse chestnut leaves* (Leicestershire, 1987), *Hazel leaves* (Dumfriesshire, 1991), *Elm leaves* (1994, Dumfriesshire), and *Beech leaves* (London, 1985). Some of Goldsworthy's leafworks were created with Tom Lang, in St Louis (1987), where Goldsworthy explored pulping plants.

A group of works made in Goldsworthy's stamping ground of Dumfriesshire in Scotland in the Fall of 2002 explored the bright yellow of elm leaves. In amongst the browns and greys of autumnal landscape and the dull, overcast light, the yellowy elm leaves stood out vividly (these leafworks, and the later ones using dark brown leaves, were made for 'the transition from autumn into winter and the damp, grey short days that are so common at this time of year in Scotland' Goldsworthy remarked [P, 134]). Goldsworthy fashioned a ring of leaves around a mossy rock; wrapped in a band around a branch (an 'old style' Goldsworthy sculpture); a square shape of leaves placed on a rock, with lines torn through them; *Elm Sticks* was a border of leaves around some elm branches supported by bark, over a stream; *Elm Leaves* was a row of leaves moving from brown through yellow to green, laid on bark over a stream. (Goldsworthy was also making work in Townhead Burn, a different stream and valley not far from his favourite spot of Scaur Water. Goldsworthy said he hadn't really noticed Townhead Burn until years after living in the area, but is 'an extraordinary place and of late it has become the source of my best of my work in Dumfriesshire' [E, 165]).

A new form appeared in Goldsworthy's *œuvre* in late 2002: leafworks which employed a new play with spatial illusions, in particular the relation between foreground and background (which was heightened by the use of bright-hued leaves against predominantly dark backgrounds), and the idea of an invisible support for a sculpture. These new works took the form of: leaves laid on top of bark over a stream (*Elm Leaves*, 2002), so it looked as if the leaf row was floating above the water; and the image that formed the cover of *Passage*: four rows of yellow elm leaves laid on top of bark over a stream. These leafworks (like the other works exploring elm leaves made from Fall,

2000 onwards) were all very small in scale, and used the brightness of the leaves against the dark hues of the autumnal landscape as the visual hook.

Goldsworthy's aim in the leaf pieces, though, drew attention to the fragility and delicacy of leaves, as well as their strength and function. A leaf, after all, is a complex biological factory, so the natural scientists suggest. 'There is a whole world in a single leaf', commented Goldsworthy.21 Goldsworthy's leafworks do not have a scientific agenda. Rather, they celebrate the presence of leaves, the being-in-the-world of leaves, so to speak. In his sketchbook of August 17, 1984, Goldsworthy wrote:

> I am beginning to get more structure into leaf work – forced to find struct-ure in leaves – No rocks or branches. The key is in the leaf veins – The leaf architecture. Amazing how geometric the structure is. (HE, 100)

Goldsworthy's leaf sculptures are, like all land art, specific to particular places. The brilliant oranges and reds and yellows in *Maple patch* (1987) or *Line to explore colours in leaves, calm, overcast* (1987) could only occur in Japan, it seems. Place and work are one for Goldsworthy: he does not distinguish between elements in a work: '[l]ooking, touching, material, place, making the form and resulting work are totally integral' (in N. Hedges, 68).

The forms Goldsworthy explored in his 1989 *Leaves* show in the UK capital included boxes of sycamore and plane leaves (with the stalks sticking out); a 16 inch cube; cones and pyramids; beech shields; seed pods; hollow globes of sweet chestnut; spiral bands; a lengthy serpent form (51 inches long); and probably the most distinctive shape of Goldsworthy's leafworks, the horn. Goldsworthy produced a special version of the leafworks display case for a collector in California in 1996.

Goldsworthy weaved in brown leaves with yellow leaves, forming a contrast between the two colours, as in *Yellow and ruddy leaves* (1986). As with so many of Goldsworthy's sculptures, *Yellow and ruddy leaves* includes in its title the mode of its making:

---

21 Quoted in P. Nesbitt, "Leafworks", in HE, 108.

[The] Yellow and ruddy leaves[:]
[I] made [the] edge [of the line] by finding [a] ruddy and yellow leaf [which
were] the same size[.]
[I] tore [the] yellow leaf in two, [and] spat underneath one half [of it,]
[then] pressed it on to the ruddy leaf[.] (HE, 64)

Goldsworthy's leaf sculptures are often at their most effective in Autumn, not surprisingly, as the dates for many of the leaf pieces demonstrate (November 1, 1986, November 22, 1987, November, 1977, October 22, 1992, November, 2003, and so on). Works such as *Line to follow colours in maple leaves* (1992) use the changing colour of leaves in Autumn as their basic structure: the leaves pinned to the fallen tree change from green through yellow to orange, red and damson. One of Goldsworthy's best leafworks was made in Illinois in 1992. It comprised of a shield of red maple leaves set in the 'V' of two tree trunks. The importance of light was emphasized in *Maple leaves* in the book *Wood* by the decision to include a photograph of the sculpture from both sides, showing the sun shining on the leaves from one side, and shining through the leaves from the other.

Sometimes the wind is a problem, blowing away works which Goldsworthy has painstakingly constructed (Goldsworthy often chooses valleys or woods or more sheltered spots for his leafworks – there are few leaf pieces on an open mountainside in the Goldsworthy *œuvre*, for instance.) Making the leafworks enables Goldsworthy to learn about leaves – leaves blown from trees, or cold, brittle leaves, or 'wet frost-fallen' leaves, or freshly grown leaves. He is careful to take only a 'few leaves from each tree.'[22] He follows the seasonal development of leaves closely, most especially in and around his studio in Scotland. Leaves, like stones or snow, teach the artist much.

> The sycamore has taught me most [Goldsworthy said]. The biggest lesson being that so much can be found in something common and ordinary. Its leaf can turn all colours; its stalks can go bright red and within its leaf structure I realised my first leaf construction. (*Leaves*, op.cit., 18)

---

22 Quoted in *Leaves*, Natural History Museum, London, 1989, 18.

Goldsworthy's art might not work in richly coloured gardens, such as British gardens like Sissinghurst Garden in Kent, or Powis Castle in Wales. In amongst the beautiful white lilies and roses, the brilliant yellow daffodils and primroses, the succulent blue of irises and pansies, Goldsworthy's poppy-red stones would not stand out so much. Goldsworthy's artworks are compelling partly because they are sited in wildernesses, not on housing estates, not on the trash-strewn verges of highways, not in the bleak streets of dreary towns. Set amongst the green grass and slate-grey rocks, Goldsworthy's blocks of snow or stitched sycamore leaves hollow out their space and influence. They could not compete with most urban environments, or with motorways or out-of-town shopping precincts. (For instance, when Goldsworthy installed snowballs on the streets of London in 2000, they were large snowballs, not small snowballs. Works in the same scale as the leafworks, for example, would be lost in the cityscape).

Goldsworthy's sculptures require specific (and controlled) contexts and environments in order to work. The foxglove petal sculpture, with its delicate pink tones (Leeds, 1977), needs to be set in amongst the grey rocks to work properly. Similarly, pieces such as the russet-coloured dock leaves, woven into bright green grass stems (Morecambe, 1978), are small sculptures, requiring close-up photography to make them live. In the case of the dark soil or peat-covered rocks, made in Japan, Lancashire and the Isle of Skye, the close-up photograph does not work so well: it is the context of these large boulders in their wild landscapes that makes them stand out: thus Goldsworthy includes the rural surroundings in the composition.

Goldsworthy's photographs, too, are carefully framed so that they miss out the electricity poles, the trash heaps, the kicked-in fences, the smashed bottles, the abandoned cars, the supermarket carts, that are a feature of every landscape everywhere in the British Isles (and many other places Goldsworthy visits), no matter how far from the throbbing centres of humanity. However far one goes, one confronts the marks of humans. Go wandering in the wildernesses of central Wales, say - one of the least densely populated places in the British Isles - and one'll find litter. One may be able to purchase a few miles between oneself and the nearest road, so that the sound of cars will fade into the susurrus of the wind. Sky above, grass underfoot, and nothing but the 1,500 foot high system of mountains.

Goldsworthy's photographs present an idealized world, veritably the pastoral world of ancient times. Goldsworthy's Arcadia, though, is definitely a Northern European pastoral realm, not the Southern, Mediterranean paradise of satyrs, shepherdesses, gods and wild animals. Goldsworthy's 'pastoral sublime', to use the phrase applied to a category of J.M.W. Turner's works, is a Northern European realm, very much in the tradition of Turner's paintings of the Alps, with lowering, gloomy skies, raging wind, snow-capped mountains and mossy riverbanks. John Martin, Thomas Girtin, John Sell Cotman, John Constable and J.M.W. Turner made many paintings of the landscapes Goldsworthy works in. Apart from Australia and Japan, Goldsworthy's art centres around cold, rain-sodden, Northern landscapes (he has made many works in Southern France, though, since the mid-1990s). True, there is much sunlight in his photographs of Australia, photographs that evoke the stereotypical colonial view of the out-back as a rugged, inhospitable place where the white people sit around camp fires. Goldsworthy's Japan is a more sublime, rarefied place, though it is still rough and distinctly non-human. (Goldsworthy does not go along with notions of the pastoral, however: nature is not a 'pastoral retreat' for Goldsworthy, it is also brutal, and cannot be controlled by humans [E, 164]).

Goldsworthy photographs his sculptures often looking down on them, so the surrounding landscape is not seen. He edits out unsightly buildings or roads, but art has always involved much more editing than many artists would admit. Goldsworthy knows that what one leaves out of a work is as important as what one puts in. Goldsworthy said that photographs were 'very important to me as a working record', and that he had a record of nearly everything he'd made, which he could look on and use.[23] 'A good work is the result of being in the right place at the right time with the right material' said Goldsworthy.[24]

---

23 10. In A. Papadakis, 1991, 250.
24 11. In J. Beardsley, 1984, 134.

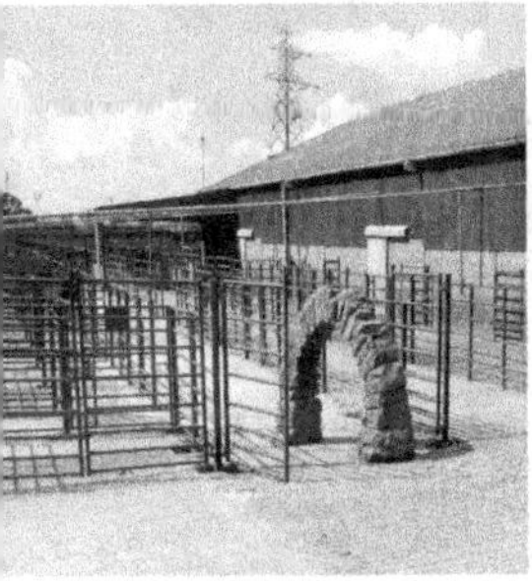

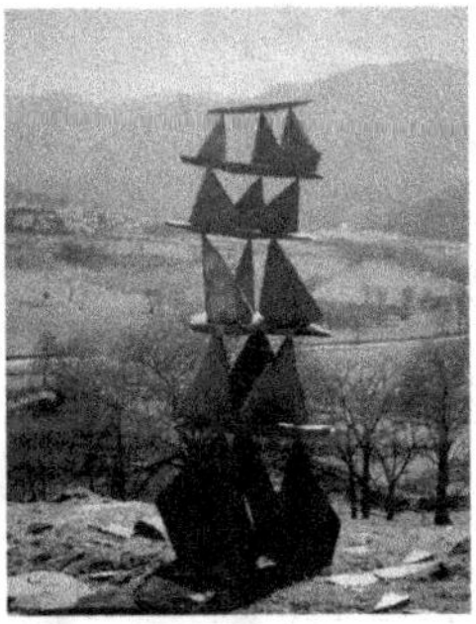

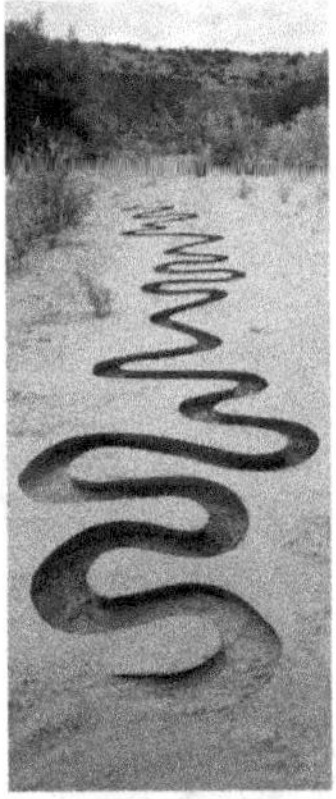

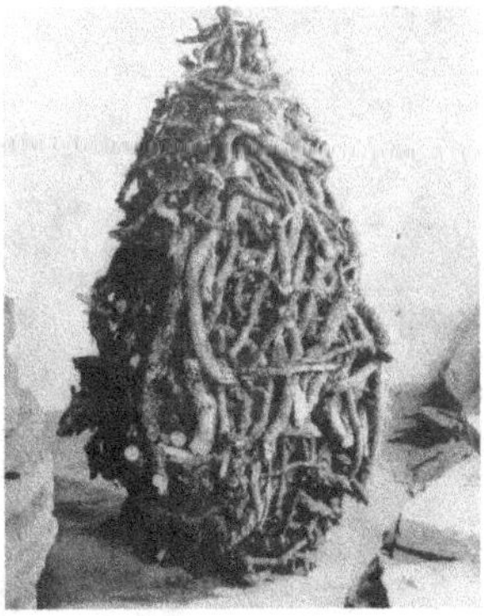

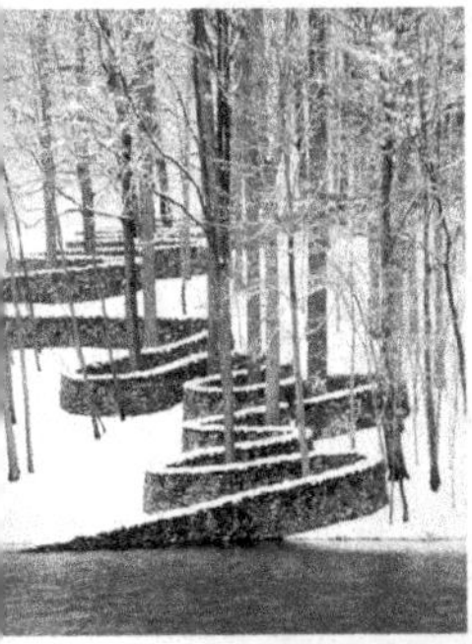

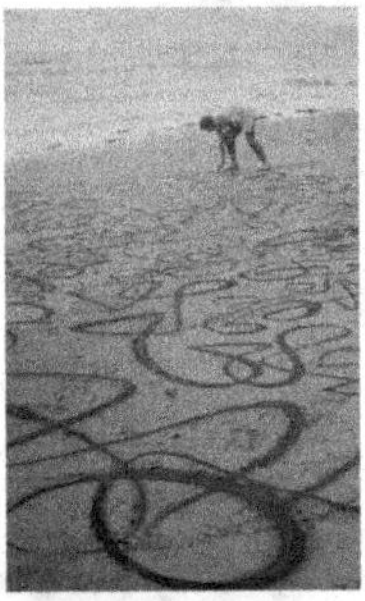

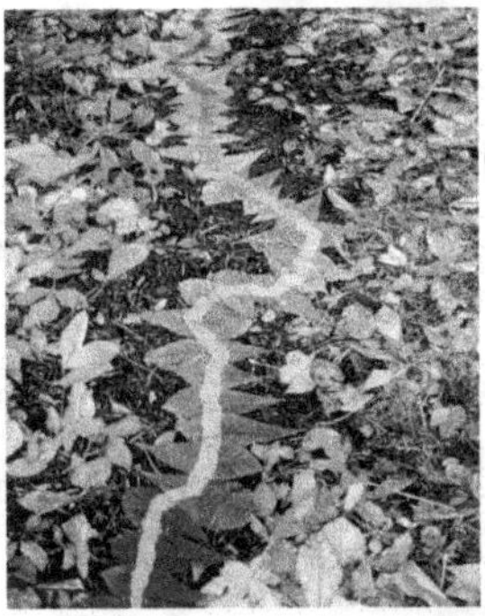

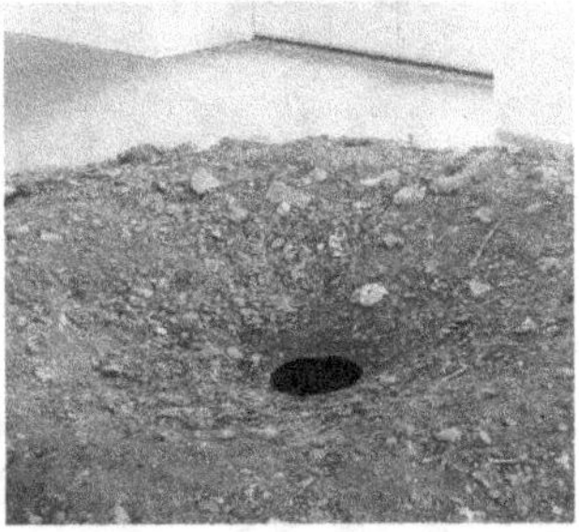

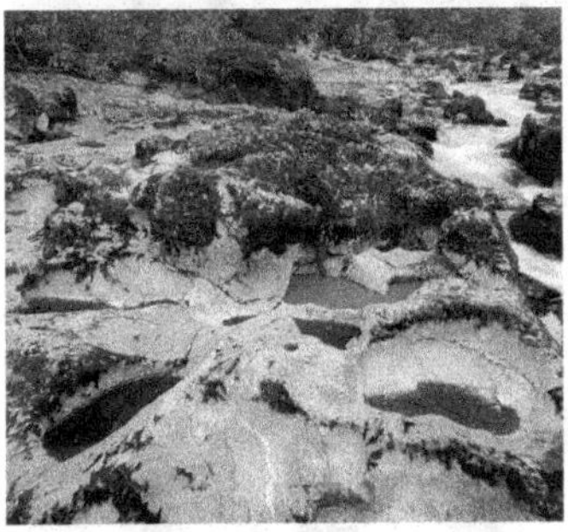

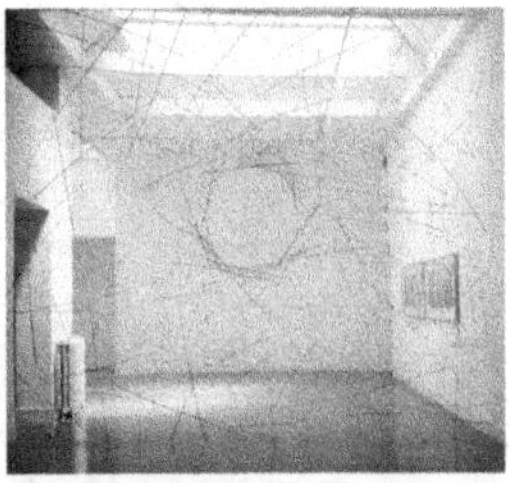

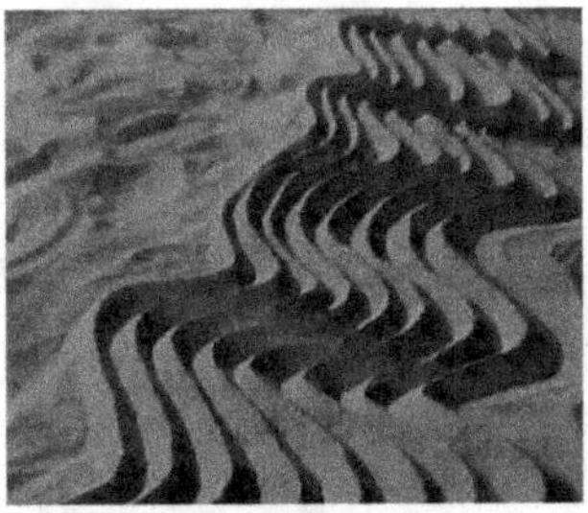

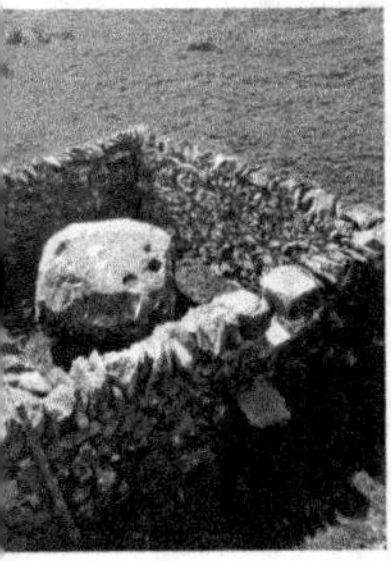

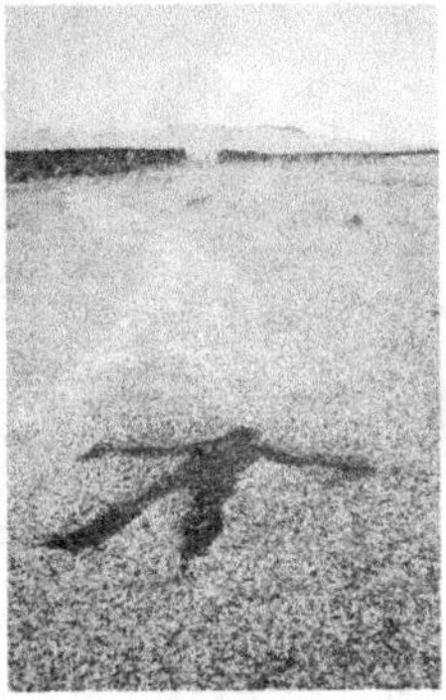

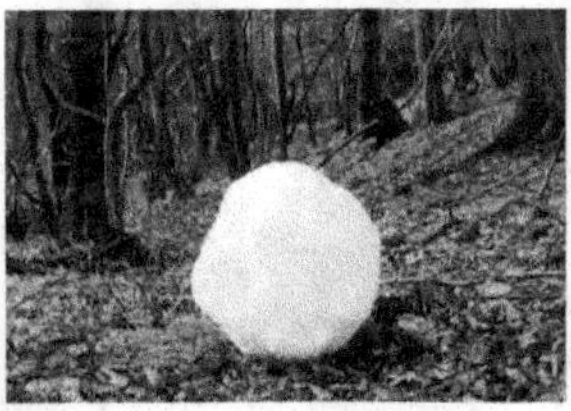

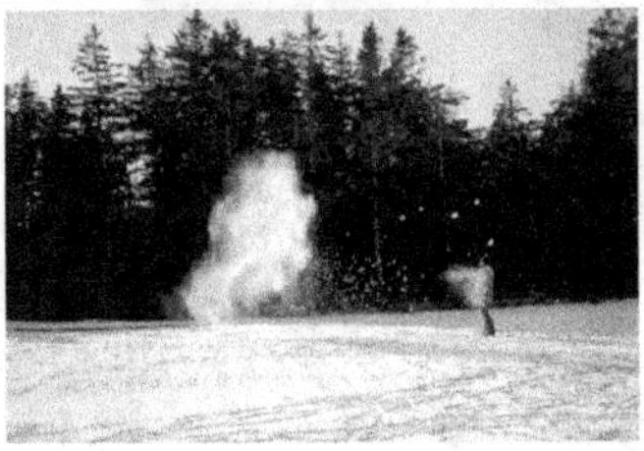

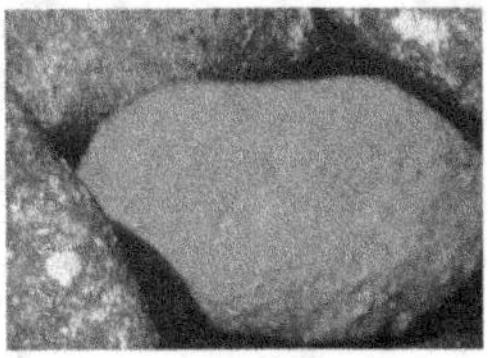

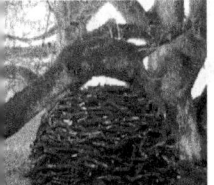

Goldsworthy's forms

The recurring forms in Andy Goldsworthy's include:

Lines. Cairns. Walls. Snowballs. Holes. Cracked lines.
Screens. Sheepfolds. Arches. Shadow prints. Throws.
Leafshields. Globes. Stained pools. Wrapped rocks.
Broken stones. Ridged sand. Sand drawings. Balanced rocks.

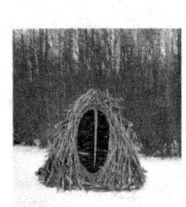

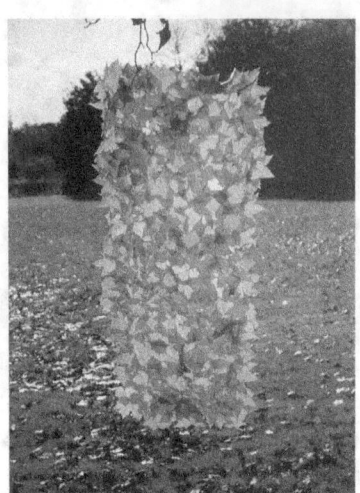

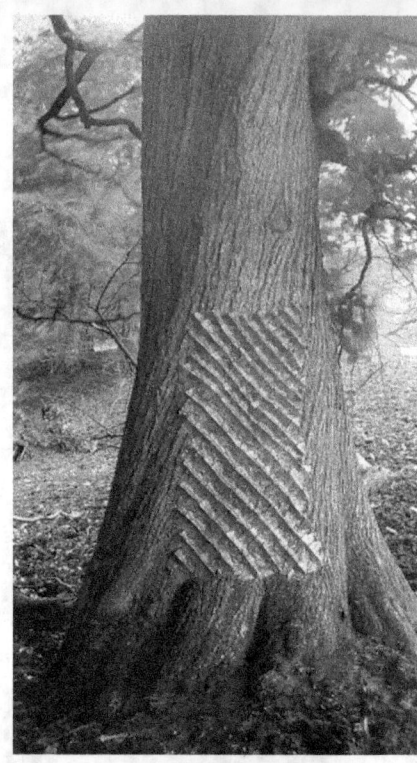

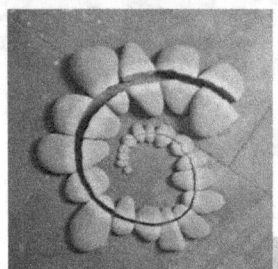

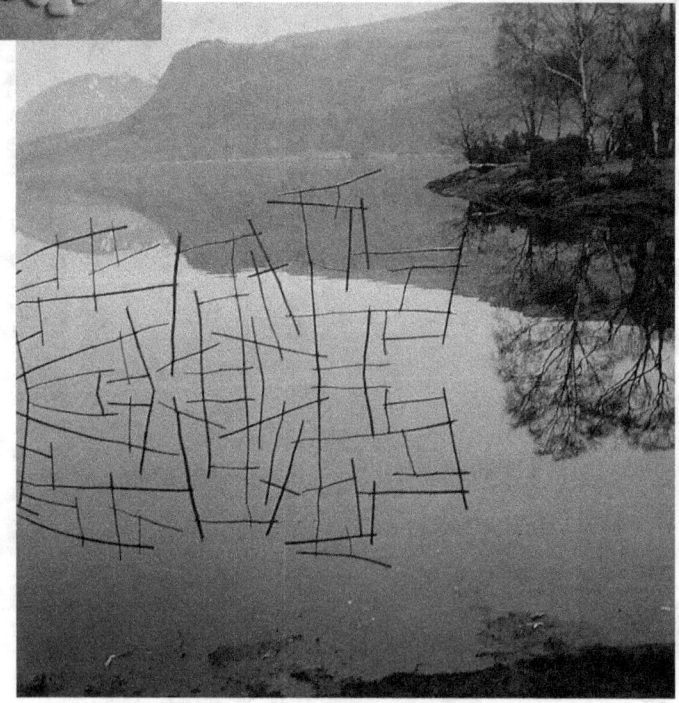

Frontality

Goldsworthy usually employs classic Renaissance space (like most
Western art since the 1300s). He often emphasizes the frontality of his
sculpture, as in the examples above: leaves pressed into the bark
of a tree; a leafshield; sticks in a lake; and broken pebbles.

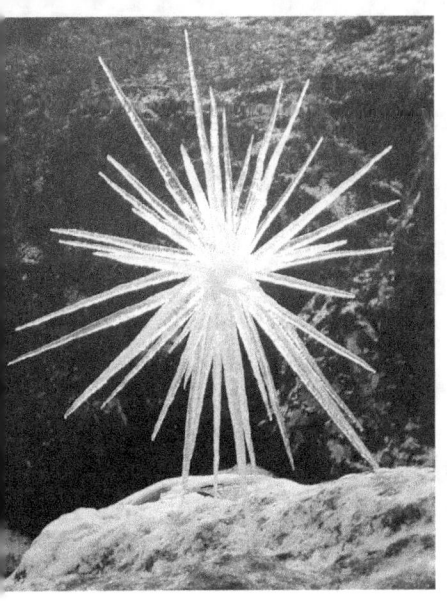 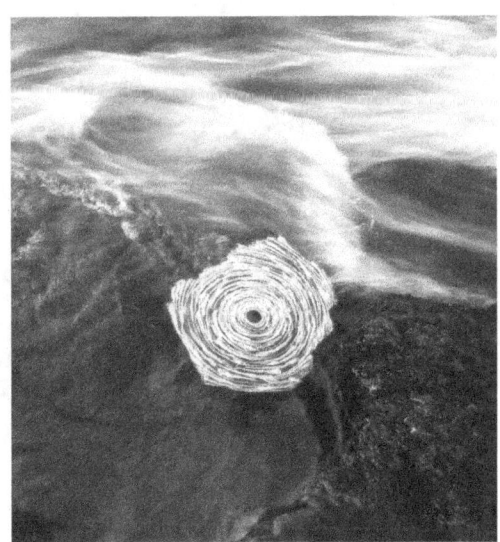

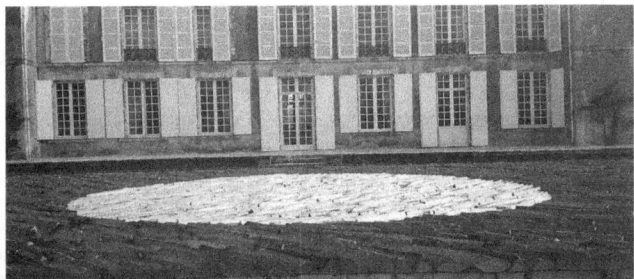

Light, shadow, contrast

Goldsworthy is often working with light as a central element
in his artworks: cloudy, shadowy light is often favoured,
as in the Roof installation; Pool of Light uses the direction
of sunlight; high contrast is deployed in the wool pieces;
and the ice pieces use backlight.

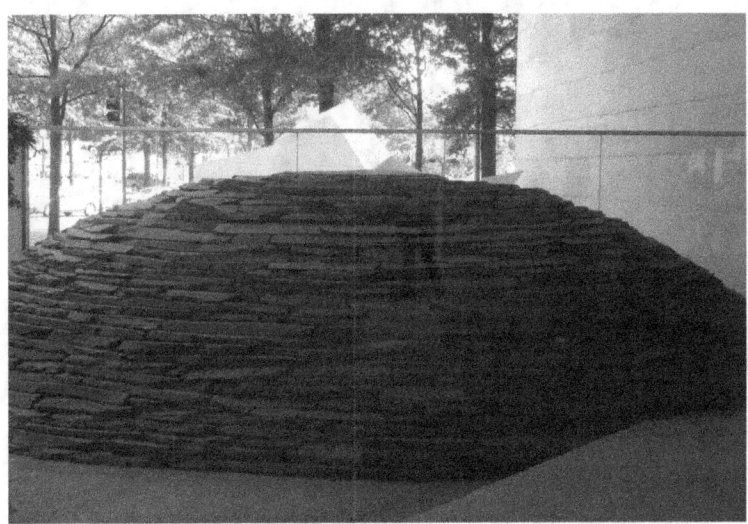

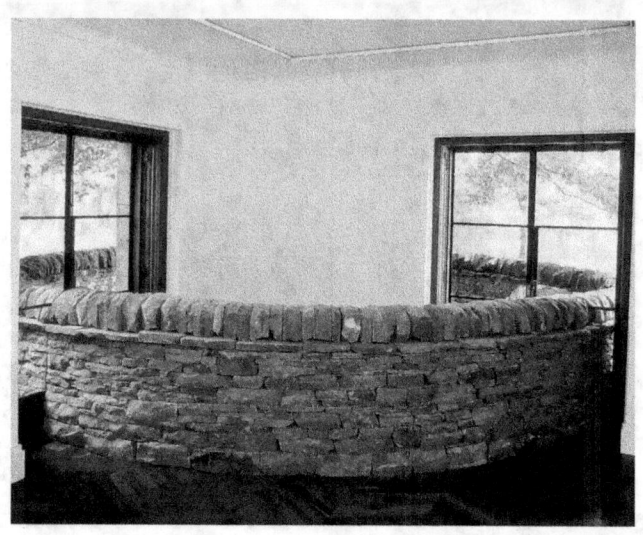

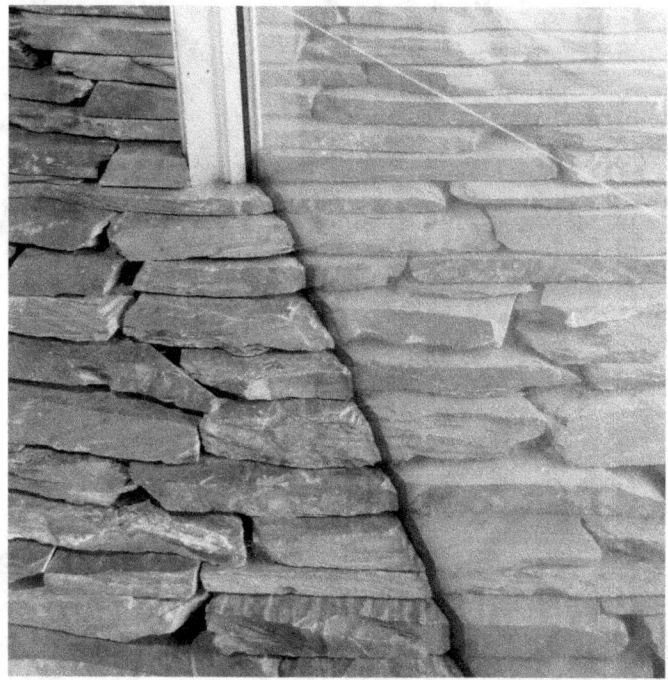

Optical illusions

Goldsworthy likes to play optical tricks from time to time:
for instance, to continue a shape or form through barriers,
as in these examples in New York state (Storm King Fold)
and the National Gallery of Art in Washington (Roof).

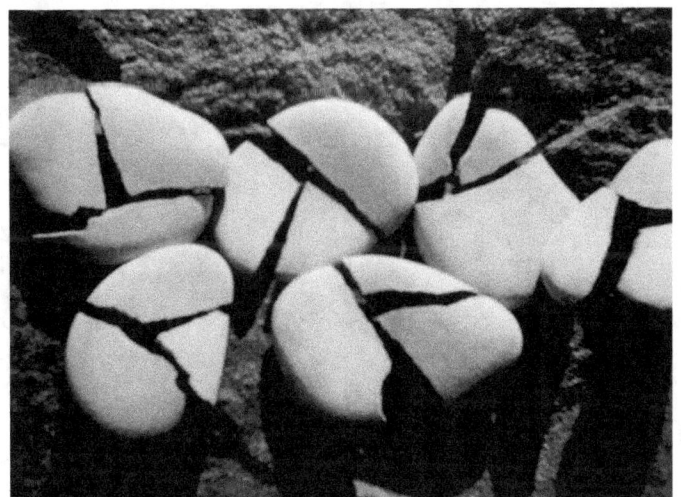

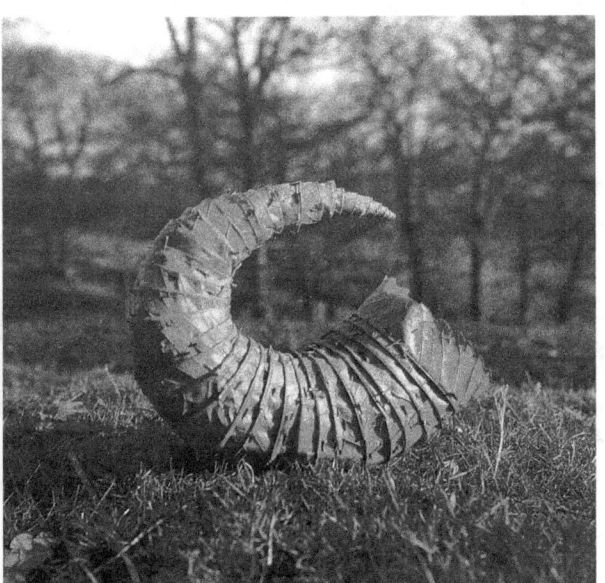

Single material

A large proportion of Goldsworthy's artworks are created from a single material: one type of stone, as in the broken pebbles; a collection of one kind of leaf, as in Autumn Horn; a Clay Wall installation; and a throw of red soil.

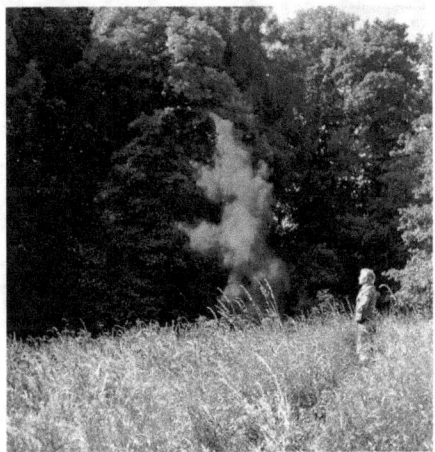

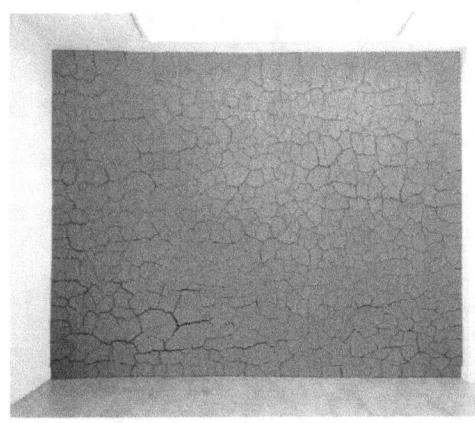

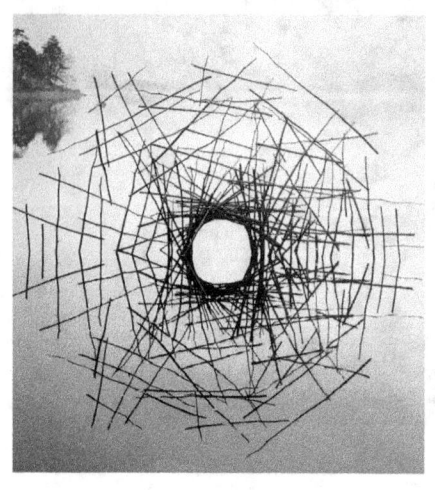

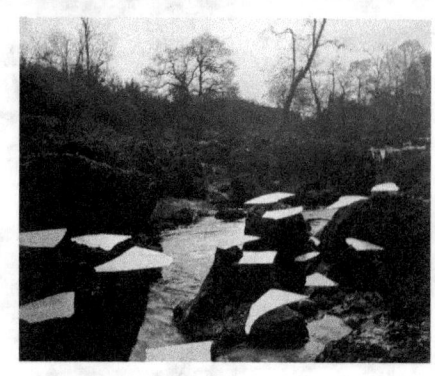

Wilderness setting

Without a doubt a central ingredient in Andy Goldworthy's art is his choice of settings, and primary among these is a wilderness setting, as in these works from Alaska; the Lake District's lakes; and Goldsworthy's homeground of Scaur Water in Scotland.

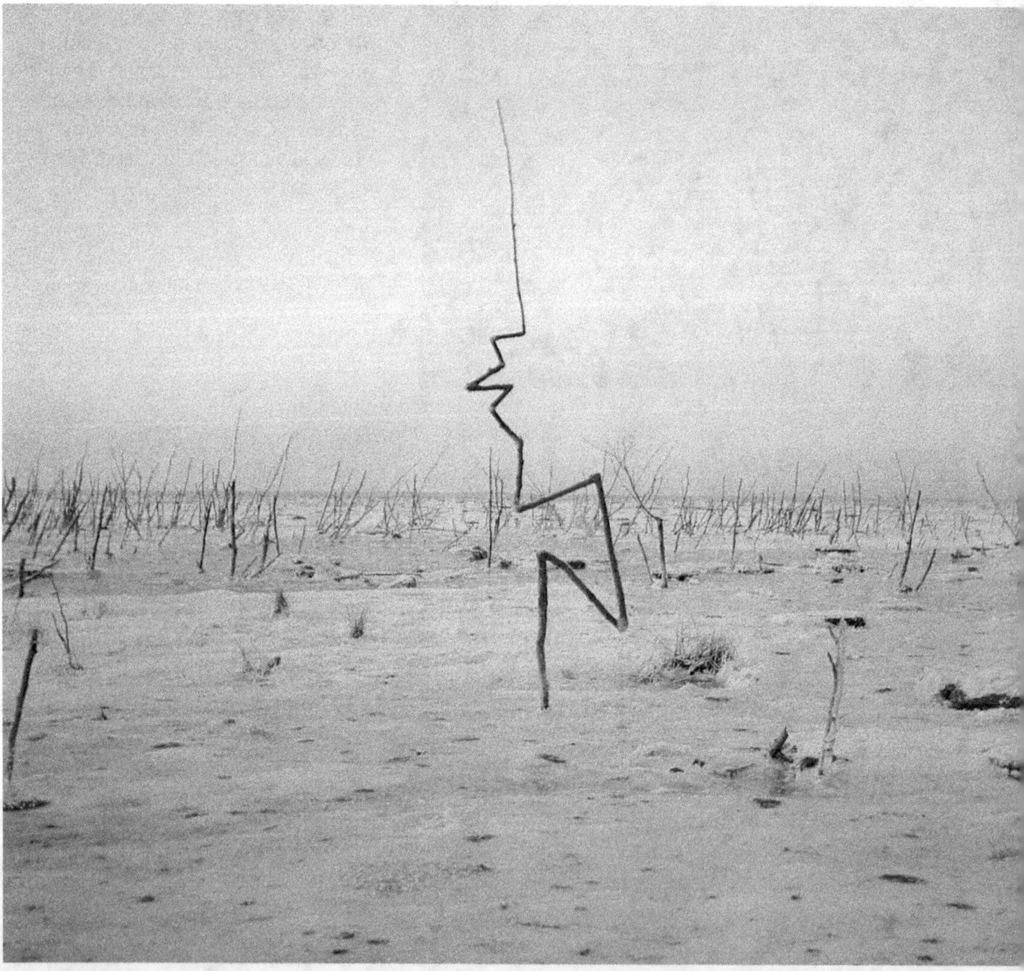

Wrapping

Goldsworthy has made an art of wrapping objects, though not yet on the scale of the king of wrap art, Christo. Goldsworthy has wrapped rocks, trees, branches, and other objects with leaves, wool, sticks, feathers and flower petals.

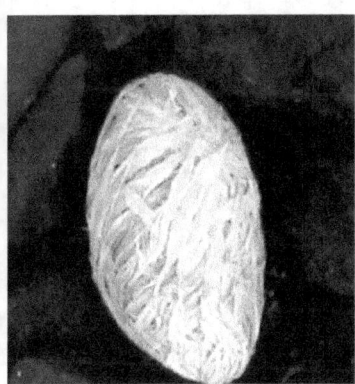

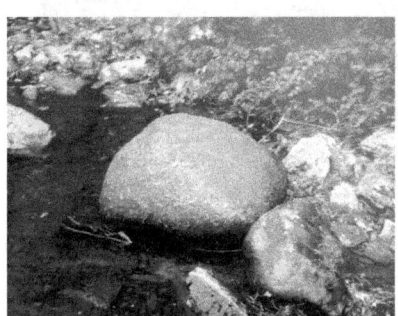

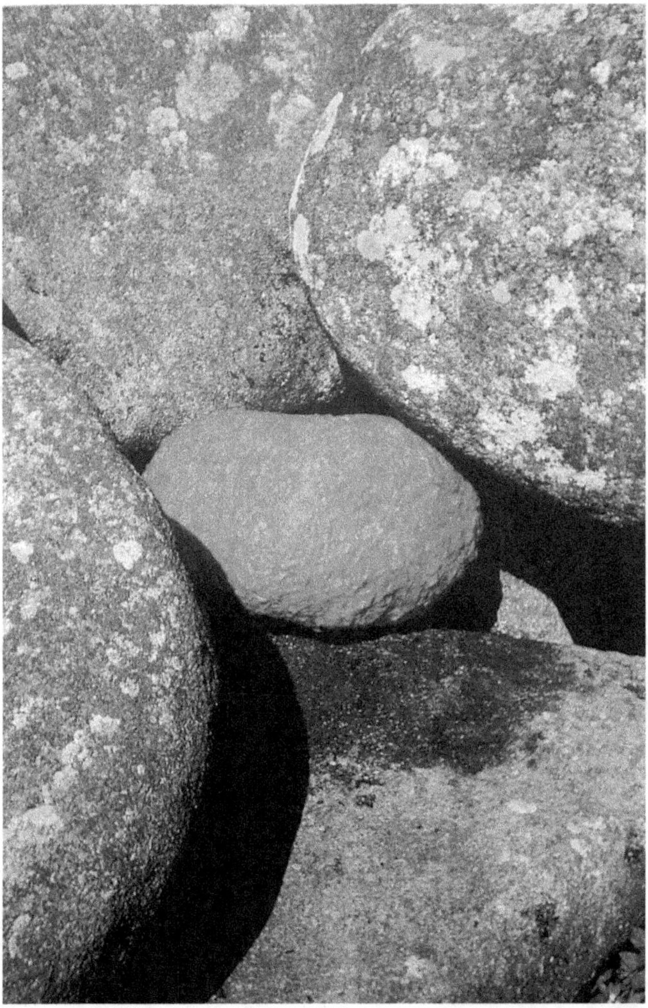

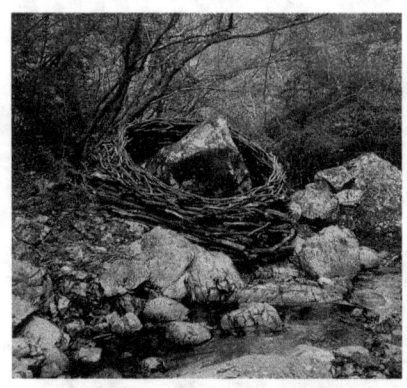

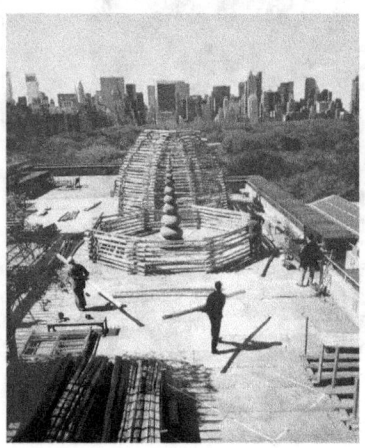

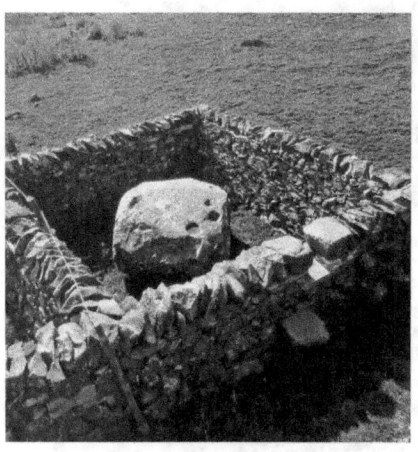

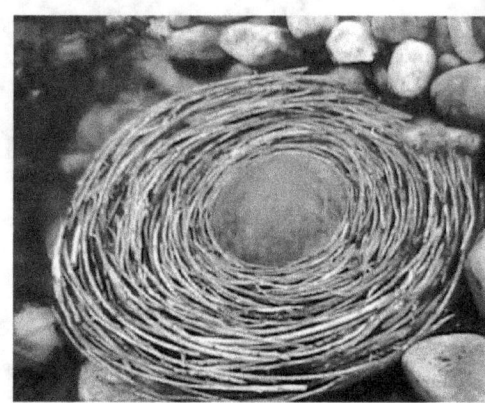

Enclosure

Enclosing an object or putting an object inside another
is a key Goldsworthy motif, occurring more and more
in his later works: such as the sheepfolds; or putting towers
of rocks inside wooden cairns, as in New York City;
or enveloping boulders with sticks.

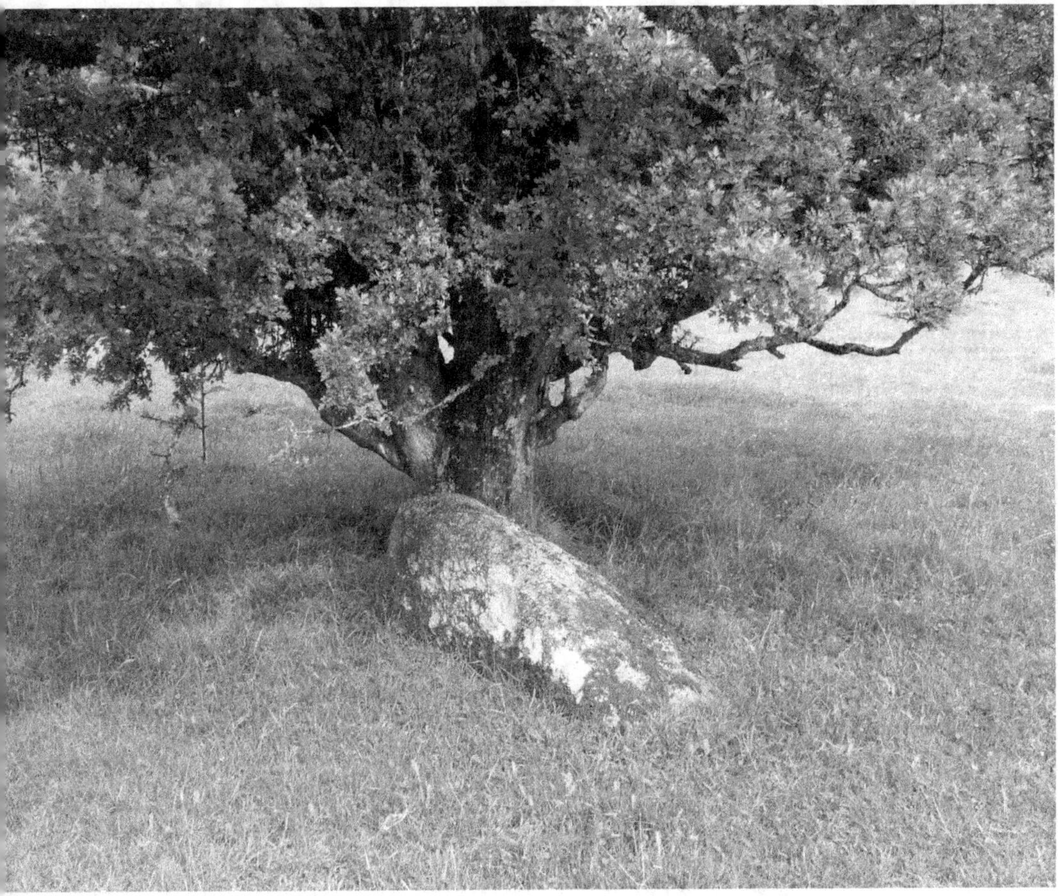

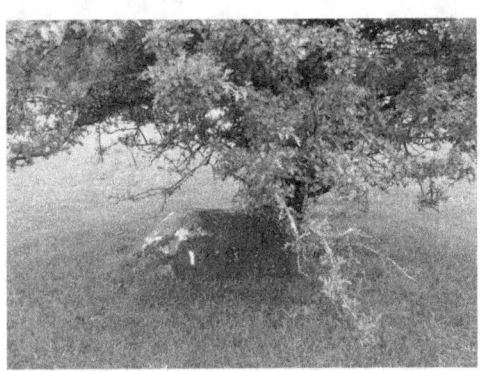

Andy Goldsworthy changes the way
you see the world. For instance,
I start to see Goldsworthy sculptures
round and about – what you might call
'found Goldsworthy' works, like this
boulder and tree I passed on a walk
in Dartmoor, near Newbridge.

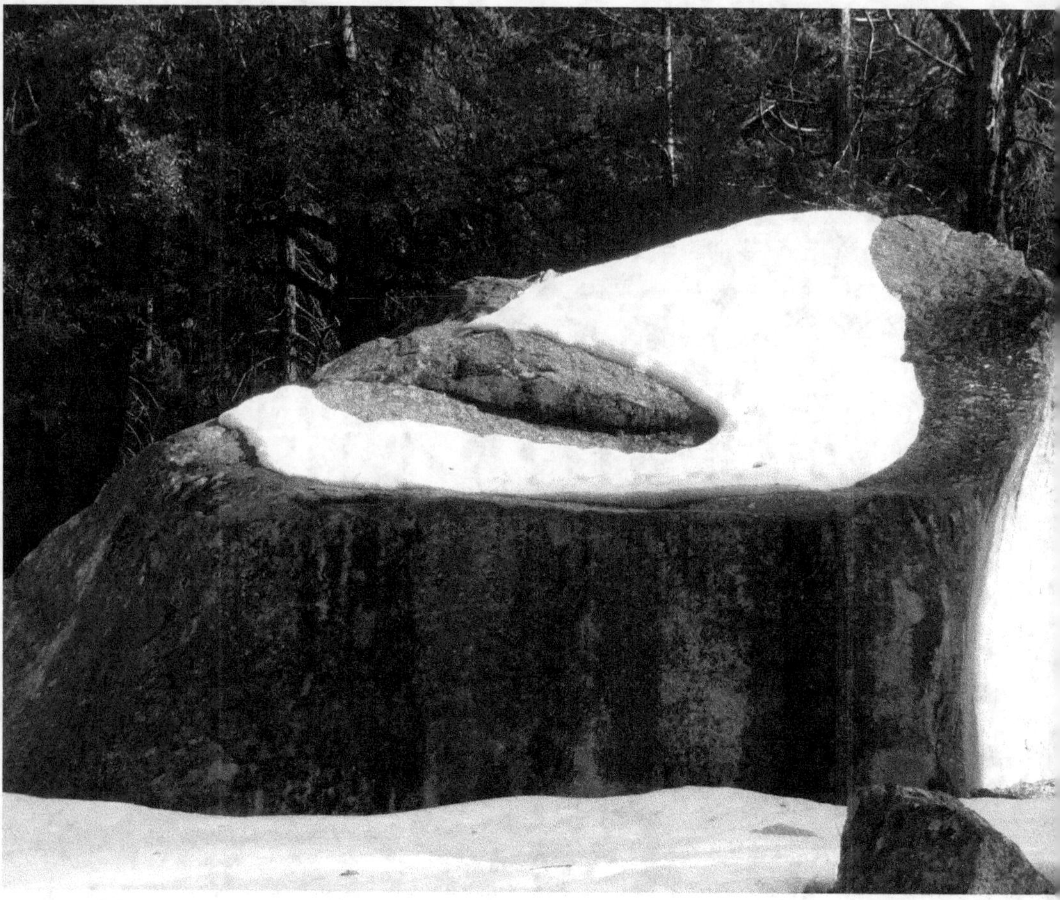

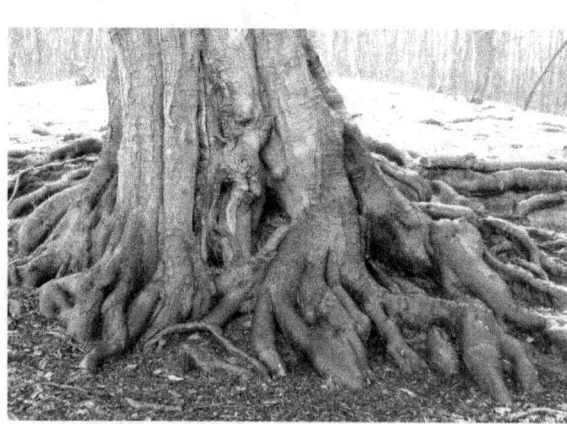
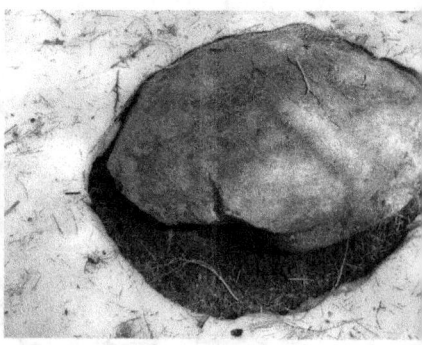

'Found Goldsworthy' pieces - boulders in the snow
in Yosemite Valley in California, and tree roots in Mereworth, Kent, U.K.

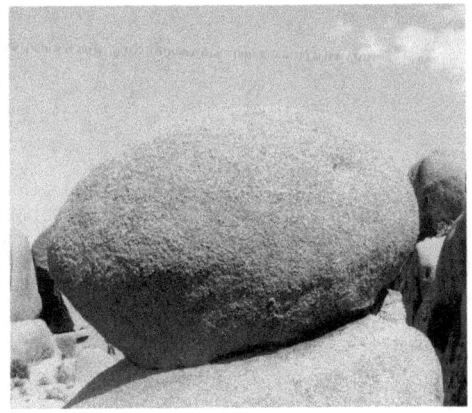

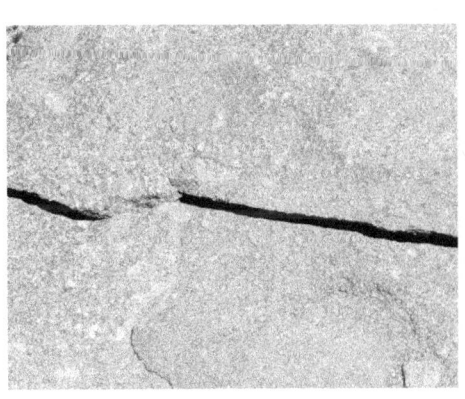

Joshua Tree National Park in the Sunshine State is a great place for finding 'found Goldworthys' – in balanced rocks, or cracked rocks, or rocks wedged into stone walls (above and left).

Sometimes you come across little sculptures made by people, like these stones in the Rocky Mountains near Estes Park, Colorado (below right).

I don't know who built the stone cairn (bottom) that I saw driving through the Rockies in Lyons, Colorado, but it must be inspired by Andy Goldsworthy.

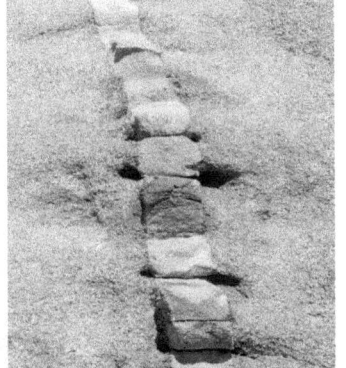

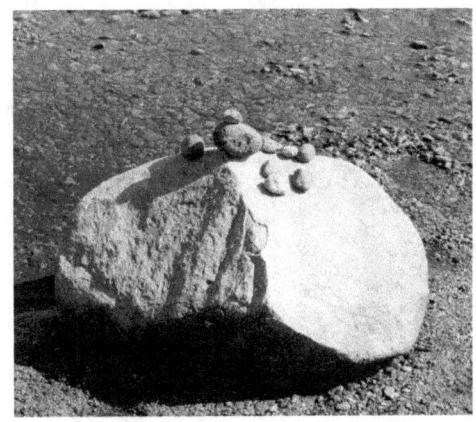

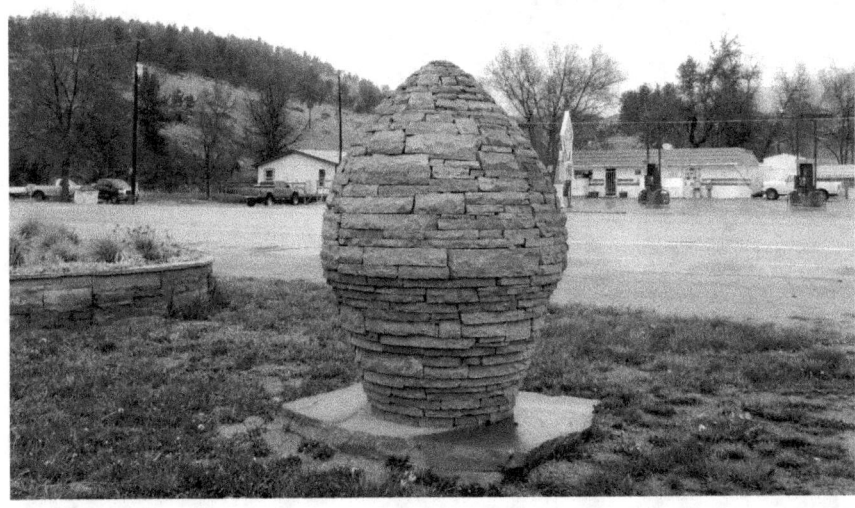

6

TREES, TIDES, PLANTS AND HOLES

LIVING PLANTS

Andy Goldsworthy is by no means the only contemporary artist who uses living plants. Some artists have installed trees upside-down (Vito Acconci) and plants upside-down in galleries (Michael Blazy, Henrik Håkansson, Sam Kunce). Some artists have trained plants to grow at odd angles (Hans Haacke, Cartsen Höller). Some artists have forced plants into vacuformed moulds (Laura Stein) and rubber foam (Ingo Vetter, Annette Weisser). Some artists have lined rooms with cages of bay leaves to produce an aromatic environment (Guiseppe Penone). Some artists have planted seeds on their naked bodies (Teresa Murak). Some artists have planted clover fields in galleries (Nikolaj Recke) and made couches from grass (Daniel Spoerri). Some artists have built parks running up the sides of buildings, complete with benches and steps (Vito Acconci); some have made enclosed indoor gardens (Knut Åsdam). Other artists have created portable orchards (the Harrisons); portable indoor vegetable gardens (N55); and crammed hothouses (Lothar Baumgarten). And some have let roses run riot over cars (Silvie Fleury). Herman de Vries is a close competitor with Goldsworthy for the artist who's created the most works with living plants.

Plenty of land artists and sculptors have used real flowers as well as Goldsworthy: Anya Gallaccio used roses (1992), sunflowers (1991) and zinnias (1992) (she's become more associated with flowers than Goldsworthy); Herman de Vries (who spread thousands of lavender flowers on a gallery floor in 1998); Wolfgang Laib with his pollen floor spreads; Richard Long, who pressed flowers flat in a field in *Brough of Birsay Circle* (1994); Jenny Holzer's *Black Garden*, a war memorial garden of very dark plants and flowers (1994); Gary Rieveschl, who planted *Heart Wave*, a line of 12,000 red tulips, in 1980; Daniel Buren also made a row of tulips, *11,000 Tulips* (1987, Holland); and Peter Hutchinson, who planted 'thrown ropes' of flowers (1996). And also Annette Wehrmann, Shelagh Wakely, Mark Dion, Meg Webster, Carsten Höller, Paula Hayes, Peter Fischl, David Weiss, Tobias Rehberger, Lothar Baumgarten, Brigitte Raabe, and Olaf Nicolai.

One of the most famous of contemporary sculptures using living flowers was Jeff Koons' giant dog sculpture (*Puppy*, 1992), constructed in Arolsen with 17,000 flowers, and standing 11.5 metres tall. 'I decided I wanted to make an image that communicated warmth and love to people. A very spiritual piece. It just came to me to make the *Puppy* out of live flowers'.[1] Although Koons' art was known for its postmodern, camp, trashy chic, Koons likened the interior of the *Puppy* to a church: 'I wanted the piece to deal with the human condition, and this condition in relation to God. I wanted it to be a contemporary Sacred Heart of Jesus' (ibid.).

---

1 J. Koons, in A. Muthesiues, ed. *Jeff Koons*, Cologne, 1992.

TREES

Many sculptors and land artists have worked with trees as well as Andy Goldsworthy: David Nash, Guiseppi Penone, William Jackson Maxwell, Robert Irwin, Jackie Winsor, Daniel Buren, Alan Sonfist, Harvey Fite, Peter Walker, Giuliano Mauri, Nils Udo, Luc Wolff, Maria Nordman, Sjoerd Buisman, Cosima von Bonin, Stefan Banz, Vito Acconci, Jørn Rønnau, Buster Simpson, Jan Dibbets, Helge Røed, Lars Vilks, Andy Lipkis, Herman de Vries and Mel Chin.

Using trees means working within a long and celebrated religious and cultural tradition.[2] For example, trees have since time immemorial been associated with spirits and religions. The Greeks believed that trees had spirits; there were the apples of immortality and trees of eternal life; Daphne turned into a tree when pursued by Zeus; Actæon was transformed into a stag in the forest when he spied Diana bathing nude; deities such as Athena, Artemis, Dionysus, Apollo, Orpheus and Cybele are associated with trees and woods. The Celts worshipped trees, and the Germanic tribes had mystical relations with trees. The Druids revered the oak, the royal tree of ancient England, and had rituals that involved oaks and mistletoe. The oak (a favourite Goldsworthy tree) was sacred to Jupiter, Hercules, the Dagda, Thor, Jehovah, Allah and other gods in their 'thunder-god' mode. Trees were associated with secret languages and religious symbolism. Fire festivals are in particular linked with trees – burning wood is central to many land artworks: there were the bonfires at the Celtic fire festivals (such as Samhain, or Hallowe'en, a fire festival inaugurating the beginning of the Celtic year which transferred in the UK to Bonfire Night); on Midsummer Day fires are lit, traditionally with oakwood; Midsummer was also the time of the sacrifice of the oak-king of Nemi. The willow is deeply associated with witchcraft (the words 'witch' and 'wicked' are derived from the same ancient word for 'willow'); the laurel is linked with poetry – the reward for great poetic endeavour was the laurel ('Daphne', in Greek, is associated with Apollo's pursuit of the Goddess

---

2 Writers on the symbolic and religious aspects of trees include Mircea Eliade (*Patterns of Comparative Religion*), Robert Graves (*The White Goddess*), James G. Frazer (*The Golden Bough*), and J.R.R. Tolkien, among others.

Daphne); laurel was also an intoxicant – the leaves were chewed to induce a frenzy – and the poet Francesco Petrarch revered the laurel tree, linking it with his beloved Laura and the longed-for notion of poetic immortality which the laurel symbolized. Particular trees have been mythologized: there was the 'holy thorn' that, as legend has it, sprang from Joseph of Arimathea's staff as he planted it in the sacred ground of Glastonbury; the wood of the Sacred Tree of Creevna, at Killura, had healing properties; naked children were passed through gaps in pollard ashes before dawn as a cure for rupture; Yygdrasill was the sacred ash tree of the Viking god Woden – he used it as his steed; in secular times trees still play a mythic role: there are the trees that hid figures such as Robin Hood and Charles I from their foes.

In fairy and folk tales, forests are places of enchantment, initiation and trial, where strange beasts and beings are encountered, spells are undertaken. The 'dark forest' or *selva oscura* occurs at the opening of the great poem of European culture, Dante's *Divine Comedy*, where the first thing the poet-pilgrim does is enter the 'dark forest'.

When land artists pick up a bit of wood, then, or use a branch in their work, they are activating a mass of associations in the fields of symbolism, legend, myth, magic and religion. Every tree and type of wood has its symbolic associations: oak, beech, laurel, willow, sycamore, ash, larch, hawthorn, holly, vine, hazel, ivy, rowan, alder and birch.

One of the most ancient religious functions of the tree was the World Tree of shamanism, the oldest of all religions. The World Tree was the mythic centre of the world of the community, it was the *axis mundi*, the pivot of time and space. The archaic shaman had many tasks: one of them was to travel to the Other World, to bring back news of what happened there, and to guide the souls of the departed to the Land of the Dead. The shaman did this by climbing up the Cosmic Tree: the shaman's magical flight to the Other World was linked with climbing the World Tree.

What has all this to do with 20th century land art? A lot. Constantin Brancusi, more influential on land art than Picasso, Arp, Giacometti, Rodin, Matisse or Maillol, worked notions of shamanic flight into his

Birds in Space sculptures, and most especially in his *Endless Column*, which is cited by many key sculptors (Judd, Andre, Morris) as an important inspiration. Brancusi's *Birds in Space* aimed to express the essence of flight, the moment when a quivering verticality is released from the chains of gravity and flies upward. One only has to look at David Nash's *Tripods*, Andy Goldsworthy's tower of rocks, Barnett Newman's *Broken Obelisk*, or Donald Judd's stacks, to see how important Brancusi's sculptures were, with their shamanic, World Tree associations.

Planting trees has become a favourite with land and environmental artists: Goldsworthy has planted dwarf oak saplings in his Holocaust memorial in New York; Alan Sonfist created various solid circles and rings of trees (*Circles of Life* [1986], *Circles of Time* [1987]); Mel Chin planted trees and plants on a landfill site in St Paul, MN (*Revival Field*); Joseph Beuys led the planting of oak trees at Documenta 7 in Kassel in 1982; Andy Lipkis planted trees in urban areas (such as L.A.), and organized fund-raising marathon runs for trees (1979); Guiseppe Penone placed a long white crystal in tree trunks, a very Goldsworthyan piece (*Light Traps*, 1994); Vito Acconci constructed a tower of trees (1996), one above the other, all of them upside-down; Robert Irwin installed nine plum trees in Seattle, WA (1983), separated by blue screens; Buster Simpson planted willow trees in drinking fountains (1993).

Daniel Buren constructed one of the most compelling of all treeworks: an olive tree standing atop a huge cube of soil in a gallery (*Untitled*, 1999), a truly spectacular (and enigmatic) work, with the tree and earth in proportion, quietly dominating the ornate room at Castello di Rivoli. *Pace* his *Sheepfolds* project, Goldsworthy remarked in 2001 that the

> planting of any tree is a gesture of optimism and renewal – growing out of stone in the protective embrace of a sheepfold will, I hope, give that gesture a potent mixture of feelings – hardship, struggle, fragility, precariousness and strength.[3]

---

3 A. Goldsworthy, *Sheepfolds* website.

Andy Goldsworthy has worked intimately with trees since the beginning of his career as a sculptor and land artist. He has his favourite trees (oak, beech, elm), with sycamore trees favoured for their leaves (for building objects such as the leaf boxes). Elm trees, for example, are Goldsworthy's chief source of yellow in Autumn (P, 127). Some of Goldsworthy's most important works have used trees as their focal point, such as the *Capenoch Tree* series, and *Sidewinder* and *Seven Spires* at Grizedale forest. Goldsworthy tended to use parts of a tree that were considered waste or unwanted, he explained; and he avoided cutting trees where possible (E, 176).

Goldsworthy has employed trees in countless works, using leaves and branches as materials in hundreds of sculptures, or trunks as easels or scaffolding. He's hung many works from trees: snowballs, shields, and lines of leaves. He's decorated trees with dandelions and snow. He's pressed leaves and sand into boles. He's extended trees with sand and clay. He's wrapped branches with petals and leaves. He's created footpaths winding between trees. He's used trees as backgrounds for carved sand drawings. He's built branches into stone walls. He's let trees define the path of his major works, such as the stone walls. He's worked in many, many forests and woods. Indeed, if you took trees out of Andy Goldsworthy's art, there would be a huge gap. In Goldsworthy's art, trees embody time, change, beauty, mystery, and place. Trees are, in short, the 'architecture of the planet'.[4]

---

4 Film director John Boorman's phrase.

THE BLACK HOLE

Andy Goldsworthy's anxious, ambivalent attitude towards holes in the ground recall the views of (usually male) philosophers on the negativity of holes and voids, which are associated with the sexual identity of women. These fears and ambiguities are found in much of Western culture: in Sigmund Freud's castration myth; in the bilious misogynist Christian theology of St Augustine, Tertullian, St Paul and Origen; or the sado-masochistic literature of the Marquis de Sade and Georges Bataille. In this view, women are vampires and witches, preying mantises and carnivorous spiders sucking up male desire and energy. Another religious view sees women as Mother Goddesses, identified with nature, the seasons, vegetation and the powers of the Earth. A deity which some feminists and British poets (such as Robert Graves and Peter Redgrove) have worshipped (though they would not use that term) is the 'Black Goddess', a divinity of darkness, night, the unknown and the supernatural.

The psychologist Jacques Lacan's notion of the 'lack' or loss, which subsequent feminists (such as Hélène Cixous, Julia Kristeva and Luce Irigaray) have critiqued, is another obvious reference to the hole. What women lack (for Lacan) is the phallus, the 'transcendent signifier' as cultural theorists call it. The art object is thus (in Julia Kristeva's interpretation) a fetish, a stand-in for the imaginary maternal phallus. Friedrich Nietzsche had similar views of the 'feminine': it was not menstruation or lactation that scandalized Nietzsche so much as the lack or absence of a visible (sexual) organ. 'What Mother Nature needs so urgently to hide from view is not so much what she has as what she lacks. Nietzsche suspects a void at the center of the body of nature.'[5] In French feminist Luce Irigaray's reading of Lacan's philosophy, what women lack is the ability to speak from/ with the phallus: the genital lack suggests an ideological or æsthetic lack, an absence which becomes cultural silence.

This masculinist fear of the black hole or void at the heart of nature

---

5 C. Koelb, "Castration Envy", in P.J. Burgard, ed. *Nietzsche and the Feminine*, University Press of Virginia, Charlottesville, VI, 1994, 79.

is very apparent in Mr Goldsworthy's statements: 'looking into a deep hole unnerves me' he wrote; the black holes of his sculptures are openings into the 'deep insecurity in nature – a fragile, unpredictable and violent energy' (S, 64). Goldsworthy is fascinated by holes: 'I enjoy the seductiveness of a hole', he said, 'which always makes me want to explore the spaces inside or beyond' (HE, 61). Goldsworthy admitted to being frightened as well as fascinated by the powers of nature. He spoke of the blackness under the Earth rising up and buckling the rim of the holes he makes in the ground and in the floors of art galleries. He made a hole in a gallery floor (in London) to remind the spectator that just below the building is the unpredictable and immense energy of nature and the Earth.

Goldsworthy dug holes at the Serpentine Gallery (London) in 1982 and 1984, at Coracle Press, London (in 1985), and at the Frank Hals Museum (in 1984). Sculptures such as the Greenpeace office commission – *Seven Holes* (1991) – are obviously about the Earth's energies (planetary as well as local forces). The sculpture *Black Water Stone* (1993) made explicit the identification between the Earth and 'feminine' discourses: the low cairn with the small hole at the summit was placed under water: the presence of the 'feminine' element, water, added another layer of connotation to the already symbolically rich sculpture (the cairn or mound; the circle; blackness; the hole; the submerged or partially out of sight setting).

The hole is also associated, of course, with death and the grave. In a portentous moment, Andy Goldsworthy said that '[i]t is possible that the last work I make will be a hole' (HE, 24). Of course the last sculpture he'll make will be a hole: then he will disappear down it, like the white rabbit. The body is returned to the Earth after death, in one way or another. After all, there's nowhere else for it to go (unless one can afford fifty million dollars for a burial in outer space).

Like a gravedigger, then, Goldsworthy scrabbles about in the soil, producing a hole in Hyde Park (1982), a hole in peat in Blaenau Ffestiniog (1980), a double hole in Cumbria (1980), and a hole just under a tree trunk in the Yorkshire Sculpture Park (1983). The sculpture *Sumach leaves* (1998), made at New York's Storm King, combined three

Goldsworthy motifs: leaves blended for hue, concentric layers around a circular hole, and a hole in the ground. Goldsworthy occasionally returned to hole sculptures, such as in a hole carved out of sand between two stones on the beach at Collieston (2000).

Andy Goldsworthy regarded his hole made at the Serpentine Gallery in the 1980s as 'perhaps the best work I ever made in a building', because he claimed he 'touched the nature of the building'.6 The Goldsworthy hole is also a key element of many of his cairns: the holed cairns are usually low circular structures with a circular aperture on the small flat summit, as in *Black water hole,* or another water hole, in the Thames (1987), or *Slate hole* (1983) and *Stick hole* (1999). Sometimes the holed slate cairns recall hearths or alchemical vessels in which the energies of nature are being harnessed. One thinks of David Nash's 'hearths' and stoves (*Sea Hearth, Snow Stove, Wood Stove, Slate Stove*, etc), and Chris Drury's shelters. (Goldsworthy has fired stones in a kiln, in order to release the stone's essence, exactly as mediæval alchemists did. It is not the spectacular nature of fire and flames that intrigues him, though, but 'the slow intense powerful heat that is at the core of nature' [S, 65]). The rounded dome with a hole at the top is also a shape that humans *live in*: one thinks not only of Eskimo igloos, Central Asian *yurts* and prehistoric 'beehive' and Iron Age huts, but also modern astrodomes and even camping tents. Other holed cairns include ones made from rowan leaves (Yorkshire, 1987) and pebbles (Japan, 1987). Goldsworthy planted a hawthorn tree in a holed stone cairn (*Dunesslin Cairn*, 1999), a work which looked forward to *Garden of Stone* (2003).

Andy Goldsworthy made a line of circular holes in Runnymede, California (1992) in dry weather. When it rained a few days later green shoots of grass started growing up through the holes. 'For me, there is something deeply interesting about a bright green grass blade growing out of a black hole' (W, 15). Another hole, *Branch and hole*, also at Runnymede (1992), looked like the shadow of the branch as it lay on the earth, or the image of the branch if projected onto the ground. *Torn Hole* (Cambridge, 1986) was a simple piece: horse

---

6 A. Papadakis, 1991, 249.

chestnut leaves stitched together on a tree in full leaf with a small circular hole torn into them. In Mallorca Goldsworthy made a stone cairn around an olive tree with a circular opening for the tree (1994). The effect was of a monument to the tree, or of a form enclosing and protecting the tree. In Central Park, New York City, Goldsworthy constructed a base of stacked sticks around three trees (1993). Also at Mallorca, Goldsworthy created a series of stone columns next to or on top of olive trees (1994), but these are not particularly distinctive works.

The most 'violent' of Andy Goldsworthy's sculptures are not the holes in floors and cairns, though they are related to them: Goldsworthy's trenches or cracks are made directly into the soil (at Yorkshire Sculpture Park [in August, 1987], and Little Langdale [1988], for example). Significantly, Goldsworthy did not pretty up these cracks by making them into spiral, circle or gentle serpentine shapes. They were jagged cracks, which resembled the fissures earthquakes make, or the trace of a lightning strike in the sky. The energy of these trenches does not flow smoothly out of the planet but comes out in ragged pulses. Like the torn stones, Goldsworthy was opening a window in the trenches into the energies of the Earth. Opening up a huge gaping hole may be too simple (as Michael Heizer has done): the zigzag lightning form is more suited to the unpredictable form Goldsworthy's version of the Earth's energies takes.

Andy Goldsworthy says he is unsettled by holes, by stones cracking open ('a deeply unnerving but beautiful expression of change' [S, 65]), by the potential in nature for destruction as well as birth. What is striking about Goldsworthy's writings, which are sometimes portentous or banal, is the number of times the word 'shock' appears. Goldsworthy is 'shocked' when a landscape is altered by a manmade lake (at Vassivière [S, 106]); he is 'deeply shocked' when a stone he was working on was smashed by another one falling from a cliff above (S, 94); he is 'shocked' when a pool of water is turned to red by rubbing two stones together (S, 83); he is 'deeply unnerved' by a heated stone splitting open (S, 65). The 'shock' of such natural events presumably derives from Goldsworthy's 'sensitivity' (he is portrayed a 'sensitive' artist in the pro-Goldsworthy criticism and media). Only someone with an exquisitely, breathlessly delicate sensitivity could be *shocked* by a little pool of water turning red, or *shocked* when a stone falls off a cliff. The jaded casual onlooker, seeing the tiny pool turn red might then say, 'well, *so what?'* But artists often work on an incredibly small and enclosed scale, in which the tiniest changes can be startling. Goldsworthy's project is to show the casual observer that a crack in the ground can be startling, to show that the 'fragile, unpredictable and violent energy' in nature can be discovered even in the smallest areas of nature. Even the little holes in the flattened domes can be windows onto the 'deep insecurity in nature' (S, 64). The world-weary viewer yawns and says, yeah, but Los Angeles, India, Russia, Iran and Japan have *real* cracks opening in the planet, earthquakes that can kill two thousand people in one day.

7

ANDY GOLDSWORTHY
THE SNOWMAN

ANDY GOLDSWORTHY AND SNOW

*When I work with winter, I work with the North. For me, north is an
integral part of the land.*

Andy Goldsworthy[7]

Much of Andy Goldsworthy's art is about and made from ice and snow
(which also means, in the United Kingdom, working mainly in
Winter). Other artists who have worked with snow include Dennis
Oppenheim above all, and Joseph Beuys and Hans Haacke.
Goldsworthy is distinctly a 'Northern' artist, who makes work in

---

7 In *Andy Goldsworthy.*

landscapes that come out of the 'Celtic fringe', out of the sort of landscapes that Celtic culture exalts: misty, rocky hillscapes; sodden Autumnal forest floors knee-deep with leaves; wild snowscapes; overgrown paths through woods; perpetual 'magic hour' light; cold, clear streams banked with large mossy boulders; and still lakes at dawn. Goldsworthy's landscapes could have mythical figures such as the Lady of Shallot, Lancelot or King Arthur or Gandalf riding through them without altering anything. They are the landscapes of Merlin, Taleissin and Morgan Le Fay, of Welsh legends such as *The Mabinogion*, of historical events shrouded in mists, of historical figures such as Robert the Bruce, Owen Glendower, King Edward and Boadiccea.

The places associated with Goldsworthy – his studio at Penpont, Scaur Water in Dumfriesshire, Carlisle, Yorkshire Sculpture Park, Grizedale in Cumbria, Leeds, Leadgate in Durham – are all Northern British sites. And the cultural stereotypes of Britain's North – grimy towns, rain, bleak moors, gloomy skies, deadpan humour, heavy industry, terraced houses, down-to-earth and no-nonsense attitudes – all chime with Goldsworthy's sculpture.

One wonders whether Goldsworthy would like to work in snow and ice more than in any other medium; some of his best and most interesting works are ice and snow. His notes and titles record many frustrations stemming from working with snow. In temperate snowlands, though, one feels Goldsworthy is very much at home. Snow has the right sort of qualities Goldsworthy looks for in a material: it is malleable, it melts and changes, its whiteness makes for good, contrasty imagery, and it seasonally alters the landscape, and later dissolves into it. (And it's free, and it's sometimes found in abundance).

In Goldsworthy's snowworks one senses also the sheer fun of working with snow. For people in most of Britain, snow is not a definite event each year, as it is in, say, Northern Russia or Alaska. For children, snow can be an exciting occurrence (while British adults always gripe about it). Snow was a perennial delight and 'shock' for Goldsworthy. In *Midsummer Snowballs* he wrote that '[e]ven in winter each snowfall is a shock, unpredictable and unexpected' (MS, 31). Goldsworthy retained the child-like enjoyment of snow falling in Britain throughout his life. While much of the UK grinds to a halt at the sight of a snowflake, Goldsworthy has the child's joy when it snows (school's cancelled, snowball fights, ice skating, sledging, and making snowmen and snowballs).

Goldsworthy speaks in wonder and awe of 'the effect, the excitement' of the first snowfall (HE, 165). Some of this excitement comes across in Goldsworthy's snowworks. He has made, for example, patterns in the snow by rolling a snowball around a field, exactly as kids (and adults) do when it snows (*Snowball trail* [Brough, Cumbria, 1982], and Yorkshire Sculpture Park [1987]). Linked to the snowball trail was a rectangular wall of snow built on the hills in Penpont in March, 1998.

Some of Goldsworthy's earliest works with snow were large snowballs. In some of these early snow works, Goldsworthy placed snowballs in areas such as woods or fields which didn't have any snow, so the snowballs stood out against the trees and grass (as in Ilkley, Yorkshire, 1981). The snowballs were sometimes carried down from higher slopes. Into some snowballs Goldsworthy inserted branches and other material (at Clapham, Yorkshire [1979], Bentham [1980], and London [1985]).

In some sculptures, Goldsworthy's snowballs are small and look like seeds placed inside the trunks of broken trees (as in the 1993 piece in *Wood*, 24). Other snowball-in-tree works include *Oak tree snowball* and *Beech tree snowball* (both Dumfriesshire, both 1994). Goldsworthy photographed these sculptures from a distance, to include the whole tree and its snowy surroundings (and also carefully composed the pictures so that the snowballs were contrasted with the dark tree trunks or walls). These are atmospheric pieces, with the white of the sky and the snow predominating.

Goldsworthy has been lucky in that there were some good, cold, snowy Winters in Britain around the late 1970s and early 1980s. 1977-78 and 1981-82 were memorable – his art might have developed differently if he had made work during milder, snowless Winters.

Other Goldsworthy iceworks include icicles stuck onto a wall (made on New Year's Eve, 1992) and *Icicles frozen to a rock* (1991). In these works, the icicles are clustered together, like a mini forest of trees. The icicle works, like the mound of stones which were dipped in water then frozen onto a rockface (S, 44-45), are testaments of endurance: the artist had to keep returning to the same place to pull the work off. *Icicles,* made on the last day of 2003 at Goldsworthy's favourite Scaur Water spot, was a row of icicles, some a few feet long, frozen to a rock (P, 18). *Ice 'fish'* was a flat curve made from little sheets of ice; *Ice column* was also constructed from sheets of ice refrozen together: the result looked like a Naum Gabo tower (both 1991, Dumfriesshire).

There was also an *Ice star,* two icicles aimed at each other ('pointing their frozen energies towards each other'),[8] small slabs of thin ice frozen to rocks in a stream and photographed to catch the rising sun (2004), an icicle that appeared to pierce an oak branch (2002), an *Ice hole* made in Yorkshire Sculpture Park, *Ice Spires* (2003), a cluster of icicle spikes frozen together, and a hollow *Ice ball* (1987).

An icicle work was made in Winter 1995-96, which Goldsworthy called '[t]he coldest I have ever known in Britain' (W, 67). This work has a privileged position in the *Wood* book, having three photographs to itself: two close-up, showing the spiral icicle in cloudy and sunny conditions, and one long shot showing its location at Glen Marlin Falls in Dumfriesshire. Goldsworthy spoke of the intensity of the sun shining onto the icicle: 'it was as if the icicle was both absorbing and generating light. This was the moment when the work came alive' (W, 10). Goldsworthy likened the moment when the icicle was illuminated to when Constantin Brancusi photographed his *Bird in Space* sculpture in his Paris studio.

To enhance the grandeur of some of his snow pieces, Goldsworthy printed them in a large, double page spread format in the book *Andy Goldsworthy* (1990). To evoke the beauty of the setting and the changeability of the weather,[9] Goldsworthy reproduced (in the same book) three double page spreads of a snow wall made at a favourite

---

8 A. Goldsworthy, sketchbook, Jan 22, 1983, HE, 146.
9 'Working in Britain means working close to change: a clear day soon clouds over, snow melts quickly, a calm morning turns windy. These qualities give urgency and energy to what I do' (AG).

spot, Blencathra in Cumbria. The full title of the work explains some of it:

> Slits cut into frozen snow
> stormy
> strong wind
> weather and light rapidly changing

The title reads like a *haiku*, like many of Goldsworthy's titles. The title, however, does not convey the Romantic power of these photographs which directly recall the oil paintings of J.M.W. Turner. Behind the slitted snow wall the viewer sees brooding cloudscapes, with the sun burning through in the second shot. In the third picture, the wall, in the foreground, is in shadow, while the sun shines onto a portion of a distant hill. Above roam clouds with softened edges, as out of Mark Rothko's abstract panels or Emil Nolde's watercolours of North Friesland.

In Anchorage, Alaska, in 1995, Goldsworthy built a series of lines from branches frozen together. The forms – curving and zigzagging columns – were familiar Goldsworthyan motifs. Later, Goldsworthy took down the stick towers and used them to form a long line of 114 sticks which stretched out over the Alaskan snow. Goldsworthy related the line of sticks to the tree line, the line of distant mountains, and the line of the estuary.

> I want the line to be made up of wood, ice, wood, ice, wood, ice. Winter, summer, winter, summer, winter, summer [Goldsworthy wrote]. I like the idea of many pieces being joined together in a continuous line, just as the seasons are. (W, 49).

This series of works culminated in a stick house in which Goldsworthy hung a 3 foot icicle made by dripping water. In his journal Goldsworthy said that the icicle was meant to be like a knife with the surrounding wood as a sheath. He also related the vertical icicle to the spine of the dancers in the *Végétal* performance, and to the stone columns (W, 10). The ice house was about the relationship between trees, water and the cold. 'The tree needs water, yet water makes it vulnerable to the cold. Water at its core, its spine: delicate, fragile and vulnerable' (W, 49). Goldsworthy spoke of the relation between stone and wood, stone and trees. 'It is no accident that I called the piece of land near to where I live 'Stone Wood'. I've always been aware of the relationship between these two materials' (Sh, 22). Note that two of Goldsworthy's major art books are entitled *Stone* and *Wood*.

The biting cold maybe gives Goldsworthy a sense of heroism, for suffering invariably enhances a work (as in, 'this work was difficult, made under adverse conditions'). After all, Goldsworthy is not an artist who makes work in the 'comfort' of a home or studio (working indoors doesn't feel 'real' to him). No: he goes out into the natural world, where it can be uncomfortable and challenging. He claims to know the landscape around his studio in Penpont, Scotland, very well, so that a snowfall does not hide the world: 'I know what lies under the snow – I know the earth beneath' (HE). Always Goldsworthy stresses the intimate relationship he has with nature. Part of this intimacy comes from returning to the same patch of land again and again. Through successive visits, layers of touch and meaning in the landscape are uncovered by the artist. The artist returning to the same space always works in time as well as space, for s/he creates a personal history of that place. S/he works with her former selves, as well as in the present – with the artist and ideas she had two years ago, ten years ago, twenty years ago. 'Some places I return to over and over again, going deeper – a relationship, made in layers over a long time' (AG). Sometimes, as he wanders round familiar spots, Goldsworthy comes upon old works (and occasionally photographs them).

The personal dimension is important in Goldsworthy's work. His work is not 'impersonal' in the sense that it could be made 'anywhere'. It is, like most land art, always a product of a relationship between an artist and a particular place. Making the art itself, the doing of it, is important for Goldsworthy. So that when people ask the eternal question, *but is it art?*, he retorts, well, he doesn't know and doesn't care, but 'it is important and necessary for me as a person.'[10] (Artists

10 A. Goldsworthy, interview, Dec 9, 1987, in HE, 163.

always leave it up to others to define their works).

Sceptics can claim that many of Andy Goldsworthy's sculptures gain much of their fire from their situation in wilderness landscapes. They would be right. Although Goldsworthy states that many of his sculptures are made in built-up areas, areas of dense population and human activity, a glance through any Goldsworthy book or a visit to a Goldsworthy show will reveal the large proportion of wilderness or rural landscapes in his art. He expunges all the trash, houses, telegraph poles, apartment blocks, cars and roads from his photographs, and presents lush streams, moorland, forests and hillsides (if his art is often made in cities, where are the buses, the graffiti, the signage, the mail boxes, the phone booths, the dumpsters?). There are no people at all in his art, except Goldsworthy himself, who is sometimes seen, with his beard, sweater and jeans (often a hat, sometimes gloves), making a piece of art.

In this sense, Andy Goldsworthy's work is not at all figurative – but neither is it wholly 'abstract', in the Mark Rothko or Piet Mondrian sense, because real, recognizable objects appear in his work. This is one of the reasons for the growing popularity of his work: apart from the Eighties ecological/ green movement, and the accessible, decorative quality of his work, it is thoroughly countrified and rural, quite in keeping with primæval desires for escape into the country, that nostalgia for nature that lies behind the pastoral and landscape tradition in the West.

Goldsworthy speaks as poets do of the spirit of place, where the place itself becomes as important as the object: 'the work is the place', Goldsworthy has stated (S, 6). Any number of artworks gain much from their setting, from Greek temples to a Caravaggio discovered in a dark, incense-smoky church in a backstreet in Rome. For the land or earth artist, of course the place becomes (identical with) the work. In the typical Goldsworthy work, though, there is usually some object at the centre of the landscape or the photograph. There is usually a rock covered in leaves, a red pool, a slate cairn in the centre. At first glance, the object seems to be the subject of the artwork and the focus for the eye. Not so: the surroundings are just as important, and these pastoral landscapes help to sell Goldsworthy's art just as much as the woven grass stalks or the sticks wrapped around a boulder.

Goldsworthy's skill is not just to 'touch nature' (whatever that means) but to touch the chords of desire for nature in people. Goldsworthy's art is popular partly because of this powerful desire among Western audiences for contact with the natural world, an appetite which is manifested in natural history programmes on television, in jaunts to zoos, gardens and wind-swept hillside car lots and beauty spots, in Hopper, Rockwell and Monet posters and prints, in gardening magazines and gardening centres and plants in the house, in the popularity of English rural novels by George Eliot, Thomas Hardy and the Brontës.

The eco/ green movement (and its associated movements in pagan/ New Age/ road, anti-capitalist, anarchist and animal activism) taps into this nostalgic love of an urban-centric culture for all things 'natural'. 'Urban living has always tended to produce a sentimental view of nature', wrote John Berger.[11] The natural world seems to be green and life-giving and untarnished by the complexities of modern life. The natural world, which is Goldsworthy's preferred world, is a place of leaves, rivers, animals and stones, a place seemingly devoid of people, the ones who fuck things up, who complicate things, who introduce the concepts and realities of neurosis, confusion, waste, violence, consumption and politics into the 'pure' natural world.[12]

It's not like that at all, but these eco, green, pastoral feelings are powerful. Goldsworthy's art, like the pastoral novels of George Eliot and Thomas Hardy, like green politics or the money-spinning popularity of Vincent van Gogh and Claude Monet, trades on the desires for an earlier, ancient Paradise, a time when things seemed to be simpler, richer, deeper. This is the 'green world' of childhood, a time of playfulness and living close to the Earth, enjoying the seasons passionately but also freely, in a relaxed manner. In mythology, it is the 'Golden Age', *il illo tempore, ab origine*, in the Creation era, at the

---

11 *The White Bird: Writings by John Berger*, London, 1988, 7.
12 'Nature for me is the clearest path to discover – *uncluttered by personalities* or associations – *it just is*', says Goldsworthy in a telling statement (my emphasis, sketchbook no. 19, 1988, HE, 150).

origin of the world, before the Fall of Adam and Eve into sin, a time before œdipal anxiety and patriarchal psychosis, a Gaia time, a whole earth time, all 'natural' and recycled and vegetarian, a holistic time, a time of social unity, when everyone felt as one in communities and loved each other, a time of maternal bliss, when women were nurturing Mother Goddesses and men could be sweetly dreaming babies without feeling embarrassed.

Goldsworthy's art books, commissions and shows trade on this pastoral imagery and desire: they allow stressed, overworked and neurotic city dwellers time out from staring at the control screens (TV, computers, cell phones, ATMs) of the megavisual world, encouraging a little day-dreaming into the soft greens and greys of wild moorlands. Goldsworthy's art may be increasingly successful because it reminds people that, yes, one does love nature after all: one came from it, one'll go back into it, in the end, in death.

Goldsworthy's art may hit home because it does *not* bombard people with telephones, computers, cars, factories, radios, TVs, microwaves, washing machines, hoovers, irons, faxes, and all those machines that connote *labour*, that are the symbols and mechanisms of working life. In Goldsworthy's green world, all is natural, untechnological, with artifacts that evoke a return to basics: stone, wood, leaves, ice.

TOUCHING NORTH (1 989)

Andrew Goldsworthy's most dramatic work to date is probably *Touching North* (1989), four circular arches made of snow. It is dramatic mainly due to its location, that space so thoroughly a masculine 'wild zone', the place of macho adventures, colonization and courage: the North Pole. The *Touching North* project was organized by the Fabian Carlsson Gallery, London (one of Goldsworthy's dealers at the time), and overseen by Fabian Carlsson. In March and April, 1989, the expedition visited Montréal, Resolute, Grise Fjord, Camp Hazen and the North Pole, and the show travelled to London, Edinburgh and L.A. through 1989.

Goldsworthy's intention with the grandeur of *Touching North* was 'to follow North to its source'. He had already encountered 'North' in 'the cold shadow of a mountain', he said, meaning he had already found the extreme cold associated with the North Pole in Scotland or Northern Britain. But there was a practical reason for going all the way North to the North Pole, and that was so that Goldsworthy could enjoy 'the luxury of constant freezing' (in Britain, snow comes and goes: it does not stay for months on end as it does in the North Pole). As Goldsworthy wrote: 'so much that I have made in ice has been frustrated by a rise in temperature. I have held ice seemingly for ages waiting for it to freeze only to let go and see it drop off.'[13] Yeah, we all know that feeling.

Although the four circular walls were the centrepiece of the *Touching North* project, Goldsworthy made other snowworks at the time. *Snow Spires* was two little groups of pyramid forms between five and seven feet tall (1989, Ellesmere Island), while *Snow Slabs* was a long line of slabs, recalling the lines of prehistoric stones at Carnac in France. Other works in *Touching North* included a wall constructed from narrow slabs of snow balanced on top of each other; flat wedges of snow piled on top of each other to form a low bridge; a series of free-standing arches placed in a row, recalling the nave of a Gothic cathedral; a cairn made from circular slabs of snow; a low wall of snow with arrow-shaped slits carved in it; another wall consisting of chevrons placed end-to-end. There were also various narrow walls of snow with slits carved in them: one in the shape of a star; another in a Goldsworthyan serpent; another with parallel zigzag lines.

---

13 A. Goldsworthy, *Touching North*, 1989, and in HE, 75.

SNOWBALLS IN SUMMER (2000)

Snowballs In Summer (a.k.a. *Midsummer Snowballs,* 2000) was one of Andy Goldsworthy's larger, more complex installations. Fourteen snowballs were gathered from the snowfields of Dumfriesshire and Perthshire in 1999 and 2000, kept in storage, transported to London and exhibited on the streets of the City of London. This, coupled with the show *Time*, at the Barbican Centre (in August-October), made 2000 the most prominent display of Goldsworthyania for some years in the British Isles. Goldsworthy liked the idea of the snowballs appearing in the middle of Summer in an urban setting (a variation on his early works of carrying snowballs down hills to place them among snowless woods). The snowballs were not 'made for people. They are about people' (MS, 33).

Sites for the London *Snowballs* show were explored on foot, with Goldsworthy planning where to position the snowballs by painting white typing correction fluid on photographs. Installing the snowballs between midnight and dawn on June 21st required a carefully organized effort involving helpers, forklift trucks, cranes and lorries. The snowballs were placed in the Barbican area of central London, including the Barbican Centre, Silk Street, Moorgate, St John Street, Long Lane, Smithfield Market, London Wall, Bunhill Fields cemetery and Charterhouse Square.

Goldsworthy wanted the snowballs to be *in situ* by dawn, so for the public they would just seem to have appeared from nowhere. Surprise was important. Goldsworthy said he aimed the snowball installation at the workers in the City who'd be travelling to work in the morning, popping out for lunch, and going home later. At that time, at five or six in the evening, the contents of the snowballs would be gradually emerging (MS, 34). The melt would be integrated into the working day of the City. The centrepiece of the *Time* show was a large wall of mud, which dried gradually, and *Red Stone*, the last of the London *Snowballs*, which had been packed with red stone powder and allowed to melt in the Barbican's Curve gallery, spreading red-stained water over the floor.

Time, change and the millennium was another aspect Goldsworthy wanted to explore in the London *Snowballs* installation: the snow would be gathered at the end of the 20th century and exhibited at the beginning of the 21st century. (Remember what a big deal the Millennium was?). Goldsworthy made other sculptures, such as arches and cairns, which were completed either side of New Year's Eve, 1999. Thus, for Goldsworthy, it was important that the sculptures bridged two centuries and two millennia (T, 12). For *Snowballs In Summer*, Goldsworthy also employed a link up on the web to images of the snowballs on the streets.

The materials set inside the London snowballs included pebbles, sheep's wool, cow hair, crow feathers, horse chestnuts, Scots pine cones, beech branches, barley, elderberries, barbed wire, chalk and ash keys. (The contents in the snowballs in the Glasgow, 1989 show included willowherb stalks, daffodils, pine cones, pebbles, horse chestnut stalks, stones, dog-wood, reeds, oak and birch twigs, slate, chestnut leaves, chalk, soil, ash keys and pine needles.) Goldsworthy also placed scraps of farming machinery he'd gathered from near his home in Penpont. Some of the snowballs melted quickly, some stayed for a day or so (June 21st was a dry, cool day, but the wind eroded the snowballs quicker than anticipated). Some snowballs were vandalized, others were moved. Some of the materials contained in each snowball related to where they were situated (cow hair, for example, in the snowball outside Smithfield market). Goldsworthy remarked that he could have easily included sensational materials in the snowballs, to give the project a higher profile (though the TV and press were there anyway).

8

ANDY GOLDSWORTHY
THE GREEN MAN

All forms are to be found in nature, and there are many qualities within any material. By exploring them I hope to understand the whole.

Andy Goldsworthy, *Winter Harvest* 14

One of the problems Andy Goldsworthy's art addresses head on is the age-old tension between the 'real world' and art, between objects as they are in the everyday world, and objects as they are represented in art. Goldsworthy encourages the viewer to look again at the natural world: not just at the beauty of it, but at the multitudinous variety of

14 A. Goldsworthy, HE, 163.

forms in nature. His sculpture is a poetry of natural forms (but notions of representation and simulation are not sidestepped, because although Goldsworthy's art is based on things 'as themselves', the use of photography sees a swift return of confusions over the politics of representation). The snowball in the *Snowballs* installations (1989 and 2000) is not plastic or concrete masquerading as a snowball, but a real snowball. Similarly, the twigs and stalks and needles and pebbles folded into the snowballs are real (but the snowballs are also art objects).

What's amazing is the actuality of nature: the variety of forms (the way the branches twist, for instance). Paul Nesbitt wrote of Andy Goldsworthy's art:

> Throughout these works the dominant theme is one of working with nature, to reveal nature itself – physical, chemical and biological. Goldsworthy uses nature's materials – rock, water (snow and ice, rain and mist), earth and the plants and animals which inhabit these; he uses nature's properties – structure, shape, form and colour; he uses nature's forces which together create, alter and animate those materials and properties – forces of light, heat, wind and gravity.[15]

Goldsworthy would have the viewer look closely at nature again. By using 'real' objects, Goldsworthy aims to demolish notions of representation and mediation. Instead of a picture of snow, one has in Goldsworthy's art snow itself; rather than paint pebbles, or sculpt them in bronze, Goldsworthy uses real pebbles.

Of course, there are problems with using objects as objects – Marcel Duchamp with his readymades confronted this problem. The dilemma is partly one of context: because, placed in a museum or art gallery, as items to be studied, enjoyed, critiqued, natural forms become art. The snowballs may not be on pedestals, but they are perceived as art objects (and intended and presented as such). The leaf sculptures are more obviously works of art, set on shelves, or photographed against paper backdrops, as bottles of perfume or Swiss watches are photographed for adverts. If one is looking at a Goldsworthy sculpture in a book or a gallery, one is a already anchored in a gallery/ art/ æsthetic

---

15 P. Nesbitt, "A Landscape Touched by Gold", in G. Hughes, 1990, 49.

mode of viewing. If Goldsworthy's sculptures are in a gallery, one sees them as art (and a particular kind of Western, bourgeois art, the sort of art that is exhibited in Western, bourgeois galleries).

Carl Andre explored the relation between real and represented objects with his controversial pile of bricks. The sculpture was 'controversial' (a journo's inaccurate shorthand for something that's really a mild argument) because the general public (whoever they are) perceived, via the media, that Andre had simply stuck some bricks into a gallery. Or rather, that British taxpayer's money had been used to purchase Andre's bricks (in the 1970s, the Tate Gallery was partly funded by public money). A pile of bricks on a building site is... a pile of bricks. A pile of bricks in an art gallery is... sculpture. Context is everything here. This is what Carl Andre explored, whether consciously or not: the *response*, affected by so much of culture, socialization, physical context, education, and so on, makes objects sculptures. People make art. A leaf simply exists, but if someone puts it in a gallery or an art book, it becomes art (as well as remaining a leaf; but being an artwork takes precedence). If people think something is art, then it's art, as Donald Judd said.

Obviously, Andy Goldsworthy's leafworks – the sycamore boxes, the sweet chestnut horns, the maple circles – are sculptures, seen and described (and sold) as sculptures. That's easy, to see the leafworks as sculptures. The petal-covered rocks, those too, are clearly sculptures. There is no mistaking the carefully crafted pieces as anything other than 'high art'. Every artwork creates a multitude of readings, but one of the dominant readings of Goldsworthy's 'real' objects is that they are 'high art' sculptures.

One of the most beautiful of Goldsworthy's works is *Rosebay willowherb* (1990), a web of willowherb stalks woven together into a circle. At the centre was an open circle made by the stalks: Goldsworthy wove the stalks together so that they expanded in gentle curves. *Susuki Grass* (1993), made in Japan, was a similar work, a wall or curtain of stalks. Related to *Rosebay willowherb* was *Woven silver birch* (fabricated at Langholm in Dumfriesshire, 1986): again the sticks were woven together to form an open circle at the centre. On the outside of the sculpture, the sticks moved off in every direction. It looked like a catherine wheel firework, with the sparks frozen in the air.

Goldsworthy produced a few of these 'drawings in air', free-standing sculptures which were practically two-dimensional. They were drawings in space, where Goldsworthy employed the fine bendy stalks to delineate elegant curves in the air. These works – *Knotwood stalks* (Holbeck Triangle, 1986), *Rosebay willowherb* and the stalks stuck in the lake bottom in the Lake District (*Early morning calm*, 1988) – were wholly dependent on Renaissance notions of perspective, space and illusion. They were flat works, best seen from one particular direction, and preferably with contrasty lighting, set against a sky, for instance. One or two stick works, though, broke out in all directions, such as *Hazel sticks* (1980), made in Cumbria, where a group of straight sticks, some six or more feet long, were bound together on a pole.

Andy Goldsworthy's sculptures used all the tricks and devices of post-Renaissance illusion and representation, including figure-ground relationships, negative space, perspective, selective viewpoint, *chiaro-scuro*, silhouettes, outlines, and so on. A good example of the strong pictorial element in Goldsworthy's art are the sculptures that use negative space to create the illusion of continuous form: these sculptures typically have loops of ice or sand on two sides of a rock or a tree. In, for instance, *Reconstructed refrozen icicles* (1999 [T, 112]),

Goldsworthy's ethics are those of Chris Drury, Hamish Fulton, Richard Long, David Nash (he has worked at Nash's Blaenau-Ffestiniog studio) and other British land artists: a mystical feeling for the landscape, expressed by an exquisite sensitivity of *touch*, that all-important component in the eroticism of sculpture:

> Movement, change, light, growth and decay are the lifeblood of nature, the energies that I try to tap through my work [said Goldsworthy]. I need the shock of touch, the resistance of place, materials and weather, the earth as my source.[16]

---

16 A. Goldsworthy, *Andy Goldsworthy*, Viking, London, 1990, no page numbers; and in N. Hedges, 67; HE, 160-1.

As Goldsworthy affirmed, he *must* touch. A world in which he would not be allowed to touch would be hateful. A world in which the trees had 'DO NOT TOUCH' signs on them would be horrendous. Significantly, Goldsworthy works mainly in areas in which the ownership of the land is not contested. He operates in landscapes where he has been given permission to work, invited (and paid) to work. No 'DO NOT TOUCH' signs for him.

For Goldsworthy, as for any number of sculptors, the personal touch, of hands on materials, is crucial:

> The work itself determines the nature of its making. I enjoy the freedom of just using my hands and 'found' tools – a sharp stone, the quill of a feather, thorns. I am not playing the primitive. I use my hands because this is the best way to do most of my work.

Indeed, when it comes to drawing on the sand on a beach, Goldsworthy will not use a stick, as many folks would. Instead, he uses his hands, kneeling or crouching on the sand. His *Dark dry sand drawing* is worked by hand, dribbled onto the sand on the Isle of Wight (1987). The result, all swirls and curves, comes directly from Jackson Pollock (the beach drawing has the sense of harmony, of each part balanced with the rest, not part having precedence over any other, of Oriental landscape painting). Goldsworthy has also drawn lines on frozen water (Nova Scotia, 1999). A lot of work Goldsworthy has done in deserts has been with carved sand (in New Mexico, Arizona, California and Australia). In a way, these drawings and sculptures of sand (in the shape of spirals, snakes, zigzags and boulders) are basically developments of the work with sand on the beaches of Northern England that Goldsworthy undertook in the late 1970s.

Many sculptors have spoken of the importance of the *making* of the sculpture, its actual construction, with real (and sometimes organic, living) materials. In some artists, the material employed also has a symbolic or added meaning, as in Joseph Beuys' *Fettecke* or 'fat corner', a sculpture with powerful autobiographical and semiotic associations.

Land artists such as Andy Goldsworthy use their hands, primarily, as their means of making art. Goldsworthy does not go out into the landscape with anything, except a knife.[17] Perhaps he should, to be really purist, make do without even a knife? Anyway, he *does* go out into the landscape with 'tools' – the camera not least among them (also spare film too, maybe a lens filter or two, and a tripod, and probably two cameras). Without that camera, the viewer wouldn't know about many of his works. Ditto with all land artists. Without the camera, their work is 'lost'. That is, not really 'lost', but the camera means the viewer too can share in the work. Without the camera, the viewer would have to rely on written texts, perhaps, as a means of 'recording' artworks. Photography is also 'a way of communicating' Goldsworthy told an interviewer, 'and we wouldn't be sitting here if I didn't take the photographs.'[18] Here Goldsworthy admits that without the photographs there would be not much communicating going on with his art: it needs photography to work.

But, as one can readily see, Goldsworthy and other land artists are not writers. Indeed, their writings are, well, often in note form, designed as a 'record' for themselves, or as notes towards some artwork. While there have been some painters and sculptors who were also good writers who provided many insights – Leonardo da Vinci, Ad Reinhardt, Vincent van Gogh, Donald Judd – Goldsworthy is not among them. So, relying on photographs, the viewer gets to find out about many works of land art that might otherwise have never known. The camera is thus an essential tool for the land artist (Goldsworthy could go out without a knife, or gloves, but he needs a camera and film).

Andy Goldsworthy also works outdoors with many other invisible tools of his craft – his awareness of land art, his education, his knowledge of other sculptors and art history, his memory of previous works, and so on. No artist works alone, culturally. Goldsworthy's art, like all land art, like all art, works within a culture and tradition and history of postwar and contemporary art. Tracing the links with Minimalism, Arte Povera and Conceptualism, for instance, is only one way of looking at Goldsworthy's art.

---

17 A. Causey, "Environmental Sculptures", in HE, 128.
18 A. Goldsworthy, *Third Ear*, BBC Radio 3, June 30, 1989, in HE, 168.

Spontaneity is the key to Andy Goldsworthy's working method – but an intentional kind of spontaneity. Just going out for a walk, with no intention in mind, is not the thing to do. In Goldsworthy's methodology, one goes out with a sense of direction, of going somewhere in particular, with the intention of making something. Intentionality, a direction or drive, a desire (the Western, Schopenhauerian or Nietzschean Will) is crucial. 'It is *very important* that I have a direction', says Goldsworthy.[19] The sense of intention or direction primes the artist, encouraging him to look attentively.

> For me, looking, touching, material, place and form are all inseparable from the resulting work [commented Goldsworthy]. It is difficult to say where one stops and another begins. Place is found by walking, direction determined by weather and season. I take the opportunities each day offers...[20]

Like many land artists, Goldsworthy waxed lyrical about particular places, which are special for him. Goldsworthy's sculptures are 'simple', in that there doesn't seem to be much going on. But, as Donald Judd wrote in his influential essay "Specific Objects":

> it isn't necessary for a work to have a lot of things to look at, to compare, to analyze one by one, to contemplate. The thing as a whole, its qualities as a whole, is what is interesting.[21]

Goldsworthy's sculptures are marked by a number of elements familiar in land art: transience, domination, penetration, circular forms (globes, circles, spirals, snakes, cones) and nature mysticism. The ephemerality of the pieces, for instance, is a key component. Snow and ice will melt away, leaves will disintegrate, stones will be blown over.

Each Goldsworthy sculpture has a date printed with its title. Not just a year, as in the usual artwork, but a specific day (we can't be sure even what year a masterpiece by Giotto or Duccio was painted, but we know the exact day, even hour, when land artworks were created).

Thus, one of Goldsworthy's best pieces, the delicious poppy covered

---

19 A. Goldsworthy, *Mountain and Coast, Autumn into Winter*, 1988, in HE, 163 (my italics).
20 *Artists in National Parks*, Victoria & Albert Museum, London, 1988, and in HE, 73.
21 10. D. Judd, "Specific Objects", in G. de Vries, 1974, 128.

boulder, has the title: *Poppy petals wrapped around a boulder held with water*, with the time and place inscribed as: Sibobre, France, June 6, 1989. The petal-covered rock, with its brilliant red colour, nestled in some mossy boulders, looking very much like one of Constantin Brancusi's 'cosmic eggs' (egg-shaped sculptures which Brancusi titled *The Beginning of the World*). The red colour revealed the rock's shape, size and form, its position amongst and relation to other rocks. Not wishing to disturb or move the rock (it's not that small really), Goldsworthy's act of covering it in wet poppy petals drew attention to this particular egg-shaped rock, *this* one and *not* the others (although the surrounding boulders also became the subject of the sculpture: attention was drawn to them as well as to the red rock). In *Poppy petals wrapped around a boulder held with water,* then, the place becomes as crucial as the centrepiece, the red rock.

Another red-covered rock, again linked with water and a river, was made at Scaur Water in 1992: *River rock* was made by rubbing a soft red stone over a small rock which was then lowered into the shallow river. Before the sculpture settled it released a cloud of red colour which was slowly washed away. Again, it was the situation of the rock, as much as the reddening of the rock itself, that did the expressive work in this sculpture. Goldsworthy used red stone ground down as the filling of the final snowball of 2000, causing red water to spread over the floor of the Barbican Centre. Goldsworthy has also released red stone powder above a waterfall (at Scaur Water, 1997), so the pool below turns ochre.

When working with rivers, Goldsworthy said, it was not the water itself that was the really interesting element, but everything that used the river, the flow of life and change around it: 'a river of wind, animals, birds, insects, people, seasons, climate, stone, earth, colour' (T, 10). Goldsworthy spoke of '[r]hythms, cycles, seasons in nature working at different speeds'.[22] Each date records a particular day (September 24, 1982, December 30, 1987, February 9, 1981, March 11, 1984, October 19, 1988); each day has its own weather, atmosphere and events, which are important for the artist.

---

22 A. Goldsworthy, *Touching North,* 1989.

9

TIME IN ANDY GOLDSWORTHY'S ART

Andy Goldsworthy 'prints' himself on the ground negatively, his body covers the dry earth, while around his body the earth (soil, stones) is darkened by the rain. Goldsworthy has also 'printed' his shadow on frosty grass in the early morning. Goldsworthy has made rain, frost and shadow prints at the Royal Museum of Scotland, Cornell University, Central Park in Gotham, Yorkshire, Cumbria, Holland, Japan, Angers (France), Australia, Denmark and Ciudad Real (Spain).

Many of the photographs in Goldsworthy's exhibitions document very short occurrences: the red earth in the river, or mud being thrown in the shallows on a beach, or on a misty hillside: *Rainbow splashes* were made with a stick in Yorkshire (1980), *Slate throws* (Cumbria, 1988) consisted of throwing slate into the air, like *Hazel stick throws* (1980) and *Leaf throws* (Tayside, 1989); *Maple leaf throw* was made in Japan in 1990. In 1995, Goldsworthy had the Ballet Atlantique dance troupe throw sticks and soil into the air at once. In California (1994), Goldsworthy threw dust into the air against the sun, which he called *Breath of Earth* works.

It is the shapes the mud, earth and sticks make in the air that fascinate Goldsworthy. He is seen in various photos, throwing the mud and earth, his legs and arms raised high, caught in a moment of release. These photos are about time, about letting something go, and capturing the trajectory. Mud and earth is not 'alive', as a bird is, but Goldsworthy seems to throw the mud and earth as if he's releasing a bird. He wants the earth to fly. It doesn't: it arcs back to the ground, but these arcs are elegant, and become the subject of many photographs.

The 'throws' are also very dependent on particular lighting conditions. In the Lake Michigan photographs (1991), Goldsworthy was photographed (by his wife Judith) against the light in a dusky sky, so that the trajectories of the wet sand in the air could be clearly seen. The *Rainbow splashes* required low side-lighting. The red mud throws at Scaur Water occurred against bright green foliage, which contrasts with the red. Colour contrasts are also central to the Mount Victor Station throws, which were made with red sand ejected into the clear blue Australian sky (1991). Goldsworthy has made fewer throws in later years, though they are still part of his repertoire (such as *Red river stones*, 1999).

The arcs or trajectories of the thrown earth become the artwork in itself. The curve of the earth against the sky actually *is* the sculpture. Similarly, Bruce Nauman (who is, like Yves Klein, another celebrated Conceptual artist) photographed himself as a water fountain (1966). Richard Long threw mud against walls, either in a curtain of mud, or in a circle. Kazuo Shiraga wallowed in mud and threw mudballs (*Making a Work With His Own Body*, 1955). Guo Qiang Cai created miniature explosions with gunpowder to evoke the mushroom clouds of nuclear explosions (1996). Bruce McLean's *Splash Sculpture* and *Mud Sculpture* (both 1968) are precursors of Goldsworthy's splashes and throws. Goldsworthy's throws offer plenty of ammunition to critics who dislike his work, because someone making splashes in a river with a stick or throwing sand or leaves in the air is the kind of art denigrated by the tabloid press in the United Kingdom.

Many of Goldsworthy's sculptures are about a 'before' and an 'after', and the interval between, the difference, the changes. For instance, there are two photographs which depict a stick in a 'before' and 'after' setting (an early work, made in January, 1981 [in AG]). In the first photo, the sycamore branch is shown on top of snow; it's one of those images of contrast (black stick against white snow) which Goldsworthy likes so much. The second picture shows the stick with its bark now peeled off, so it looks white. Meanwhile the snow has melted, so the white shows up against the dark earth. Twenty years later Goldsworthy was fabricating the same sculptural idea: a fallen branch in a stream covered with powdery snow (2001), and branches wrapped with leaves in a Massachussetts brook (2001) or a Scottish stream (2003).

Aligned to Andy Goldsworthy's use of melting snowballs are the clay-covered rocks which Goldsworthy exhibited in 1993 in San Francisco and Japan. The stones were covered in wet clay which was rubbed smooth: they looked like huge brown dinosaur eggs. As the clay dried, it cracked and fell off. The exhibits highlighted natural processes – such as the apparent randomness of nature (a bit of clay falling off the stone here, but not on that rock over there). Another installation using clay (at San Jose, California) consisted of hollowed clay spheres, with the characteristic Goldsworthy sharp interior edges. The series of globes dried out and shed chunks of clay. Later hollow spheres include *Sand stones*, built in Holland in 1999.

Andy Goldsworthy tried different methods of actualizing or exploring the space around and within stones, the light and weather around them, the 'window' that's opened into their secret nature (HE, 167). Sometimes he covered a boulder completely in bark, or branches (as at Lake Tahoe in 1992 [S, 7-9]). A boulder wrapped in small sheets of ice became a kinetic sculpture as the ice melted and slipped off (S, 13).

In mid-September, 1991, Goldsworthy made a sequence of stoneworks at the same site in Laumeier Sculpture Park, St Louis, Missouri: first he layered wet leaves, in the usual Goldsworthy colours (red, yellow and green), onto a large boulder which was partially buried in the river bank (the boulder was the focus of the work). The Autumnal colours recalled many of Goldsworthy's previous leafworks. Over the next few days Goldsworthy explored different ways of responding to the stone: he walled it in with flat rocks, photographing it when the river was empty, then with the tide coming in; a day or so later he wrapped wet green leaves around the rock, in the rain, with the river rising; Goldsworthy returned the following Summer, and enclosed the rock in a circle of sticks (S, 26-33).

Andy Goldsworthy can be expected to explore more collaborations, such as live performance, dance, maybe video, film or installations and the like. The Digne *Réfuges d'Art* and Cumbrian *100 Sheepfolds* projects are huge commitments, that will keep the sculptor busy for years. But the core of Goldsworthy's art, the spiritual heart and the essence of it, will continue to be his work within the landscape. That means working mainly on his own (as he has done throughout his career), and mainly in South-West Scotland (as he has done since the mid-1980s).

PART TWO

ANDY GOLDSWORTHY'S WORKS
IN THE U.S.A.

10

INSTALLATIONS AND LARGE-SCALE WORKS

Like other land artists, Andy Goldsworthy works in the landscape, so there are numerous problems when he shows work in a city. The city is definitely *not* the obvious Goldsworthy place. The photographs and prints, then, point always towards the outdoors, towards the ideal Goldsworthy space, which is some wilderness – Scotland above all, and the North Pole, Japan, France, Cumbria, and America.

The snowball prints (which Andy Goldsworthy produces by allowing snowballs to melt onto big pieces of paper) are disappointing, really. A snowball melting on a sheet of paper is too random and easy, perhaps. The combination of a natural act of melting and the framed piece of paper in a gallery, with the gallery's art historical context, is problematic. The viewer might prefer to see Goldsworthy making these prints, or combining them with other forms. Then they would make more sense (on their own, they're a little lean). Perhaps a photograph of the artist making the print would suffice. As it is, the snowball prints are full of suggestions of things they cannot deliver. They are, like Goldsworthy's photographs, a record of something that occurred elsewhere. And what occurred elsewhere is of course what *really* interests Goldsworthy.

No land artist can be satisfied with written accounts of art made in the landscape, just as no painter would be satisfied with photographs or written accounts of their paintings. No, they must have the paintings themselves, the actual flesh and blood of the painting, so to speak, the very feel of the oil on canvas, the shape and size and texture and reflectivity and proportion and tactile qualities of the actual painting. Photographs of paintings only disappoint the artist. Ditto with the land artist. Goldsworthy's photographs and prints are not what they're really interested in: the work is elsewhere, in the landscape (note that Goldsworthy has participated – in London and Bristol, for instance – in group shows which focus on photography as sculpture).

LARGE-SCALE WORKS AND INSTALLATIONS

Andy Goldsworthy has stated that he is not against long-term art:

> That art should be permanent or impermanent is not the issue. Transience in my work reflects what I find in nature and should not be confused with an attitude towards art generally. I have never been against the well-made or long-lasting.

Domination a n d *penetration*. These are familiar terms describing patriarchal actions or constructions or ideologies used by feminists. Is Goldsworthy, seemingly so delicate in his touches, dominating nature? He insists he isn't:

> By working large, I am not trying to dominate nature. If people feel small in relation to a work, they should not assume that there is an intention to make nature itself small. (AG)

Yet, clearly, Goldsworthy, and the American land artists (Michael Heizer, Walter de Maria, Robert Smithson, Charles Simonds, Alice Aycock), do dominate nature. James Turrell's *Roden Crater* or Heizer's gigantic *Double Negative* will clearly be around for a long time, unless someone or something destroys them (an earthquake could destroy any land artwork in the blink of an eye). Goldsworthy's stone pieces, too, may stay around for a while. There is a sense of gloating when Goldsworthy says:

> Fourteen years ago I made a line of stones in Morecambe Bay. It is still there, buried under the sand, unseen. All my work still exists, in some form.

Daring not to change or affect the natural world, land artists do just that, all the time. They 'interact' with nature, but their 'interactions', however small scale, can't help changing nature (all artists change nature if they work in it). 'I like the idea of using the land without possessing it', said Richard Long, ever the idealist.[23] Goldsworthy's aim is to 'touch' something in nature, the essence of nature itself, to

---

23 R. Long, in *Words After the Fact*, in R. Fuchs, 1986, 236.

understand it, and the identification of himself within nature.[24] Thus, about the 'lake pieces', the stick and stalk sculptures he was commissioned to do in the Lake District in 1988, he remarked: 'I felt I really got through in the lake pieces. I had touched it, and understood it'.[25]

Andy Goldsworthy, like James Turrell, Alice Aycock and Hermann de Vries, has made some huge pieces, such as the long 'snake' and the 'pool' or maze, in Country Durham, large works which take up a lot of space, and certainly *dominate* the surrounding landscape. Goldsworthy's large-scale outdoor works often use the serpent coil as a fundamental form. Goldsworthy maintained, however, that his 'snake-like' or serpent-shaped sculptures does not refer directly to snakes.[26] Instead, he preferred to call one of his favourite motifs a 'river of earth', or a tree root, or a river (RA, 113).

Whatever the artistic intention, however, it is impossible to limit readings of sculptures such as *Sidewinder, Lambton Earthwork,* the *Storm King Wall* or the serpentine shapes in the British Museum's Egyptian Hall to responses to the environment.

The serpent as symbol connotes time, change, seasons, cycles of birth-and-death-and-rebirth, eternity, sexuality, evil, the cosmos, and so on. Goldsworthy might wish to determine how viewers read his serpent-shaped forms, and emphasize the response he makes to the natural environment, but consumers of art will make any interpretation they like, and some artists might wish to suppress (snakes also connote dirt – they slide on the dust; and excrement; the alimentary canal; eating and defecating; poison; reptile life, and so on). In 1998, Goldsworthy confessed:

> after working for many years, I have to admit that I have a fascination for the snake. For me it is perfect sculpture. It's so simple. The way it moves on the ground or in the water, it draws the place. It's so expressive of the place it moves through. It's not like any other animal. It actually moves with the

24 'Goldsworthy's pieces dig at the roots of our relationship with nature, he is conducting an interrogative process with the fundamentals of our world – water, stone, earth, growing things and – latterly, in his work with volcanic rock and 'fired' stones – fire' (P. Whitaker, 1995, 109).
25 In B. Redhead, 19.
26 'Some works have qualities of snaking but are not snakes. The form is shaped through a similar response to environment' commented Goldsworthy (AG).

surface of the land. (RA, 113).

While Goldsworthy insisted that he wasn't interested in the symbolic associations of the snake, or in the snake as an animal, he did link his use of the snake to Constantin Brancusi's birds and fish (Brancusi sculpted radically simplified, abstract versions of birds and fish). For Goldsworthy, the serpent wasn't a totemic or symbolic creature, but a form that expressed 'the energy of movement' (RA, 113).

None of the monuments, cairns, sheepfolds, walls or other permanent works would be signposted. Goldsworthy figured that the people who knew about his stuff wouldn't require signs, but the works could still have an impact for those not in the know. It's part of a move, from the 1960s onwards, to avoid signing artworks, and let the pieces stand alone, and speak for themselves (along with titling every artwork *Untitled*). It was OK, though, Goldsworthy said, for his monuments to be marked on the map (Sh, 21). Again, Goldsworthy's acknowledgment of Ordnance Survey maps is part of the ethics of 1960s art, and land art in particular (land artists, including Goldsworthy, spend hours looking at maps).

WALLS AND INSTALLATIONS. Other large-scale Andy Goldsworthy works include the installations *Slate Wall* and *Clay Wall* (1998, Edinburgh), and *Clay Wall* (2000, London).

In the U.S.A., some of Goldsworthy's other large-scale commissions include: *Clay Wall* (1996, San Francisco); a *Stone River* at Stanford University (2001); and a *Stone River* in Aspen, Colorado (2006), at the Doerr-Hosier Center. The 'stone rivers' were snake-shaped walls, typically of red sandstone – stone versions of forms Goldsworthy had developed in sand in the 1980s and 1990s (such as the British Museum pieces in 1995).

The *Spire* project, built in the Presidio in 'Frisco in 2008 (with an exhibition in 2008-2009), was a 100-foot tall tower fashioned from Cypress trees. Goldsworthy had developed this form of a wooden spire back in the 1980s (*Seven Spires*).

The *Fall Creek* installation, at the Herbert F. Johnson Museum of Art at Cornell University (in 2000), comprised a group of low holed mounds fashioned from hundreds of branches on the floor. Goldsworthy has worked at Cornell a number of times: the university has a long history of land art links: one of the important land exhibitions, *Earth Art*, took place in 1969 (it featured Richard Long, Dennis Oppenheim, Roberts Smithson and Morris, and Michael Heizer).

ARCHES

The idea of balance, of objects being held aloft, defying gravity, fascinates Andy Goldsworthy so much it becomes one of the central motifs of his work. He makes arches from thin pieces of slate (such as the *Slate Arch* [1985, Cumbria], and *Slate Arch* [Wales, 1982]), or has arches stretching up four steps (*Slate Arch*, 1990, Tarbes). *Over the stone* (1993) was a large arch made from loose stones found on the hillside at Scaur Glen: it was built over a large boulder, the internal form of the arch echoing the shape of the boulder. *Over the wall* (1993) was an arch that leapt over a stone wall; *Tree arch – river stones* (1993) was an arch of three components, leaning up against a tree of two trunks; *Between two trees* (1992, Pennsylvania) was a shallow arch wedged between some trees; *Out of the stones* (1993) was an arch leaning against the boulder that Goldsworthy used in *Over the stone*: it was two-thirds of an arch (these arches were made in the Winter of 1992-93 in Dumfriesshire [S, 98-99], apart from *Between two trees*).

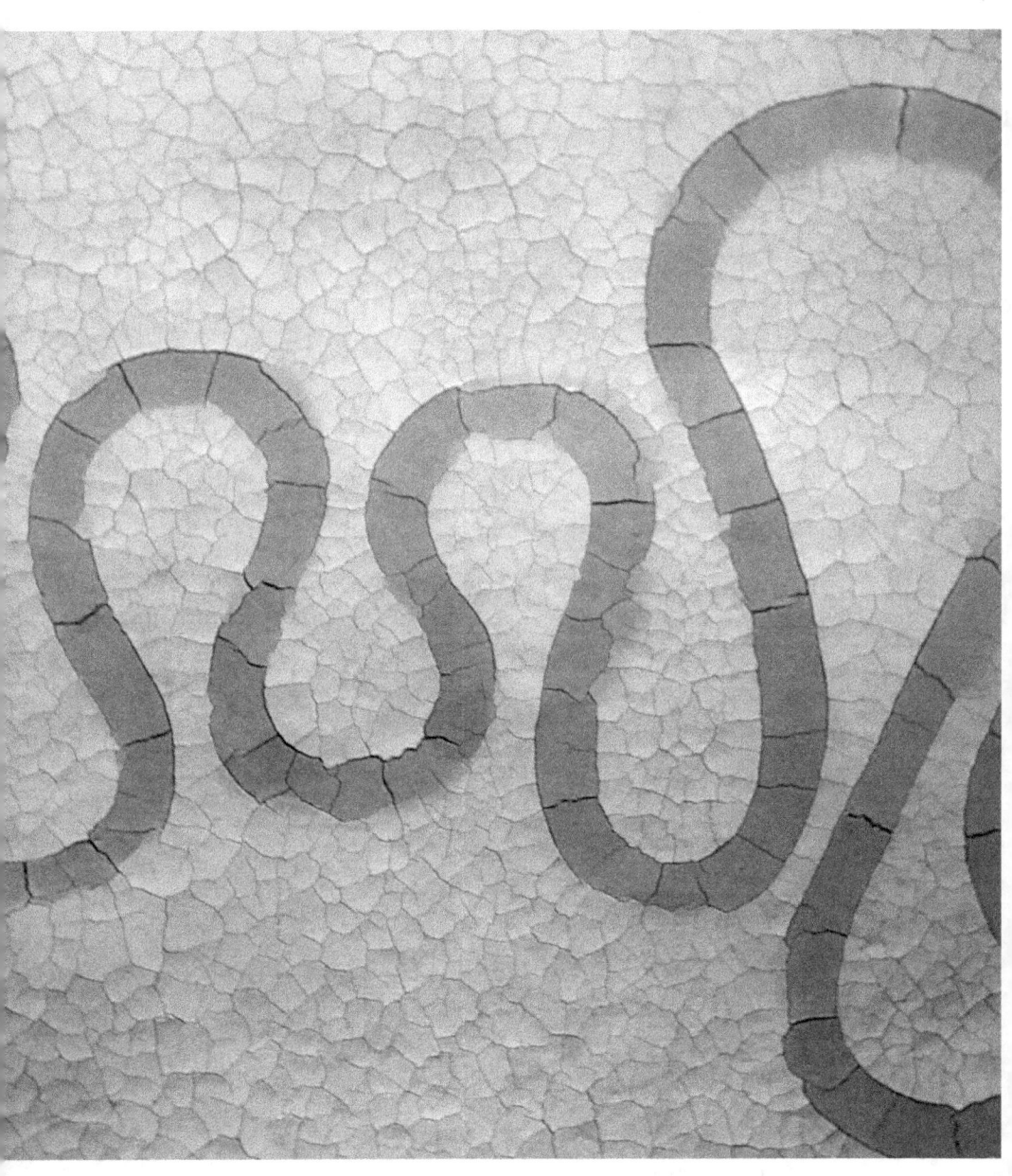

Andy Goldsworthy, Clay Wall

11

GARDEN OF STONE, NEW YORK CITY

One of the most important of Andy Goldsworthy's later commissions was the installation *Garden of Stone* (2003) at the Museum of Jewish Heritage in Lower Manhattan. *Garden of Stone: A Living Memorial* was a group of 18 hollowed Vermont granite glacial boulders, with an oak tree inside (dwarf oaks, which only grow very slowly, and might take 100 years to reach twelve feet). Goldsworthy explained: 'I've resisted the temptation to put in mature trees... there's something very beautiful and profound about a flick of growth emerging out of a huge boulder, the fragility of that life.' The trees were planted at the top of each stone, with the hollow space below for the roots. The largest boulders weighed 13 tons. The trees will give out acorns in four years, which could be used to plant new trees when the trees in the boulders die. (Why 18? Because 18 corresponds to the Hebrew letter for *chai*, a symbol of life).

Garden of Stone was situated on the second floor garden, over-looking the Hudson River, with socio-political icons such as the Statue of Liberty and Ellis Island easily visible beyond.

Garden of Stone cost a million dollars (the Public Art fund collaborated with the museum), making it easily Goldsworthy's most expensive commission to date. Jacob Ehrenberg was project manager.

The glacial granite boulders were taken from Vermont (near Barre). They were then transported to a Connecticut quarry (Stony Creek) where Ed Monti, a guy in his seventies, hollowed them using a cutting torch. The bases were flattened so that the rocks would sit properly on the ground (Goldsworthy said that in trimming the stones, he aimed to retain as much height to each stone as possible).

Ivy Barsky, the deputy director of the museum, said they were looking for 'something nonprescriptive, with no text or literalism – a personal space, not a space that told people what to think.' Goldsworthy presented his idea to the committee of trustees and Holocaust survivors and they liked it. 'He totally got the idea of memory, that it's about future generations,' remarked Barsky.

Goldsworthy allowed the marks made on the boulders by their journeys and hollowing to remain. That was part of his preference for retaining evidence of the transformations materials undergo. It was part of the social project of Goldsworthy's art: it was important for the artist where the stones came from; the source was part of the overall sculpture. Hence the boulders were collected from fields and the landscape, rather than quarries (the more obvious place to shop for stones): 'how the sculpture is made and the journey of both the ideas and material are also important', Goldsworthy remarked in *Passage* (65).

Goldsworthy also wanted to maintain the integrity of his garden of trees and stones, and was concerned about the planting the Museum of Jewish Heritage planned for the borders of the site. Goldsworthy said he hoped to retain the 'sense of barrenness' of just the stones and the trees, and the introduction of other plants would compromise his sculpture, as well as the look of the building (P, 69). Originally, Goldsworthy planned to have all of the stones roughly the same size, but the idea developed to having a range of sizes, with the larger ones acting as 'guardians or leaders in the group' (P, 67).

The trees require quite a level of maintenance, as Tom Eccles of the Public Art Fund pointed out, which's unusual for a public art work (you can't just leave the *Garden of Stones* and paint it every few years, like some public sculptures). Eccles added that it was 'an incredibly fragile work for a public commission'.

Garden of Stone was made as a memorial for the victims and survivors of the Holocaust. Goldsworthy was an unusual choice, perhaps, for an artist to tackle such a massive political and ideological issue. Goldsworthy has not been known for addressing issues such as the Holocaust in his art. Certainly he could not be described as a high profile political artist. He has also not had much of a connection with Jewish culture or history (or with the Holocaust).

Goldsworthy said he didn't want *Garden of Stones* 'to be too specific'. And talking about trees, he said: 'When I see these things in the land, I learn from that about nature and life's ability to survive.'

A group of Holocaust survivors were invited at the opening of the exhibit (September 16, 2003) to plant the saplings in the stones. (Goldsworthy's mother Muriel also planted a tree). *Garden of Stone* brought together two of Goldsworthy's favourite materials, trees and stones, and obvious (but no less noble) themes of change, growth, transformation, burial and rebirth.

The impression that *Garden of Stones* makes is of a garden that's smaller than it looks in photographs. It is set in a gravel space with shallow grey stone steps at the museum end. There's a thick wall, topped with gravel, along one side. The stones vary in size, and some are very big. There's a hole in each stone, with a tree growing out of it. Some of the trees were a few feet tall when I visited the sculpture in 2008 (maybe three or four feet). All of the stones were irregular. There's two or three feet between each boulder. The stones are evenly spaced throughout the garden. No other plants or flowers or trees or bushes are in the garden, giving the impression of a Zen Buddhist or Japanese garden. There is a garden on the other side of the wall, with willows and other trees one floor down.

Garden of Stones is at the very tip of Manhattan, and the views are spectacular – of the Statue of Liberty, Ellis Island, and New Jersey, and Staten Island, and New York harbour. It's a big panorama. Boats going by all the time. A sense of movement, of light on the water.

The *context* is profoundly Jewish – the whole museum is devoted to Jewish culture and history, with an emphasis on issues such as intolerance and the Holocaust. It's a powerfully *political* space, which Goldsworthy isn't usually associated with – a white guy from North Britain. He seems very Gentile and non-Jewish.

But the sculpture works in terms of look and feel – partly because of the museum building – all grey stone, granite, and tastefully reserved vegetation. There is little colour to distract from the space, but the water and the sky and the setting beyond the museum is one of the most spectacular of any Goldsworthy work.

Indeed, in terms of setting this may be the most impressive in all Goldsworthy's art – even including the works set on romantic mountains. Go up to the third floor of the Museum of Jewish Heritage, and look out over the *Garden of Stones*. You can't help looking up and around at this enormous harbour setting, with all its river craft, distant Jersey and Staten Island, a big sky, plenty of light, and historical icons like the Statue of Liberty and Ellis Island. If you said, 'pick me the most impressive site in New York City', this might be one of them.

CAIRNS

Garden of Stones is linked to the cairn, one of Andy Goldsworthy's key forms. Many Goldsworthy cairns are fabricated from slate (such as *Slate cone*, 1987, 1988); others from branches (*Oak branches*, 1990); or sandstone (*Sandstone*, 1990). Others are put into groups (such as the proposals for stone cone groups at Vassivière, Newcastle and Penpont). Later cairns include the commissions *Logie Cairn* (1999) in Aberdeenshire, *Penpont Cairn* (2000), *Three Cairns* (2002) in the US, and *Hollister Cairn* (1999) in California.

The first cairn Goldsworthy made (in Cumbria) he related to the rock formations in that part of North-West England (called the Nine Standards). He had also made a balanced cairn in Wales that referred to the Nine Standards. For Goldsworthy, that pile of stones were guardians – and the idea of sentinels watching over the landscape has remained with the sculptor ever since, becoming the fundamental interpretation of all his cairns and cones. Part of the *Sheepfolds* project were the *Nine Pinfold Cones*, stone cones sited within pinfolds made in 'counterpoint and dialogue' with the Nine Standards. As well as 'sentinels', guardians of a place, the cairns were also memorials to a place, or a people (Goldsworthy has linked stone cairns to burial mounds [RA, 89]), or monuments that crown a summit. The cairn 'has become one of the most repeated and well-travelled in my art,' Goldsworthy recalled in *Enclosure* (59). So you can see why Goldsworthy chose stones for his Holocaust memorial.

The cairn/ cone form is also about the process of growth and energy. It is a form that celebrates for Goldsworthy 'the fullness, vigour, heavy ripeness and power generated from a centre, deep inside' (S, 37). Like D.H. Lawrence and Friedrich Nietzsche, Goldsworthy here makes the age-old links between 'ripeness' in nature and femininity and pregnancy. The Goldsworthy cone, then, can be seen as another expression of female fecundity, in the Lawrencean manner, an equivalent for a pregnant woman (like the prehistoric "Stone Venuses", the squat, callipygous figurines): in short, stone Mother-Goddesses. Fullness, fruit, growth, ripeness ('ripeness is all' in *King Lear* [V, 2, 9]).

As the cairns were being constructed, Goldsworthy explained, all sorts of irregularities would introduce themselves. Like many artists say of their works, Goldsworthy said when he completed a cairn, he only saw the mistakes. But it was precisely the accidents and mistakes which 'give the form a tension and energy' (RA, 101). The perfect artwork was a practical as well as philosophical impossibility. Goldsworthy said was often surprised by the final result: '[e]ach cairn is a shock, and not what I intended' (ibid.). Getting the belly of the cairn right was critical, Goldsworthy remarked, and the foundation and beginning was usually tricky, but the most important part was the top, the last three feet: '[t]he top draws the energy of the stone to a peak, just as the apex of an arch becomes a focus for its energy' (RA, 103).

Goldsworthy often spoke of searching for the perfect form in his cairns. Every time he built a cairn he said he was looking for the ideal form, and tried to attain it, but always fell short. Goldsworthy seemed more anxious about the shape of his cairns than almost any of his other sculptures. 'I set myself an almost impossible task: to make the perfect form by eye and hand', Goldsworthy said in *Passage* (10). That's it: the artist started out with too high ideals, which could never be accomplished (he didn't begin most other works with the same high goals).

The anxiety perhaps also sprang from the fact that the cairns were built by hand and judged by eye, not from architectural plans. They were intuitive forms, and the shape each cairn took was always being negotiated during construction. Thus, Goldsworthy often talked about work starting slowly at first, about getting the foundation level, about working upwards to the belly, about wondering exactly when he should start working inwards, about putting particular stones in particular places, and feeling anxious again as the cairn approached completion.

In another passage in *Passage*, Goldsworthy acknowledged that starting a work was always a somewhat anxious, uncertain time. Each big project tended to be different, with its own set of challenges and limitations, so that Goldsworthy always had to explore the possibilities of the project first for a few days before finding the right forms and methods. It wasn't a question of doing the same thing every time, with the same materials, in the same forms.

OTHER CAIRNS. 'Cone' is perhaps not quite the right term for an image or expression of fullness and ripeness: Andy Goldsworthy's 'cones' look more like fruit. The imagery of fruit would accord with Goldsworthy's 'ripeness' discourse. 'Cairn' is also not quite the right word either, though some of the 'cones' on rocky mountainsides (such as *Cone to mark day becoming night* at Glenleith Fell, and *Cone to mark night becoming day*, Scaur Glen [both 1991]) have affinities with natural cairns and outcrops of rock.

Some of the cairns were built at night, to be seen at night, as hymns to the night, or the dawn, or the sunset. Working on the Yorkshire *Ice hole* (1987), Goldsworthy spoke of 'working with the moonlight' which was a 'very strange intense light'.[1] Working at night, Goldsworthy described approaching 'the most beautiful point, the point of greatest tension, as one moves towards daybreak'.[2] The *Clearing of Arches* installed at Goodwood sculpture park in Sussex (1995) were made to be viewed in moonlight.

In Australia Goldsworthy constructed cairns 'for the moonlight', or 'for the day' (S, 43). Like the mulga tree branches edged with red sand to catch the setting sun, these stone cairns were made for particular lighting conditions: the orange-coloured stones fashioned into a cairn were associated with (and completed by) the setting sun. The stone cairns were the sculptural equivalent of lighting a fire in order to celebrate Midsummer or sunset; or erecting a little shrine for a minor deity. They were small-scale celebrations of the daily festivals of dawn, moonlight, noon and sunset, sacred moments that occur every day, but which are no less holy for their common recurrence. Here Goldsworthy is working, like many a land artist, 'with the sky', with large-scale events such as nightfall and moonlight.

How different from Goldsworthy's *Seven Spires* is another group of tree trunks tied together, Jackie Winsor's 1971 piece *30 to 1 Bound Trees*. Here, the binding of the trees, as in much of Winsor's work,

---

1 1987, HE, 147.
2 In Y. Baginsky, 1989.

relates to autobiographical, childhood experiences, often painful, as well as the formal aspects of density, weight and repetition.[3] If Goldsworthy's works have similar autobiographical themes, they are hidden: the artist himself rarely talks in a personal, emotional manner (he doesn't make his own life the subject of his art, like Tracey Emin or Mary Kelly).

Andy Goldsworthy does talk in autobiographical terms about his work, however, from time to time. For him, art and life cannot be easily separated (a common philosophy in modern art). One feeds the other, in a symbiotic relationship. One cannot say for certain where Goldsworthy's art ends and his life begins. He sees art as a continuation of life, where the feelings artists of the past had about nature (for example, J.M.W. Turner and John Constable and the British landscapists) feed on the same source as artists working today (that is, nature itself). Some people made their life their art (or was it the other way around?): Yves Klein, Joseph Beuys and Carolee Schneemann among artists, and personages such as Quentin Crisp and Anaïs Nin. Andy Goldsworthy is definitely not a larger than life personality like Anaïs Nin or Quentin Crisp (yet). He does, however, keep a diary, and carefully records the progress of his art, and the manufacture of each work. Around each sculpture, then, is an autobiographical residue, which is partly constructed from the title which includes details of the time and place of creation.

3 See R. Parker, 1987, 316; L. Lippard, 1976, 203.

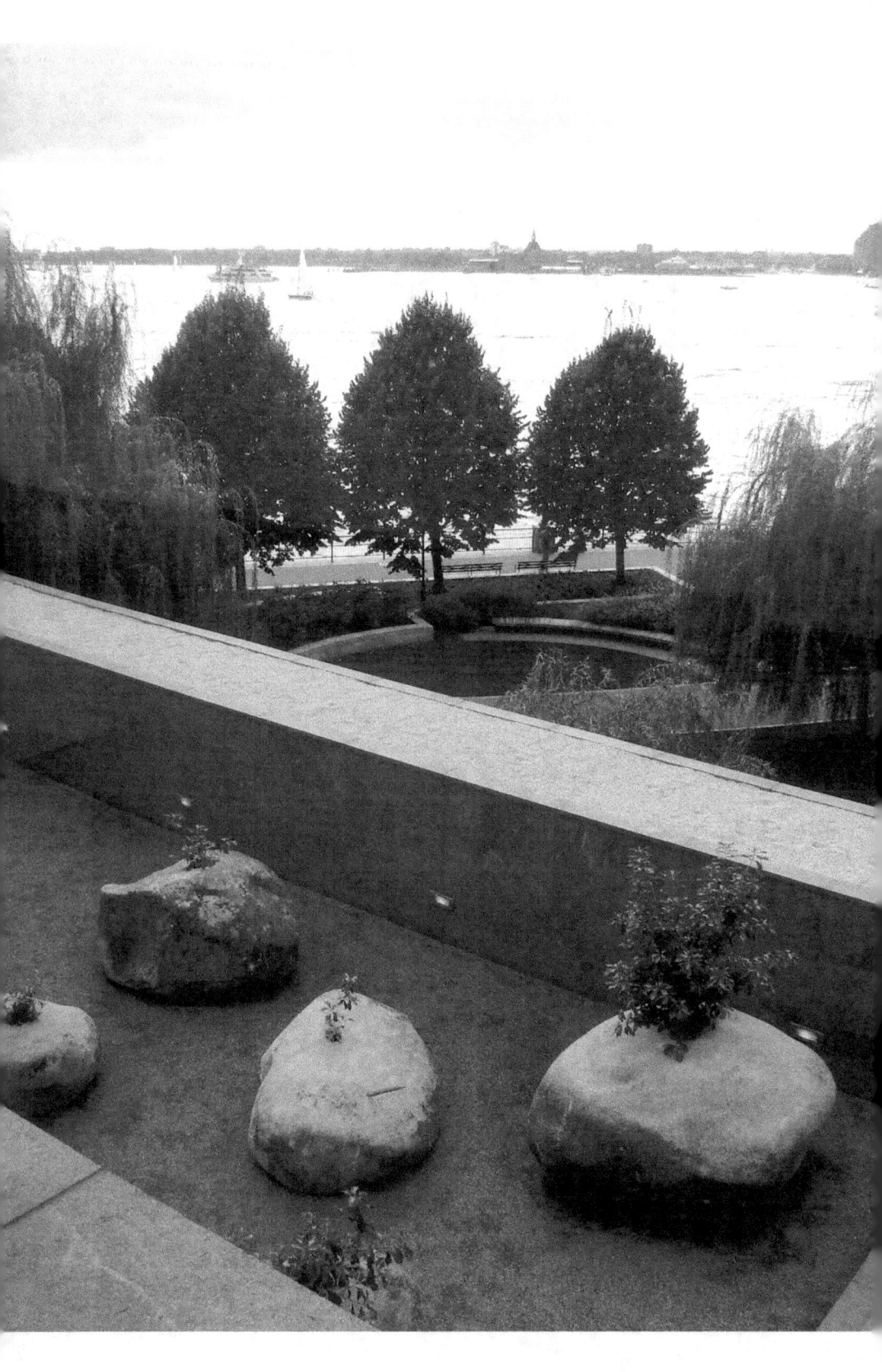

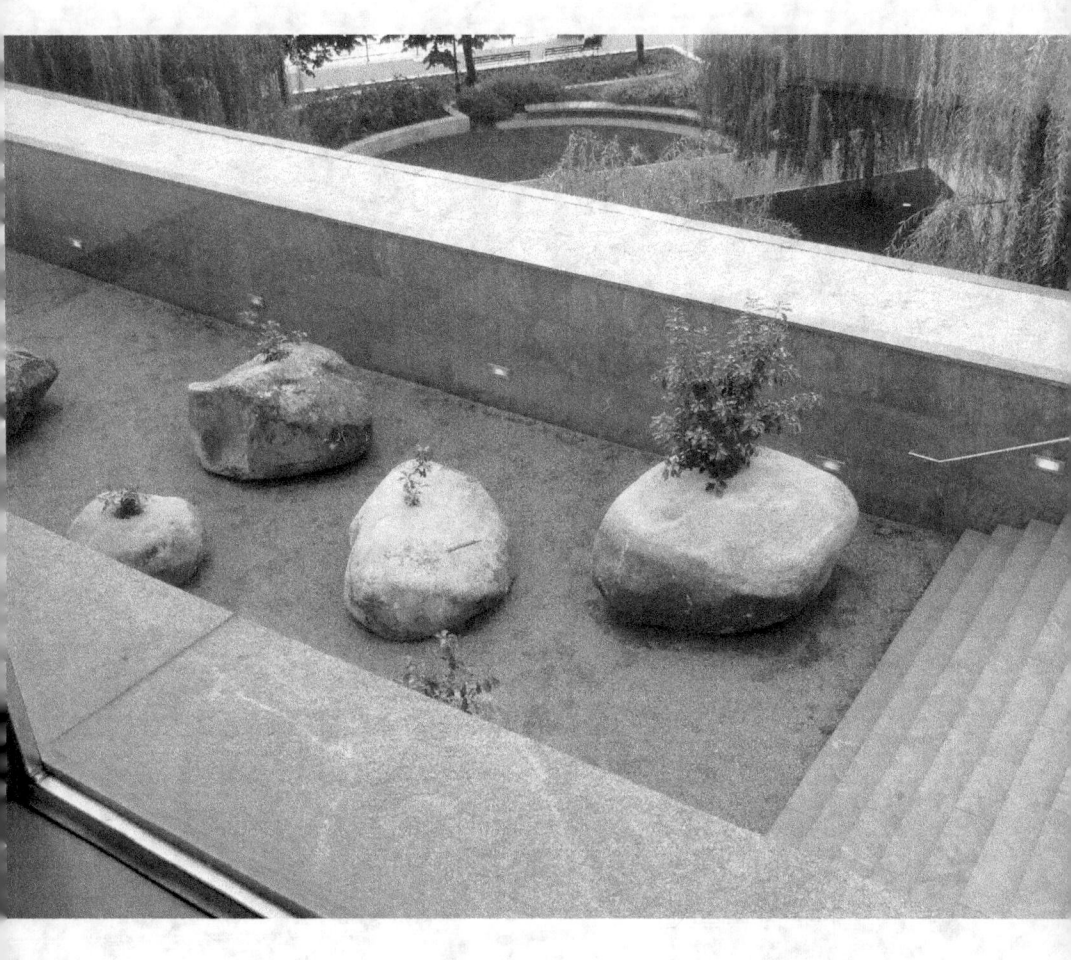

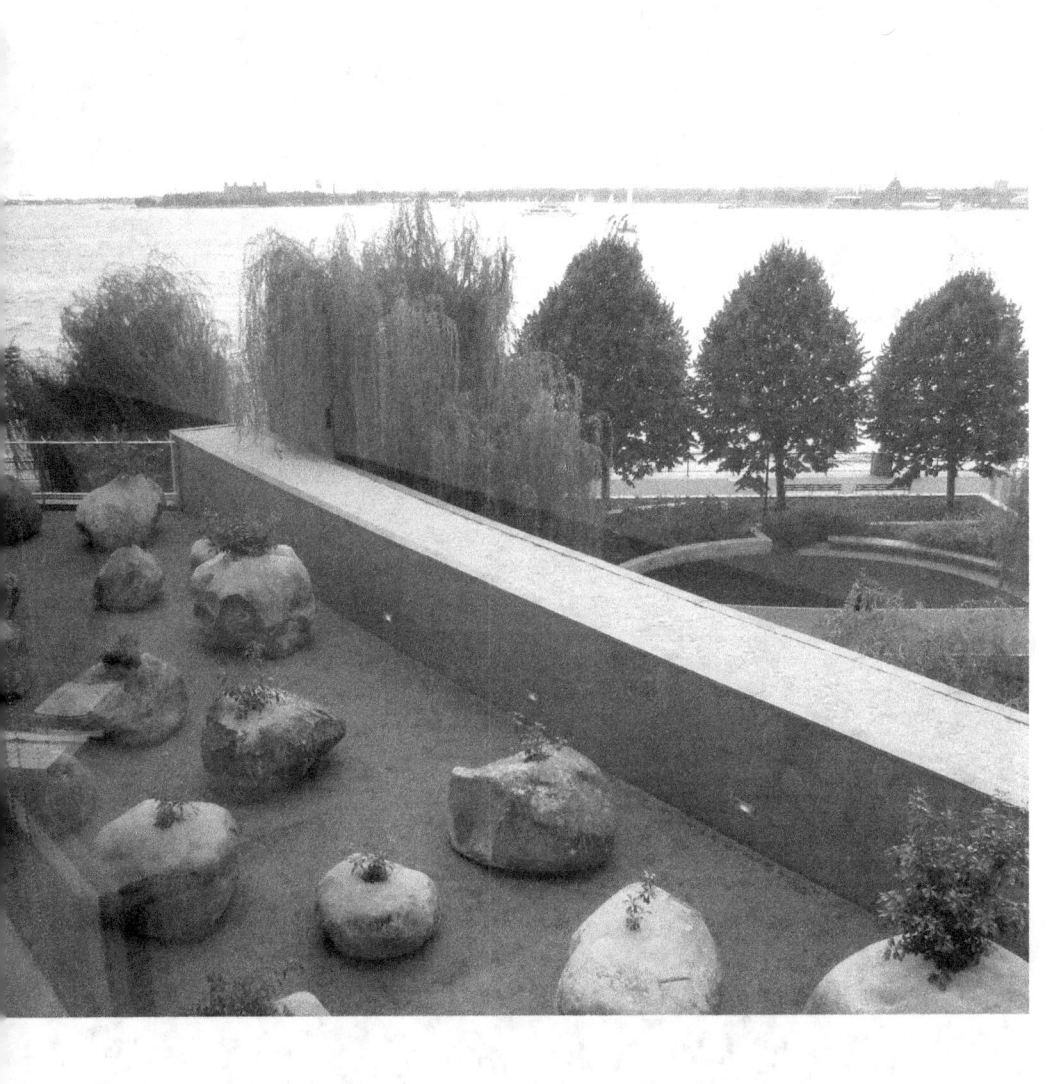

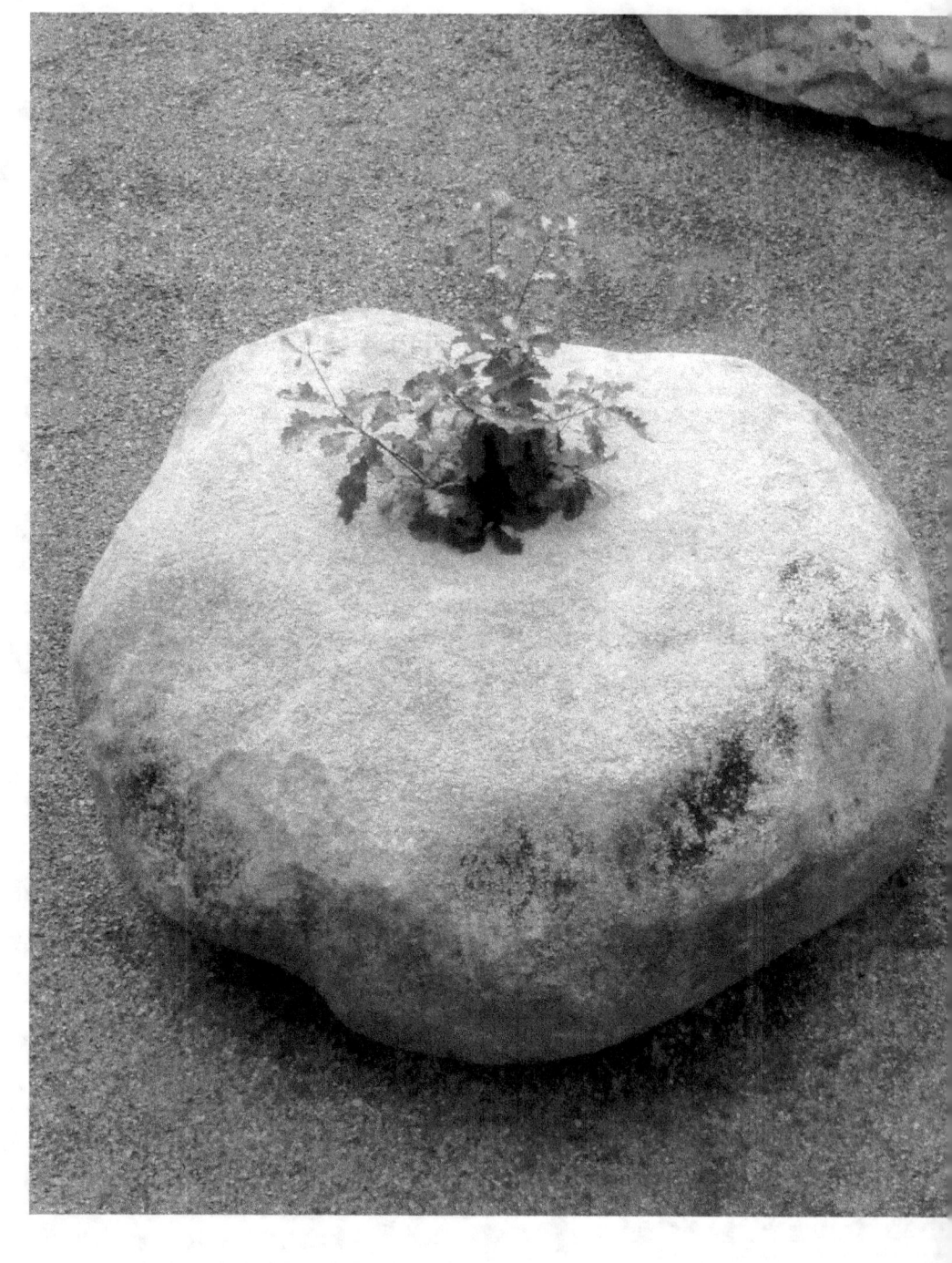

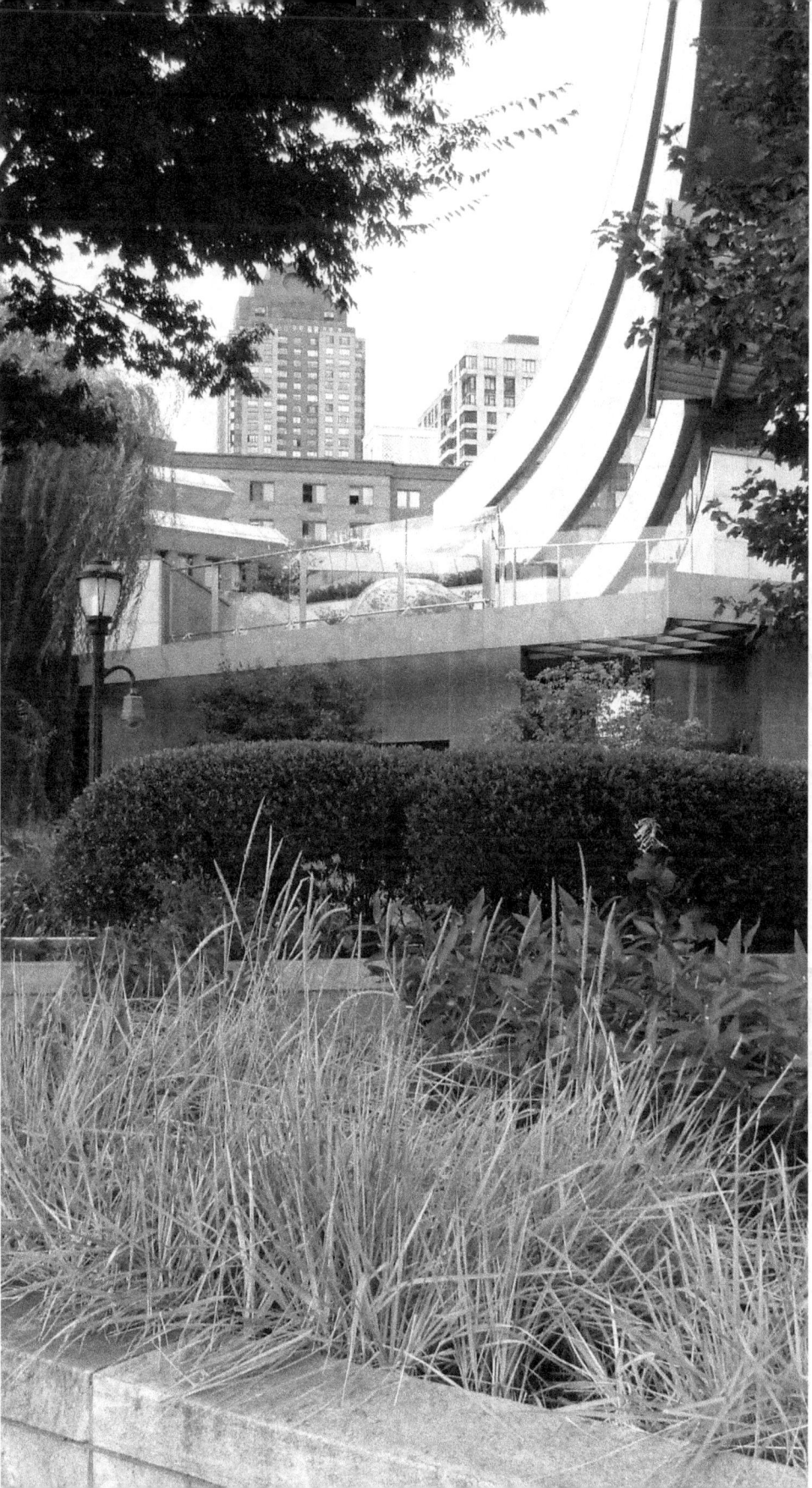

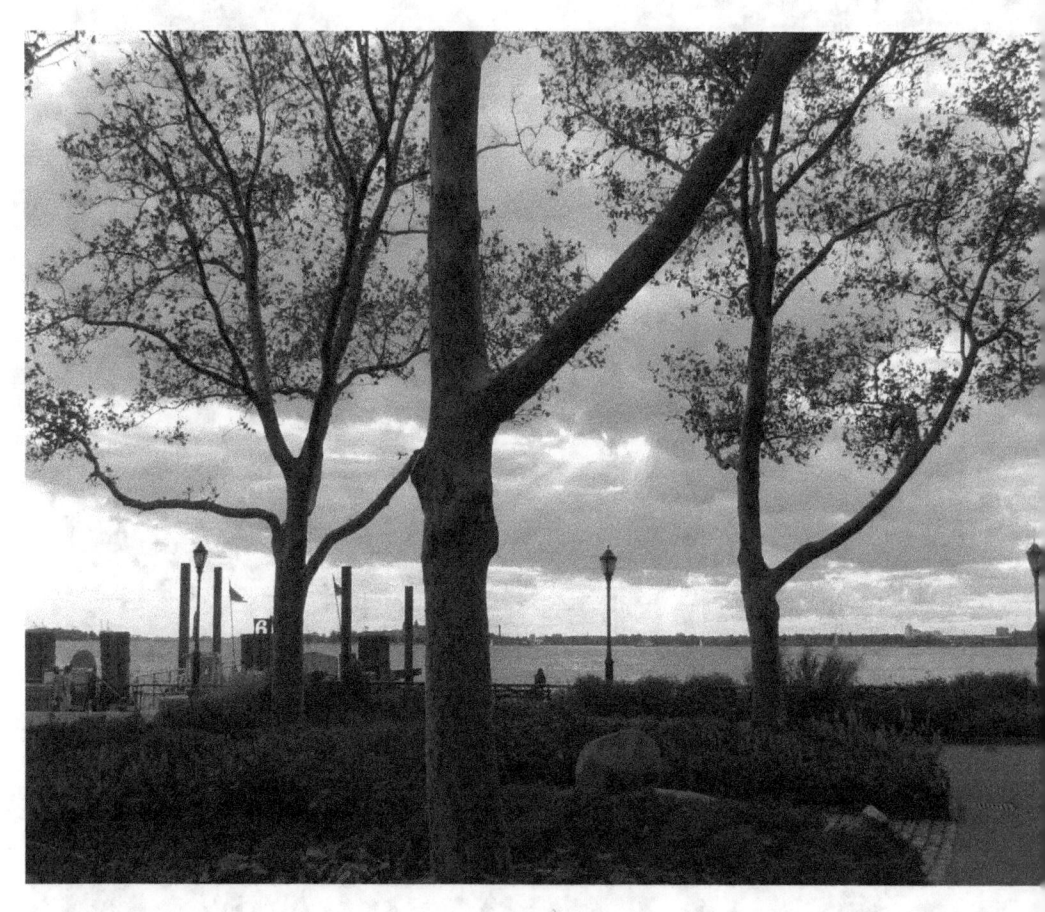

12

STONE HOUSES, NEW YORK CITY

Stone Houses (2004) was a prestigious commission from the Metropolitan Museum of Art in Gotham, for its roof garden. The rocks were taken from Glenluce Bay in Scotland and transported to the US, but the wood (white cedar) for the *Stone Houses* was from New England. The Iris and B. Geald Cantor Roof Garden overlooked Central Park and the formidable skyline of Manhattan, so the sculptures had plenty to contend with visually. This setting certainly wasn't the undulating hills around Penpont or the windswept beaches of Scotland or California, but one of the most famous cityscapes in the world. (The roof garden is a very pleasant spot to visit, to take a break from looking round one of the great museums of the world. There's a café, and it's a happy place to have a drink in the afternoon sunshine, right in the middle of Manhattan).

The two columns of granite stones were about thirteen feet high. They were fashioned in the familiar Goldsworthy form of a tapering column, decreasing in size so that the topmost stone was a pebble. Around the columns of stones Goldsworthy constructed an octagonal 'house' – basically a domed-shaped shelter structure which enclosed the columns (they were eighteen feet tall). The cedar wood had been split into rails, with each end overlapping.

The roof being open to the elements, the materials an artist employs will have to be durable – hence Goldsworthy's choice of chiefly wood and stone (materials he uses all the time in his art anyway).

Other artists who have exhibited at the roof garden include Ellsworth Kelly, Sol LeWitt, Frank Stella, Jeff Koons and Roy Lichenstein (mostly white, male, American artists, one should note). So that Goldsworthy was chosen is significant, being one of the few non-Americans to be honoured.

Having a semi-permanent installation at the Metropolitan Museum of Art is about as prestigious as you can get for a contemporary artist. In terms of sheer numbers of visitors, for instance, or in terms of the immense cultural caché of an institution such as the Met. Because this is a grand museum without any superior, and only a few – such as the Louvre, the Hermitage, the British Museum – can be placed in the same class. If you want to see everything properly at the Metropolitan Museum, set aside a few days. The European paintings alone will consume at least a couple of days: there are Rembrandts here, and Vermeers, and Cranachs, and Caravaggios, and Angelicos, and Ruisdaels, and an astonishing collection of Early Netherlandish painters: Joachim Patinir, Gerard David, Joos van Cleve, etc. Then there's a superb group of modern and French painters, such as Gustave Moreau, Vincent van Gogh, Jean Baptiste Corot and Claude Monet.

So Andy Goldsworthy is in very good company. Sculpture-wise, the Met has a ton of Rodin and Degas and Maillol, and numerous others, and plenty of ancient world statuary, not to mention the incredible ancient Egyptian halls.

The context is important to consider here – viewers of *Stone Houses* will already have seen plenty of other art by the time they reach the roof of the Metropolitan Museum: access to the roof is through the modern art galleries. The context of a mega-museum like the Met alters the response to Goldsworthy's art: this is not a one-man show in a space the artist can exploit on his own. Visitors will have come to see many other artists, or maybe just to visit the museum itself, not necessarily just to see Goldsworthy's *Stone Houses*. With the attractive bar and the stupendous views of Manhattan and Central Park, the roof is going to be a favourite destination for many New Yorkers anyway, regardless of who's showing their work there.

Deborah Solomon remarked of *Stones Houses*:

> Usually we gaze out at a landscape. But in this case we gaze inward, into the quietly romantic domes. It's the reverse of Central Park, another assembly of wood and stones, and the sprawling backdrop for the piece. In the end, *Stone Houses* allows you to look at once at a city landscape and a rural landscape, and to feel the affinities between them. I asked Goldsworthy to define the word 'landscape,' and he replied, a bit cryptically: 'A landscape does not have to involve land. Time is a landscape.' (2004)

Roberta Smith, a critic I admire, wasn't so keen on the *Stone Houses* in Gotham:

> a strange beast: a tentative step forward for the museum and a definite step backward for the artist... Mr. Goldsworthy might best be described as the Fabergé egg man of site-specific art, a magician of the earth, trees and stones whose efforts are poised between the commercial and the pure. But *Stone Houses* plays down his mystical razzle-dazzle, relocating his work in the more pedestrian realm of semiportable, vaguely figurative works produced by a host of contemporary sculptors, including Martin Puryear, Richard Deacon and Tony Cragg. (2004)

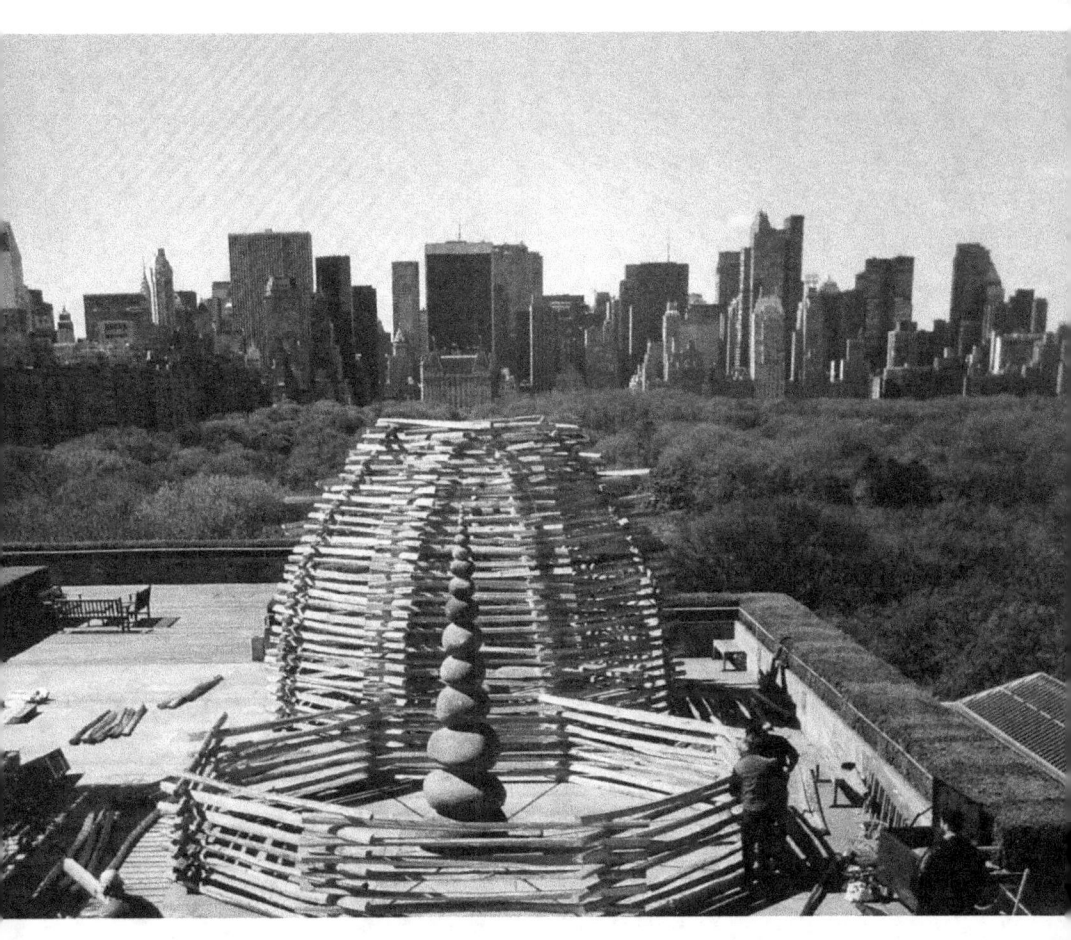

Andy Goldsworthy, Stone Houses, New York City, 2004

13

ROOF, WASHINGTON, DC

Andy Goldsworthy continued his series of prestigious exhibitions in the United States of America with *Roof* (2005), at the National Gallery of Art in the nation's capital. *Roof* consisted of nine slate domes which were basically very large versions of a form Goldsworthy had developed years ago: low, hollow domes of pieces of slate stacked on top of each other, with circular holes at the top. It's a permanent installation – in stone, as most of Goldsworthy's permanent install-ation tend to be.

Goldsworthy related the dome shape of *Roof* to the famous domes of downtown Washington, including the West Building of the National Gallery, the U.S. Capitol, the National Museum of Natural History and the Jefferson Memorial. For the *Roof* project, Goldsworthy used stone (Buckingham slate) from the same source as the materials for the domes of the Smithsonian Castle and Ford's Theater. That meant that Goldsworthy was using his regular method of choosing source materials that have some link to the site of the installation. In this case, however, Goldsworthy was working in one of the most famous historical centres in the Western world, as well as one of the centres of global political power. So the associations with historical buildings such as Ford's Theater, where President Lincoln was assassinated, or the U.S. Capitol, or the Jefferson Memorial, contain far more political punch (or affinities of a different sort) than re-using the old stones from a dry wall in Cumbria for a reworked sheepfold. Sheep on a windswept Cumbrian hillside are one thing, but the buildings where Presidents of America worked and great political events took place is something else.

Goldsworthy had begun the commission by visiting Government Island, Stafford, Virginia, in 2003, where he made some ephemeral sculptures. Goldsworthy has created many works specifically for particular lighting conditions, for moonlight, for sunrises, or the sunlight shining through a forest canopy. Working in Virginia in October, 2003, for instance, on leaf and clay sculptures in a wood, Goldsworthy made light one of the elements he'd explored. He spoke of the light as 'extraordinary, at times hypnotic, even nauseating' (P, 75). As he worked in the Government Island location, Goldsworthy said that he had learnt about 'what I find the most difficult of lights – sunlight through trees' (ib.). Goldsworthy said he had achieved 'a great lesson in time, colour and light' by creating a pointed stone edged with red leaves (*Red Leaves*, 2003). It was the way the sunlight created shadows on the floor of the copse, and over his sculpture, that intrigued Goldsworthy. It was also the *changes* in the light, from sunlight to deep shadow: to illustrate this, Goldsworthy printed a series of photographs in his book *Passage* (76-79). (And not only of *Red Leaves*, but also of other works created in Virginia: a group of pictures depicting a serpentine line of clay placed in a cut in a rock at various times during the day [P, 80-82], and a clay chevron [83-85]).

The *Roof* installation comprised a group of large, low domes or mounds or cairns constructed from slabs of grey slate placed upon each other, in layers, and tapering gradually, to form low, sloping mounds. The domes are maybe five and a half to six feet high (they are roughly twenty-seven feet in diameter).

Roof is set in a terrace or garden behind a very long glass wall (a wall of glass and metal window frames), to the North side of the lobby of the East Building of the National Gallery of Art. Beyond the installation is a high wall, perhaps eight feet tall. The mounds fill up the entire (irregular) space. As it's a roughly rectangular space, and the structures are circular, Goldsworthy has chosen to have the mounds intersect each other, as well as to end abruptly at the walls. Yet he also has two of the mounds extend through the glass wall.

Goldsworthy could have opted to use smaller mounds, or fewer mounds – with much more space between them. Instead, they are packed in, like they're crowded into that space, or squeezed in by some other force. The intersections of the domes form lines of slates at adjoining mounds. The glass wall also acts as a barrier, but only a virtual boundary, as the mounds continue beyond the glass in two cases (as if nothing can stop them, as if they can pass through glass).

So the slate domes continue into the lobby of the National Gallery of Art a foot or two. The glass wall also reflects its surroundings – people, and other artworks. The foyer is busy and echoey, filled with visitors walking to and fro.

Beyond where the mounds are is stillness, watchfulness. The mounds are silent and still presences. They are waiting, perhaps, for something – for their moment. They are not shelters, not spaces or structures for humans to shelter in. And there is no human interaction, either – the glass wall is solid, a barrier. These sculptures are not for touching, or getting close to.

Beyond the stone wall are trees. and the buildings of downtown Washington, around the National Mall. Plants grow along the top of the wall. From the mezzanine level, you can see more of downtown Washington, and the traffic hurtling along Constitution Avenue.

One of the domes extends about six feet into the lobby. The layers of slate are continuous beyond the glass. Each slab of slate is a foot or so long, and an inch or two thick.

You can't quite see the top of the domes, unless you're tall. You have to go up a floor to do that. This is well worth doing – walk to the far side of the mezzanine floor, and you can look down on the *Roof* installation. Now you can see that each dome has a hole in the top of it about 18 inches in diameter. The holes have been cut into a single (larger) piece of slate. Beyond the holes is – blackness. Maybe the domes are hollow, or maybe not.

The holes are worked by hand, and are not perfect circles, as usual in Goldsworthy's art (that is, it would have been relatively easy to draw the circles perfectly and cut them that way). The edges of the holes are wafer-thin, again as usual in Goldsworthy's art (compare with his sand sculptures, for instance).

Around the holes the surface of the slate's been rubbed away. The holes are all places in a single piece of slate which's had its edges broken off to form a rough circle. The flat pieces form the top layer of each mound. 'For me there has always been a relationship between energy, heat and black. The black of a hole is like the flame of a fire; black equates to both growth and decay,' Goldsworthy wrote in 1997 (E, 94).

The summits of each dome are flat, making a flat space about five feet wide. Each mound is roughly the same size and circumference. That's significant; it's not like two parents, say, or one leader, bigger than the others. It's a group of equals.

I visited the National Gallery of Art in Washington many times, and every time the *Roof* installation was always in shadow (being on the North side of the building). Maybe it's different at other times of the year, but not being in direct sunlight gives the installation a distinctive atmosphere.

Maybe Goldsworthy has created the image of silent sentinels here, in the middle of a busy, crowded Western city, rather than in his sculptures on the sides of mountains, in the wilderness. Because although the cars and trucks and taxis rush by, these nine domes ain't going nowhere; they're not bothered by the noise and the movement. They stay still, silent, immobile.

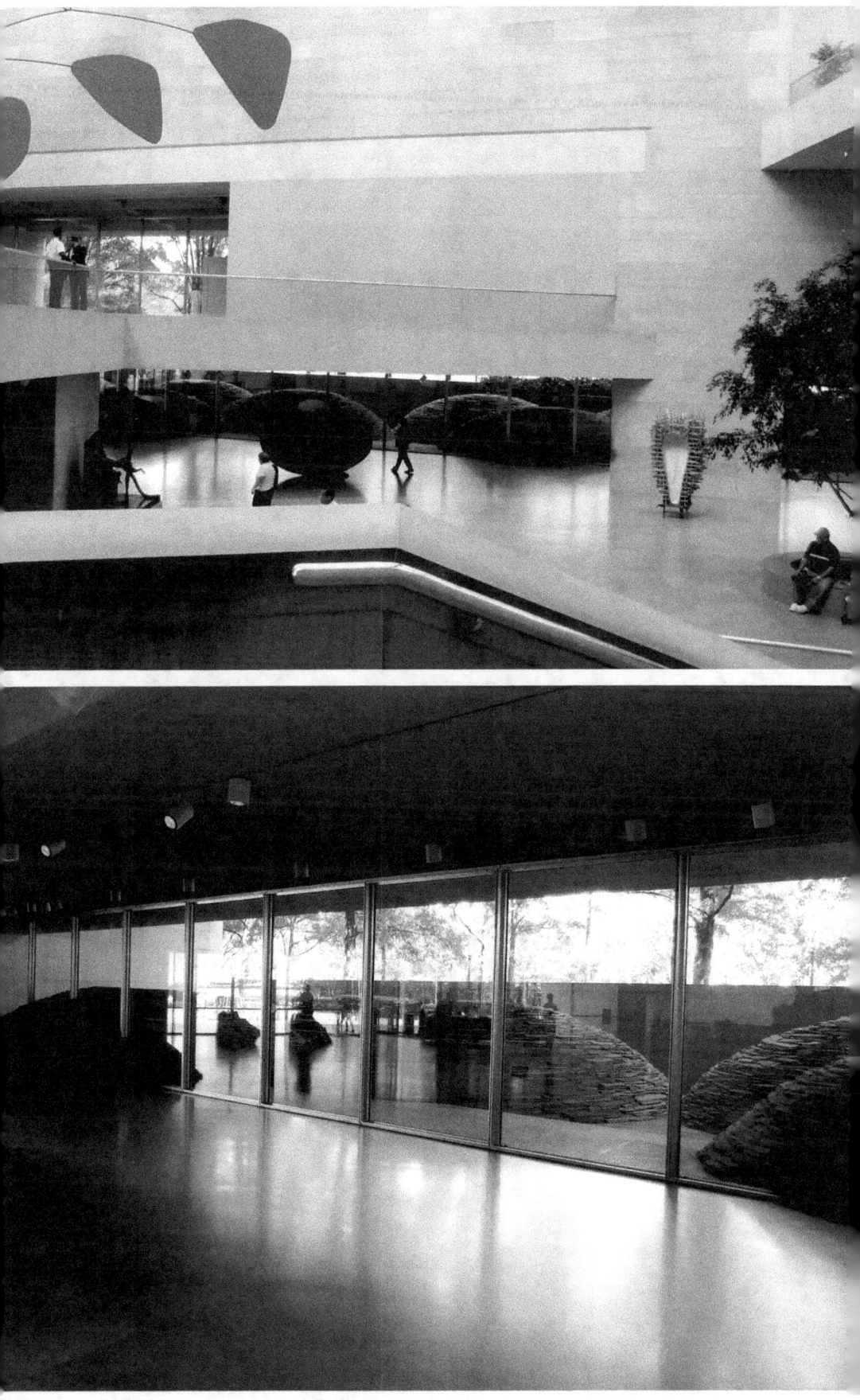

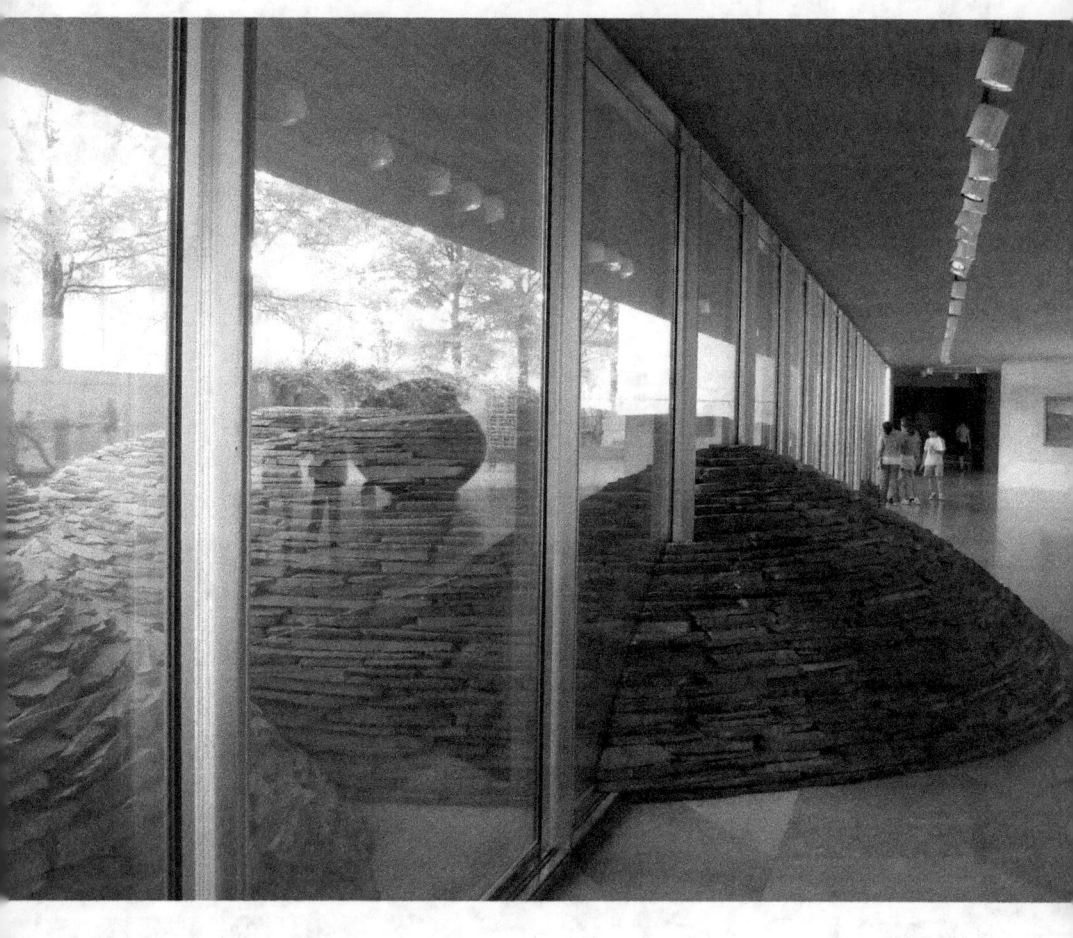

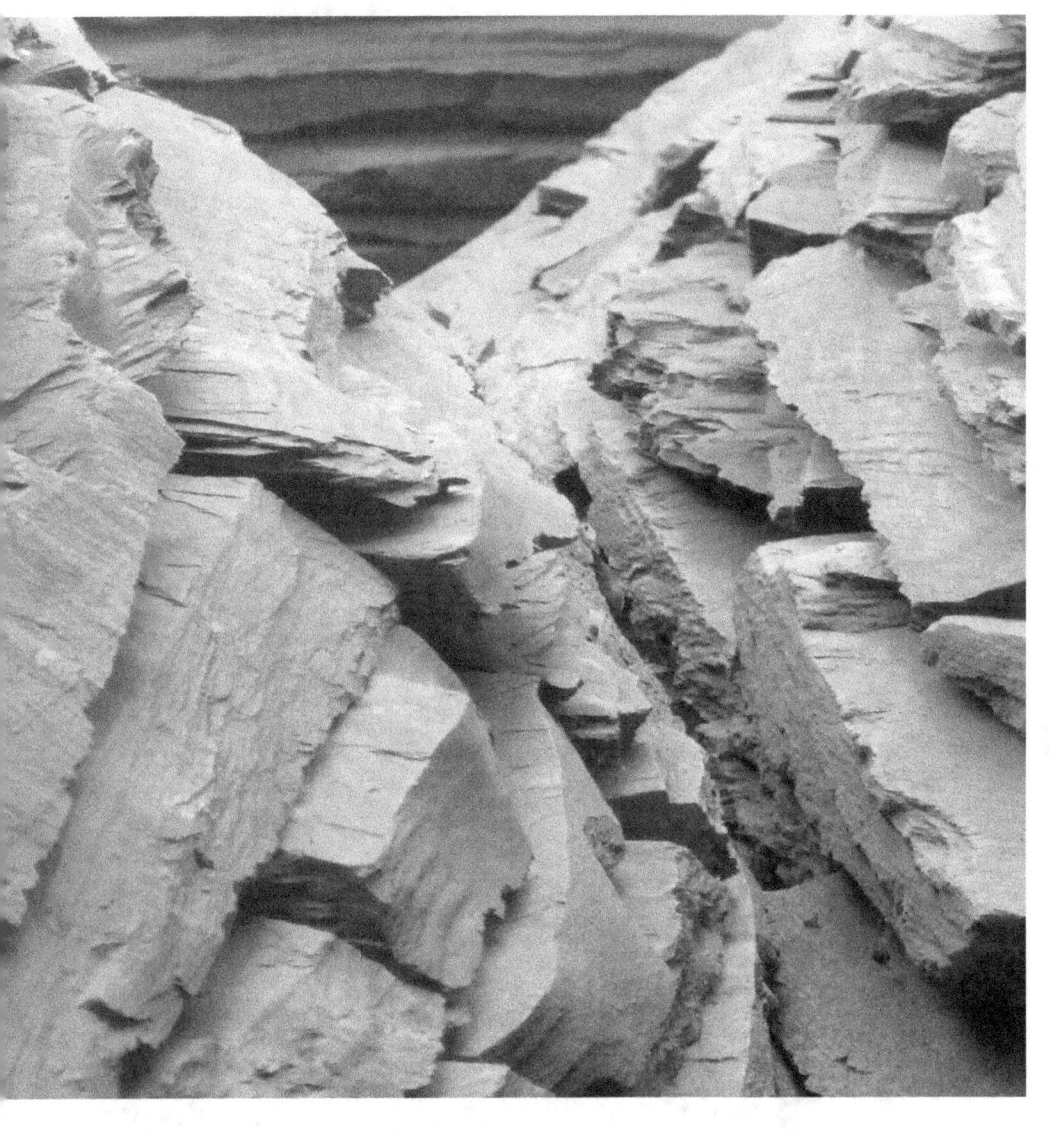

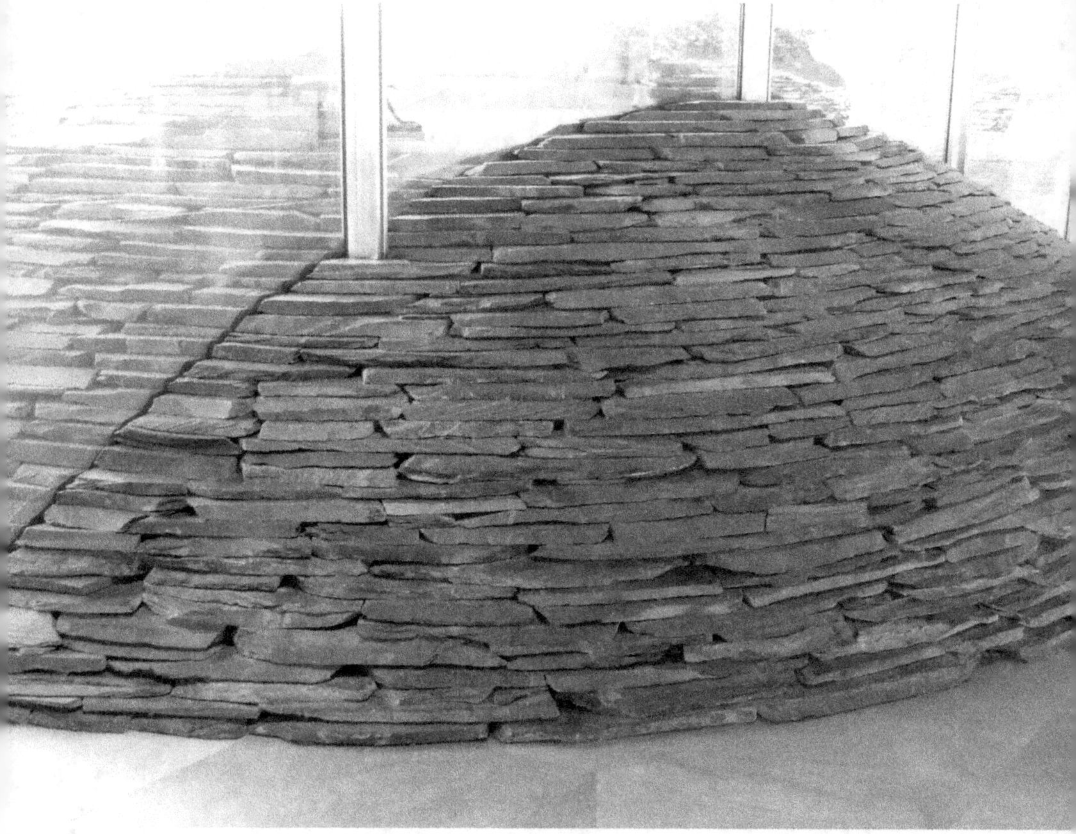

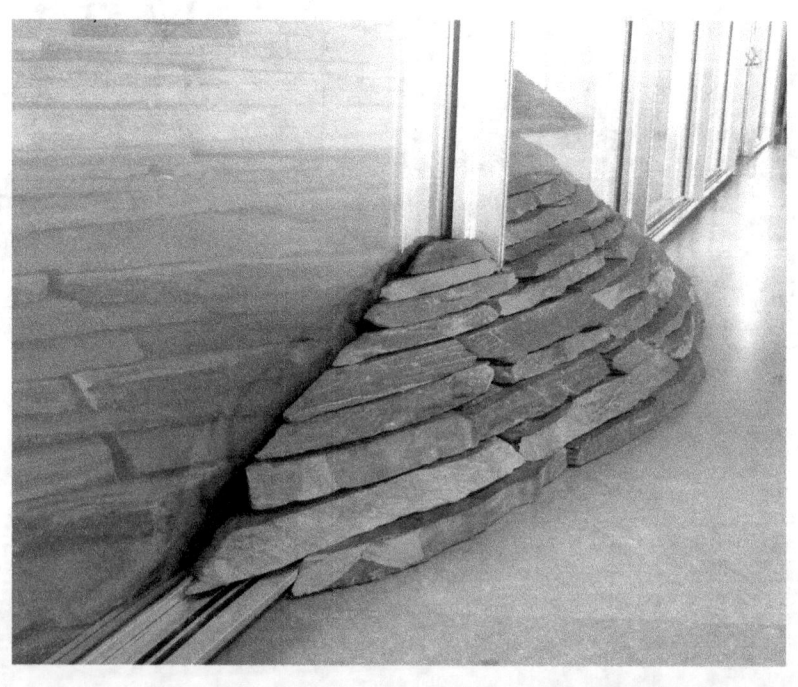

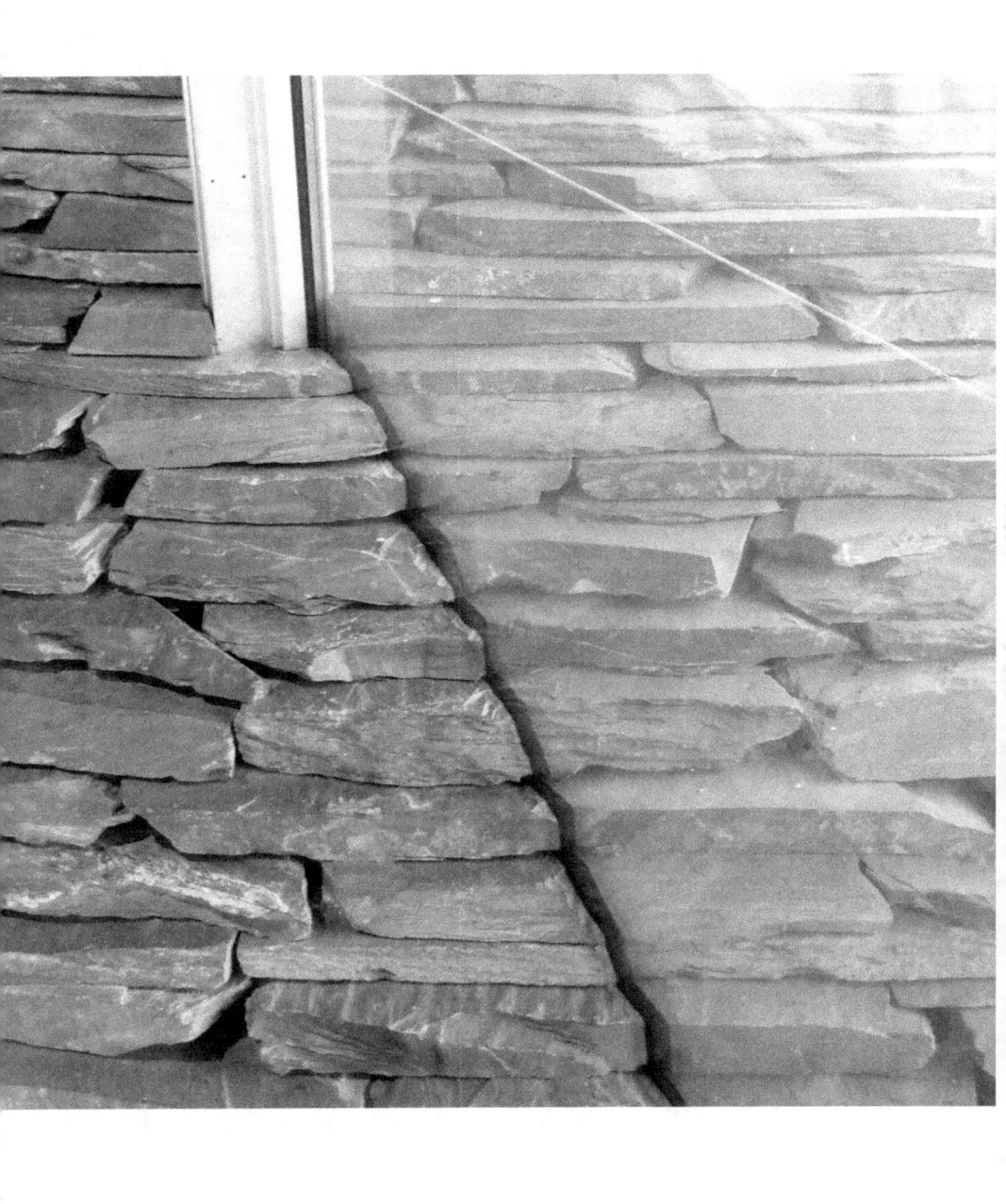

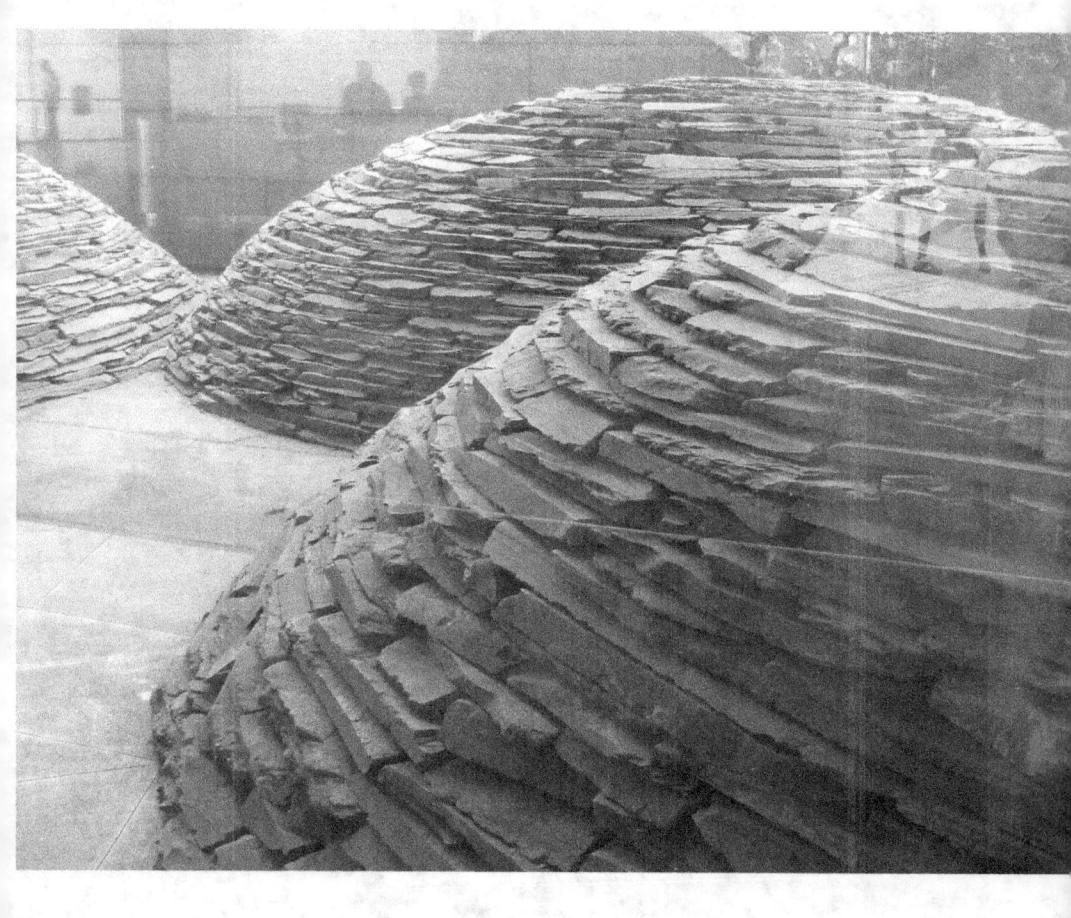

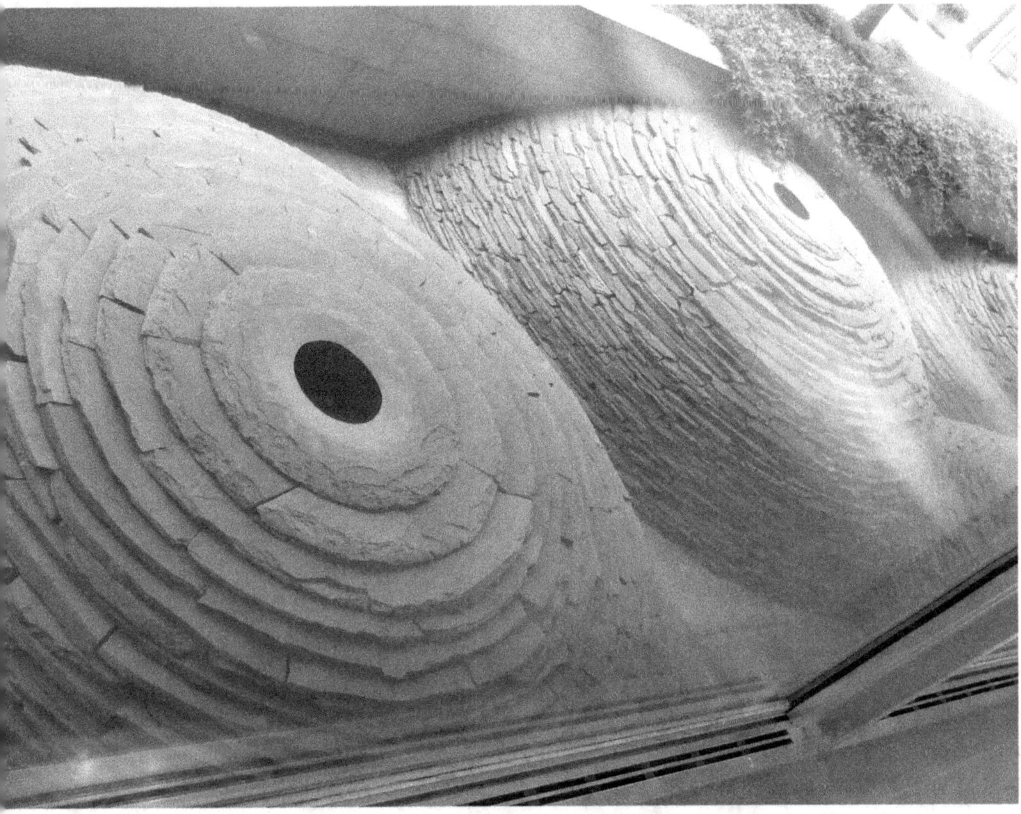

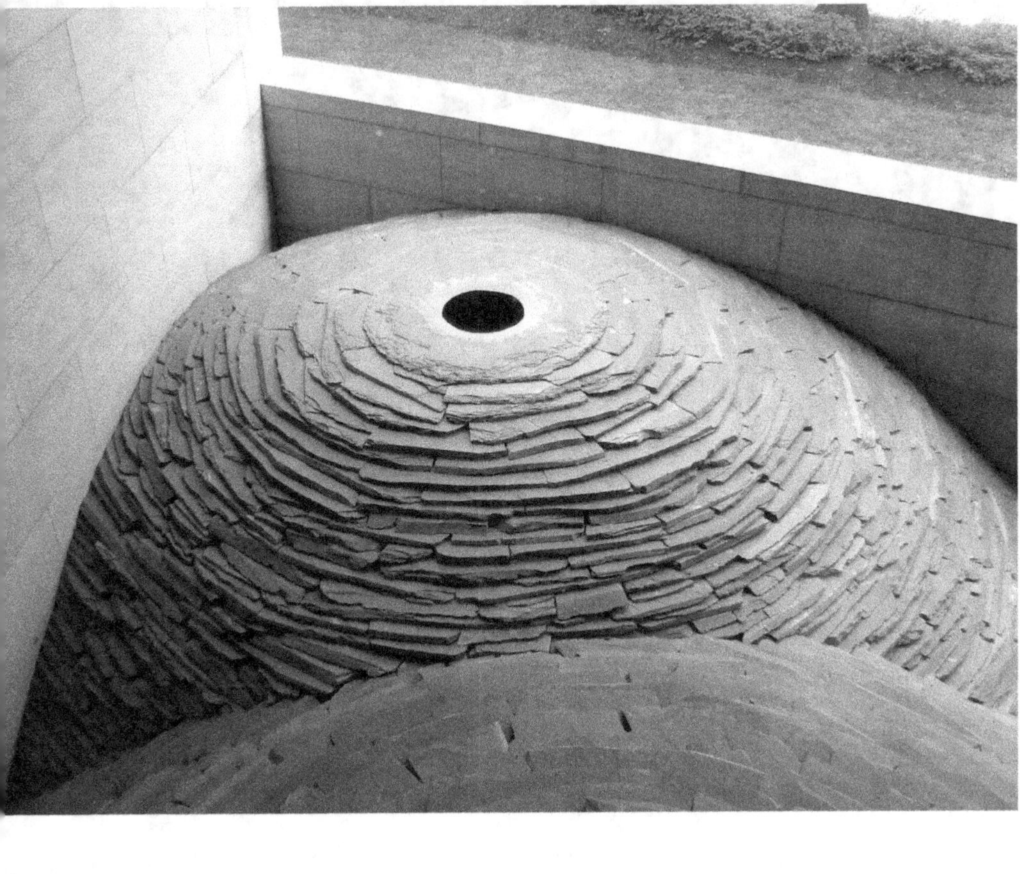

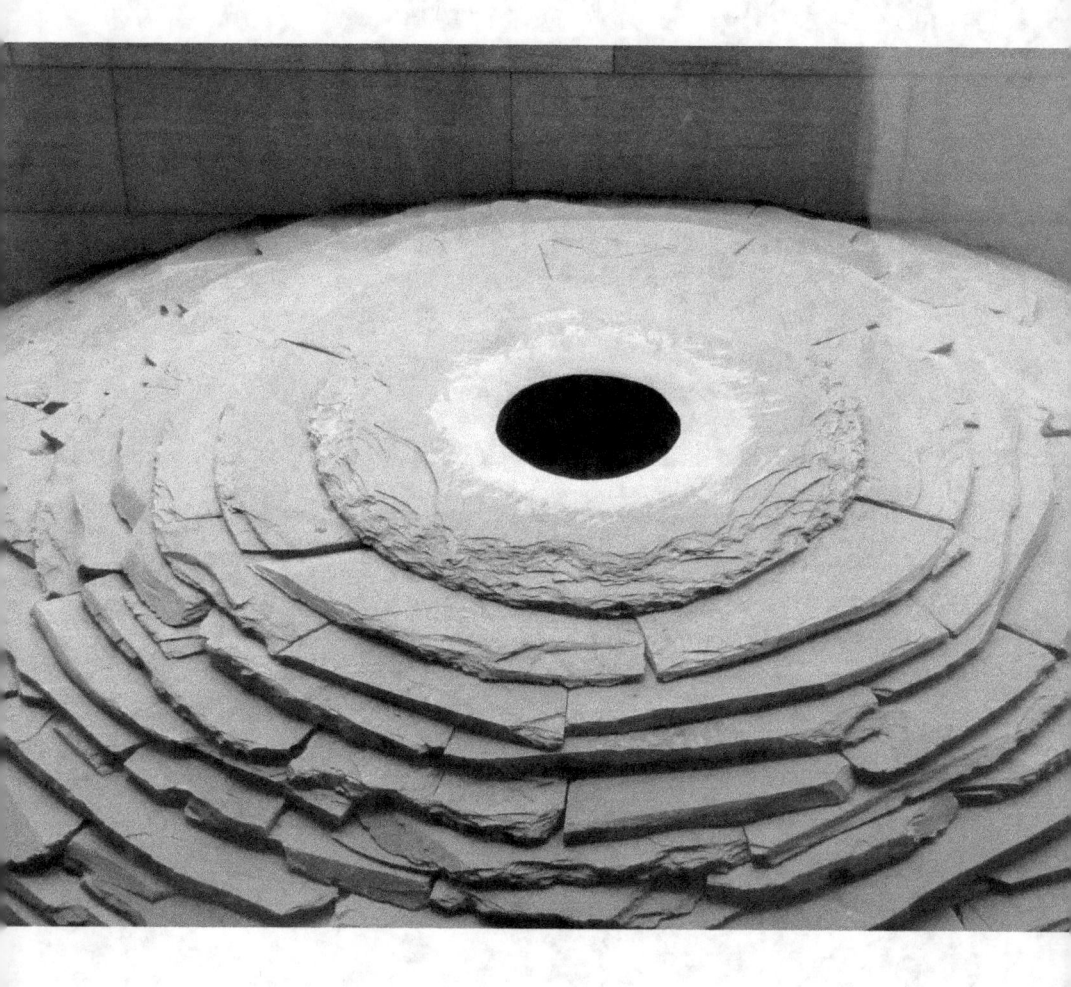

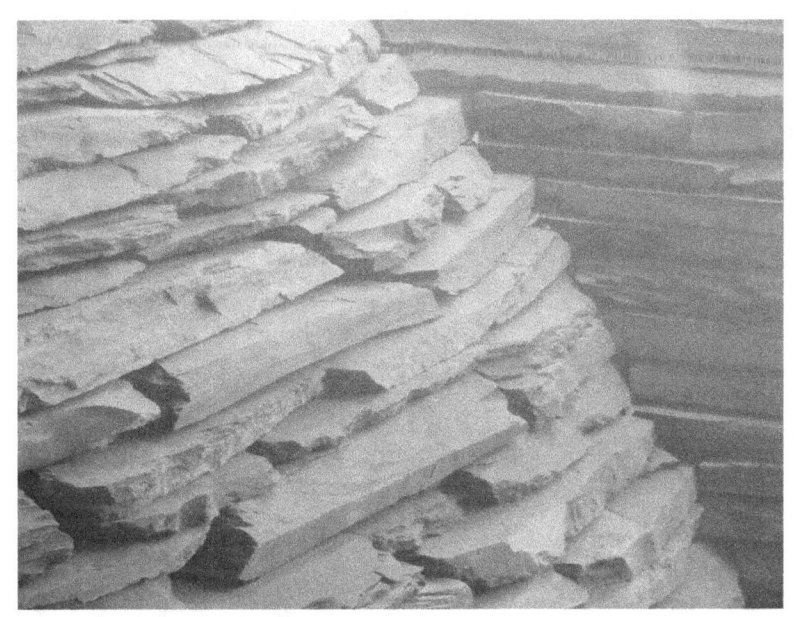

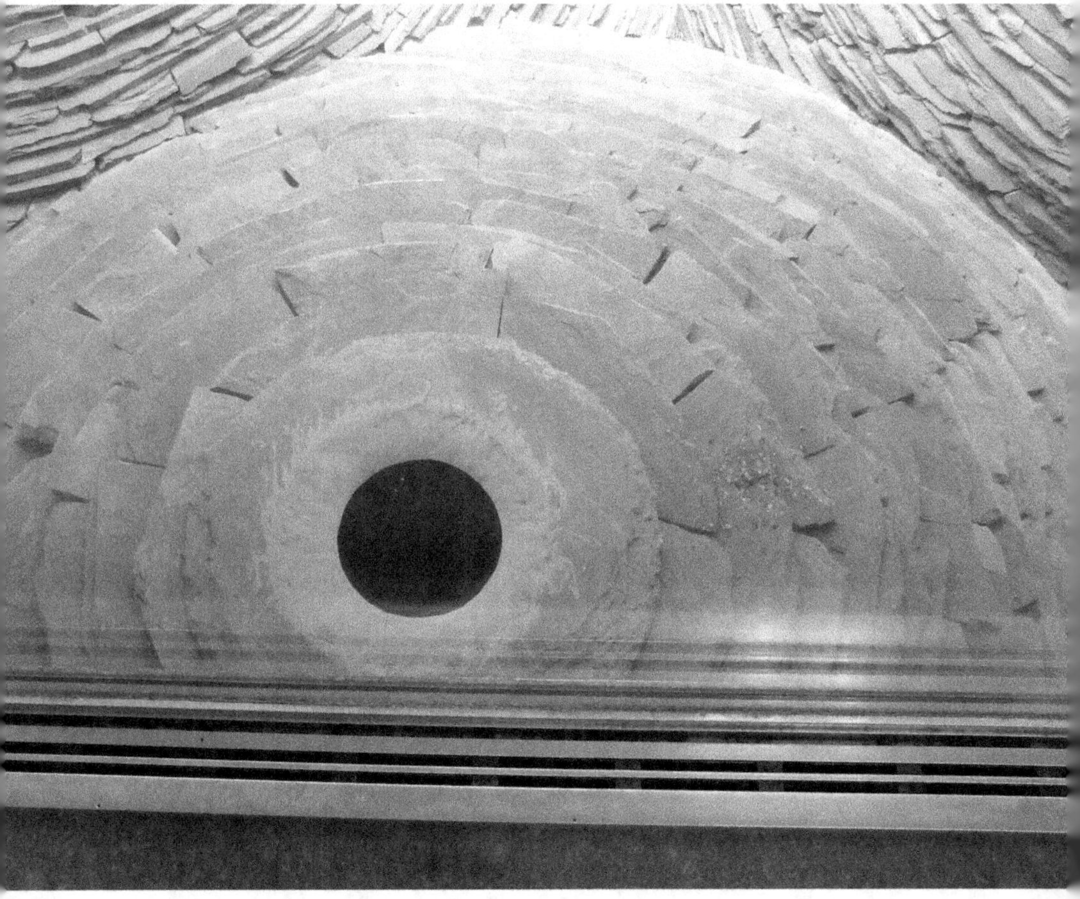

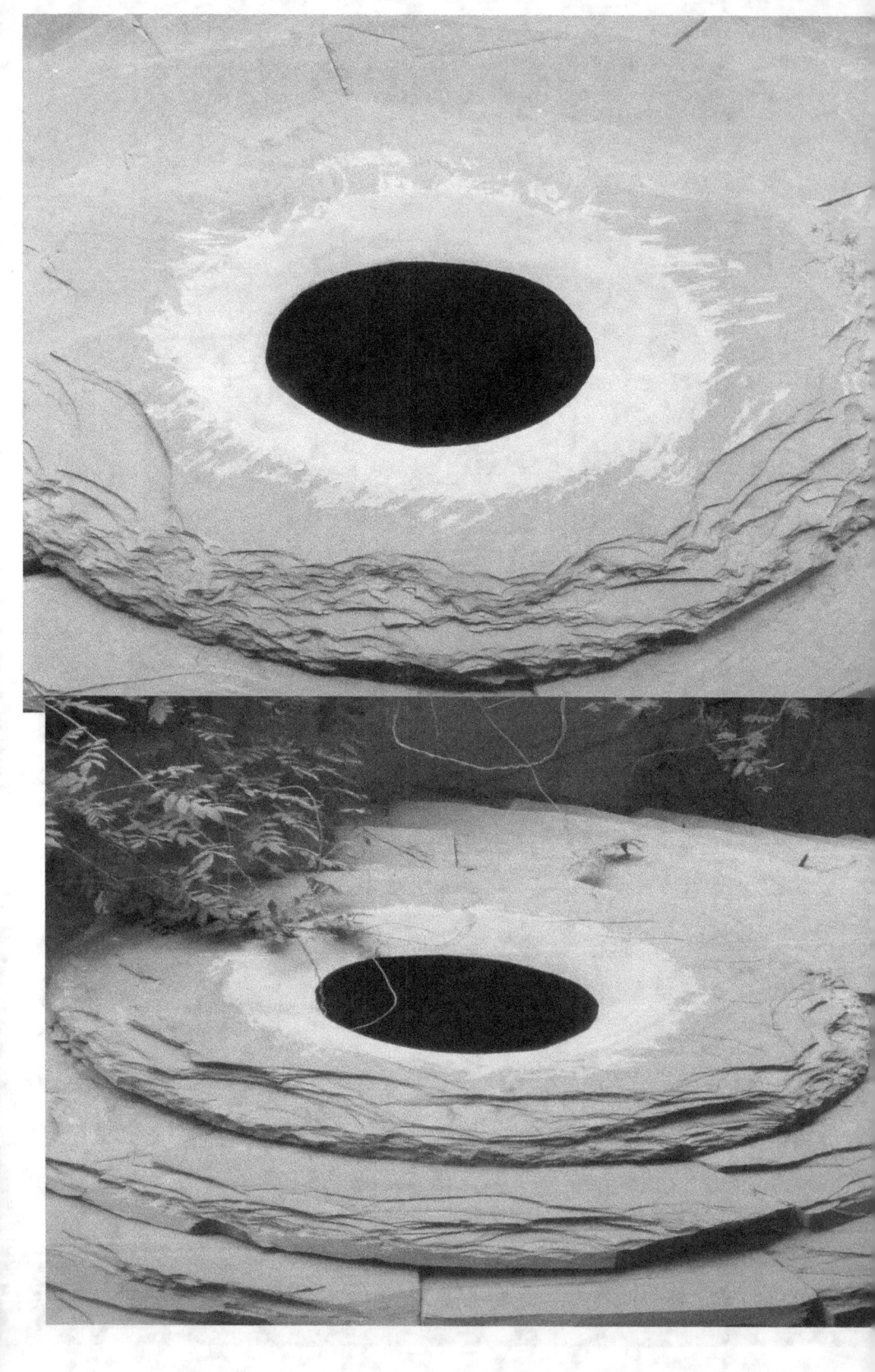

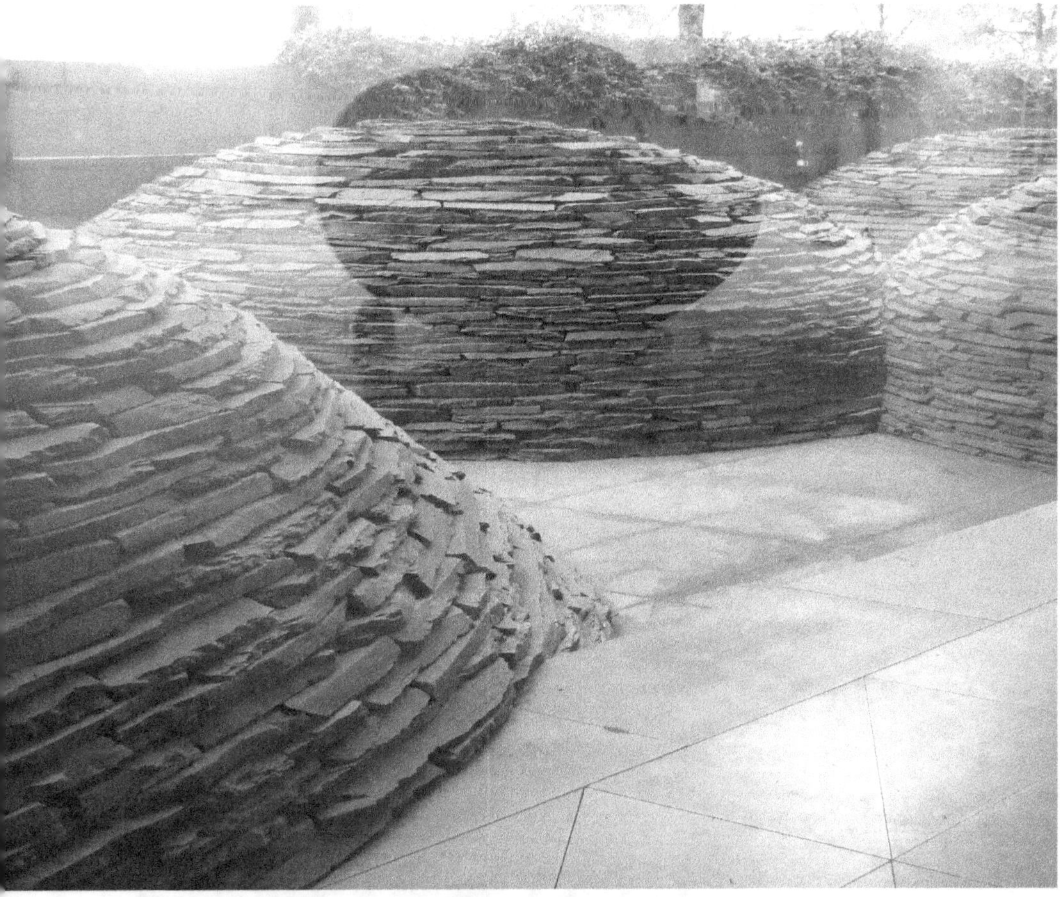

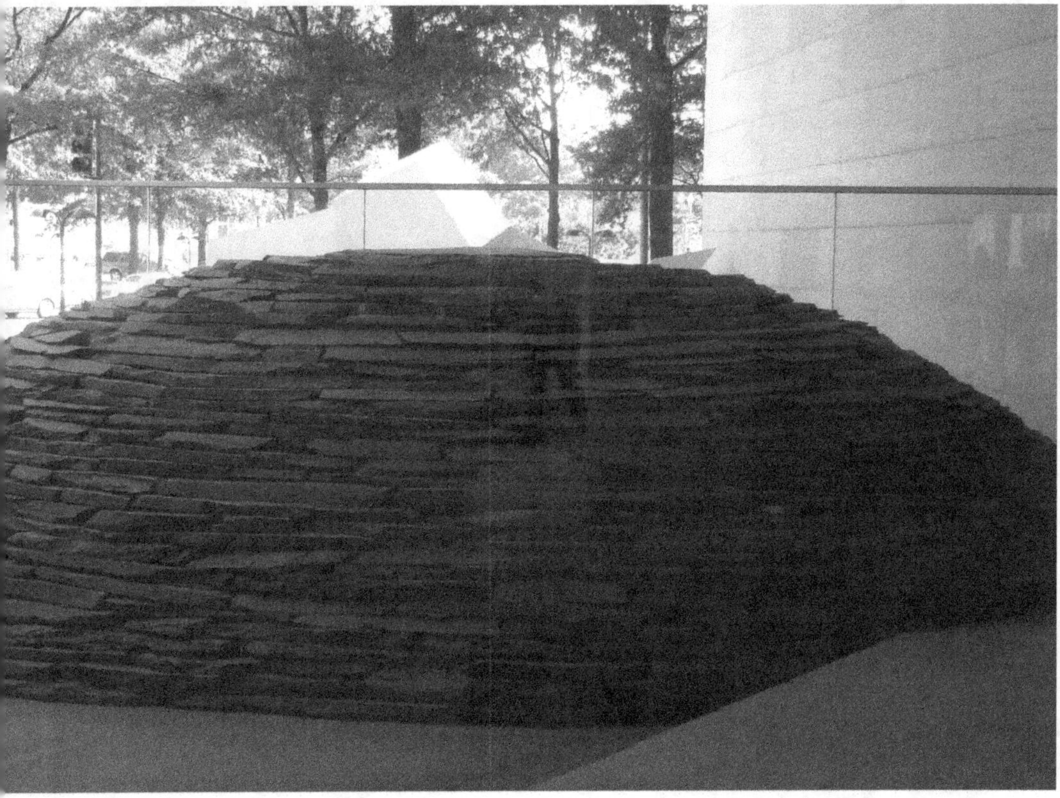

14

THREE CAIRNS, U.S.A.

Three Cairns (2000-02) was an important large-scale commission to construct three cairns in the United States of America: one on the West Coast (in California), one on the East Coast (in New York state), and one in the Mid-West (at Des Moines, Iowa). *Three Cairns* was a collaboration with three cultural institutions: Des Moines Art Center, Neuberger Museum of Art, Purchase, New York, and La Jolla Museum in San Diego. In the event, Goldsworthy built six cairns: apart from the three permanent pieces, there were three ephemeral sculptures: two were tidal, on the East and West coasts, and the third, in Iowa, was built on the prairie, which was set alight (with fire replacing water as the natural force which engulfed the sculpture. However, the stone cairn survived the fire). The *Three Cairns* in Des Moines is easy to visit, being in the centre of Des Moines. You can also drive out to the *Prairie Cairn*, which's out on I-80, East about 40 miles East of Des Moines.

The project had a conceptual basis, with the cairns linked up. They wouldn't be able to be viewed at the same time, in the same space, and thus part of *Three Cairns* 'will to an extent always exist only as an idea', as Goldsworthy put it (P, 118). Goldsworthy defined the cairn for him again: '[t]he cairn is a marker to the flow of change, life, growth, decay, death and renewal of the prairie landscape' (P, 94).

Three Cairns is one of Andy Goldsworthy's major works in the United States of America. Situated at the Des Moines Art Center, *Three Cairns* was constructed in 2002 by Goldsworthy and a team of dry stone-wallers There are four structures in *Three Cairns*, all built from Iowa limestone. There is a cairn at the centre, and three rectilinear constructions which resemble containers, recesses and walls. The cairn is larger than average human size, and looms over the spectator by a few feet. The recesses are even larger and wider.

Three Cairns is situated behind the Des Moines Art Center, in the centre of Des Moines, in a small park. There are many trees nearby, and paths, beds of plants, and so on. It is surrounded by the grass of the park. There's a plaque on the ground, describing the work, as is usual at sculpture parks. And a notice pinned to the trees which asks visitors not to climb the artworks. No fence or boundary surrounds the sculptures. I visited it in classic Goldsworthy weather – drizzle.

I highly recommend visiting the Des Moines Art Center as well as *Three Cairns* – there are some wonderful pieces here, including favourites such as Mark Rothko, Edward Hopper, Donald Judd, Sol LeWitt, Morris Louis, Brice Marden and Eva Hesse. So Goldsworthy is in excellent company (it also places the work within a contemporary art/ modern art context, and associates Goldsworthy with the great contemporary artists.)

You might think of endless vistas of flat fields when you think of Iowa, and the state is like that in large part. More fields than you've ever seen before. So an art museum as sophisticated as the Des Moines Art Center can appear a little surprising in this context. This is not New York, Chicago or San Francisco, after all (Des Moines has a population of about 209,000). If you're going to chose an art museum in which to situate a work like Goldsworthy's *Three Cairns*, there are other possibilities, of course: St Louis, Indianapolis, Kansas City, etc.

Three Cairns is of course a *conceptual* piece. That is, the *idea* of it is essential to understanding what the artist is aiming for. The 'three cairns' of the title, for instance, are *not* on display at the Des Moines Art Center. One of the three cairns is here, but the other two on the opposite coasts of the continental United States.

The cairn at Des Moines Art Center takes pride of place in the centre of the group of stone structures. It then becomes clear that the two recesses or containers on the West and East side of the cairn are meant to relate to the cairns on the West and East coasts of America. Those cairns aren't here, but their containers are.

The fourth structure also makes sense now: the container relates to the central cairn. So each cairn in *Three Cairns* is paired with a recess or container. Which raises all sorts of questions: what is the relation of the cairn to its container/ recess? Is it a pairing? Is one emerging from the other? And why are the recesses facing *inwards,* towards the central cairn, and not *outwards,* to the cairns that are 1,500 miles away on each coast of America? (Only the central cairn faces its own container.)

The conceptual aspect of *Three Cairns* is vital to the full comprehension of the piece. The viewer doesn't need to know about the other cairns on the coasts of the Land of the Free, but it enhances the work greatly. A full appreciation would entail visiting those cairns too, of course (plus the *Prairie Cairn*).

Each recess or container has an opening shaped like a cairn. The recess itself is a shape resembling the cairns, as if you could keep a giant Easter egg in there. A big, hollow space which's in human scale: the relation to the cairns is further emphasized by the way that each recess is constructed, with the layers of stone slabs placed to echo the central cairn outside. For example, the floor of the recess comprises stone slabs placed in concentric circles, just how the cairns are constructed. In fact, the visitor is invited to enter each of the recesses: there is a stone step up to the recesses, which're about a foot and a half off the ground. The feelings once inside are of enclosure, shelter, a resting place, perhaps (though there's nowhere to sit), a place to stand, perhaps. And also a viewpoint to look at the other structures.

The *Prairie Cairn* was constructed especially for the burn (the cairn and burn was managed in collaboration with Grinnell College and Faulconer Gallery). Andy Goldsworthy has often combined stones and heat – he's fired stones in stoves, for instance, and was fascinated by the process of hollowing out the glacial boulders for *Garden of Stones* with a cutting torch. In the event, the burning of *Prairie Cairn* was hot enough to melt part of Goldsworthy's camera, and he didn't get the shots he wanted of the prairie on fire around the cairn. Goldsworthy also failed to capture the collapse of the tidal cairn in the West, so the series of ephemeral U.S. cairns was in some way a failure. 'The series remains one of my strongest achievements and yet contains great failures' (P, 95).

Prairie Cairn was built near Kellogg, Iowa, at Grinnell College's Conrad Environmental Research Area. You can visit the *Prairie Cairn*, which's situated about 40 miles East of Des Moines. The art center provides directions for visiting *Prairie Cairn*. This is the permanent cairn that Goldsworthy and his team constructed.

Goldsworthy photographed *Prairie Cairn* over 18 months. The 16 prints of the *Prairie Cairn* were exhibited as *Prairie Cairn/ For My Father/ Newton, Iowa* (2002).

For Goldsworthy, it's not just sculpture on its own that's important, it's also how it's photographed and presented. Goldsworthy usually photographs his sculpture himself. Many artists hire someone else to do that, but Goldsworthy likes to choose the angles, the framing, the lighting and all the rest of it himself. He's not, as he acknowledges, a techno whizz, but he does have a Hasselblad (120mm) camera, a panoramic camera, lenses, tripods, etc. He also likes to choose the exact moment for photographing his work. He speaks of feeling anxious if he can't snap an ephemeral sculpture at the right time (for instance, with the cairns built for the incoming tide, Goldsworthy prefers to capture the precise moment of collapse, and worries when he's got to change the film over, in case he misses it). If a film doesn't come out, it's disappointing. When he was photographing his *Prairie Cairn* in Iowa in 2001, it was cold enough for his camera to slow down (P, 95).

The *West Coast Sea Cairn* was constructed at Half Moon Bay in California in August, 2001. The tidal process was central to the cairn, as with all of Goldsworthy's sculptures made on the seaboard. It was built to collapse with the next tide, and, as ever, capturing the moment of the downfall photographically was crucial. It was a paradox that something as solid and enduring as stone could be so ephemeral. That was part of the conception of the stone cairns built on beaches: stone and water, the permanent and the impermanent, solidity and fragility.

As with his *Réfuges d'Art* sculptures in France's Digne, and the walls built at Clougha Pike in Lancashire (1999-2001), Goldsworthy constructed some limestone walls with hollowed-out spaces, which surrounded the permanent *Midwest Cairn* at Des Moines Art Center. At Digne and Lancashire, Goldsworthy had built walls with vertical elliptical cavities, large enough for a person to stand in (there was a step just below the space to help the visitor up). In Iowa, Goldsworthy turned the elliptical hollows into cairn-shaped spaces. Now each wall had a recess in the middle of it shaped roughly like half an egg. The limestone walls were grouped around the central cairn in the familiar Goldsworthyan guise of guardians or sentinels

Each cairn-shaped cavity related directly to the exact shape of the three cairns, as if the cairns from the East and West coasts could be brought to Iowa and slotted into the walls, as if the coastal cairns had a womb-like resting place waiting for them in perpetuity in Iowa, as if the cairns on the coasts had travelled outwards, away from Iowa, and the Iowa walls were 'home'.

The *East Coast Cairn* (2001), built at the Neuberger Museum of Art, took on personal associations for Goldsworthy, because his father had died recently (in October, 2001). The cairn, constructed under a large tree, became something of a memorial for his father (Goldsworthy also discussed the events of September 11, 2001 in relation to the work – *East Coast Cairn* was created a couple of months after the attacks on New York and Washington [P, 112, 115]).

The *West Coast Cairn* was built outside the Museum of Contemporary Art in San Diego in early 2002. The California cairn was constructed under another tree: Goldsworthy spoke of the tree in his usual terms of sheltering and guardianship (P, 118). Scale was always an important consideration in siting a sculpture beside a tree: the tree shouldn't dominate the sculpture, and the sculpture should be able to assert itself.

Some of the poetic links artists make in the course of their work are sometimes obscure. Goldsworthy liked the fact that the San Diego cairn was made of limestone, which was created, geologically, on the seabed, and the cairn was near the ocean (P, 117). It's a connection an artist can discover over time, because s/he's working on the piece for hours or days, but one wonders how many visitors to the Museum of Contemporary Art would make the link between limestone and the nearby Pacific.

Of the *East Coast Cairn*, Benjamin Genocchio commented in 2003:

> Mr. Goldsworthy created similar sculptures in Des Moines and San Diego in an effort to traverse the country in cairns. The thinking behind this axis of obelisks is a bit fuzzy, at least on my reading of the catalog, although it is worth noting that in Des Moines the cairn is encircled by three blocky limestone walls. From each of the walls a hollow has been cut matching the shape of the cairns on the West and East Coasts. I haven't seen this egg-cup Stonehenge, although I imagine the experience is stirring.

OTHER TIDAL WORKS

Some of Andy Goldsworthy's earliest works (of the 1970s) were tidal, beachbound sculptures which relied very much on the power and majesty of the sea to make them work. Some were sculptures which required the action of the tide to complete them. They were fabricated specifically so that the sea would cover them up. They involved Goldsworthy working very fast, usually arriving at a beach site at lowest tide, to give him the most time to complete a sculpture (it was thus best when low tide coincided with early morning). Beaches were often good places for materials, too (always an important consideration for an artist): sand and stones aplenty, and wood, and flotsam and jetsam. Building the sculpture was only half of the work, though: Goldsworthy always stayed around for the moment when the tide came in, photographing the sculpture throughout its immersion. The moment of collapse was particularly important for Goldsworthy, and he was disappointed if he didn't witness it.

Although the tidal works are dealing with big themes, of time, change, decay, the sea, nature, lunar power, and so on, there is also something undeniably childlike about such sculptures. They're reminiscent of children (and adults) who build castles, boats and walls from sand below the high tideline, so they can watch them (or stand in them) when the waves approach. Thus, Goldsworthy's tidal works are some of his most fun art: they can be regarded as serious explorations of nature and time, or larking about on a beach, building stuff then watching it disintegrate.

At Morecambe Bay in Lancashire in October, 1976, Goldsworthy buried a serpentine line of stones and photographed them as the tide came in. Another work, at Heysham Head, comprised the now-familiar Goldsworthy motif: a series of rocks on a tidal pedestal: as the water rose, the sculpture altered. Goldsworthy's later sea sculptures of balanced rocks are essentially no different from these early Lancashire works. The early works, like the latest sea pieces, employ the formal elements of the littoral environment: the presence of the sea, the changing levels in water, the reflectivity of the water, the colour of the sea, and sky, the movement of the water, the constantly changing light, and so on. These environmental elements are incorporated into Goldsworthy's sea sculptures.

Later tidal works included *Eleven Arches* (1992, Carrick Bay), *Sand Stones* (1992, California), *Beach Holes* (1990, Morecambe), *Balanced Rocks* (1993, Porth Ceiriad, Wales), *Sand Holes* (1997, Rockcliffe), *Cairn* and *Stick Dome Hole* (both 1999, Nova Scotia), and the *Three Cairns* project (2001-02). In Collieston (Aberdeenshire) in 2000 Goldsworthy produced a group of ephemeral beachworks: a rock covered with smooth sand, or ridges of sand, or a negative circle of sand. Each sand work was washed away by the tide. Goldsworthy's very early works were consciously irregular and 'organic' in shape and form, rather than the more geometric forms he later adopted (such as circles, spirals and lines).

Many (land) artists have worked with the tide apart from Andy Goldsworthy: Barry Flanagan, Christo, Dennis Oppenheim, Michael McCafferty, Michelle Oka Doner, Chris Drury and Jan Dibbets. Jan Dibbets had a tractor plough the sand on a beach which would then be covered by the tide, in a film made for television (in 1969), for a *Land Art* exhibition.

Goldsworthy's Welsh *Sea Cairn* (1993) was a 'feminine' cairn built on a pile of barnacled rocks right next to the ocean: when the tide came in, it surrounded the cairn. The sculpture was another 'before and after' work, and could hardly fail: like the cover of *Stone* (*Balanced rocks*), *Sea Cairn* was seen against and beside the ocean. The presence of the surging waves gives the stone sculptures a grandeur they certainly would not possess if they were sited in a slate quarry (although Welsh slate quarries, such as those around Blaenau Ffestiniog, have their own special atmosphere). When a cairn made on the beach in Nova Scotia in 1999 didn't collapse when the tide came in (as was usual), Goldsworthy said he found the event 'profoundly altered the way I see things. My art has shown me so many things that were hidden to me' (T, 104).

In going out to work in the landscape everyday, Goldsworthy said he was learning, bit by bit, about the natural world, creating 'an intensely personal knowledge' (the pedagogical aspect is emphasized in many of Goldsworthy's writings). He didn't feel he was 'breaking new ground', but neither did he feel 'the weight of history'. Goldsworthy said that if possible 'I make a work every day' (T, 7). Goldsworthy said he didn't want to be seen as 'some sort of romantic in the landscape, escaping from the city', and that he enjoyed working on 'patches of waste ground' in cities (ibid.).

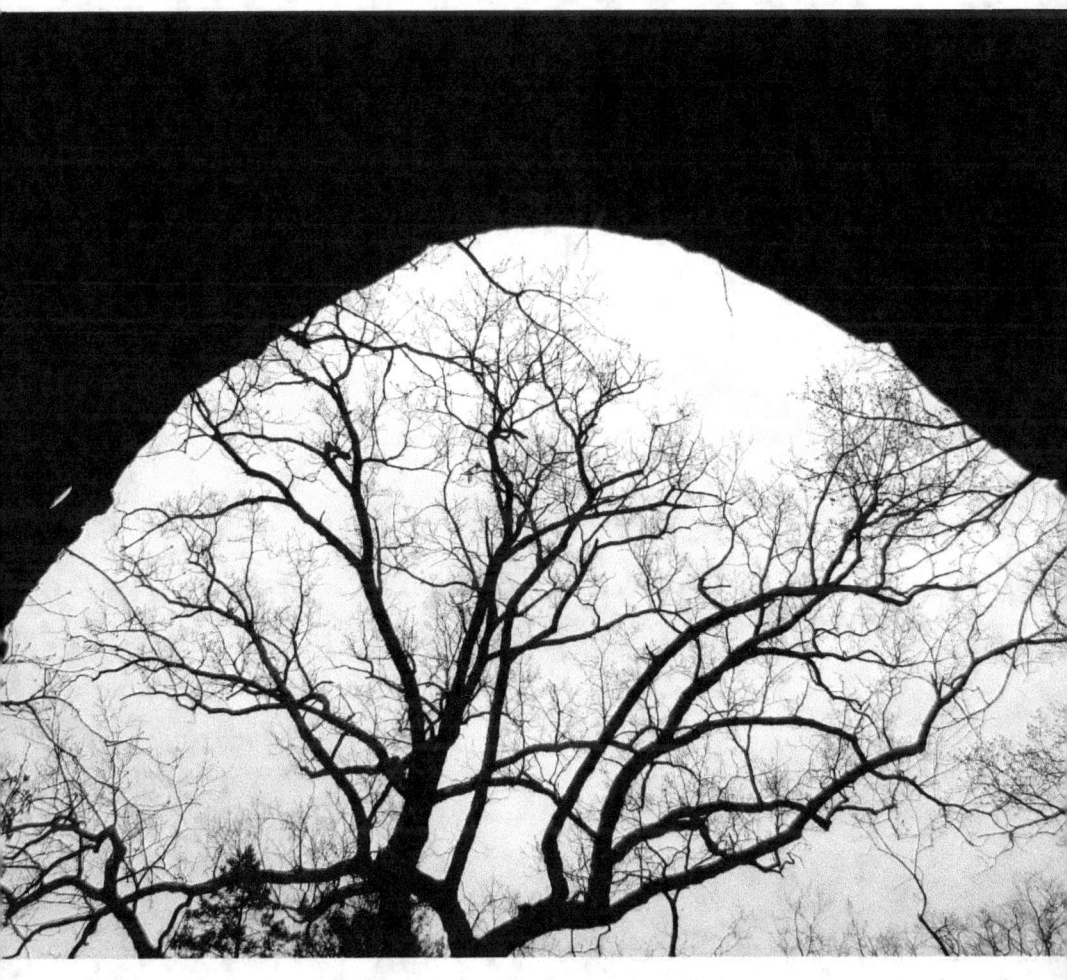

Three Cairns (2000-02) was an important large-scale commission to construct three cairns in the United States of America: one on the West Coast (in California), one on the East Coast (in New York state), and one in the Mid-West (at Des Moines, Iowa). Three Cairns was a collaboration with three cultural institutions: Des Moines Art Center, Neuberger Museum of Art, Purchase, New York, and La Jolla Museum in San Diego. In the event, Andy Goldsworthy built six cairns: apart from the three permanent pieces, there were three ephemeral sculptures: two were tidal, on the East and West coasts, and the third, in Iowa, was built on the prairie, which was set alight (with fire replacing water as the natural force which engulfed the sculpture. However, the stone cairn survived the fire).

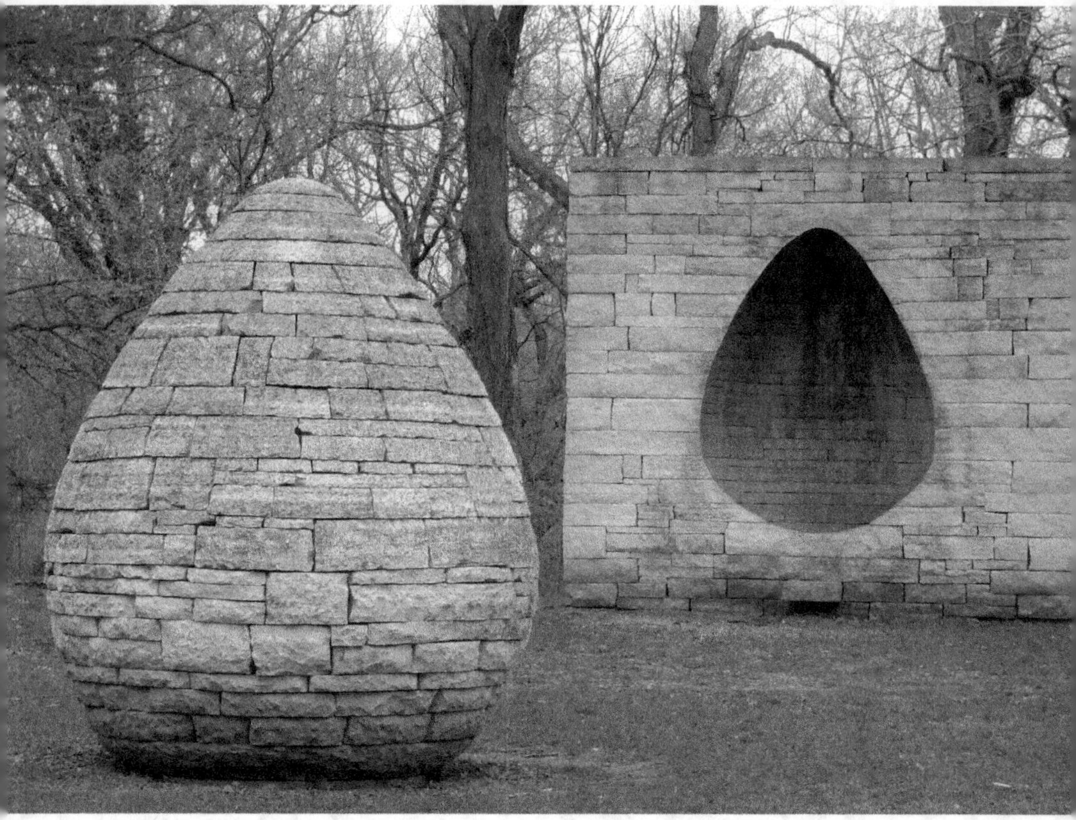

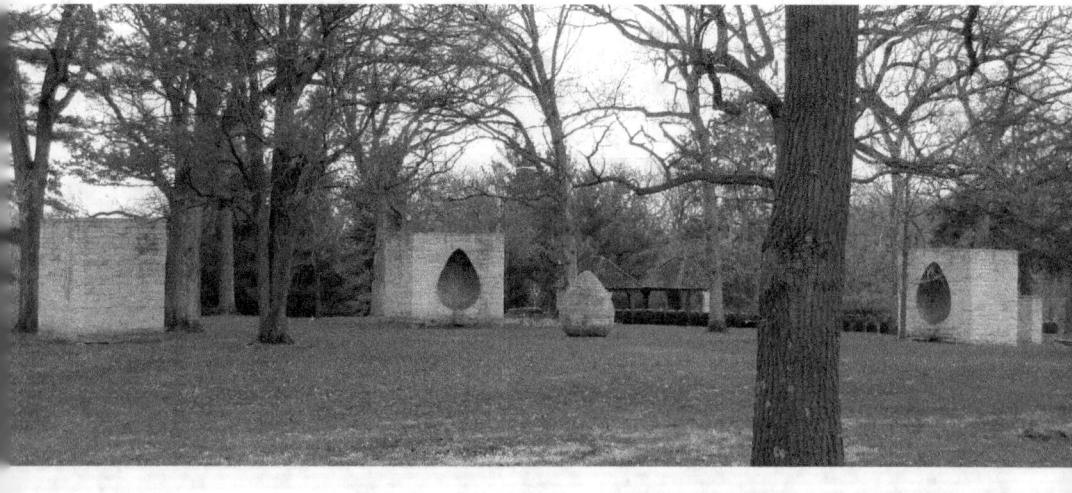

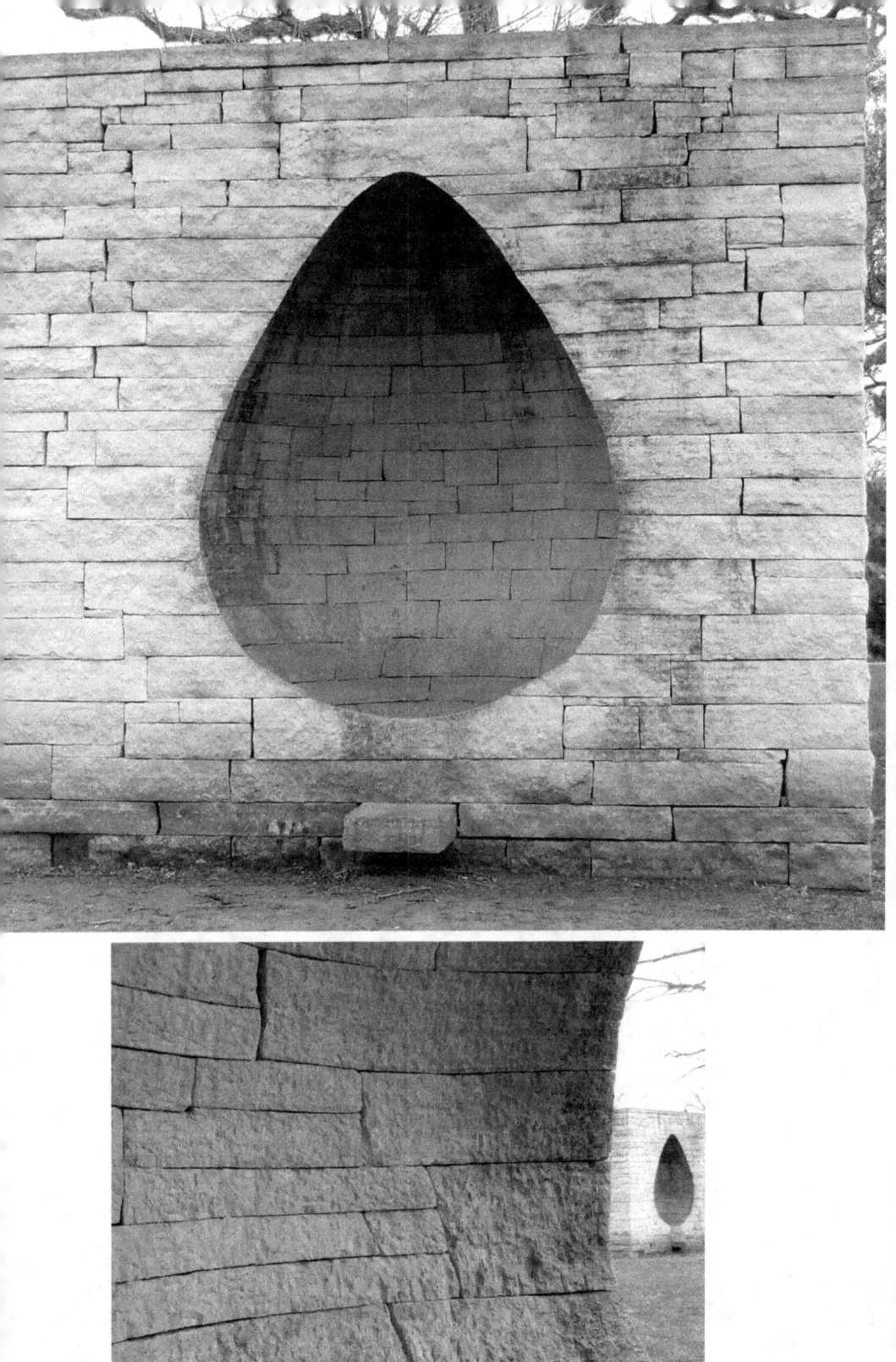

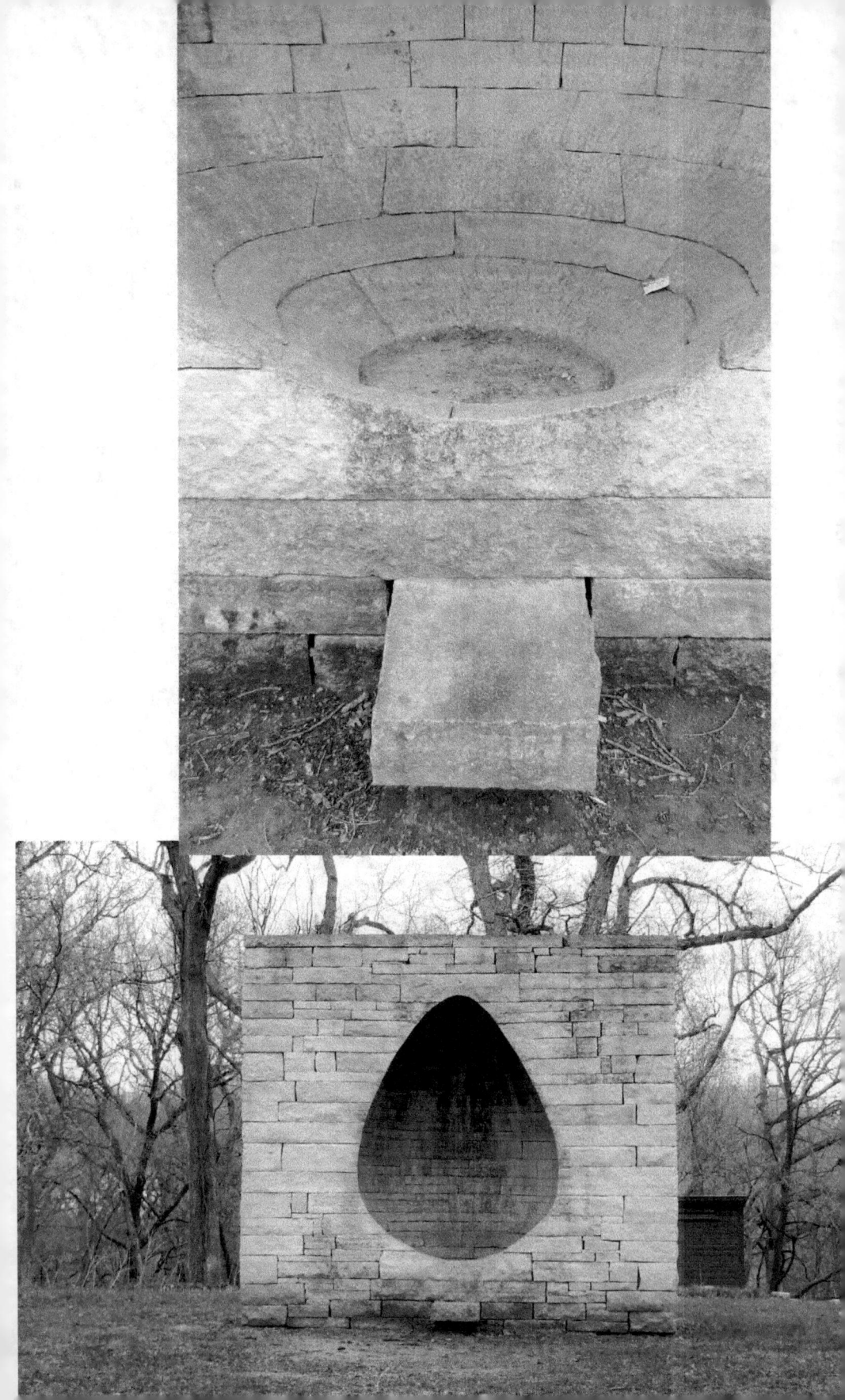

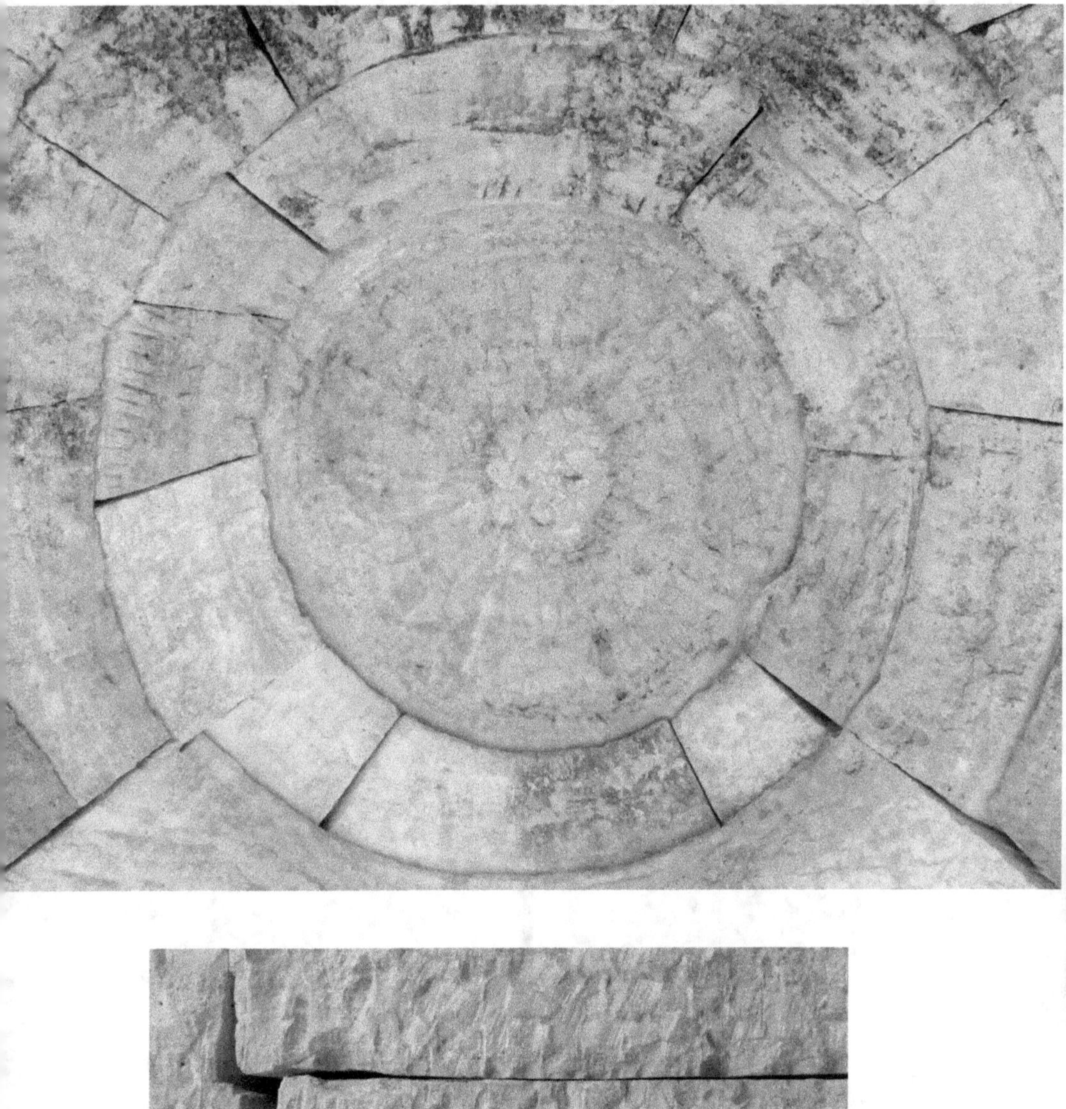

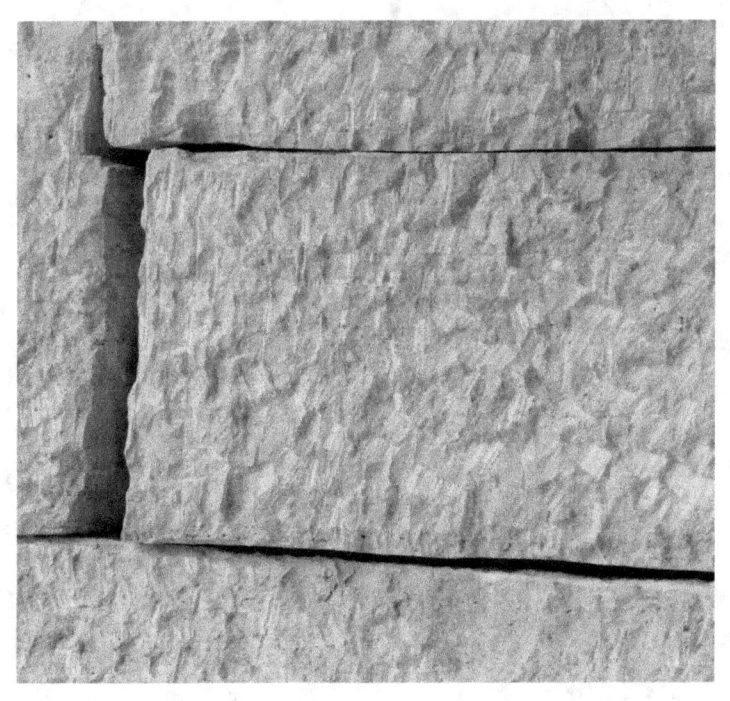

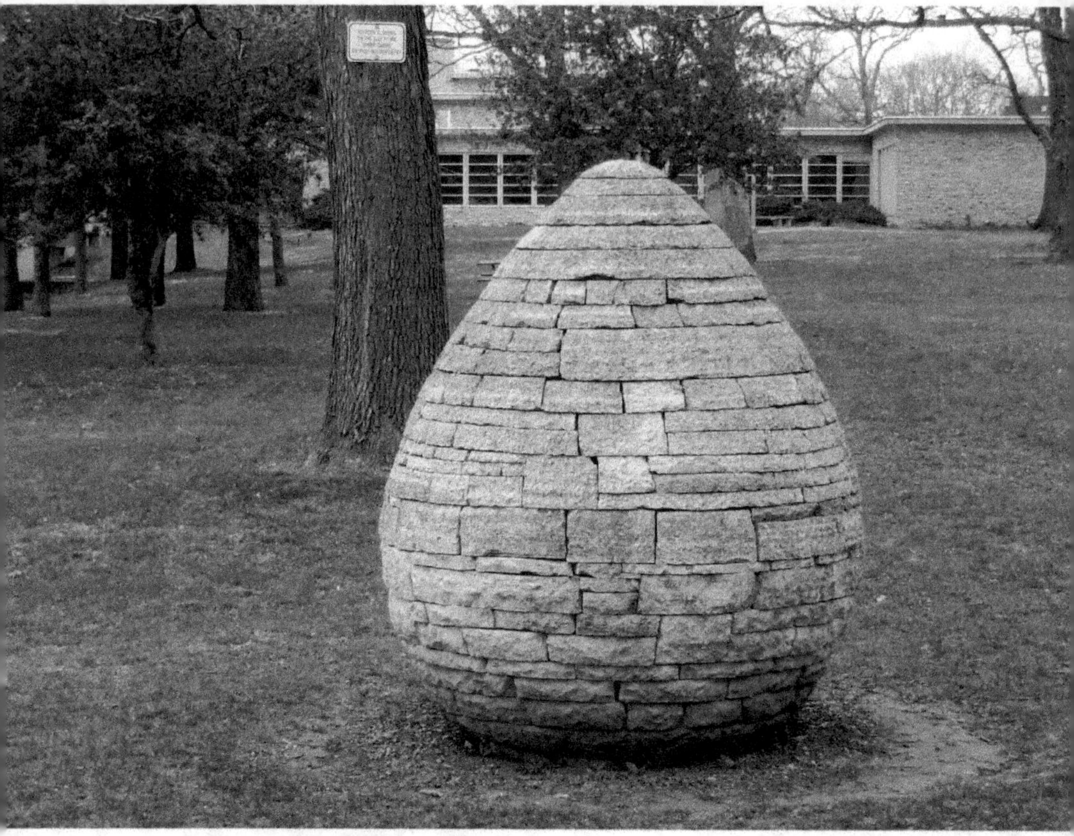

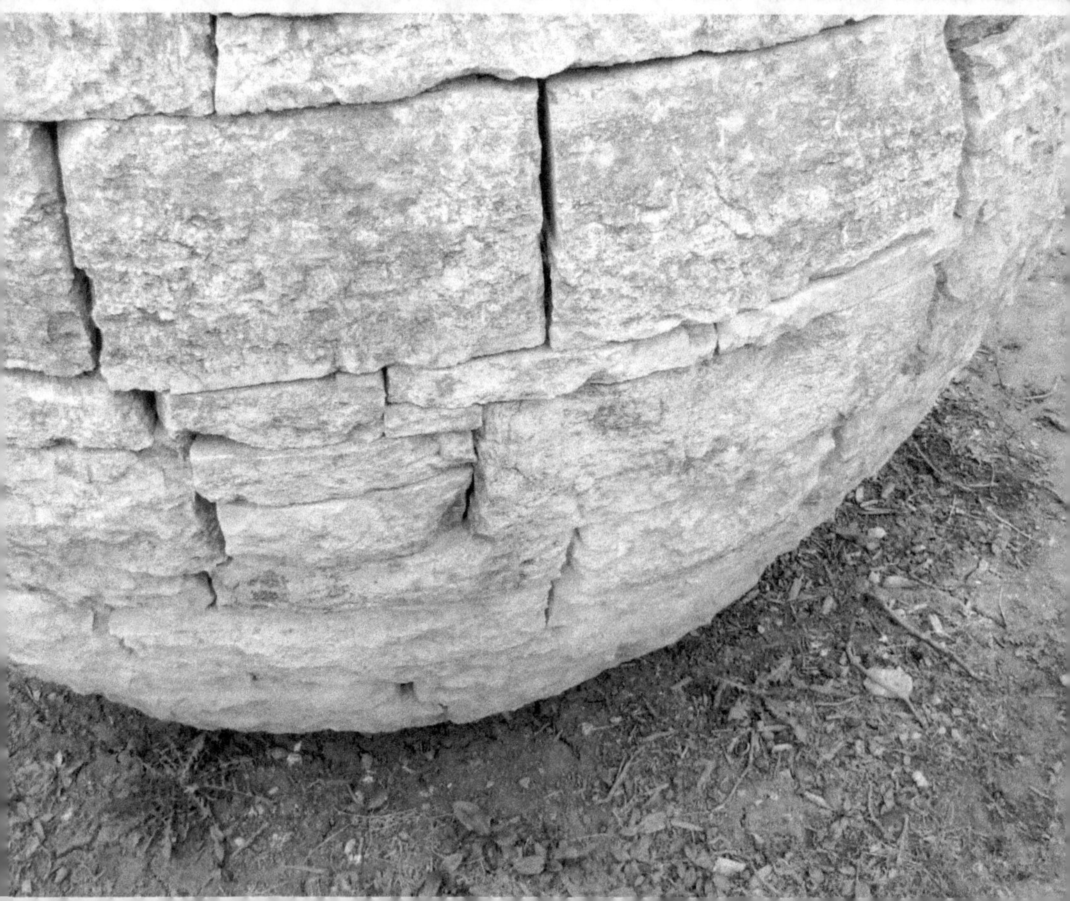

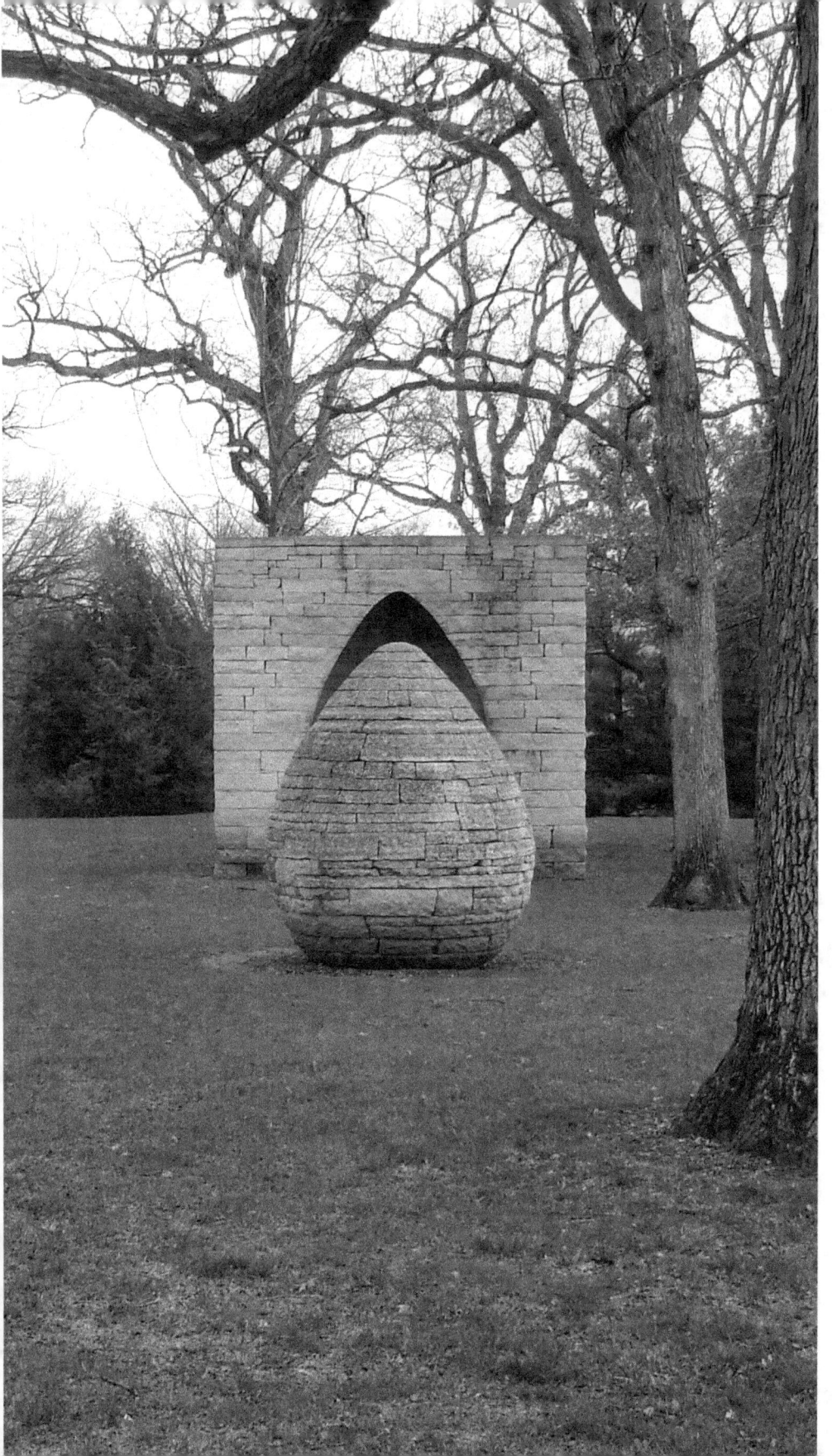

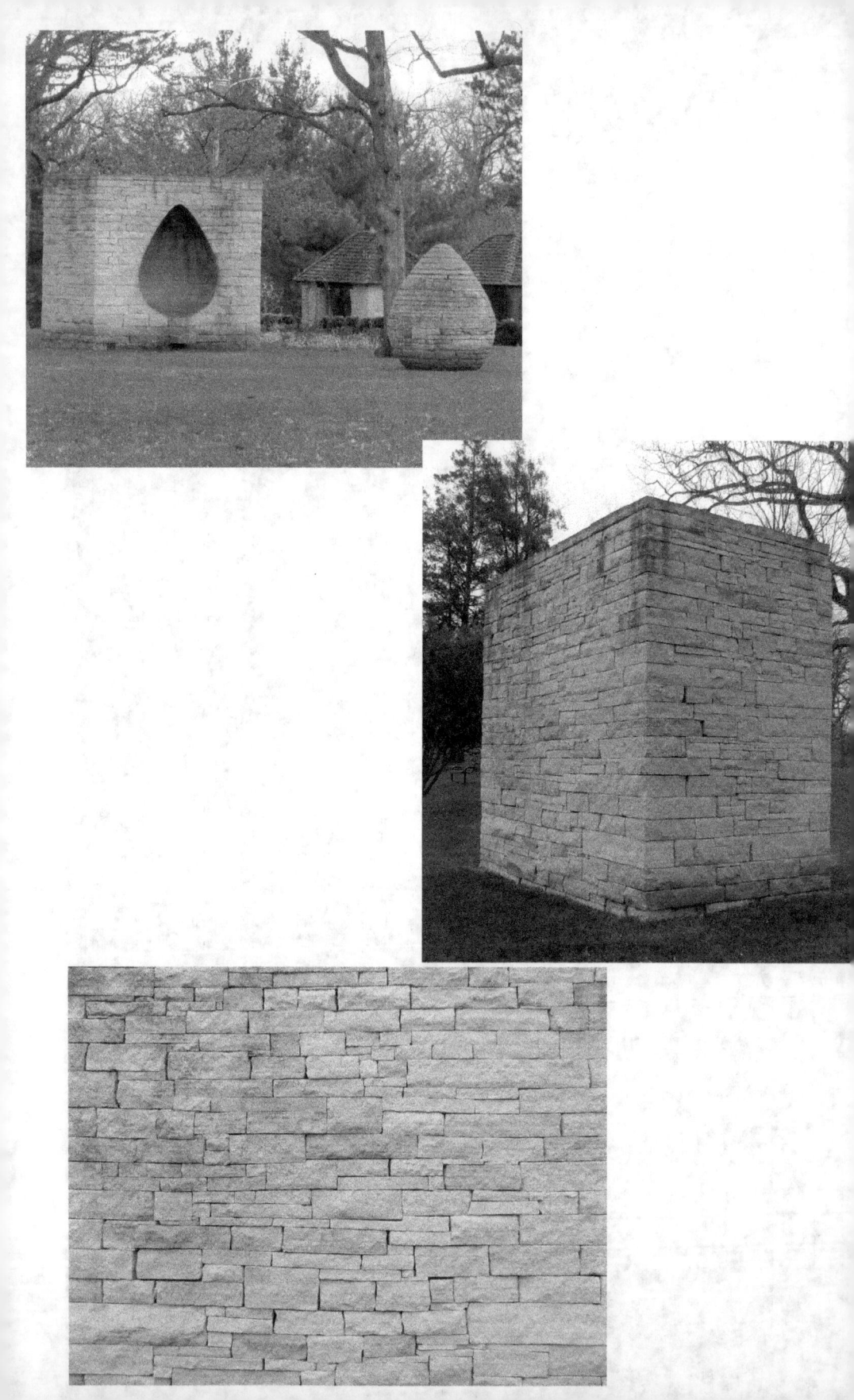

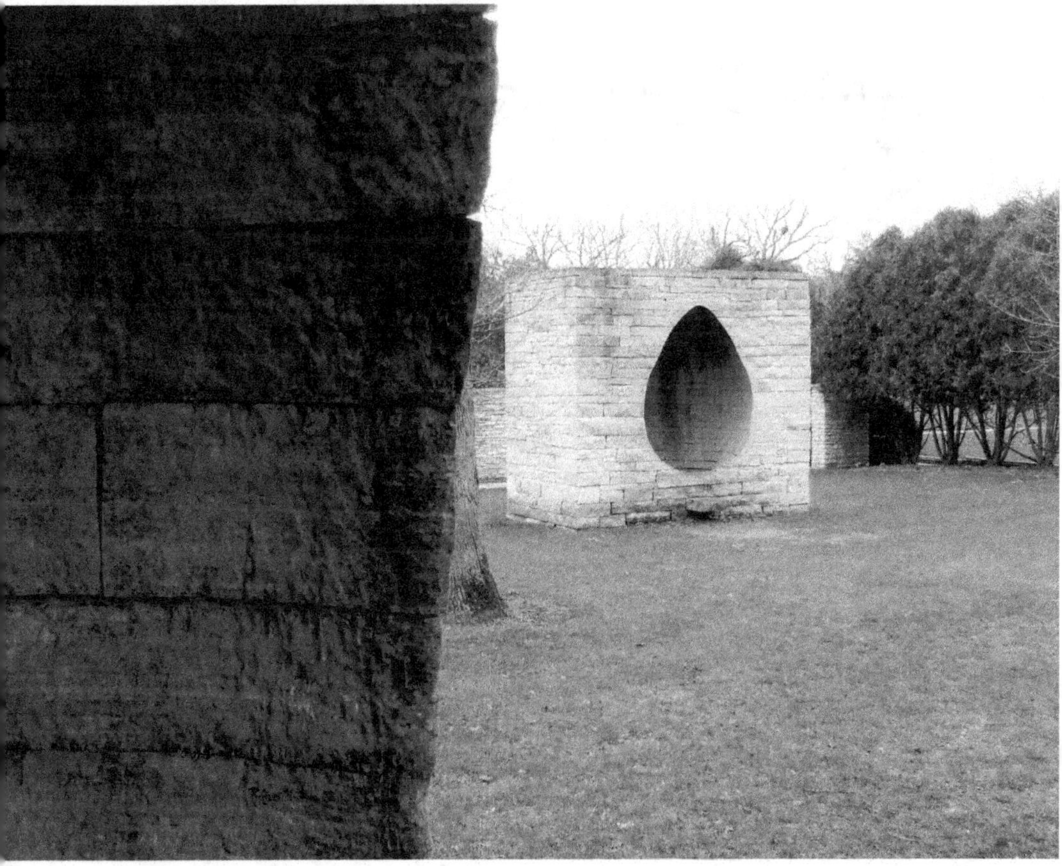

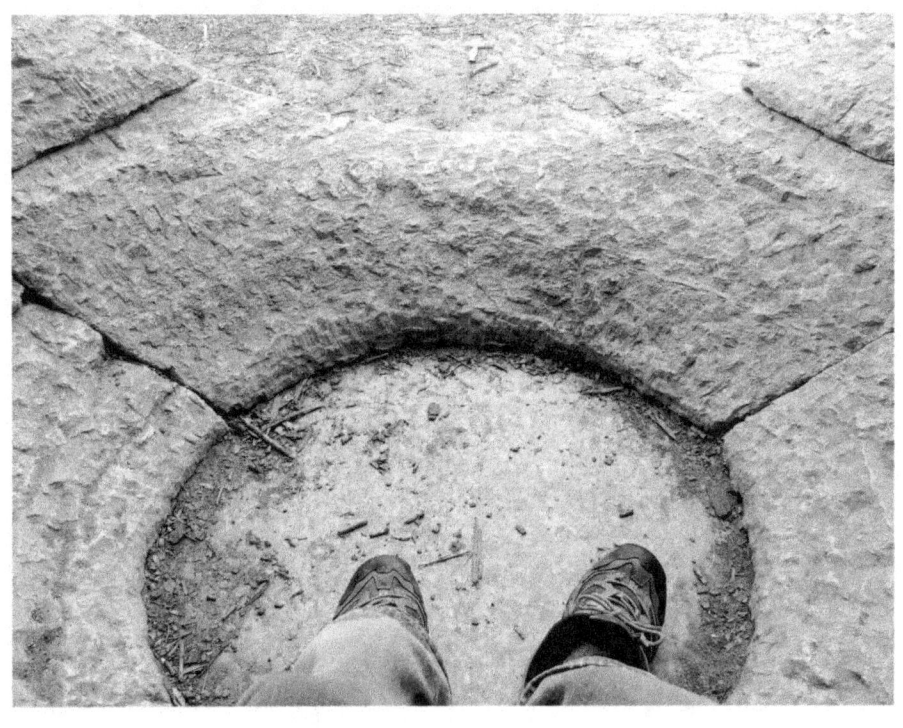

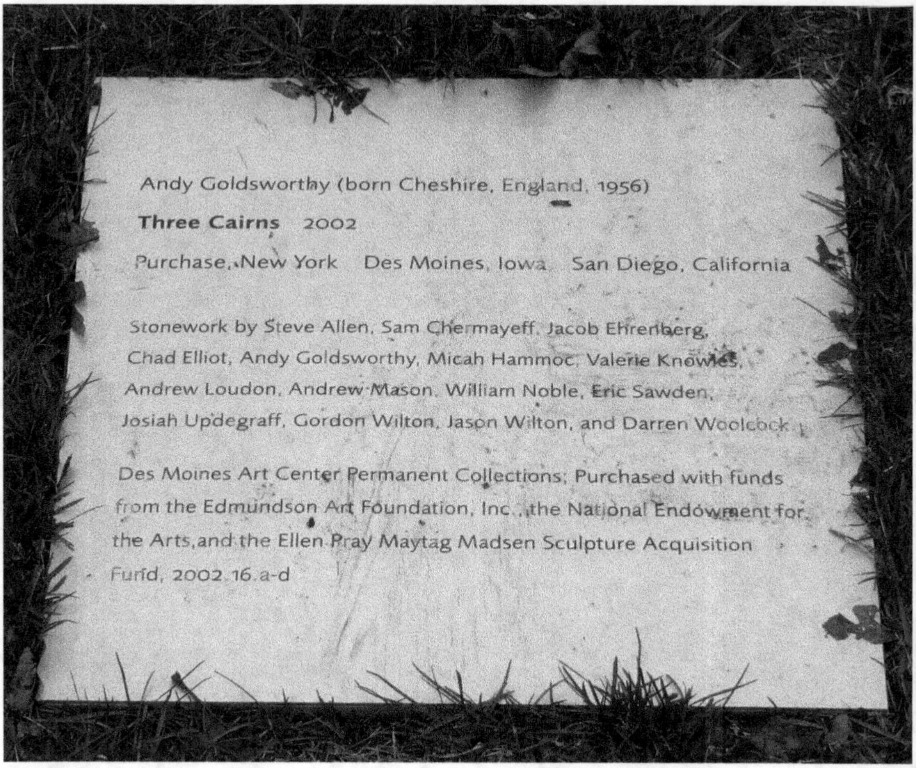

Andy Goldsworthy (born Cheshire, England, 1956)

Three Cairns   2002

Purchase, New York   Des Moines, Iowa   San Diego, California

Stonework by Steve Allen, Sam Chermayeff, Jacob Ehrenberg,
Chad Elliot, Andy Goldsworthy, Micah Hammoc, Valerie Knowles,
Andrew Loudon, Andrew Mason, William Noble, Eric Sawden,
Josiah Updegraff, Gordon Wilton, Jason Wilton, and Darren Woolcock

Des Moines Art Center Permanent Collections; Purchased with funds
from the Edmundson Art Foundation, Inc., the National Endowment for
the Arts, and the Ellen Pray Maytag Madsen Sculpture Acquisition
Fund, 2002.16.a-d

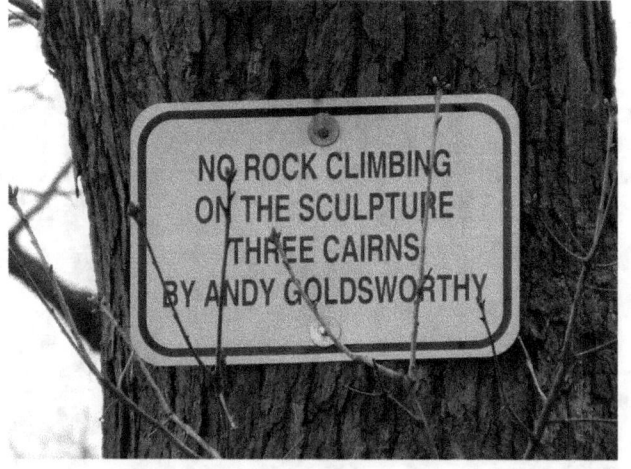

NO ROCK CLIMBING
ON THE SCULPTURE
THREE CAIRNS
BY ANDY GOLDSWORTHY

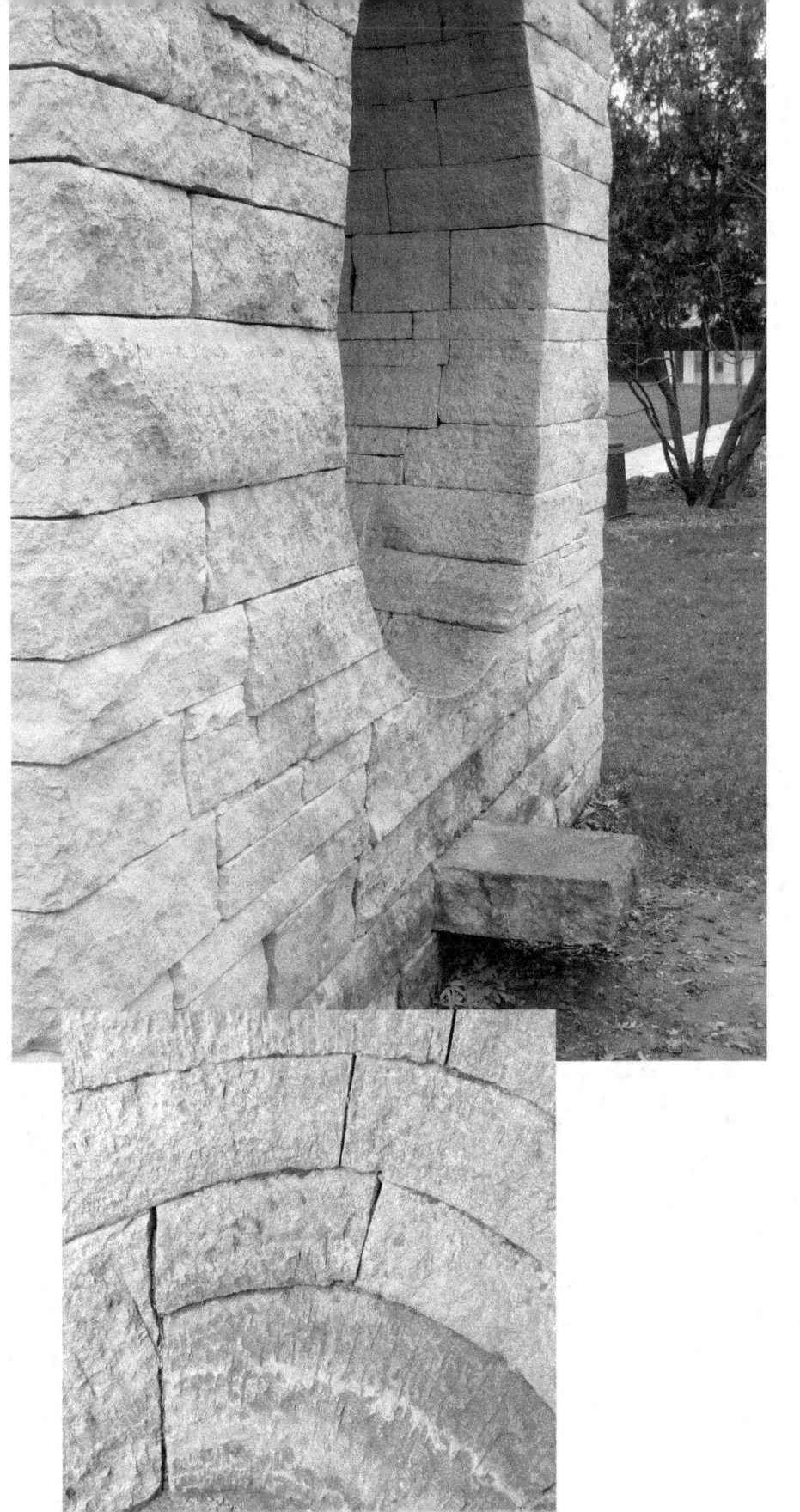

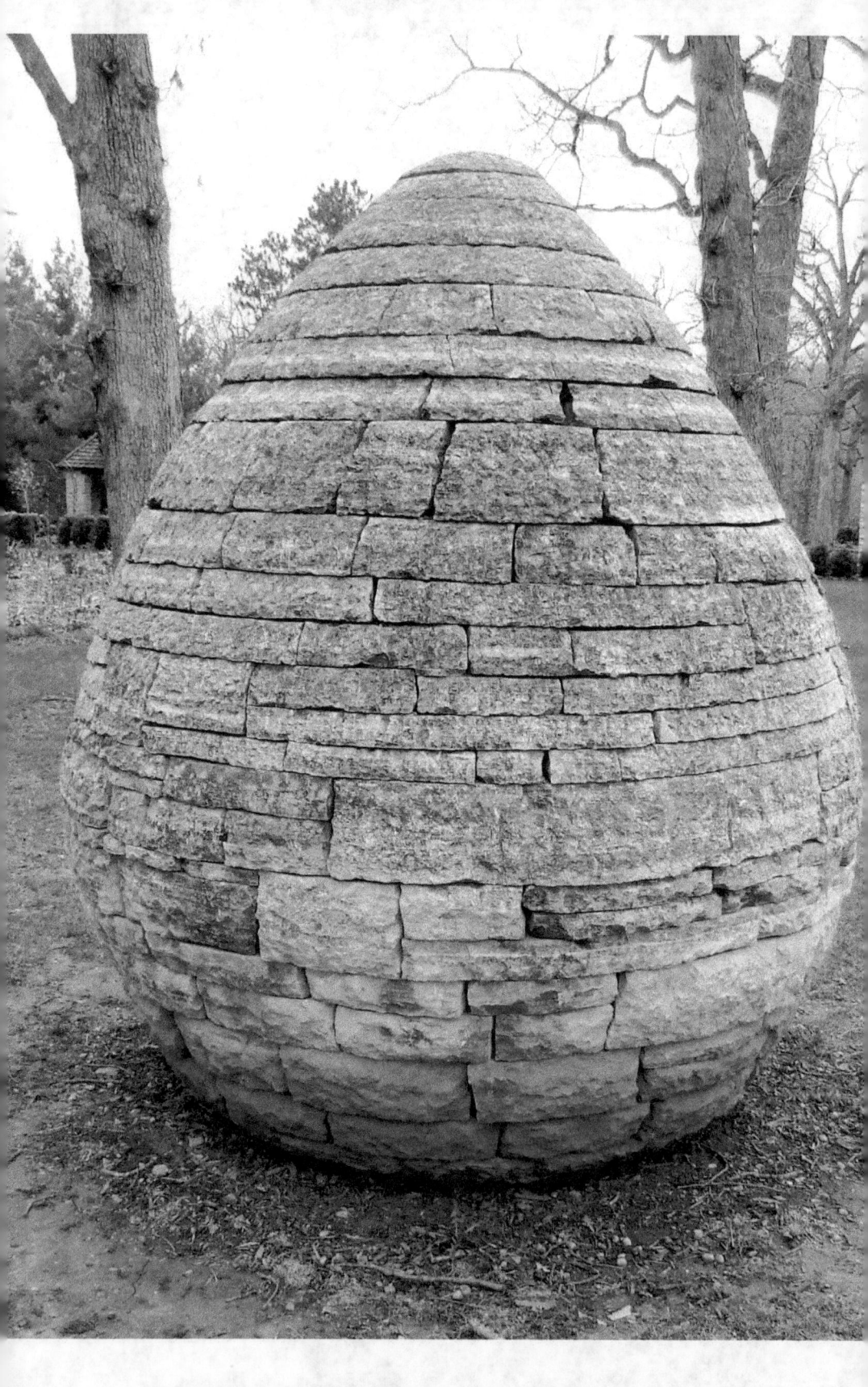

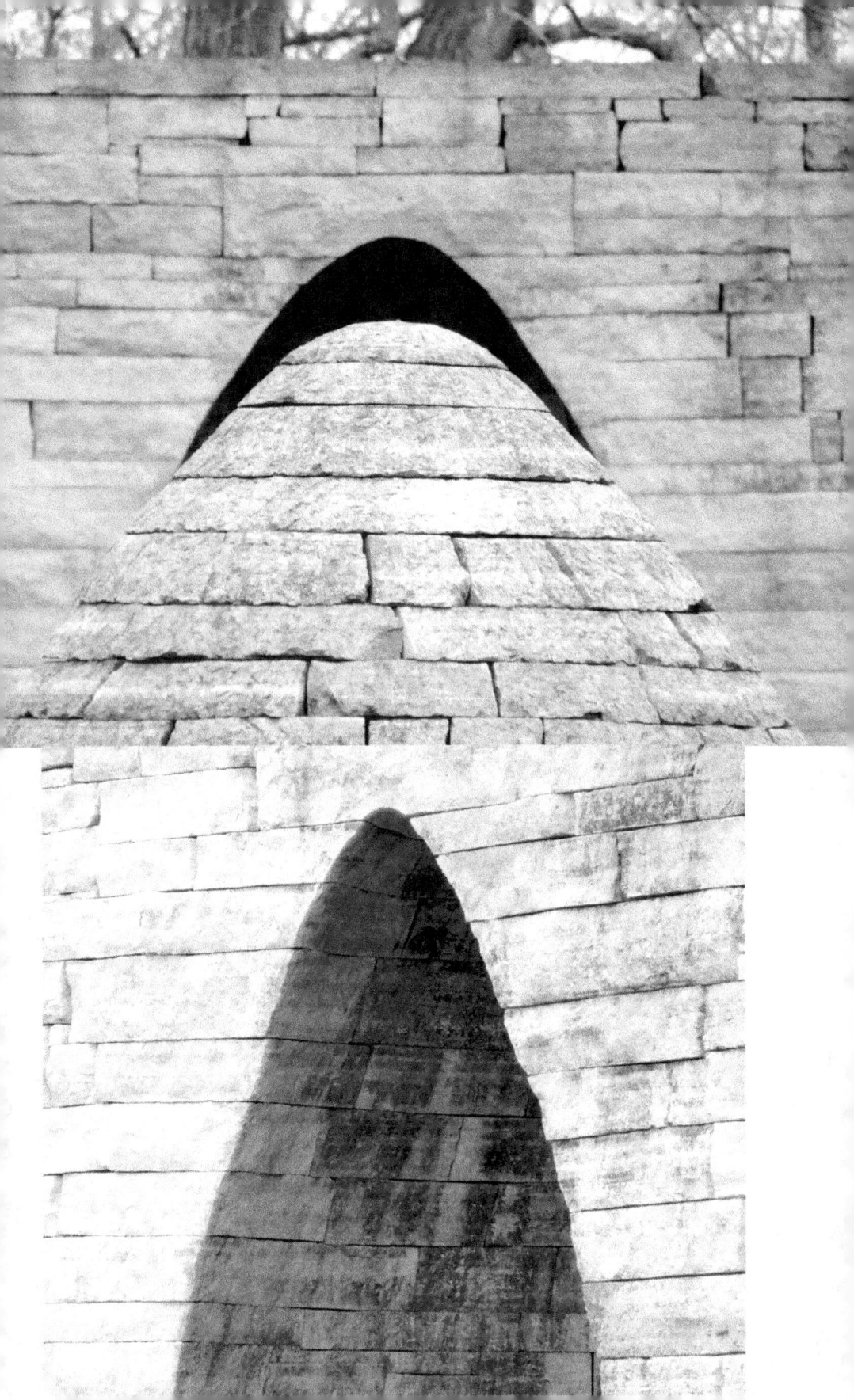

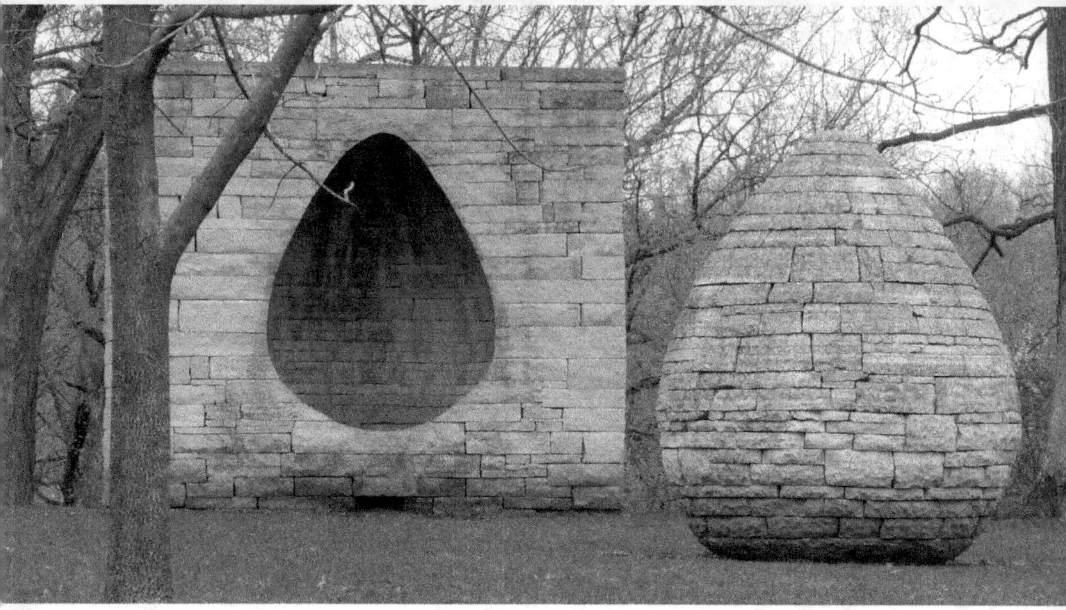

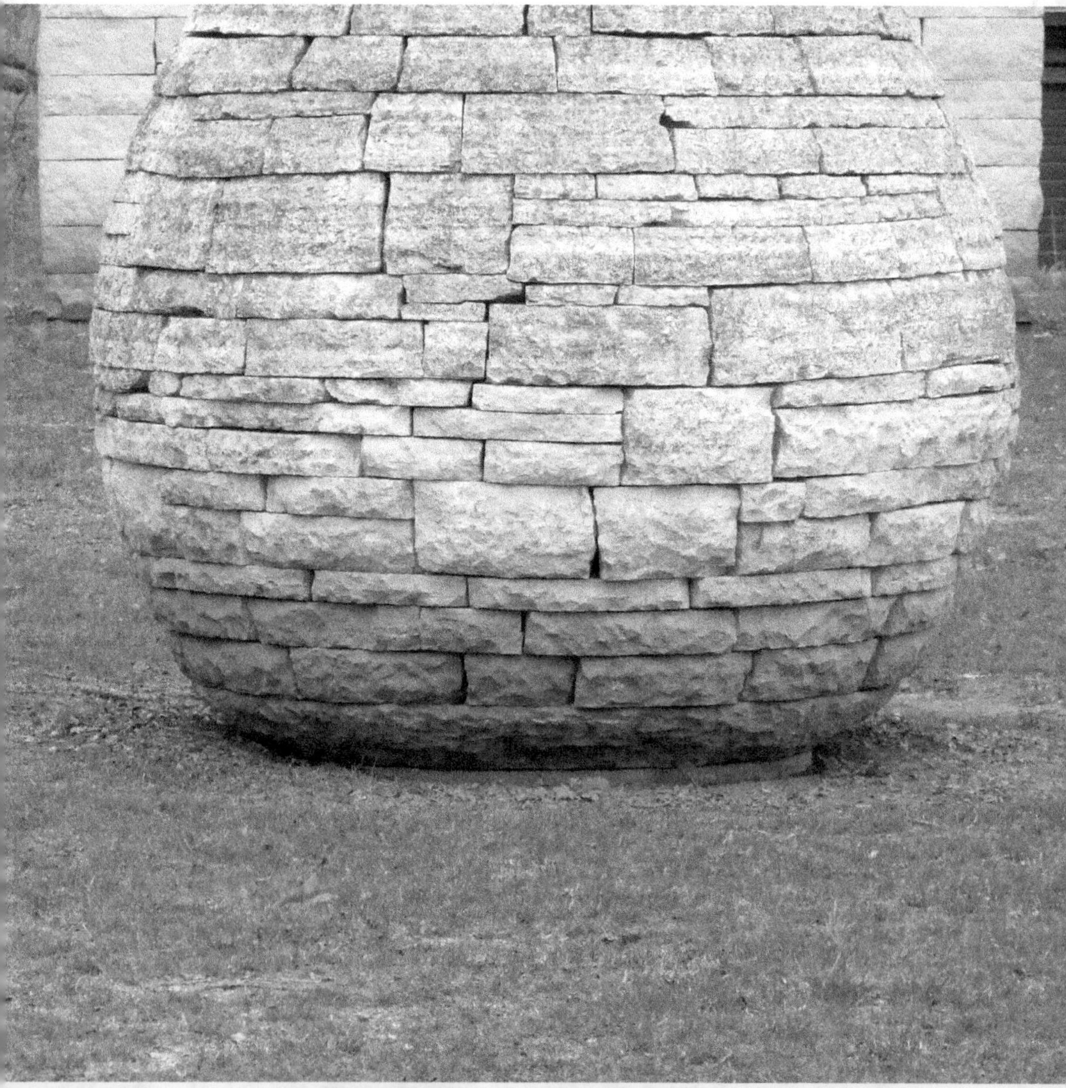

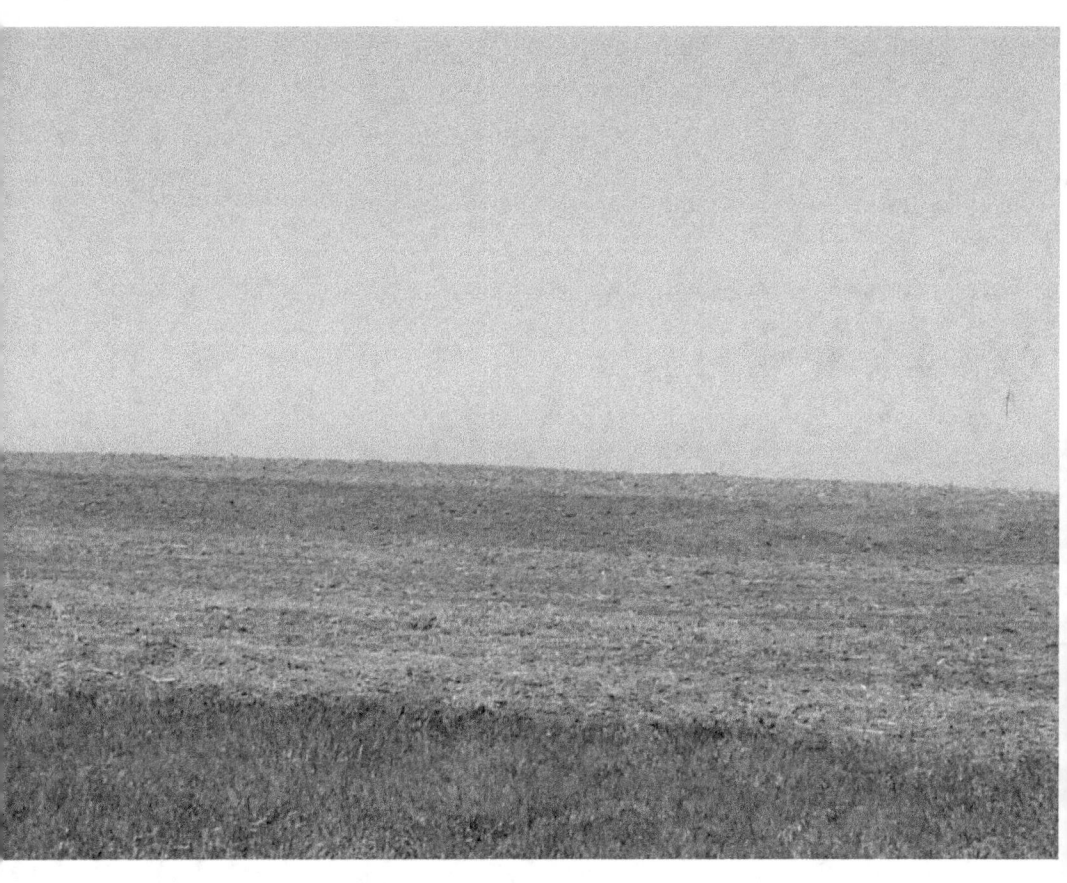

The Iowa prairie, off I-80, near Des Moines

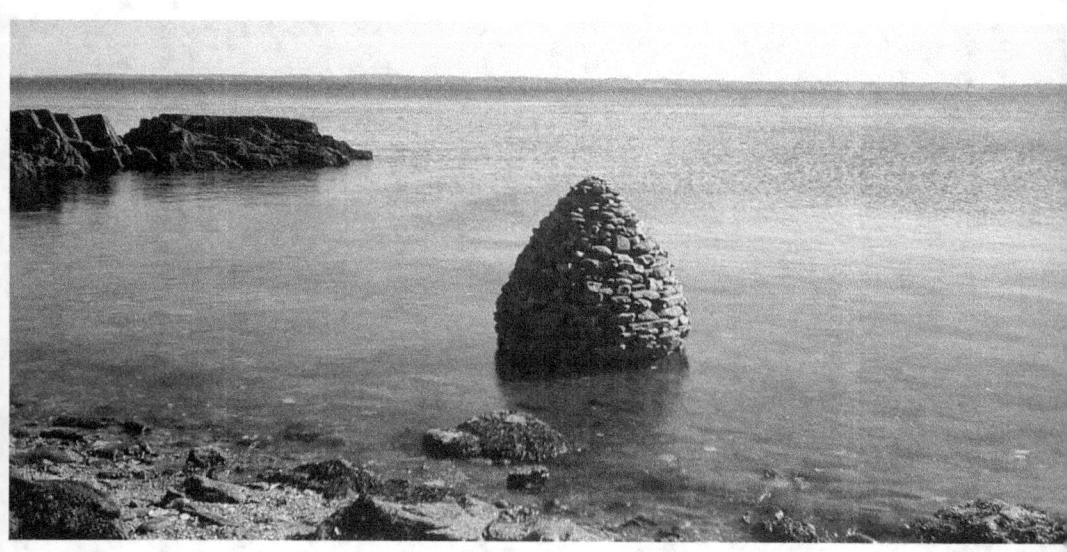

Andy Goldsworthy, Tidal Cairn

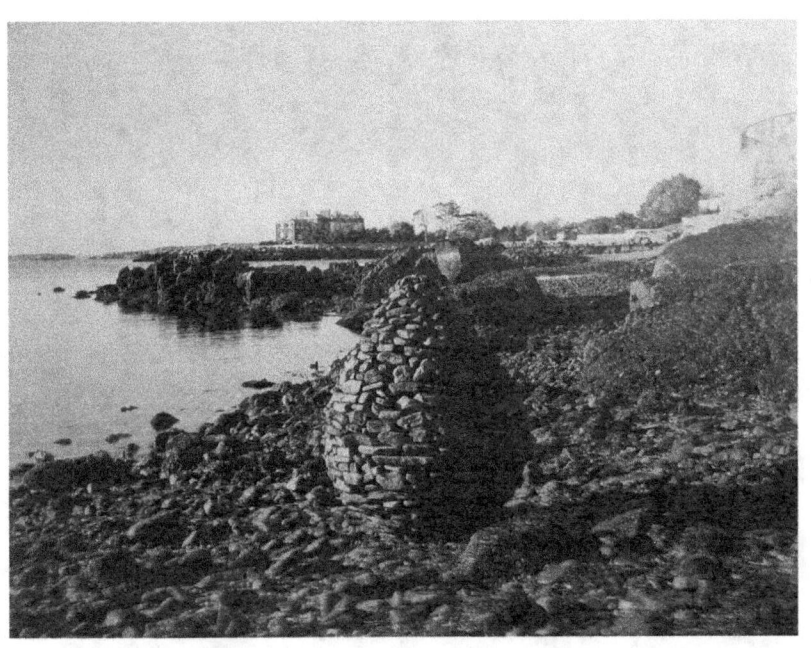

Andy Goldsworthy, East Coast Sea Cairn, New York, 2001

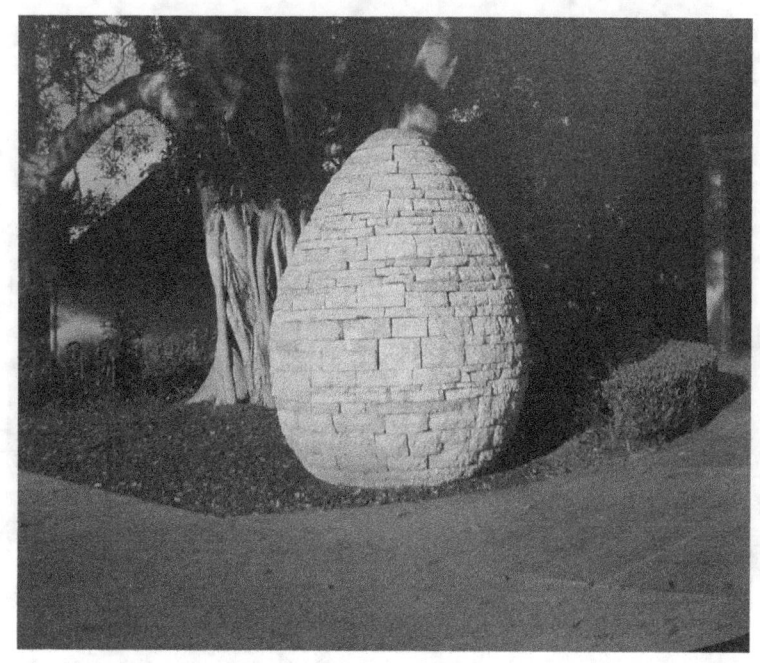

Andy Goldsworthy, West Coast Cairn, San Diego, 2002

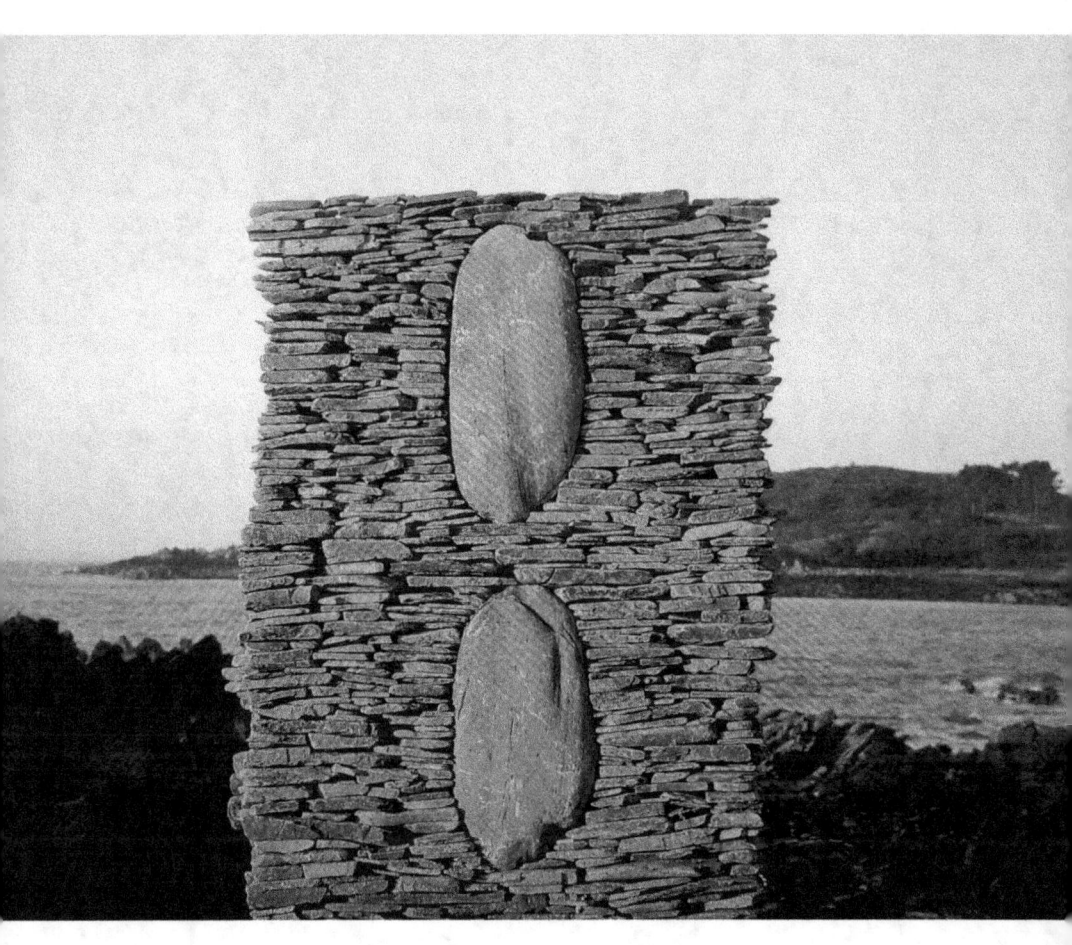

Andy Goldsworthy, Stone Stack, 1996

15

DRAWN STONE, SAN FRANCISCO

In San Francisco, Andy Goldsworthy was invited to participate in the re-opening of the M.H. de Young Museum (part of the Museum of Fine Arts) in 2005 by creating a site installation. A number of other artists were also asked to contribute to the re-launch of this major museum in San Francisco's Golden Gate Park, including James Turrell.

The de Young Museum was founded in 1895, in a beautiful part of San Francisco. The Golden Gate Park also houses the Japanese Tea Garden, the Strybing Arboretum and Botanical Gardens, a golf course, lakes, and a stadium. It's a big park of joggers, sports, strollers, kids playing. At the end is the enormous expanse of Ocean Beach.

Goldsworthy designed a series of stones which would have a crack running through them and through the paving stones they stood upon, in the forecourt and outside the entrance to the refurbished museum.

Entitled *Drawn Stone* (2005), it is an impressive, large-scale install-ation. Inevitably, given California's geological situation and the many earthquakes that have occurred there, some viewers linked the cracked line to tectonic plates.

The boulders (8 stones from Yorkshire in England – they were Appleton Greenmoore stone) are flattish, and are spaced throughout the irregular-shaped entrance area. They are about 18 inches to two feet high, and serve as benches for visitors. (That's significant – that this is a Goldsworthy sculpture that the public is invited to touch and sit on).

The affinities of *Drawn Stone* with works such as *Garden of Stone* are immediately apparent: the sculpture is a group of individual objects arranged to form a group, which are all set on the ground. Each stone is left irregular, but their placement within the group is clearly carefully worked out.

Placing Goldsworthy's sculpture outside the entrance to the de Young Museum has them act as an intermediary and lead-in to the museum itself: *Drawn Stone* is thus both an indoor and outdoor sculpture, part of the museum but also situated just outside it. It's the same with *Roof* in Washington: those domes are obviously part of the National Gallery of Art, yet they are also placed outside the walls of America's premier museum.

When you visit the de Young Museum, you can follow the crack in the paving and the boulders that Goldsworthy and his team produced, and no doubt people do just that. It begins, actually, outside the museum, and there's a bit of info explaining the work. The crack leads from that spot on the path and takes the visitor into the entrance area and the boulders themselves.

Again, that is something that Goldsworthy often does in his permanent sculptures: he likes to create trails or journeys for people visiting his art. So the visitor to Storm King Art Center is encouraged to follow the *Wall* down the slope, to the lake. And in earlier works such as *Lambton Earthwork* in Durham, the visitor can walk along earth embankments in Goldsworthy's customary snake shape. Then there's the *Chalk Trail*, and so on.

Goldsworthy doesn't insist on the trail or journey every time in his art – you could stand back from the *Storm King Wall* and admire it from a distance. But some of his sculptures, such as *Chalk Trail*, strongly suggest it. Indeed, you can only get the full effect of *Chalk Trail* if you do explore the path. And you'd be missing some important elements of the *Storm King Wall* if you only view it from far away.

With other Goldsworthy sculptures in the United States, however, you are not allowed to wander around the piece, as with *Roof* i n Washington. And with *Garden of Stones*, the view from the third floor is so spectacular, that would probably be enough for some people, and they wouldn't need to descend a floor and wander in amongst the stones.

Goldsworthy is not thought of usually as an artist who makes artworks that the public can participate in, but he does it more often than one might think. He wants visitors to be able to wander in amongst some of his works, while others, such as the cairns of wood and stone, are too potentially fragile to sustain that. It would take a lot of wear and tear from visitors, though, to substantially alter *Cracked Stone* – those boulders are pretty solid and durable.

Spire (2008) was not related to the de Young Museum commission: it was a 100-foot tall tower built from trees in the Presidio area of San Francisco. Not the easiest place to find (the Presidio, a former military zone, is a large maze of small streets), it's best to aim for the golf course HQ. The *Spire*'s nearby, along a path. Definitely worth a visit, though.

The cracked line that Andy Goldsworthy created at the M.H. de Young Museum in California in 2005 was photographed in March, 2008 and April 2010.

I have also included pictures of the setting of the wonderful de Young Museum in Golden Gate Park, as well as some of the artists featured there, such as James Turrell and his *Skyspace Three Gems.*

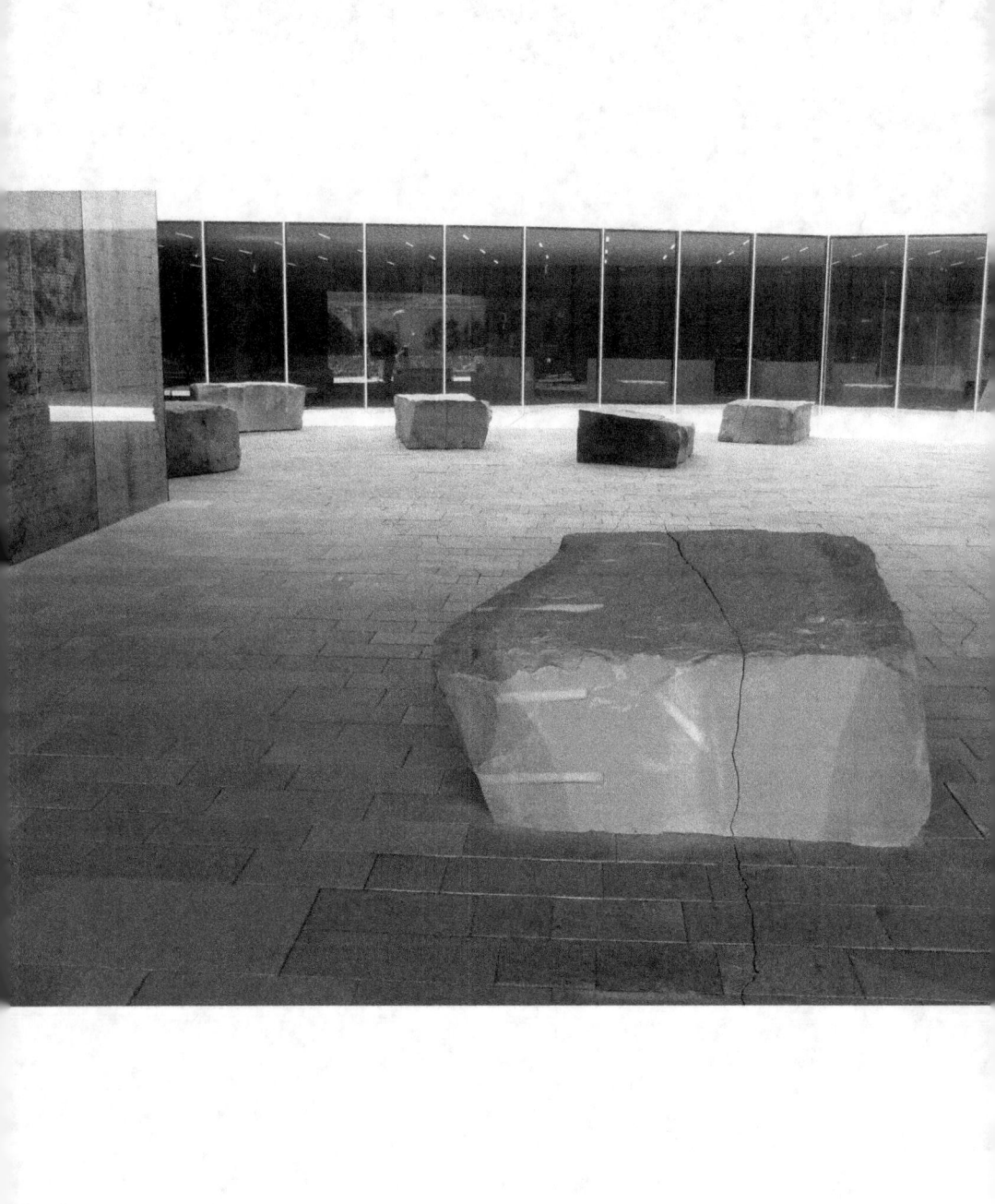

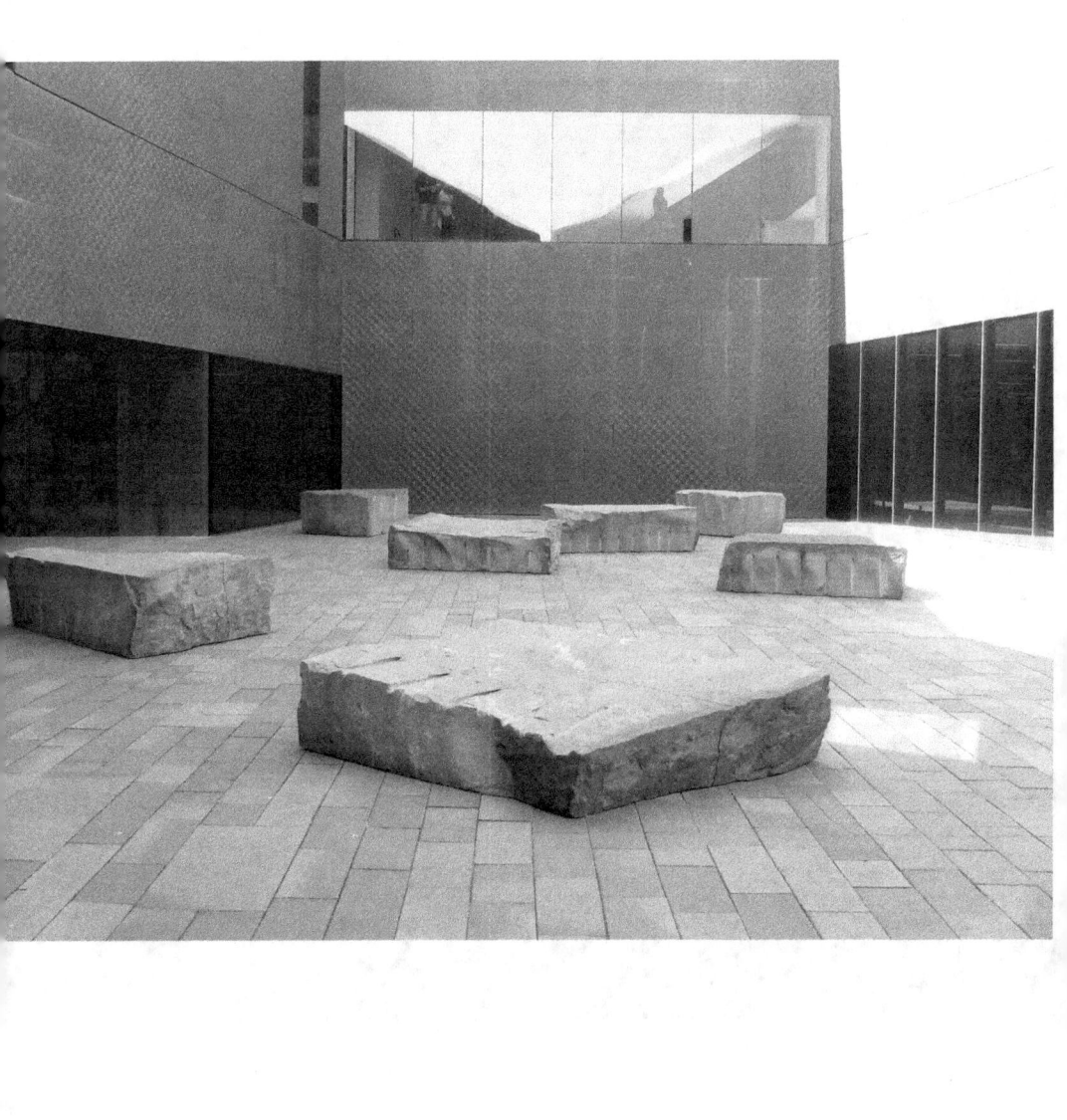

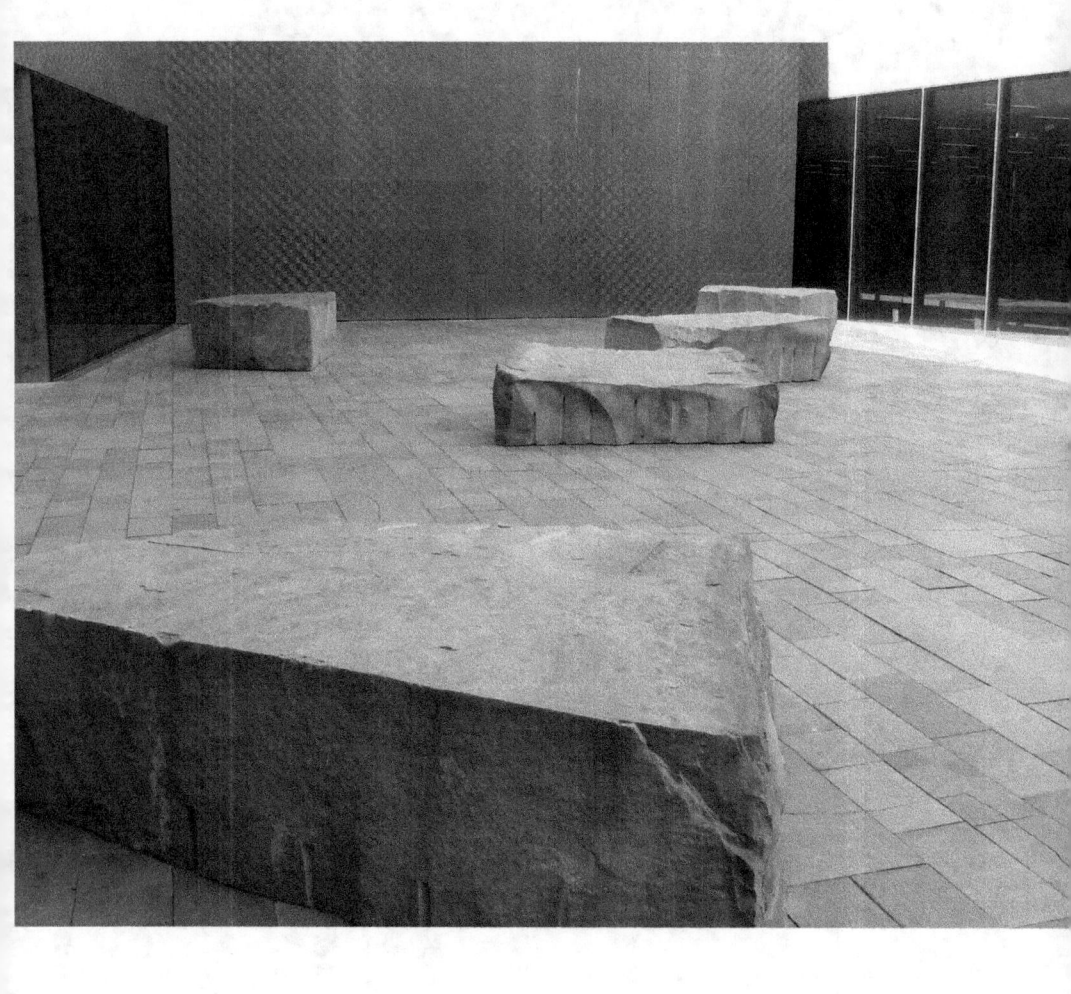

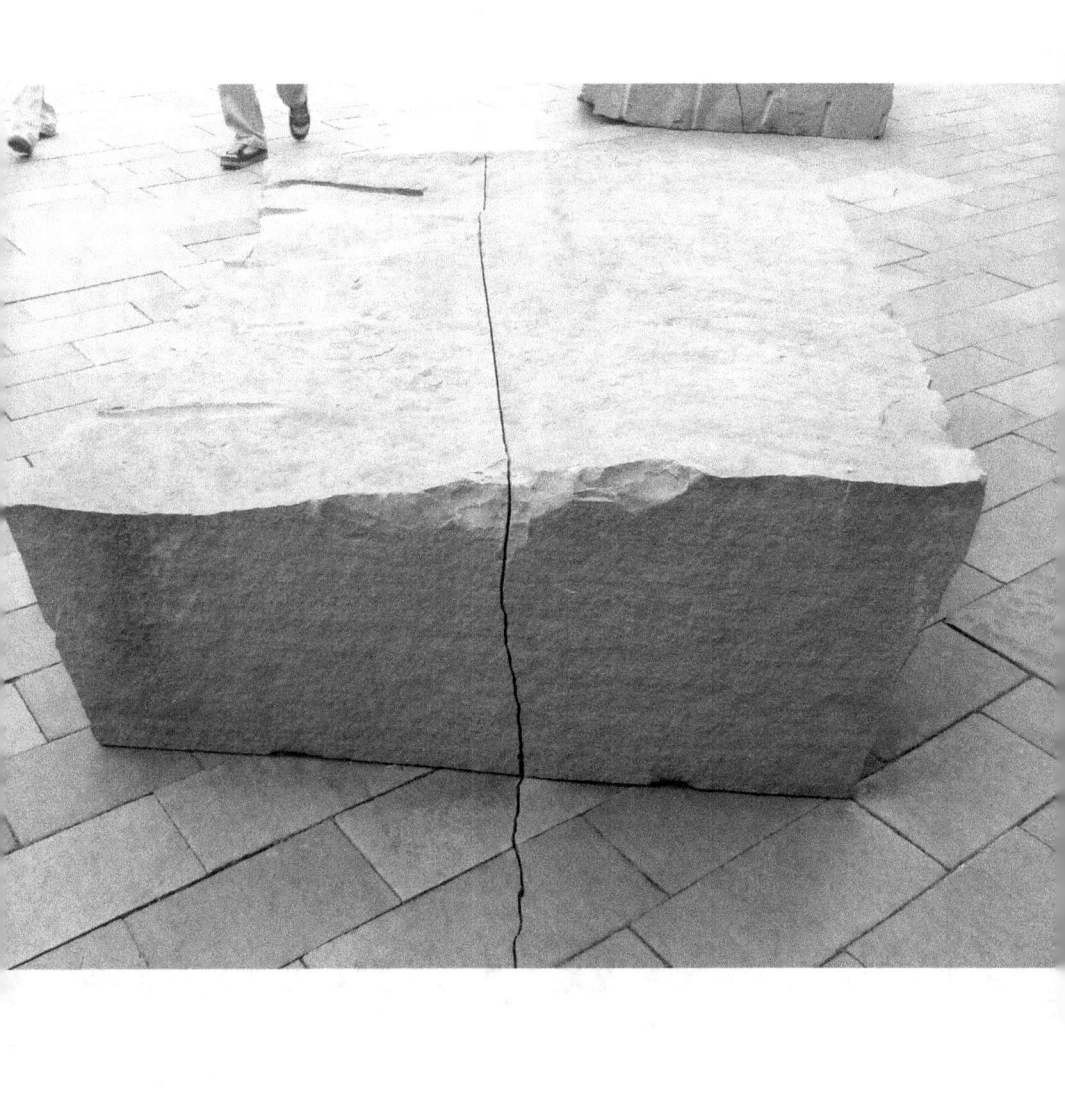

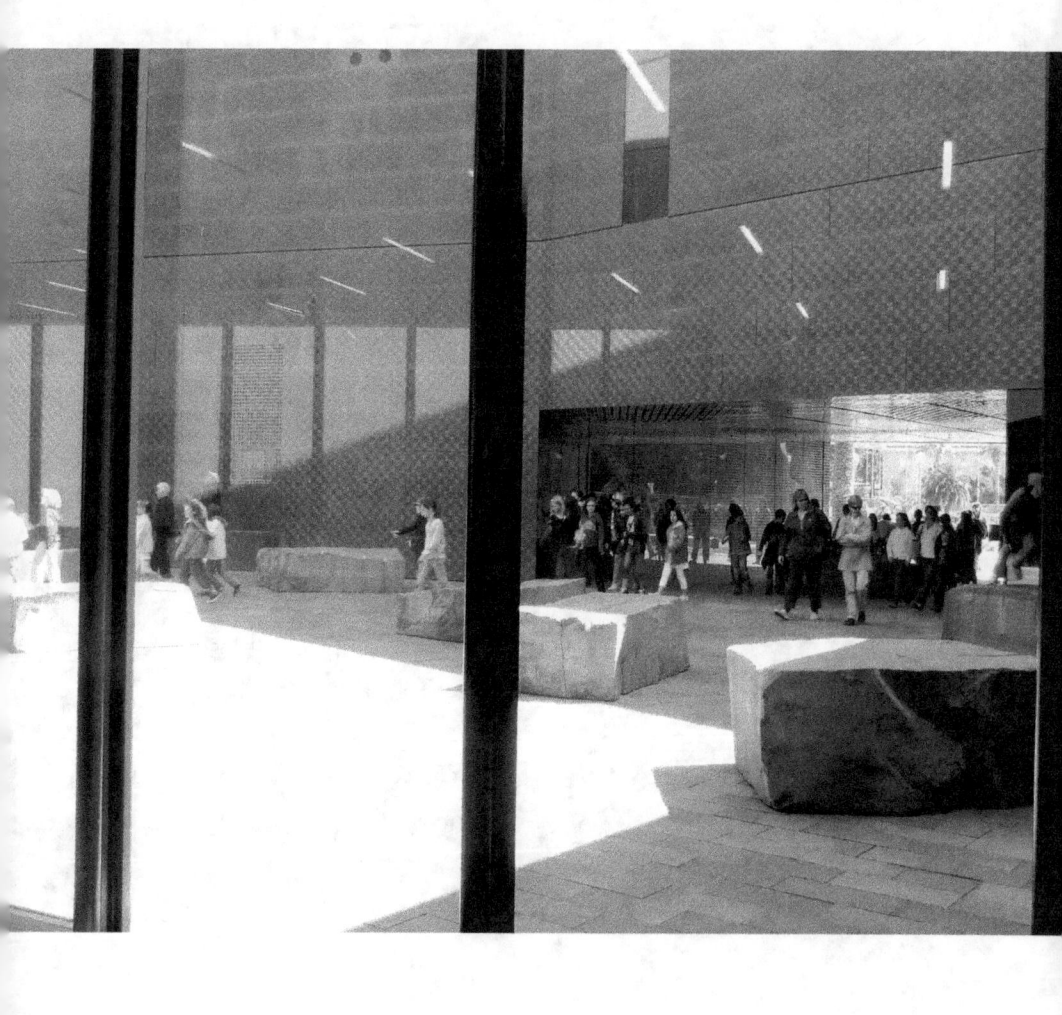

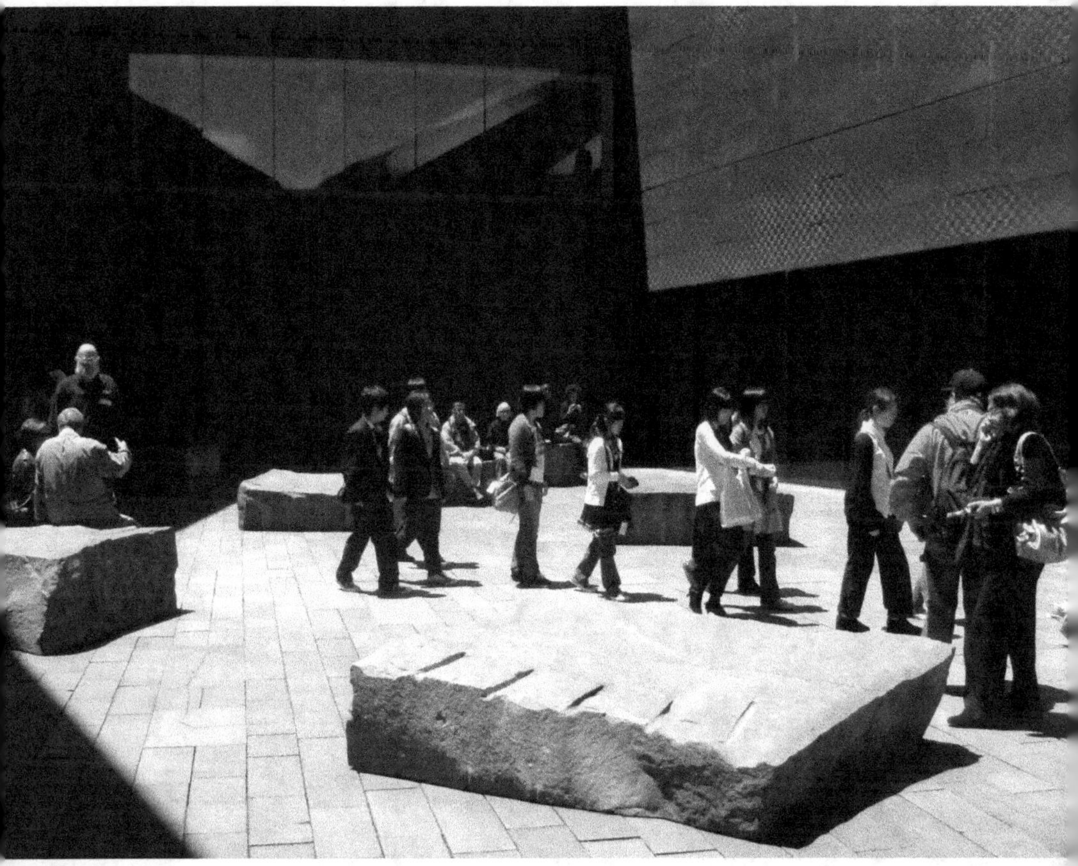

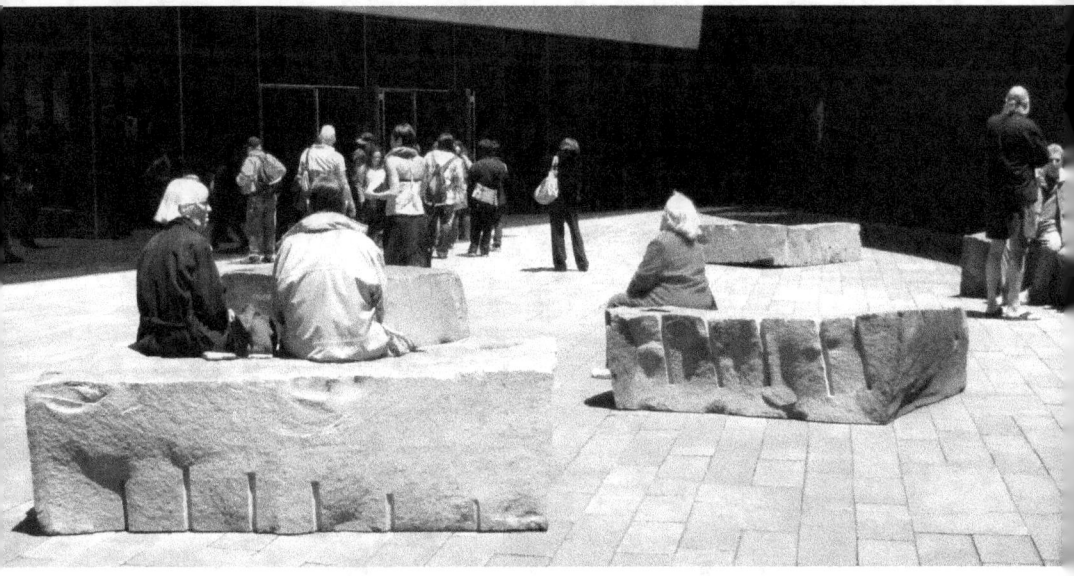

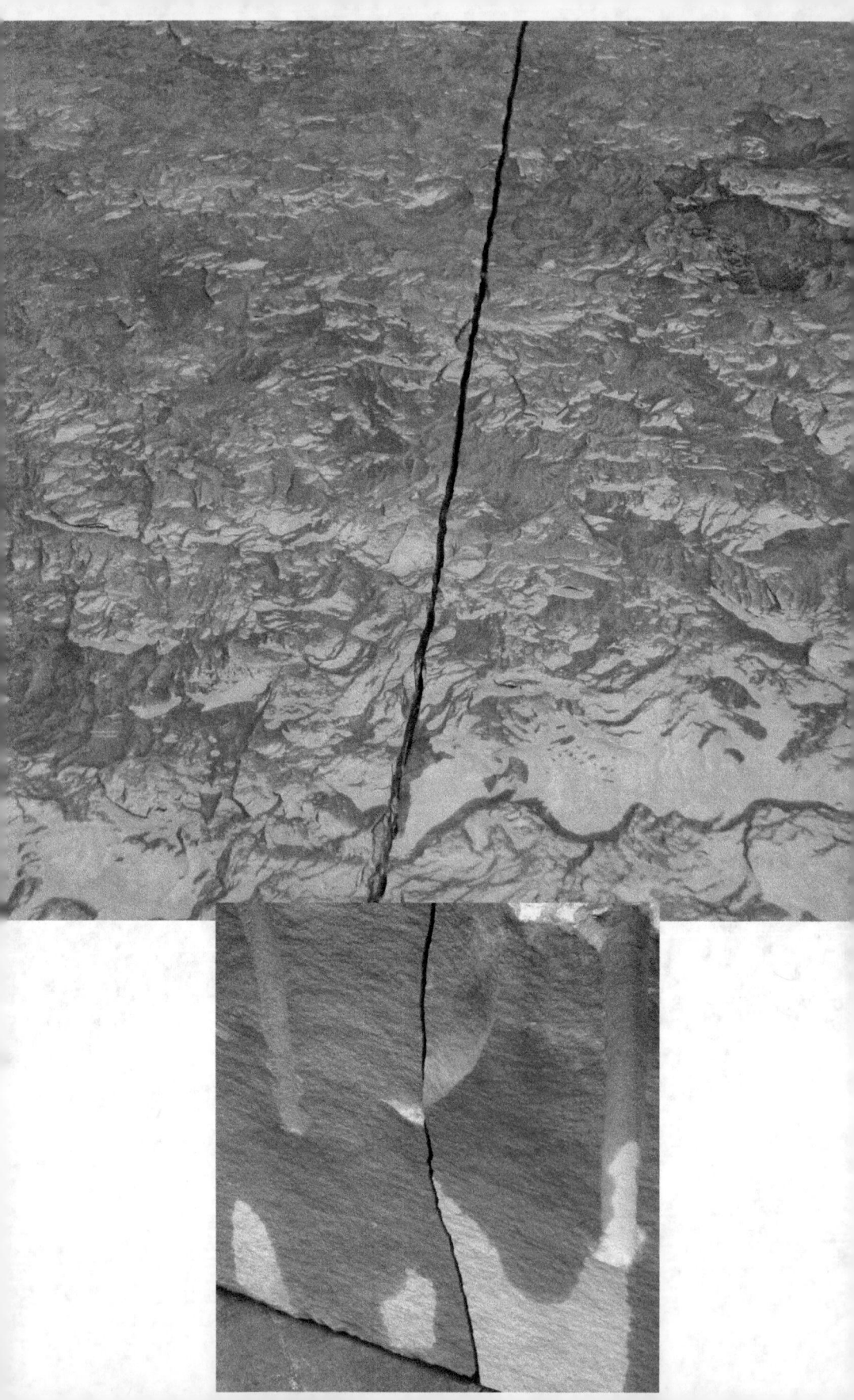

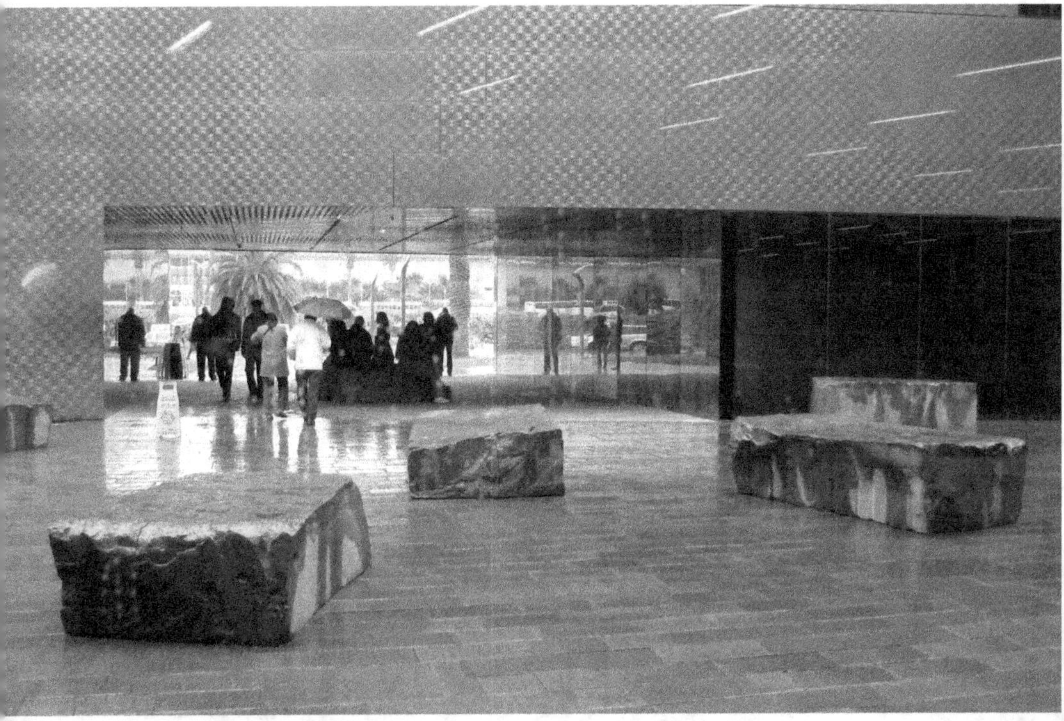

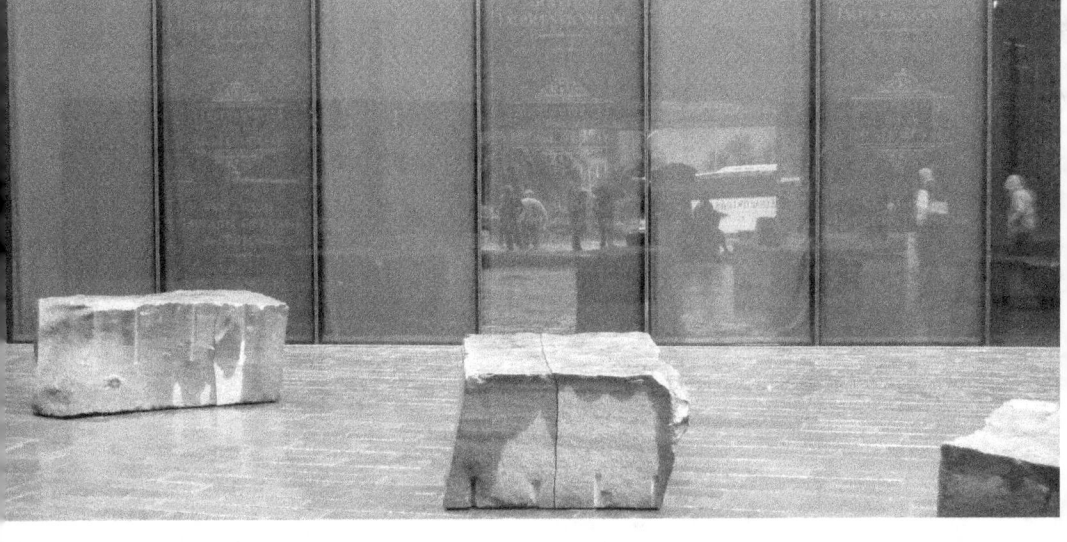

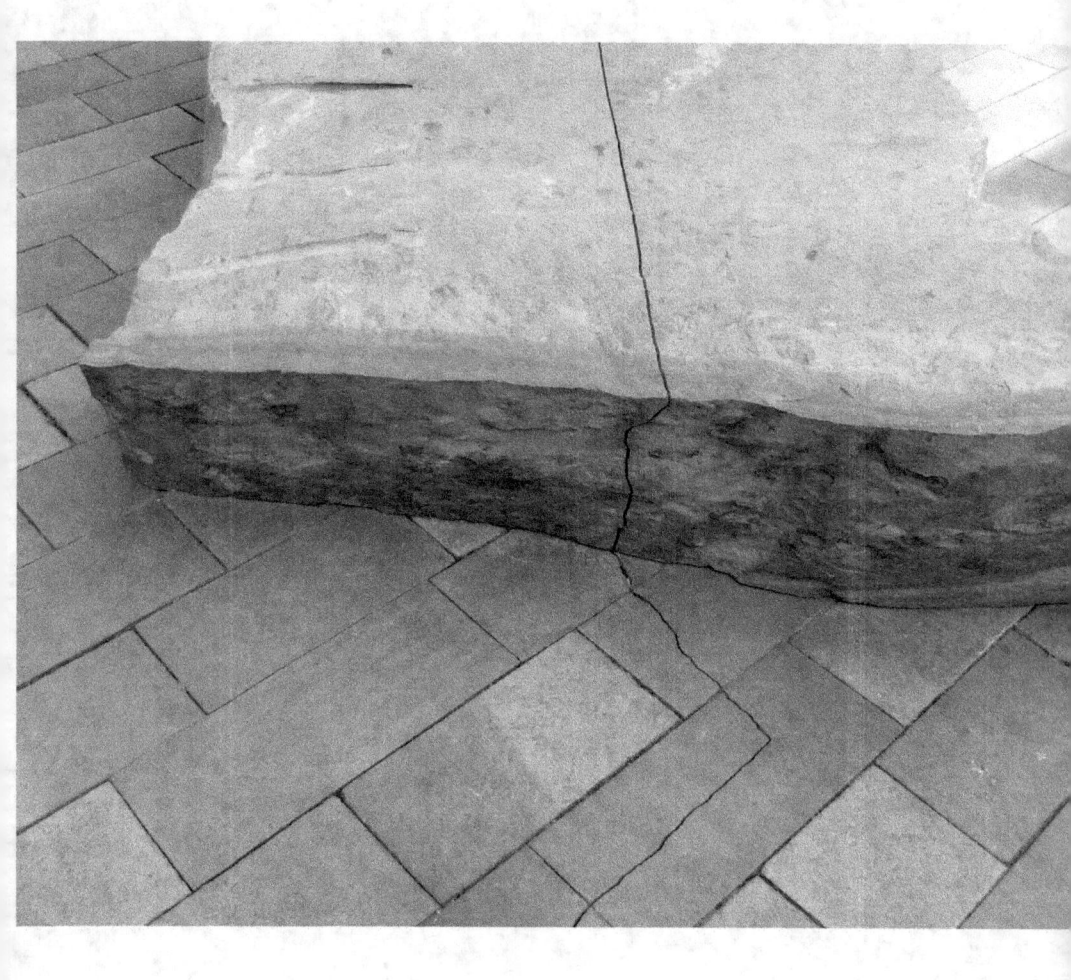

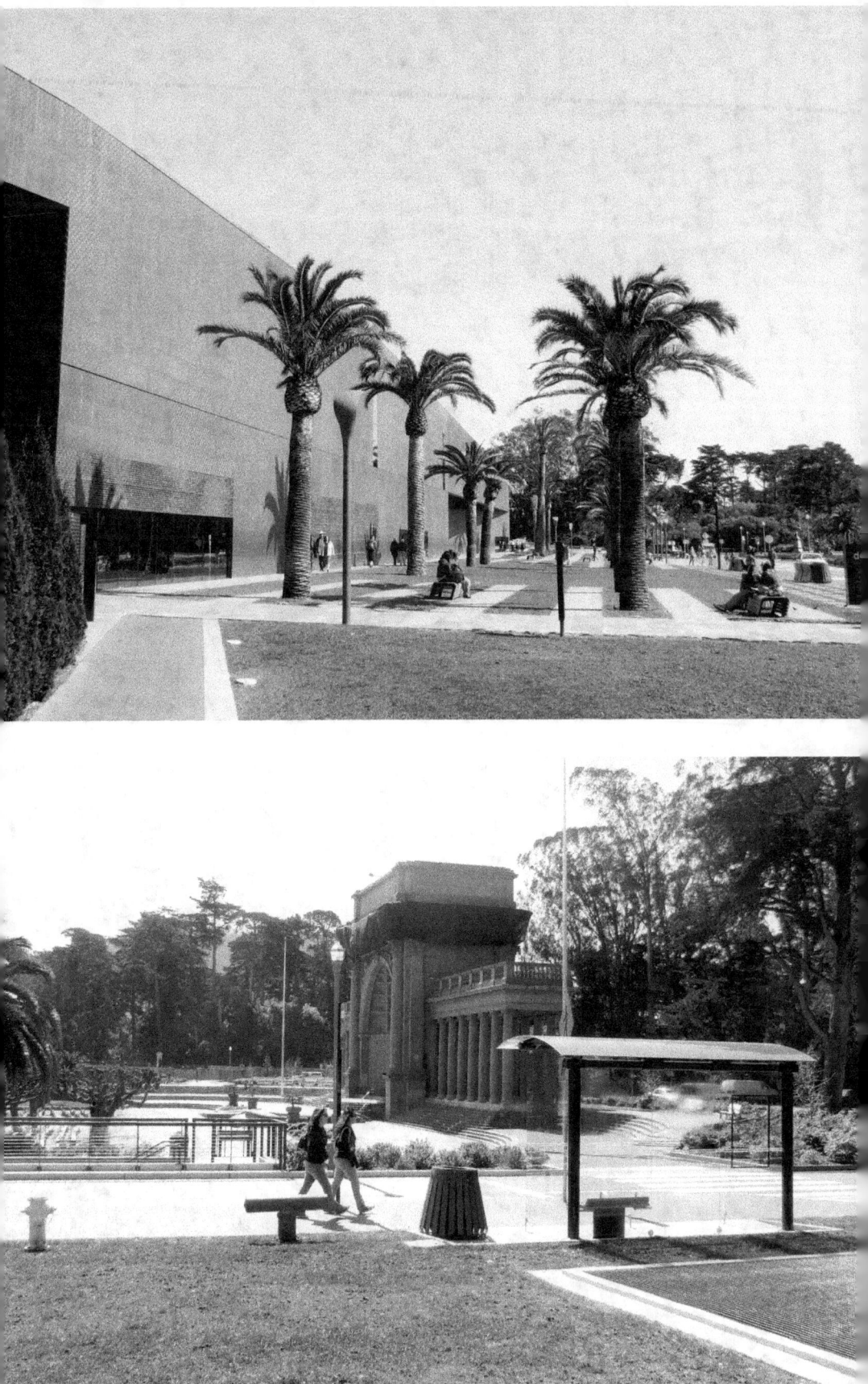

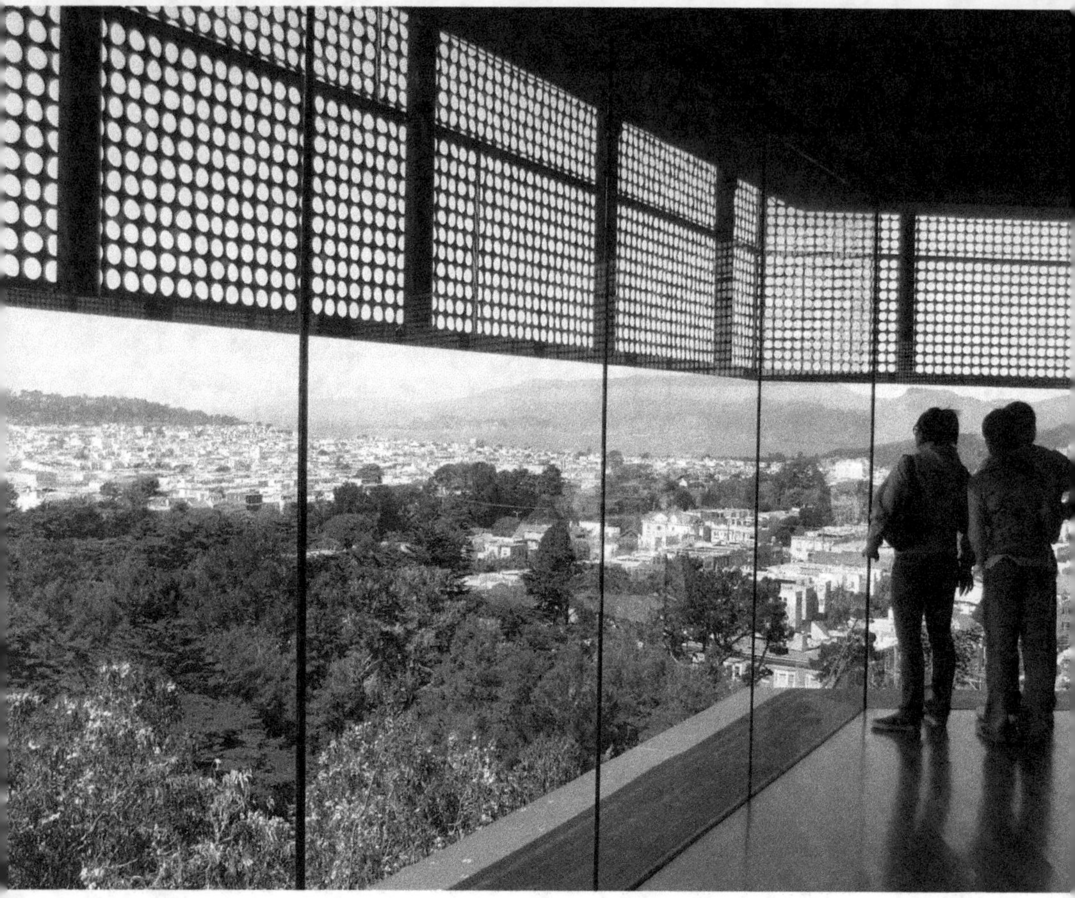

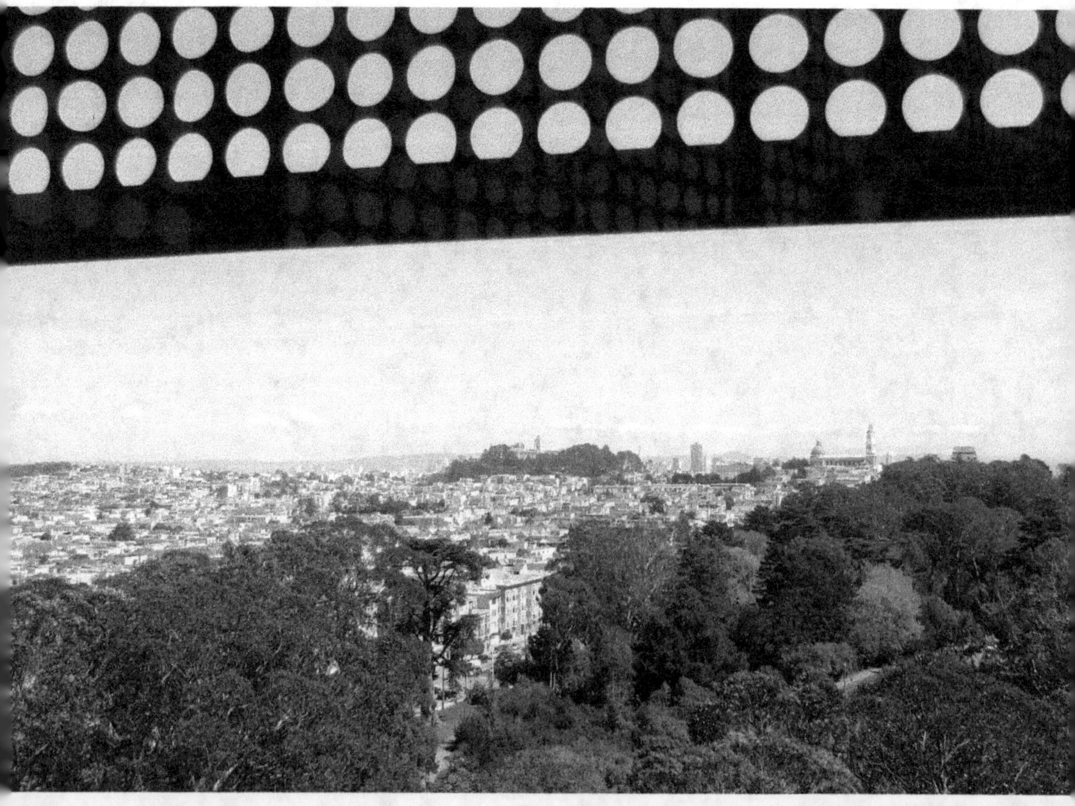

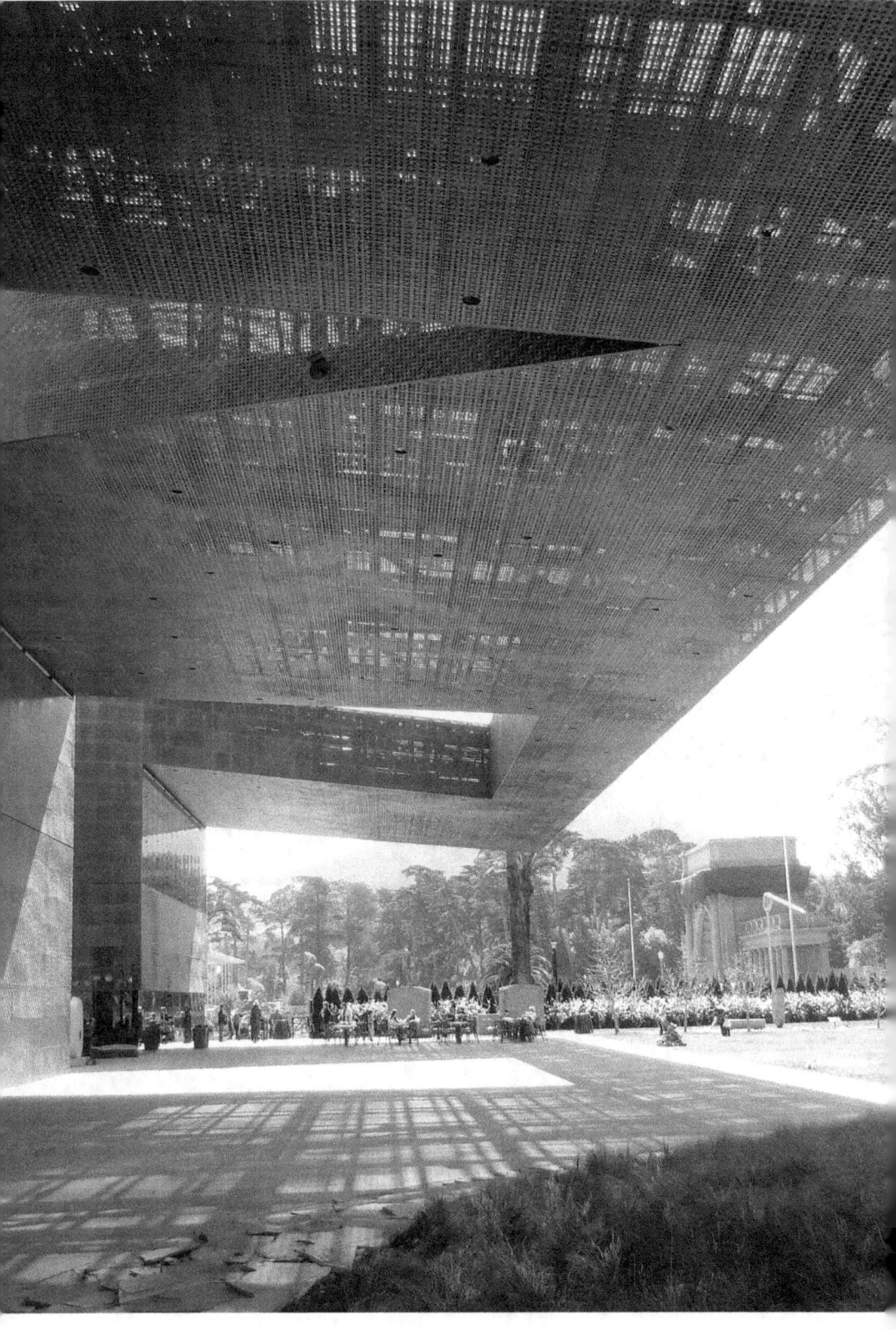

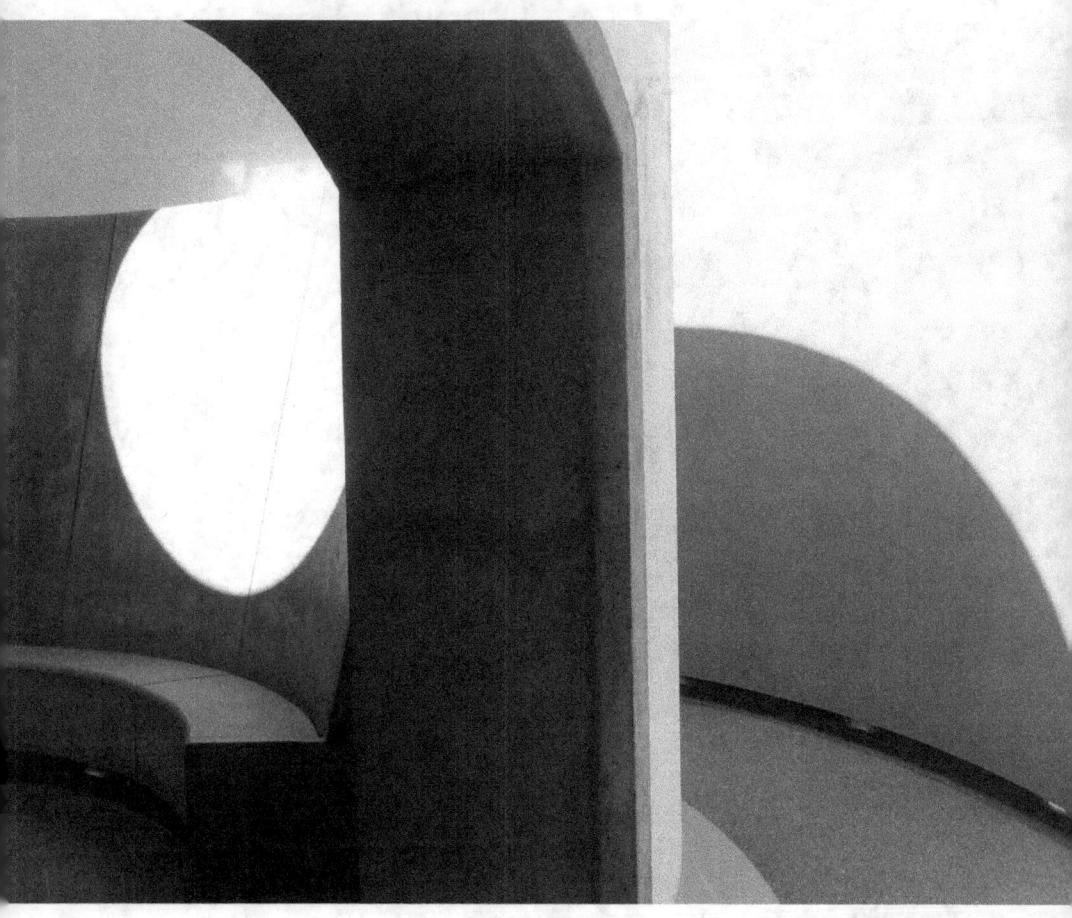
James Turrell's skyspace at the de Young Museum in San Francisco

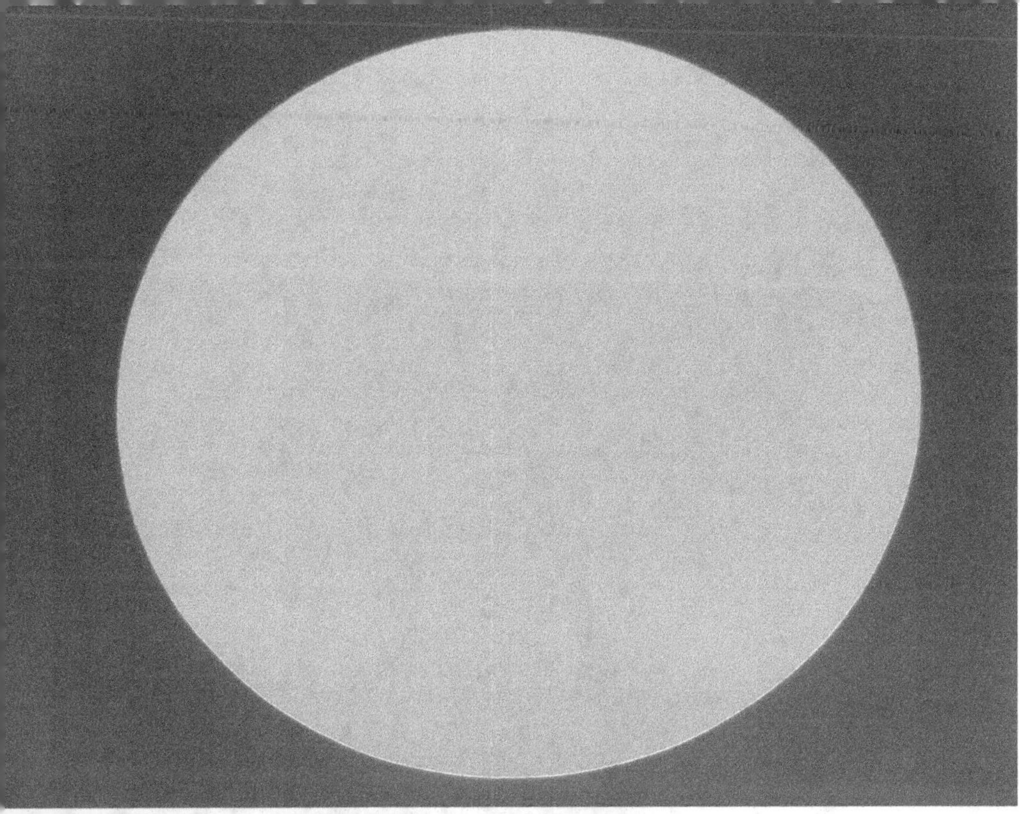

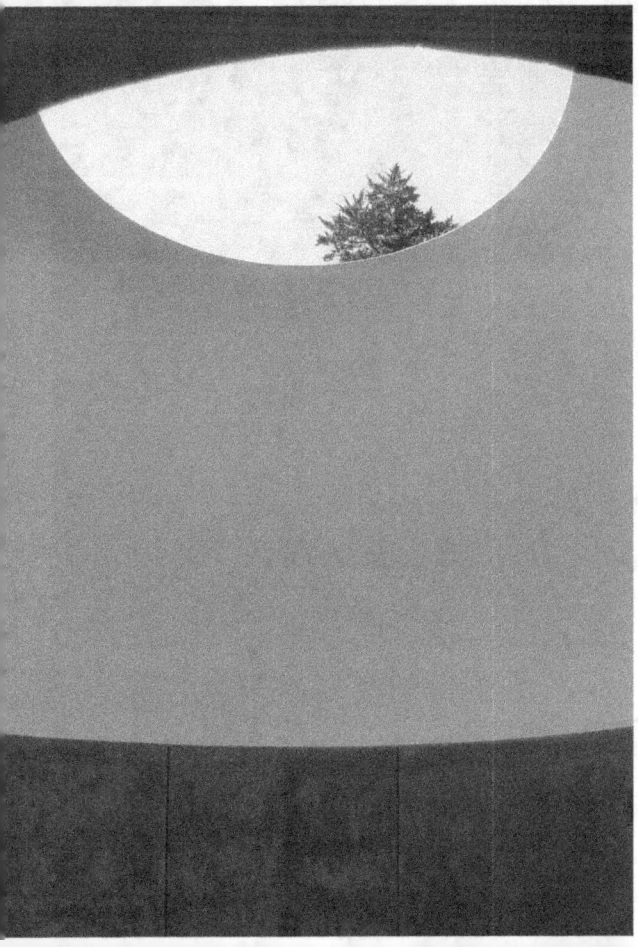

James Turrell's skyspace
at the de Young Museum
in San Francisco
(Photo: Cassidy Hughes)

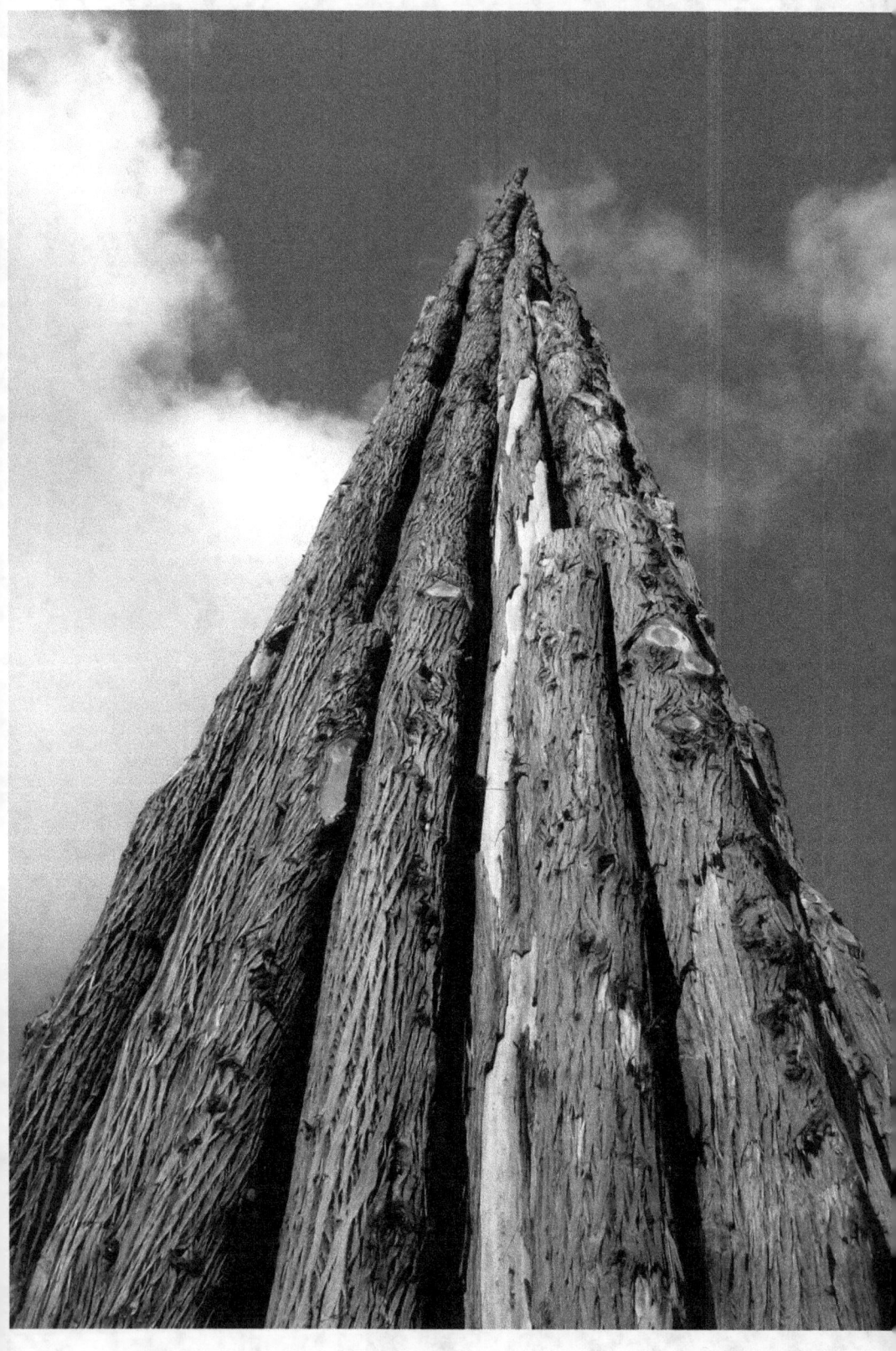

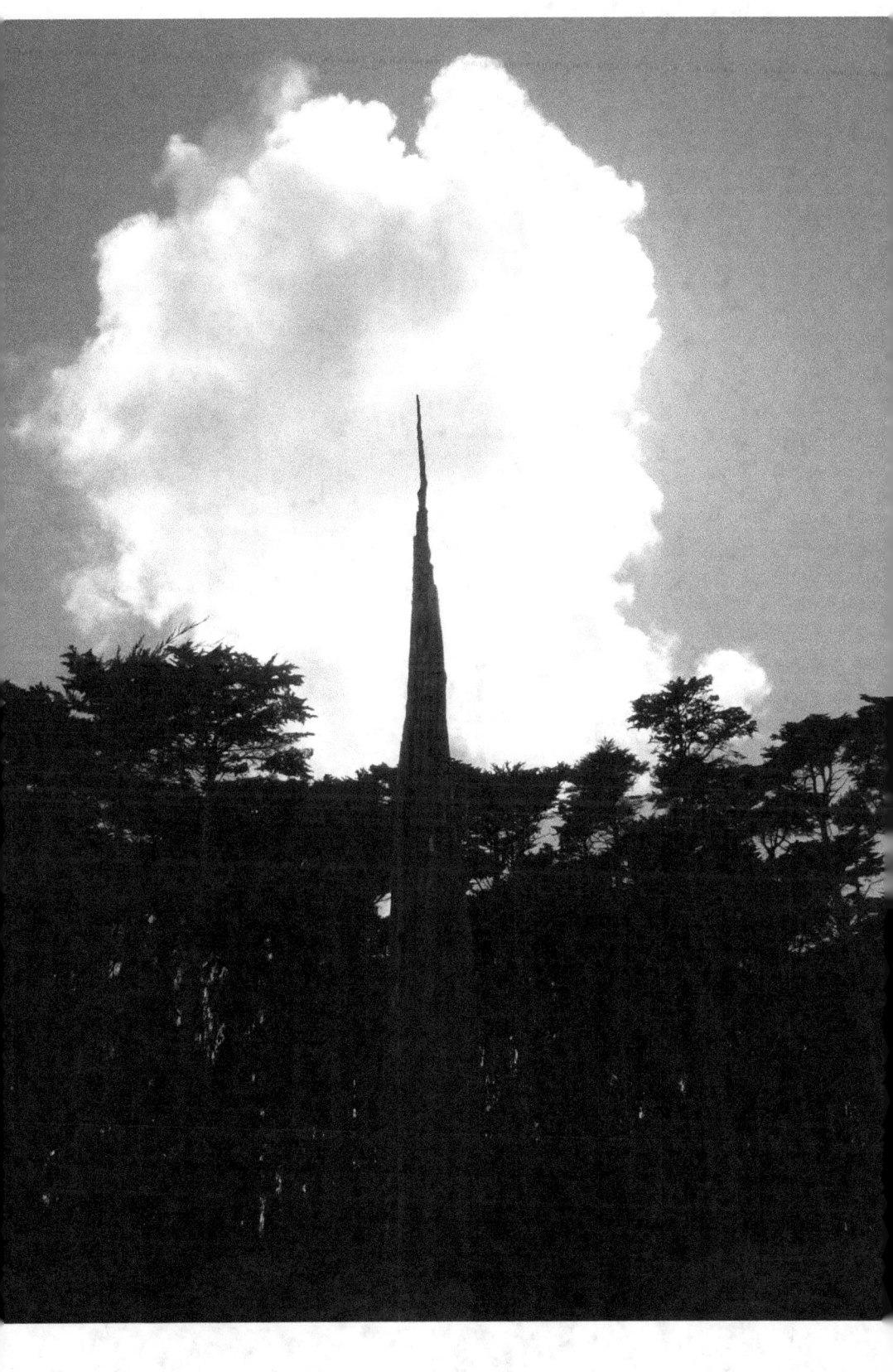

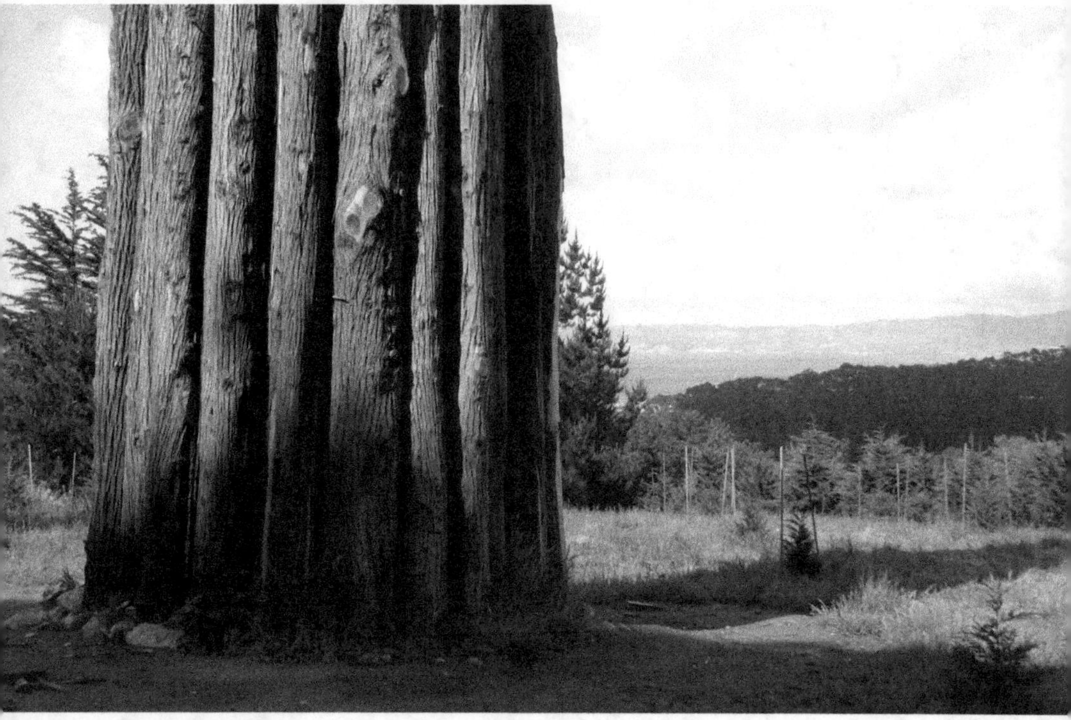

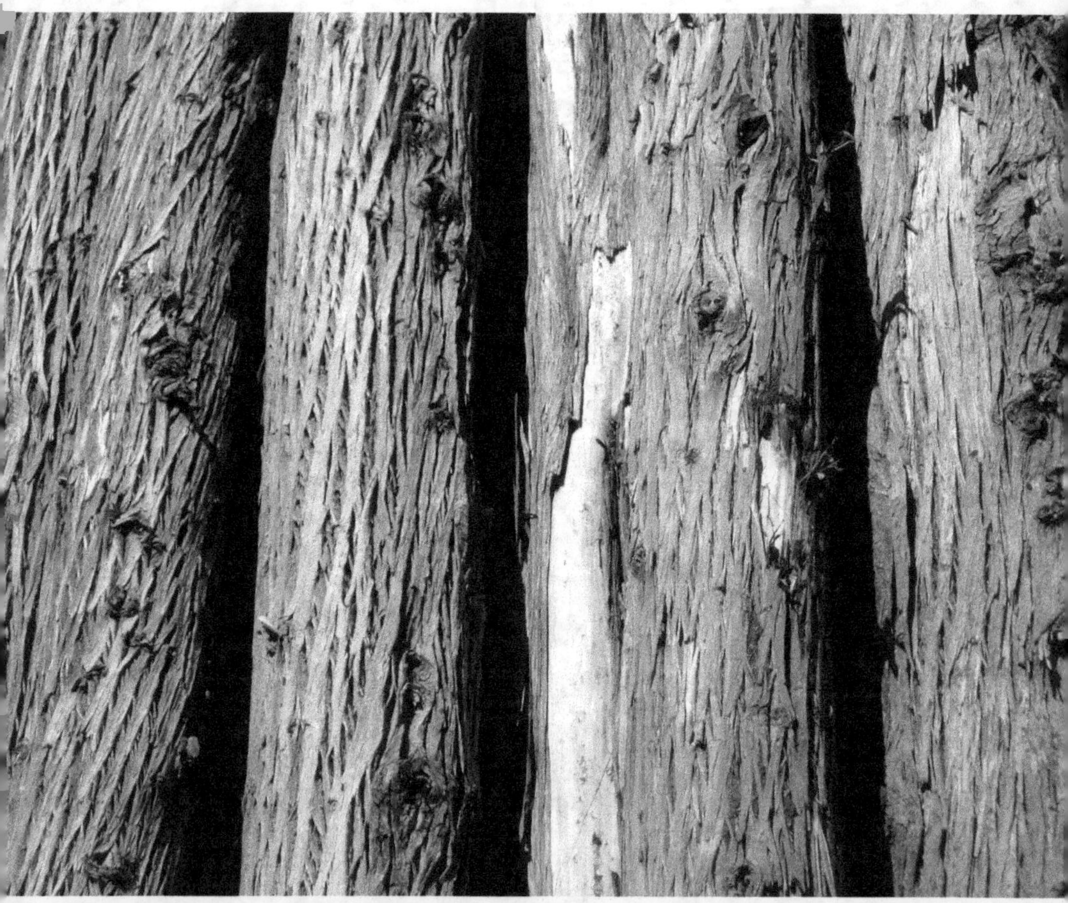

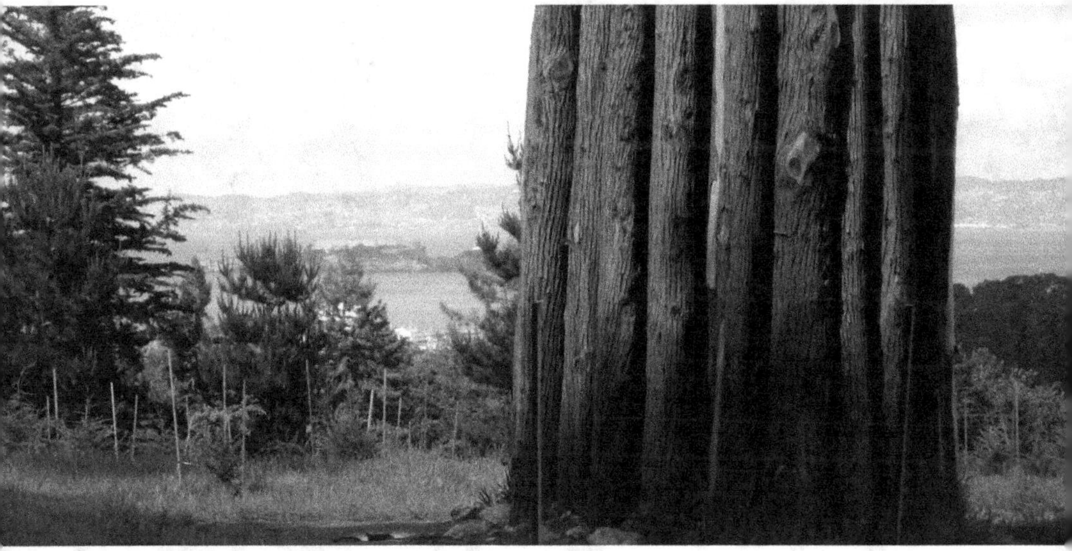

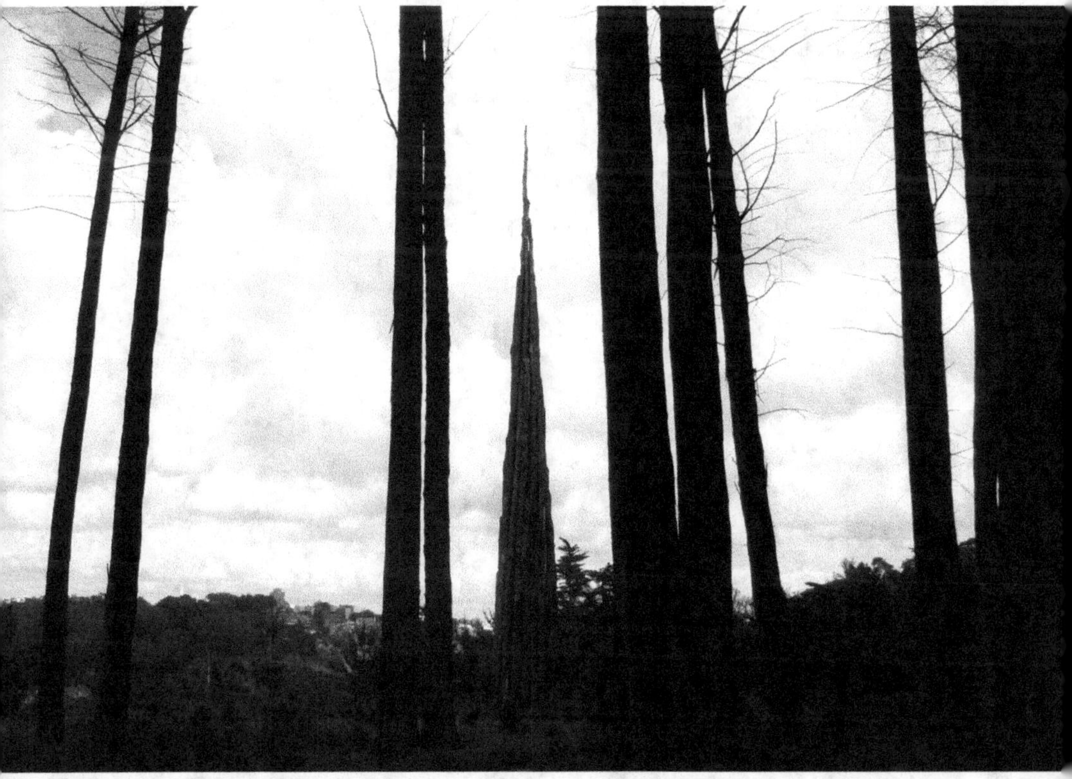

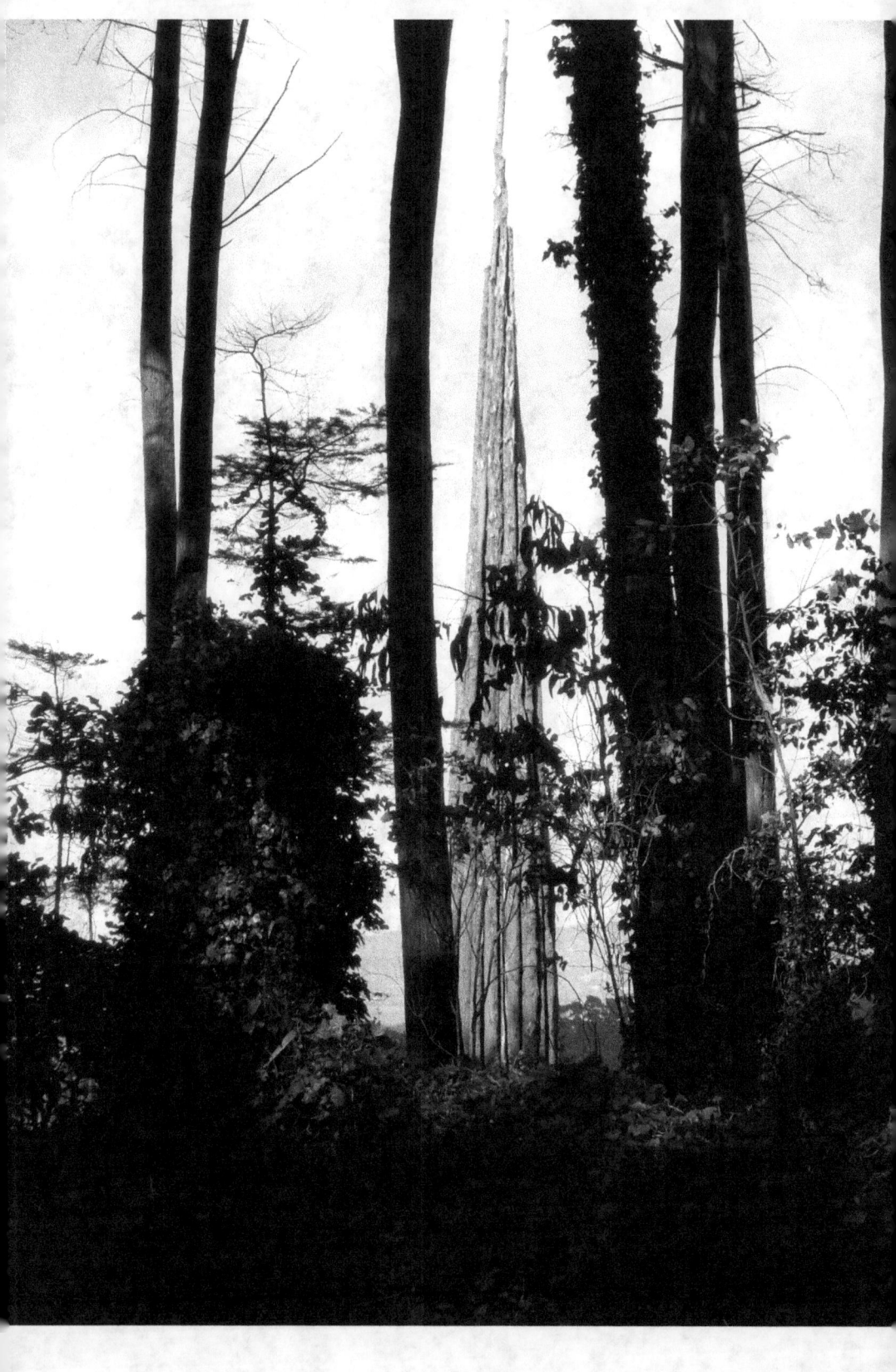

16

THE STORM KING WALL, NEW YORK STATE

One of Andy Goldsworthy's favourite structures is the stone wall. The wall he built (his first) between his land and a neighbouring farmer's at Stone Wood, Penpont, in Scotland, was a snake-like sculpture (*The Wall*, 1989). *The Wall* (a.k.a. *The Give and Take Wall*) was a 'monument to walls',[1] a neat way of creating, on Goldsworthy's side of the wall, a sculpture, and on the farmer's side, a sheepfold. Goldsworthy's walls have a dual purpose: practical, and æsthetic. The walls are boundaries or sheepfolds as well as artistic objects. Their æsthetic derives from their practical applications (S, 106). While later walls (such as *Room* or *The wall that went for a walk* or the *Storm*

---

1 A. Goldsworthy, quoted in T. Friedman, "Monuments", in HE, 154.

King Wall) did not have a 'practical' or agricultural function, Golds-worthy still related them to the practicalities of stonewalling. Goldsworthy spoke proudly and sentimentally of the practice of stonewalling: he talked in terms of 'tradition', 'history' and 'years of experience' (S, 106).

Another wall, related to the first, was made at Île de Vassivière in France: *Two folds* (1992) comprised two curl-shapes, like two question marks, which mirrored each other, as in *The Wall*. The upper fold enclosed some trees, as in other Goldsworthy wallworks, while the lower fold became flooded with water. This is a work that will decay, though: the lake will erode the wall, and the roots of the trees may alter the upper fold.

The *Two folds* wall united three of Goldsworthy's favourite elements: water, stone and earth. The stone curves linked together the earth and the water, and both the seemingly 'weaker', more transient elements – water and trees – will change and even destroy the apparently 'stronger' element, the stone of the wall. For Goldsworthy, stone is hard and unyielding (the traditional view), but also 'flowing, changing, malleable', if, he adds, one is 'prepared to understand it in those ways' (Sh, 12).

The wall that went for a walk (1990, Grizedale, U.K.) was a 150-yard long wall that literally snaked through the forest. The serpentine form of *The wall that went for a walk* related to *Lambton Earthwork* and *Sidewinder* (another Grizedale sculpture). *The wall that went for a walk* has no 'proper' function – i.e., no 'practical' function. It weaves between the trees and follows the lay of the land. Instead of ploughing through trees or rocks, Goldsworthy's curving wall assiduously avoids them. 'The wall itself is an expression of movement; a line moving through the landscape', Goldsworthy said (Sh, 12). However, the wall doesn't need to be there in the first place (a notion that Goldsworthy cannot quite resolve: in the book *Stone* he related *The wall that went for a walk* to the old fields that were at Grizedale before the forest, but it's not a convincing argument).

Some of Andy Goldsworthy's wallworks are circular enclosures, derived mainly from agricultural sheepfolds. There is no direct agricultural function to these circular enclosures, however, so they must be regarded as, God forbid, 'decorative', as works of art. Though they are made with the assistance of traditional dry stone wallers such as Joe Smith and Steve Allen (who have built many of Goldsworthy's walls), the spectator can see immediately that these are not rural artifacts, used by farmers. Rather, Goldsworthy's circular enclosures, such as *Stone gathering* (Northumberland, 1993), *Rock fold* (Dumfriesshire, 1993), *Slate dome hole* (Edinburgh, 1990) and *Room* (Pennsylvania, 1992), are about creating shelters and particular spaces in an outdoor environment. *Refuge* (2006), a show in Paris, was another variation on the enclosure theme of the sheepfolds: oak branches were enclosed by rectangular walls of slate. 'The space is made quiet and intense by the containing wall, giving a sense of protection and care', remarked Goldsworthy (S, 106).

Like the sheepfolds, Goldsworthy's circular enclosures are about marking a space separate from, yet a part of, the landscape, a sanctuary from the elements. Indeed, in *Stone gathering*, large boulders were placed inside the circular wall, just like cattle or sheep sheltering from the wind and rain. *Rock fold* encircled an excavated outcrop of rocks. *Slate dome hole*, in the Royal Botanic Gardens in Edinburgh, combined two Goldsworthyan motifs: the shallow dome with a hole at the summit, made from slate, and the circular dry stone wall. The central, sheltered rock in the Goldsworthy enclosure was compared by a critic to an altar or sacred centre (A. Causey, 140). Another Goldsworthy motif is to bury tree trunks and branches and boulders within his stone walls (as in New York state [1993], and at Storm King [1996]).

Another stone wall made by Joe Smith from Goldsworthy's drawings was *Room*. This was a human-height stone wall situated in a wood of young, slender trees. It was another of those large-scale works, like those at Grizedale forest, which Goldsworthy enjoyed building under the trees, so it was always partially obscured by tree trunks. The circular enclosure of *Room* added to the already confined atmosphere of the forest. The use of five, not four, doors, indicated that this work was not about the four cardinal points and directions, like the snow circles at the North Pole: five is the symbolic number of magic, the occult pentacle, the human form (head and four limbs) and the cosmos.

At 2,278 feet long, the *Storm King Wall* in the United States was not only Andy Goldsworthy's biggest wall, it was one of Goldsworthy's most significant works. Other artists who had worked at the Storm King Art Center in New York state included Richard Serra, Louise Nevelson, David Smith, Mark di Suvero, Isamu Noguchi, Alice Aycock and Alexander Calder. (There is plenty of Calder and Smith sculpture here, as in many of the museums in America. The Calders are enormous and very impressive. One aspect that bounces out of the Calder sculptures immediately is their *colour*; while Smith, Serra, di Suvero *et al* might retain the natural colour of untreated metal for many of their works, Calder happily covers his pieces with bright red and yellow).

The Storm King Art Center, founded in 1960 by Ralph Ogden and H. Peter Stern, is a stunning collection of mainly sculpture in upstate New York. If you haven't been, I highly recommend it. Every sculpture has plenty of space around it, including the pieces nearest the Visitor's Center. Goldsworthy's *Wall* has no other sculpture near it for hundreds of yards, and no other art can been seen from the *Wall* (the next sculptures to Goldsworthy's are Richard Serra's slabs, *Schunnemunk Fork* (1990-91) and Magdalena Abakanowicz's coffins).

Near to the Storm King Art Center is the DIA Foundation at Beacon, another spectacular centre for art, in particular for American Minimal and Postminimal artists (Robert Smithson, Michael Heizer, Agnes Martin, Donald Judd, Robert Ryman, etc). DIA in Beacon would rank as one of the premier sites in the world for contemporary art. There you can see some of the major American land artists, such as Michael Heizer and Robert Smithson, with important works by those artists (once you've seen Heizer's deep geometric holes in the gallery floor, you won't forget them. And Smithson's mirror non-sites are terrific. These are iconic examples of contemporary art, and rare to see in many museums and galleries).

Reaching Storm King is a cinch from Manhattan – just follow the

Hudson River North, heading for Newburgh and Albany. I took Route 9W, on the West bank of the river, which's very picturesque (but also slow and winding); I-87 will get you there quicker.

The key to the Storm King Art Center is the landscaped grounds, beautifully designed and maintained. Andy Goldsworthy's *Wall* is situated at the far side of the sculpture park, next to the artificial lake (you can reach it on foot or using the tram).

The *Storm King Wall* begins as a line of stones upon the ground, which rises to become a regular stone wall (about four feet high). It's as if it's coming out of the ground – as if the Earth is giving birth to it, perhaps, or as if it's an animal slithering out of the soil. Or maybe it's simply that Goldsworthy thought it looked better to have the wall tapering to a single line of stones at its end, instead of a blunt, vertical end. The more fanciful allusions – that this 2,228 foot long stone wall has snake-like elements – are only that, only fancy and musings. However, the *Wall* at Storm King does rise out of the ground, and snakes its way down a hill, to a water source, like an animal coming out of the ground, looking for water, and moving down the slope to drink.

It is a thick, solid, traditional dry stone wall, that you might see in 100s of places. There are tracks around it (gravel roads, really), and the wall has gaps to allow the tracks to pass through.

The area here at Storm King is woodland, falling away down a slope on one side, and the open grassland of the park on the other. *The Wall*, though, stays under the trees, as if hiding, or sheltering. It skirts the edge of the trees, but always remains under them. The trickiest part, one imagines, would be building the curving wall on the steepest parts of the slope, near the lake. The trees will eventually break the wall – it is very close to some of the trees. *The Wall* is very much about the relationship with the trees, as Goldsworthy explained in the documentary *Rivers and Tides*.

The *Storm King Wall* is a very big sculpture – one of Goldsworthy's largest anywhere. The curving of the piece begins after the first gap, winding between tall trees of maple and beech. The wall is four-to-five feet high. Some of the curves of the wall are very tight, like oxbow curves in a river. *The Wall* weaves around the trees. The curves create enclosures like Goldsworthy's sheepfolds. There's a rope fence around much of the wall (maybe to stop erosion). There's a small gap by the lake for people to walk through. At the lake the *Wall* slopes into the water, like Christo's *Running Fence*.

All in all, the *Storm King Wall* is a hugely impressive sculpture. It both stands out from its surroundings as a work of art, and becomes part of the landscape. It doesn't have a 'function', like a sheepfold or something agricultural, but it manages to assert itself as something with presence and solidity in itself.

Of the *Storm King Wall*, Goldsworthy was happy to contemplate its demise:

> Although it took him two years to complete, he is cheerful contemplating the prospect of its ruin. 'Eventually when it falls down, whether that happens in 15 years or 300 years, it will be a tumbled-down line in the ground,' he said. 'I like that idea, of a faint trace left in the land. (D. Solomon, 2004)

The atmosphere of the site when I was there included the sound of cicadas. And rain – it began to rain at noon, and continued throughout the day and night. That drove most visitors back to the Visitor's Center on the hill. Rainy, cloudy weather usually suits Goldsworthy's art – he's spoken of that kind of weather as being appropriate for his work. Certainly many of his sculptures have been created in that kind of weather (rain and wind and cold and cloud is the norm for much of the time in Northern Britain and Scotland – well, across the whole of the British Isles). So that long, winding stone wall suits the rain and wind just perfectly (and vice versa).

And there's the constant roar of the nearby New York State Thruway. So it should be remembered that the pictures of the *Storm King Wall* are loud with traffic.

A turkey vulture makes slow, lazy circles above. The place is surrounded by the thickly wooded hills of the Hudson River Valley. For me, the situation in the exquisite countryside of the River Hudson contributes much to the impact of the sculpture.

And one should always remember that this sculpture by Goldsworthy is just one of many at the Storm King Art Center. That is, the visitor has already walked past giant Alexander Calder sculptures, smaller grey David Smith pieces, the mysterious 'wooden coffins' of Magdalena Akabanowicz, and Richard Serra's distinctive rusted slabs. So Goldsworthy's piece is amongst many others – yes, but he's also in very good company (the best, in fact).

The second time I visited the *Storm King Wall* was in Spring, 2009. A fiercely cold wind blew through the park. There were few visitors, and most of them stayed near the Visitor's Center. It really wasn't what you would call wonderful sightseeing weather. Later, it began to snow in light flurries. Snow and cold are of course recurring aspects of Andy Goldsworthy's work. It's certainly worth visiting Goldsworthy's art at least twice, because the first impression is usually modulated by the second. Perhaps many visitors to museums, art galleries and sculpture parks would think of the ideal conditions as being a warm, sunny day. But Goldsworthy's art is very much an art of all weathers, and cold, rain, wind and snow are just as much a part of it as sun, warmth and Summer.

I recommend walking beyond the *Storm King Wall* down to the lake, and around the other side of the water. Here you can look back at the *Wall*, and track its course as it winds through the trees. You can observe the wall which emerges from the lake on the other side, and climbs up the bank, continuing towards the Interstate. This too is an important aspect of the sculpture; it expresses a recurring motif in Goldsworthy's art: the form that continues through a wall, a window, a boundary, or negative space.

I have included some photos of other aspects of Storm King Art Center, including some of the works on display.

SHEEPFOLDS (1 996–)

At Storm King, Andy Goldsworthy also produced one of his sheepfolds. The half-in-half-out sheepfold was constructed out of red stone from Dumfriesshire. In the mid-1990s, Goldsworthy developed the *Sheepfolds* project: building and renewing a hundred sheepfolds in the North of England. The *100 Sheepfolds* project was funded by public money from Britain's National Lottery (who contributed a grant of £340,000 or about $544,000. A portion of the National Lottery ticket money went to arts projects). Steve Chettle, Public Arts Officer for Cumbria County Council, was chief shepherd of the project which included exhibitions in Cumbria, St Albans and London, TV documentaries, and books by Goldsworthy (*Sheepfolds* and *Arch*).

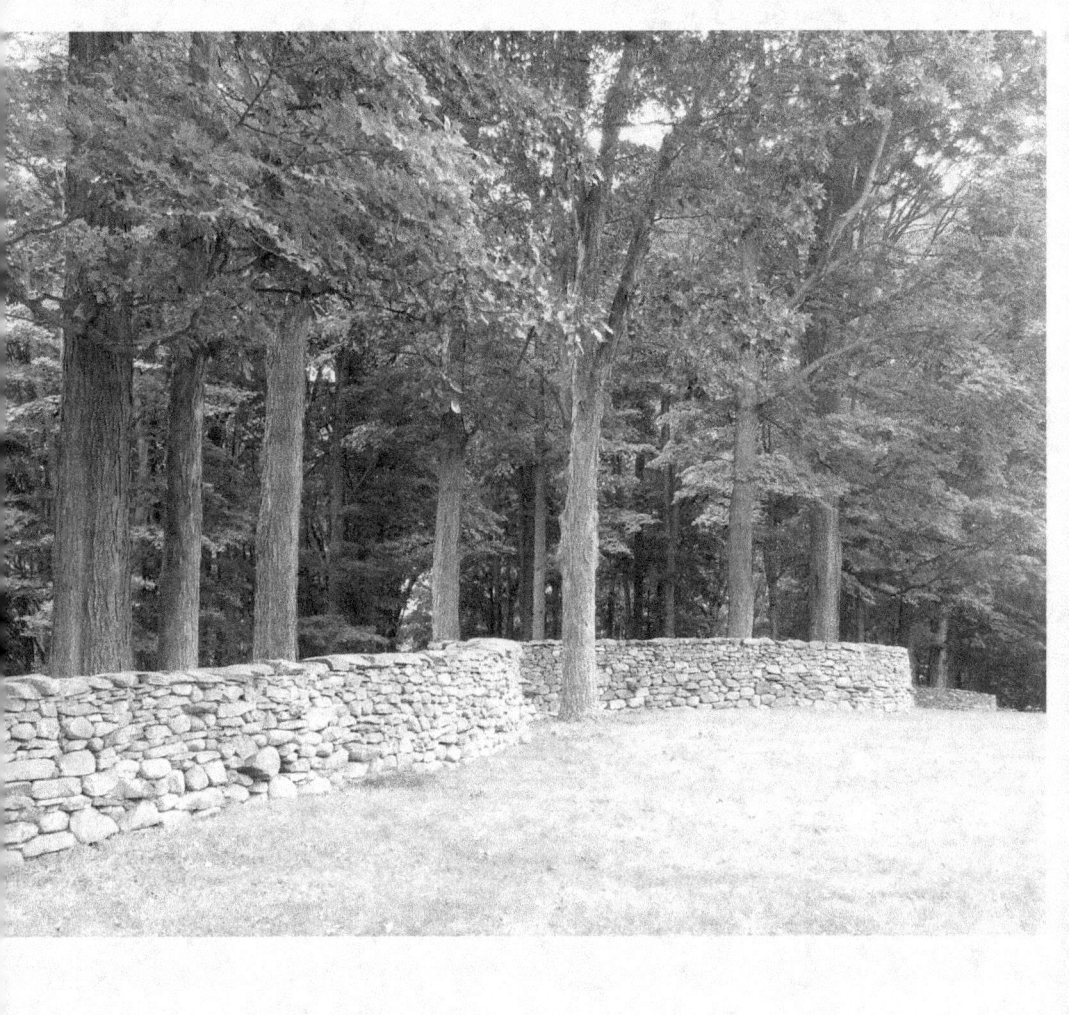

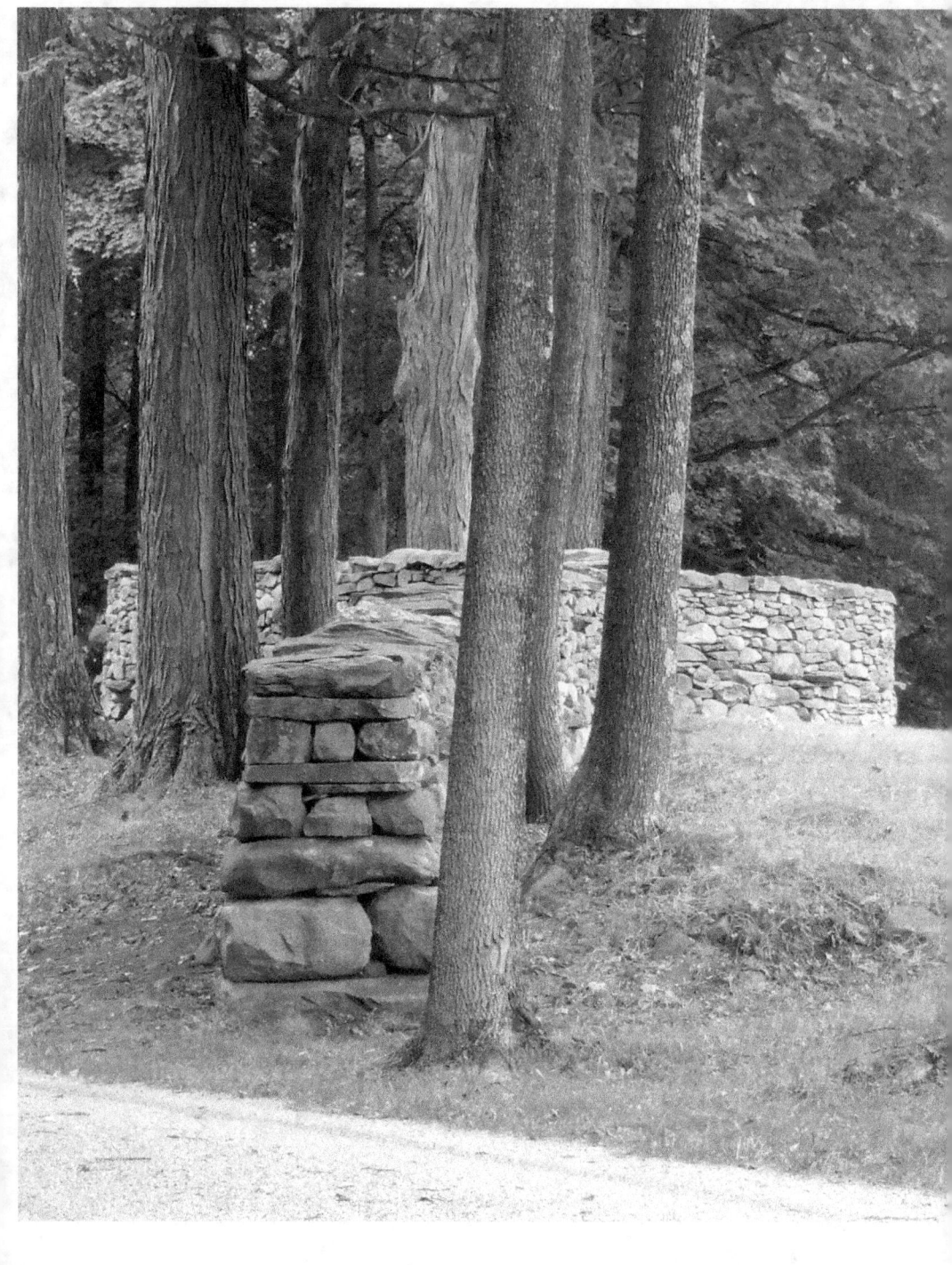

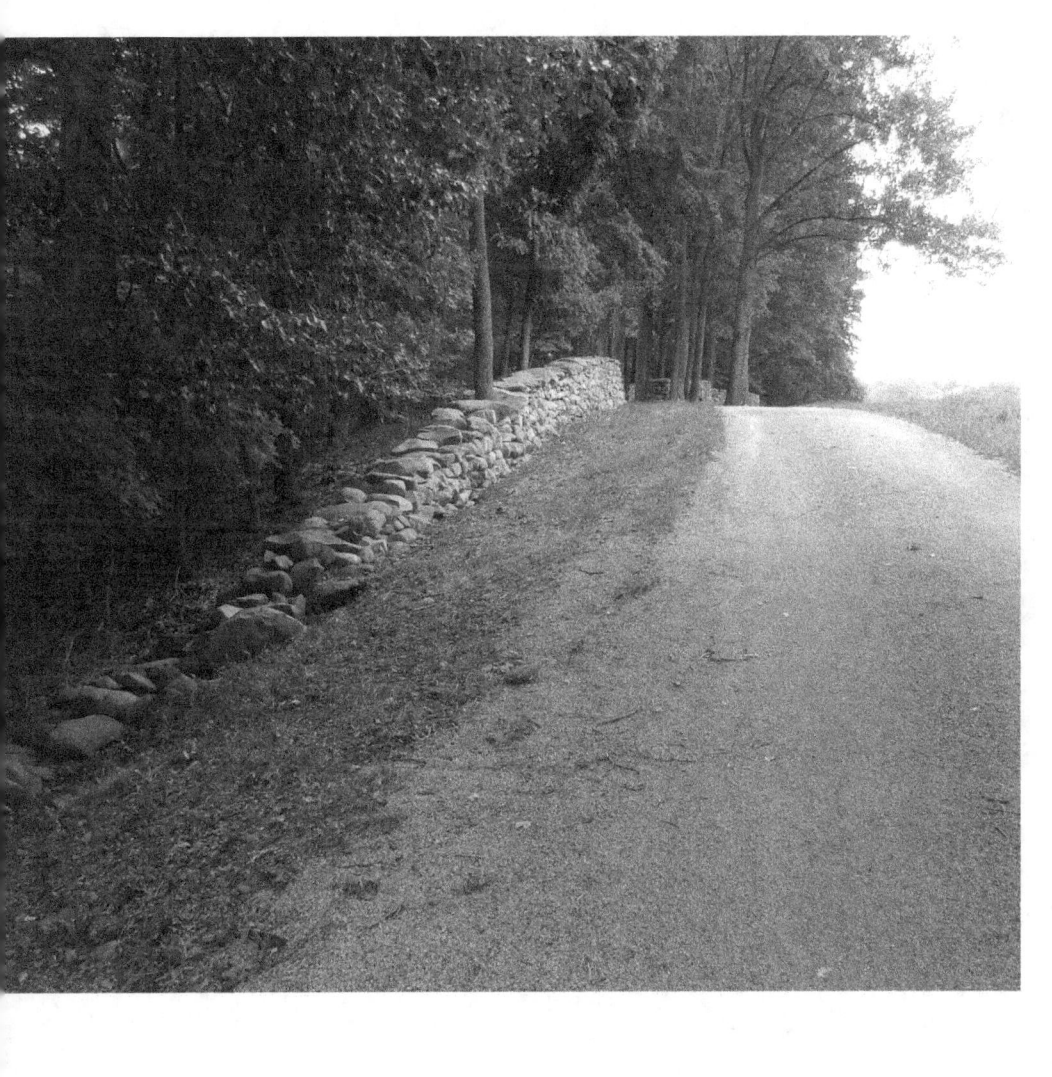

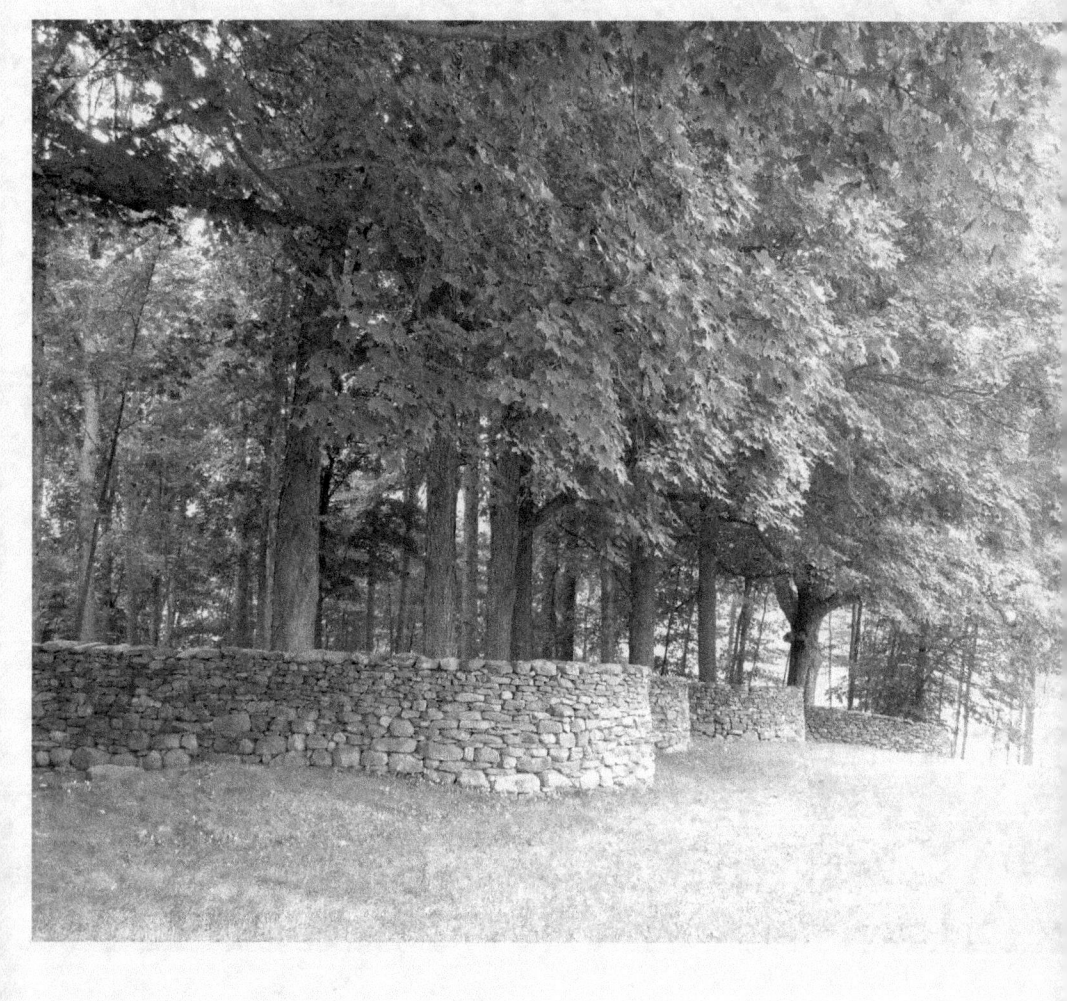

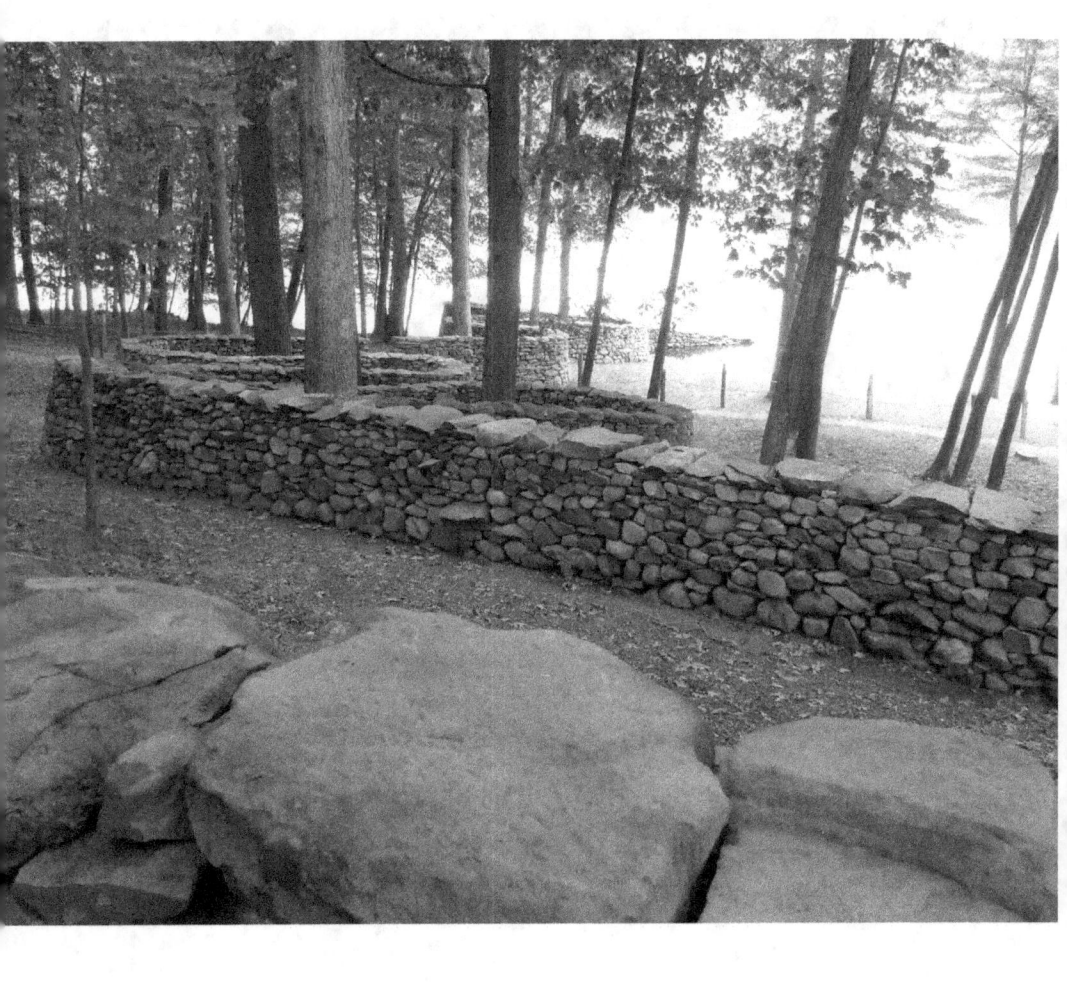

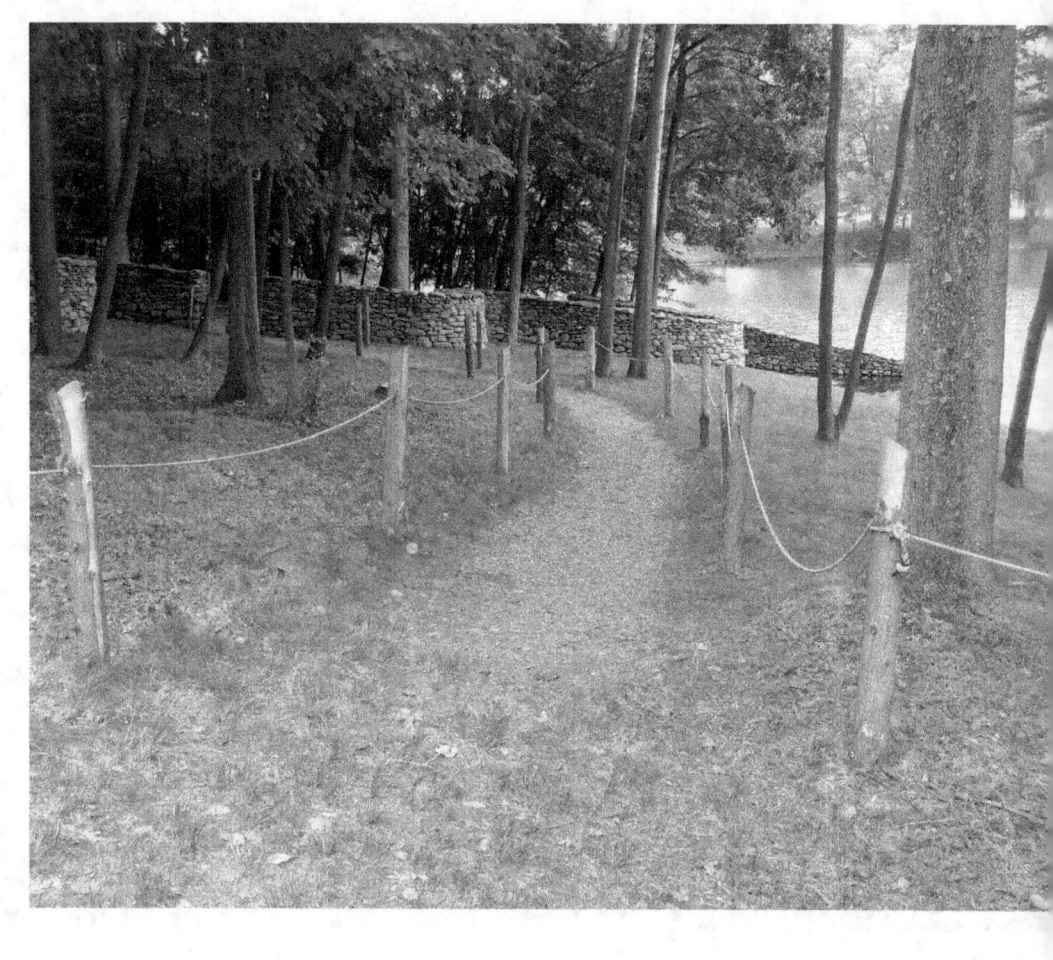

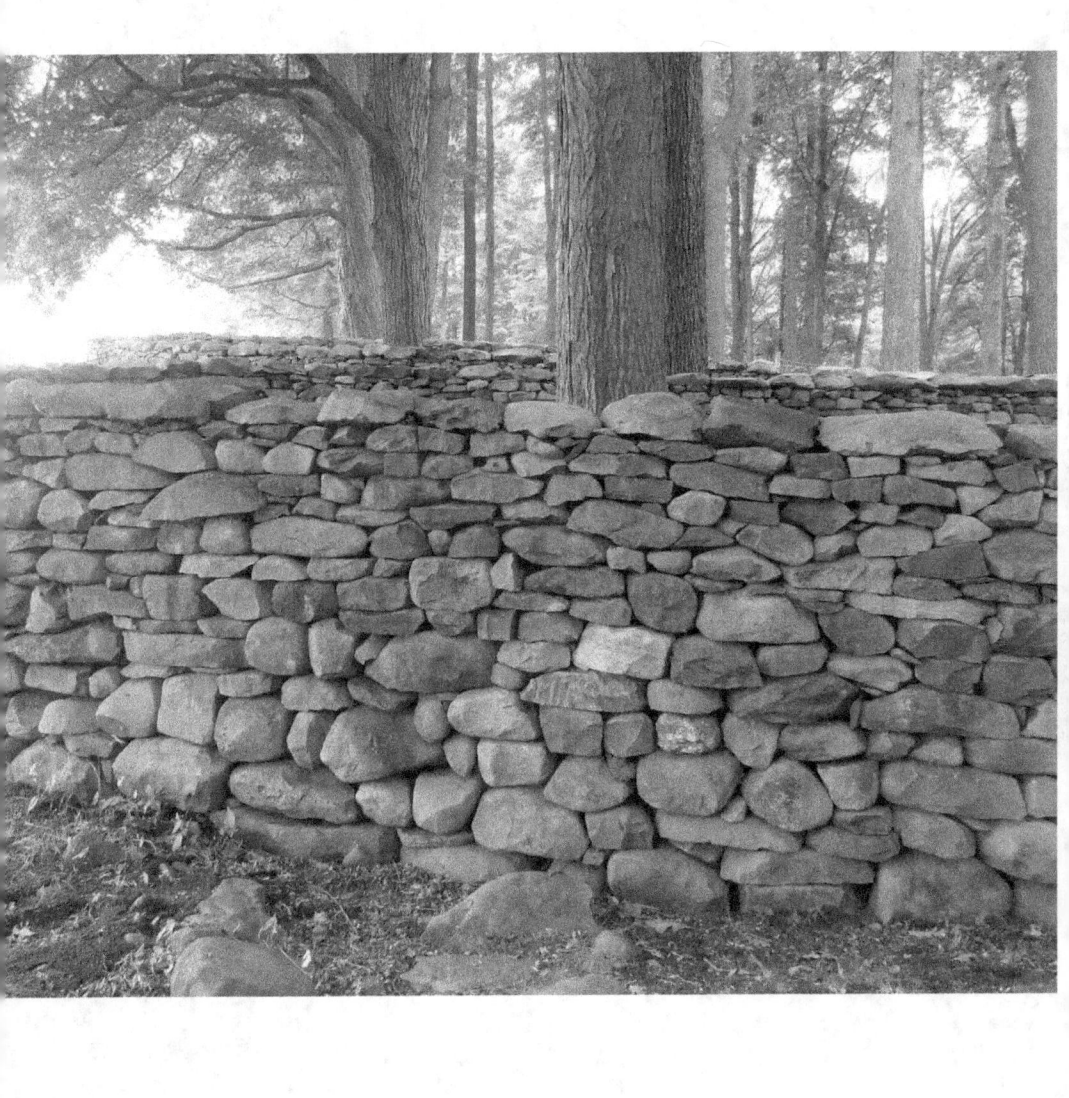

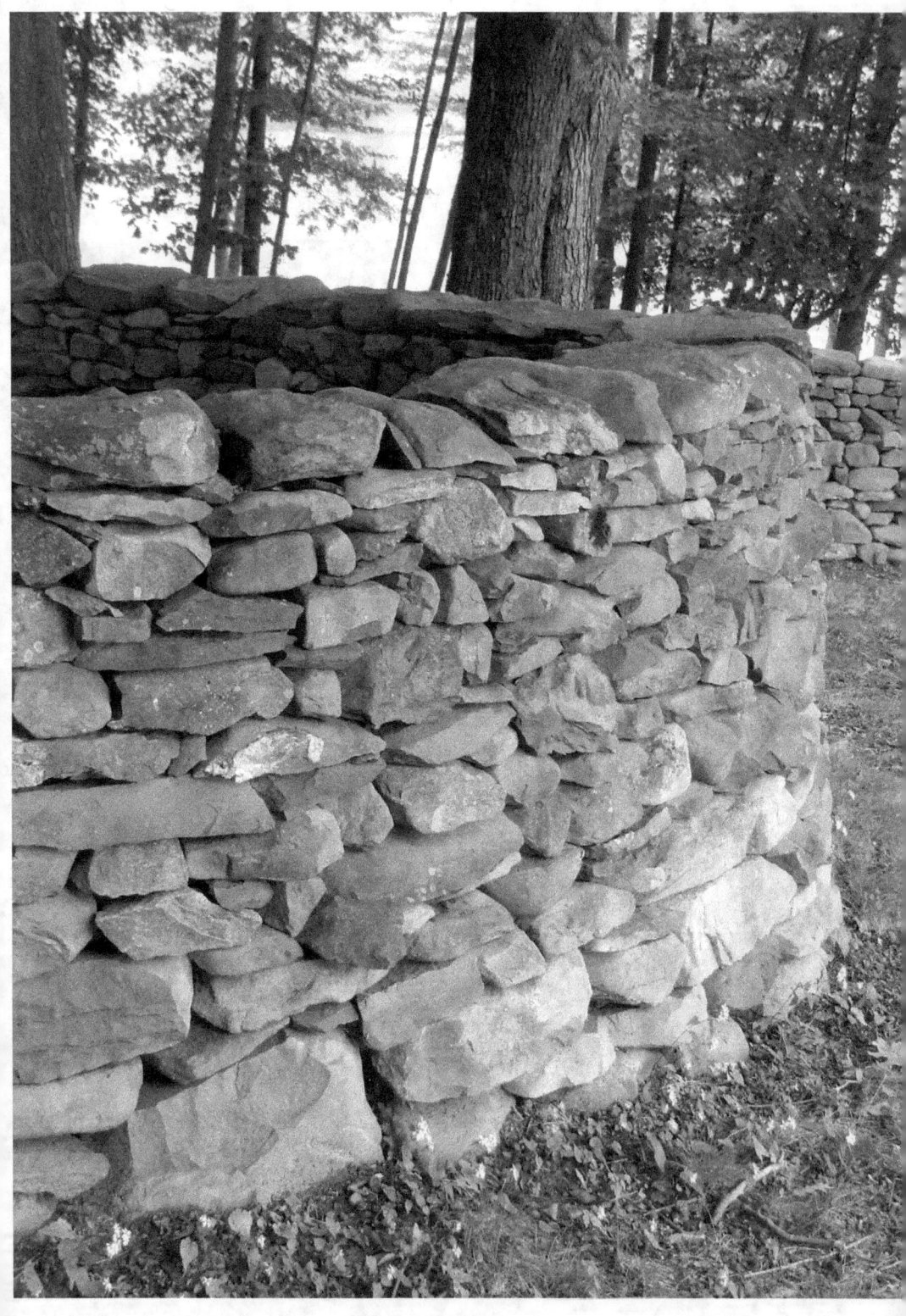

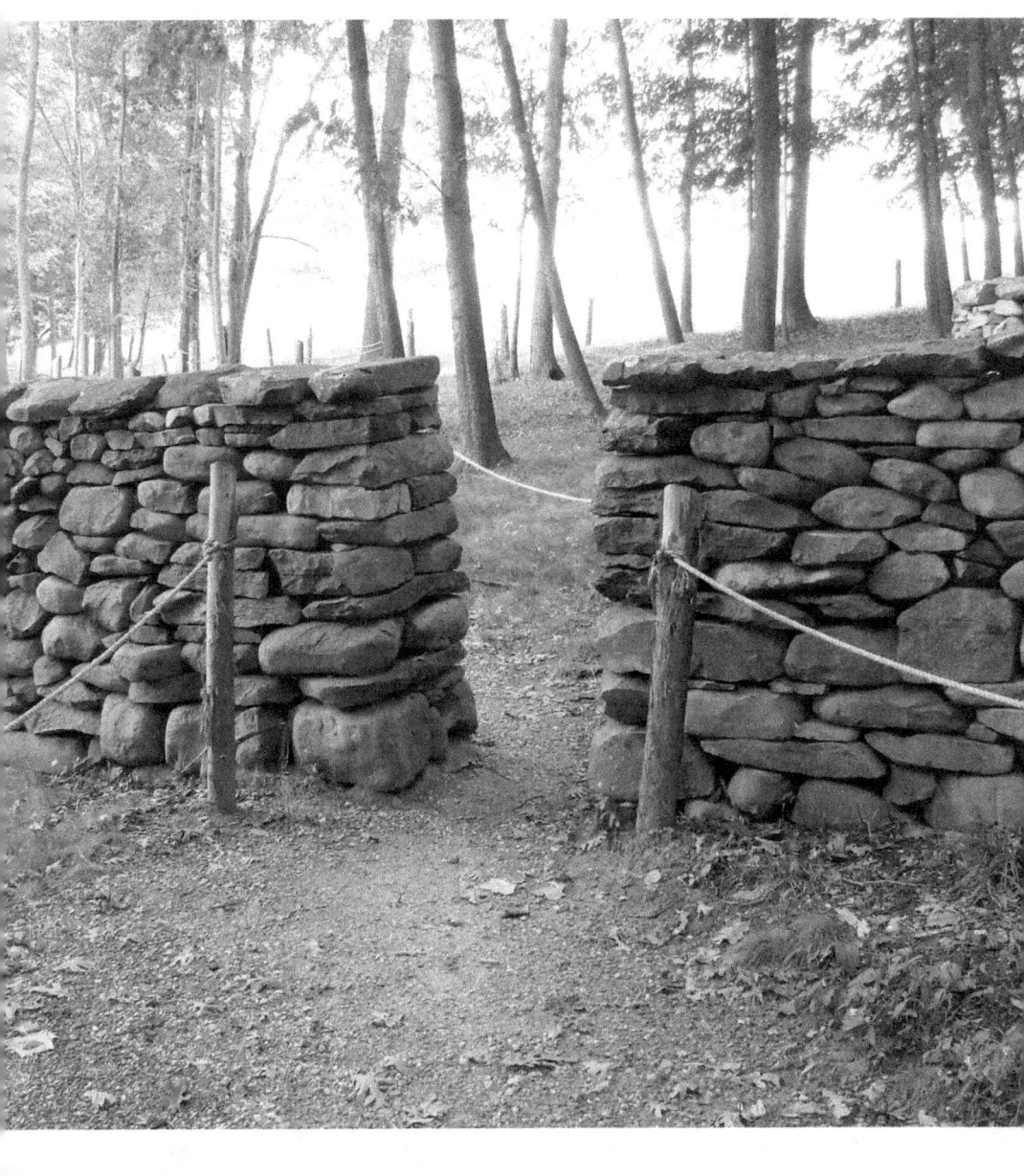

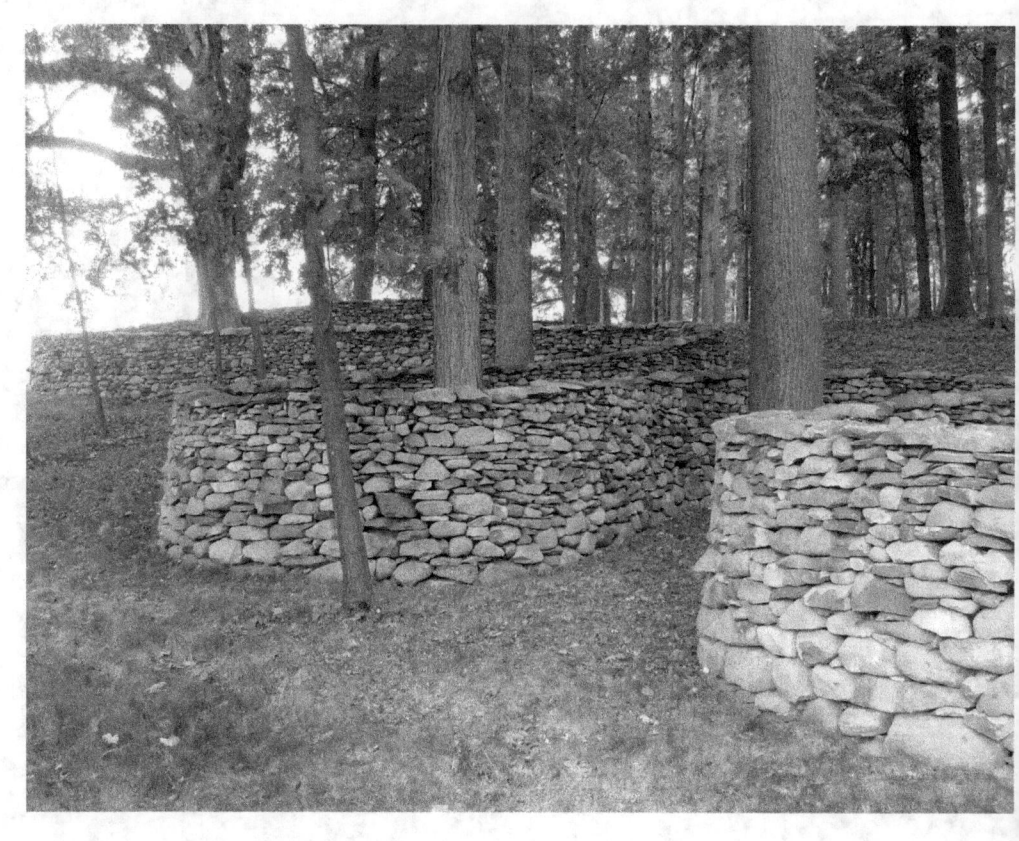

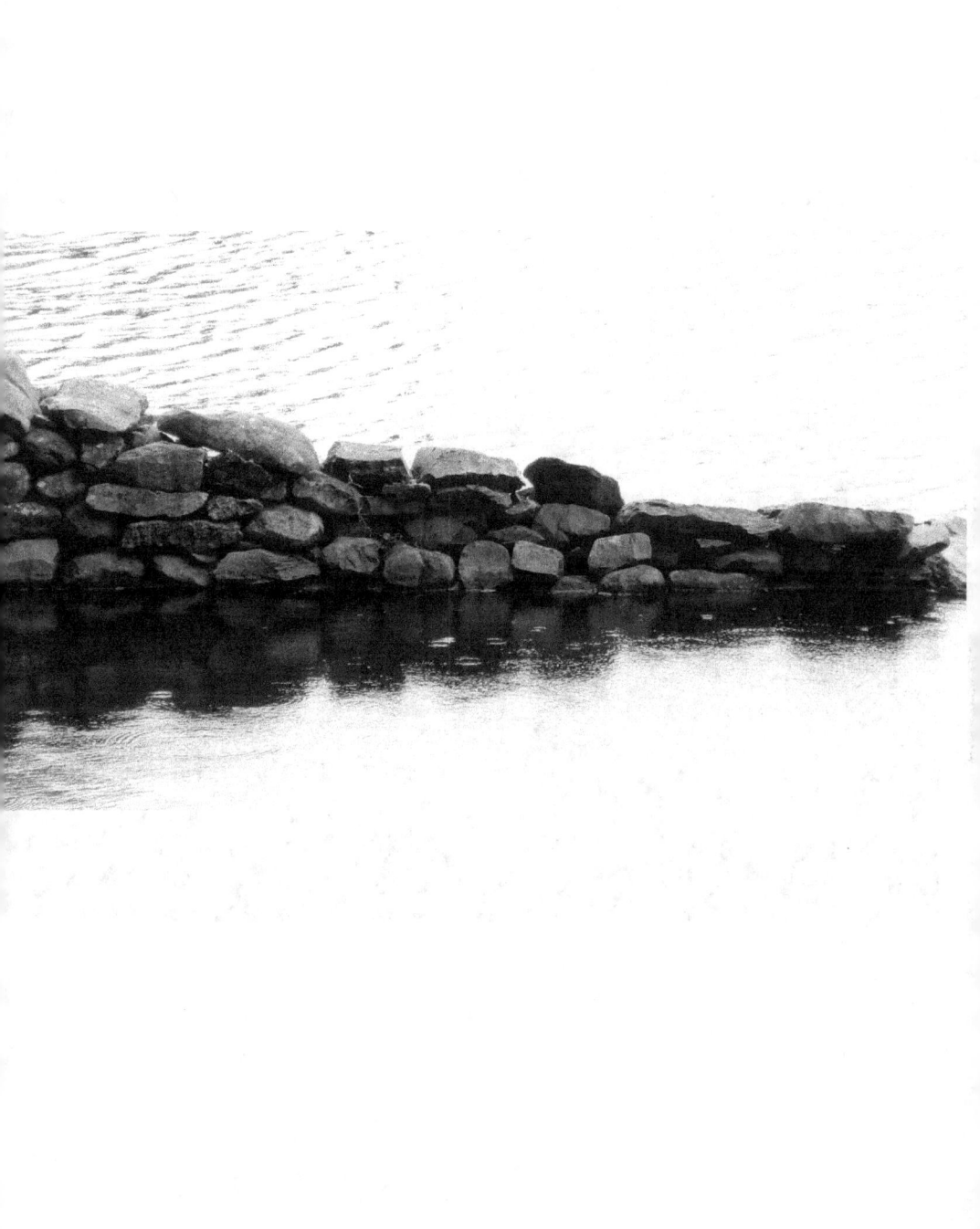

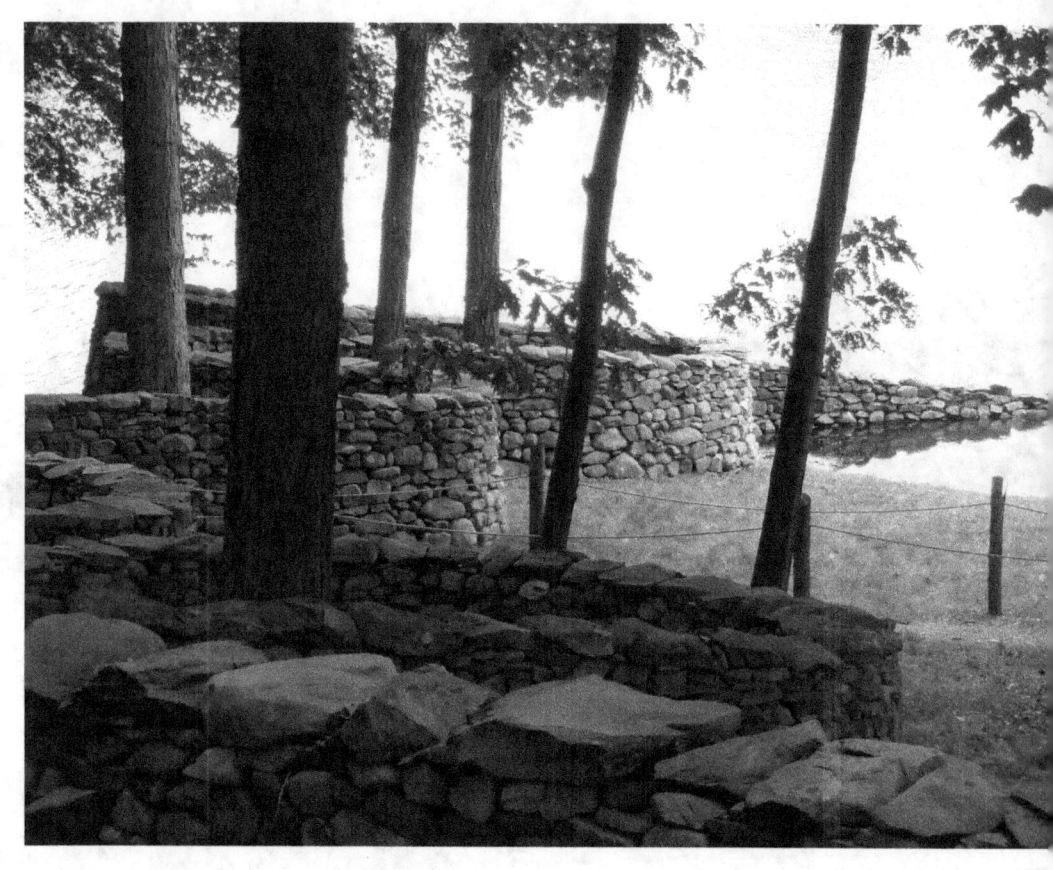

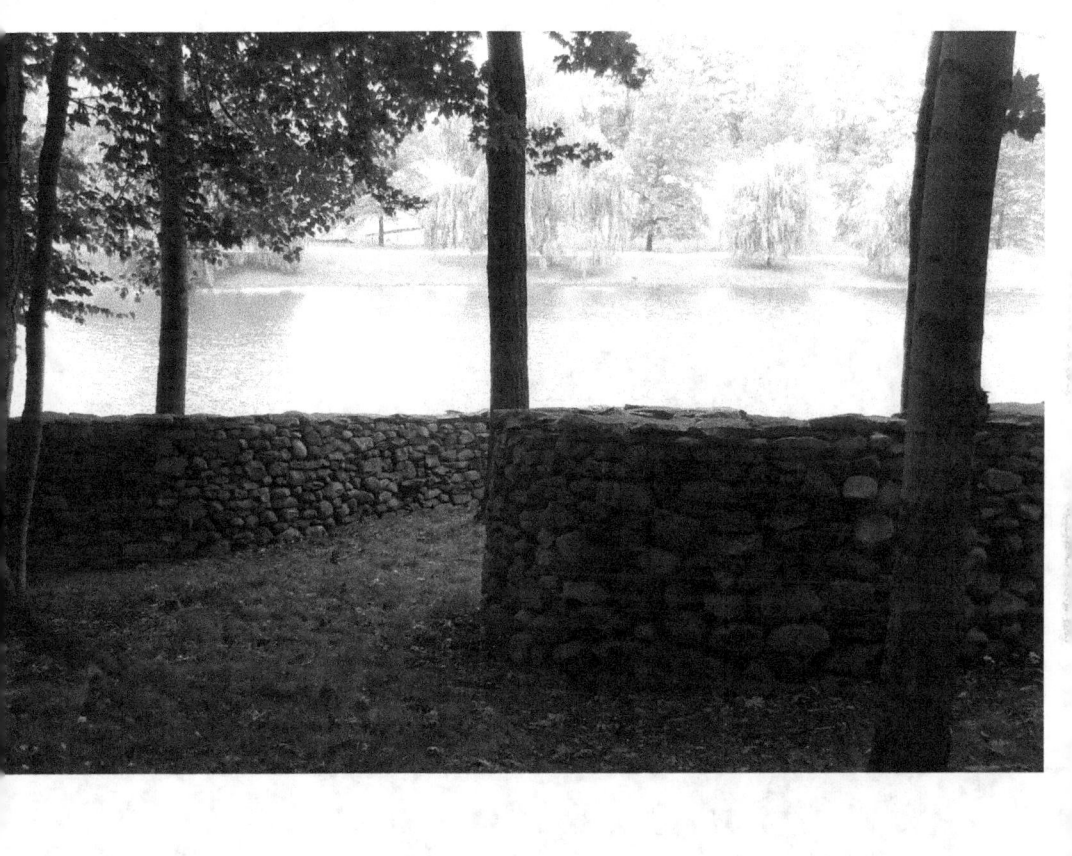

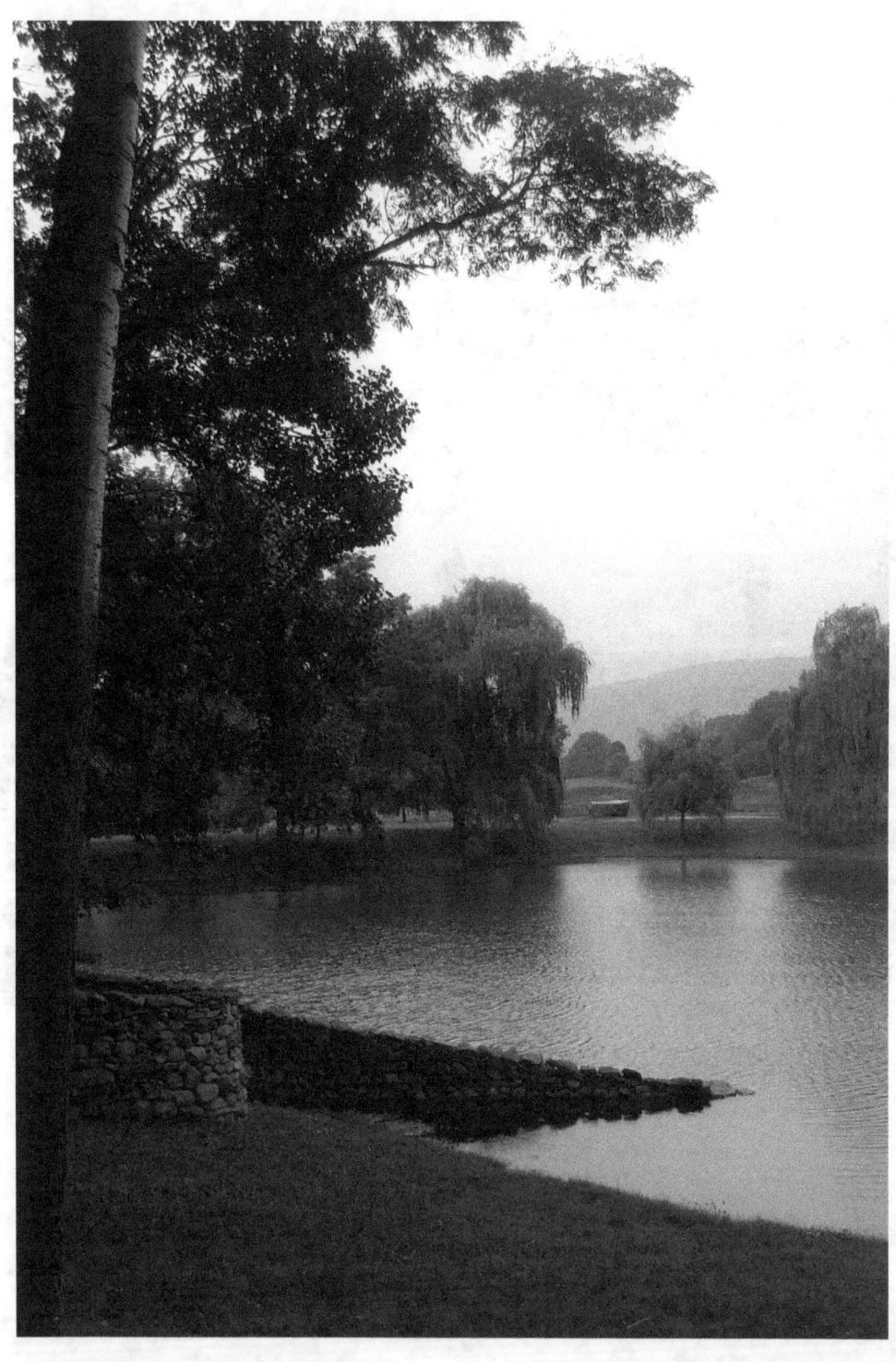

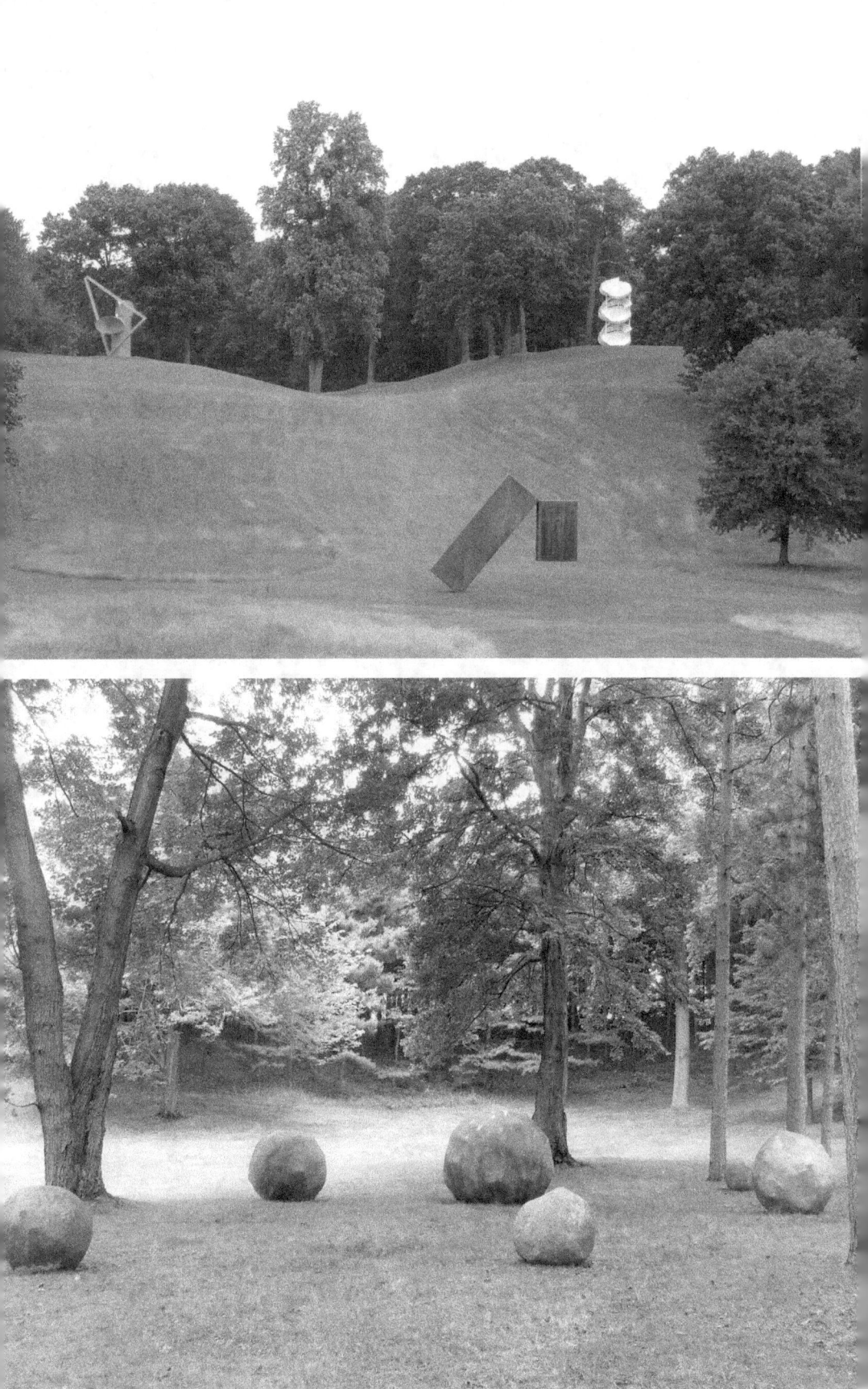

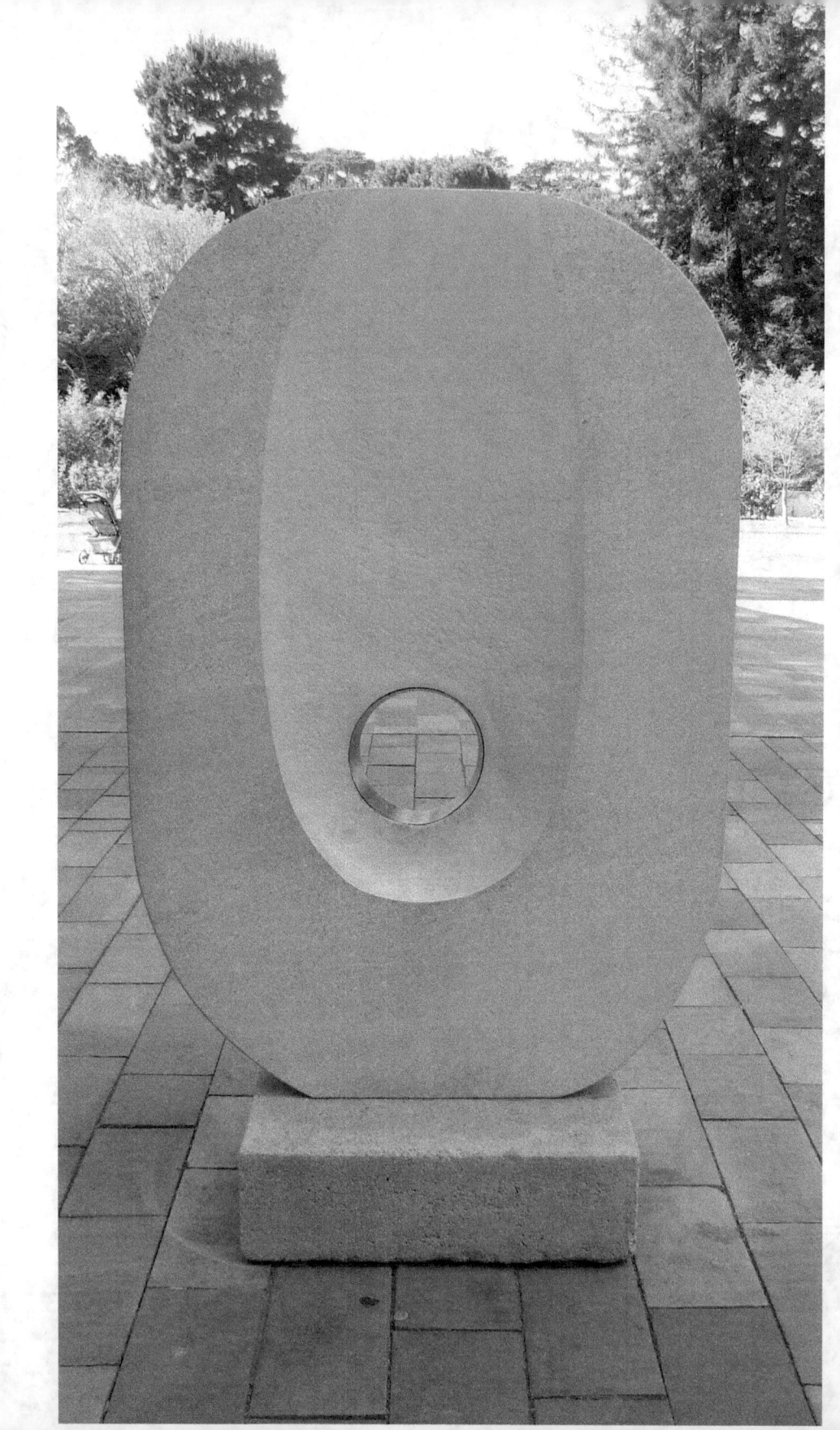

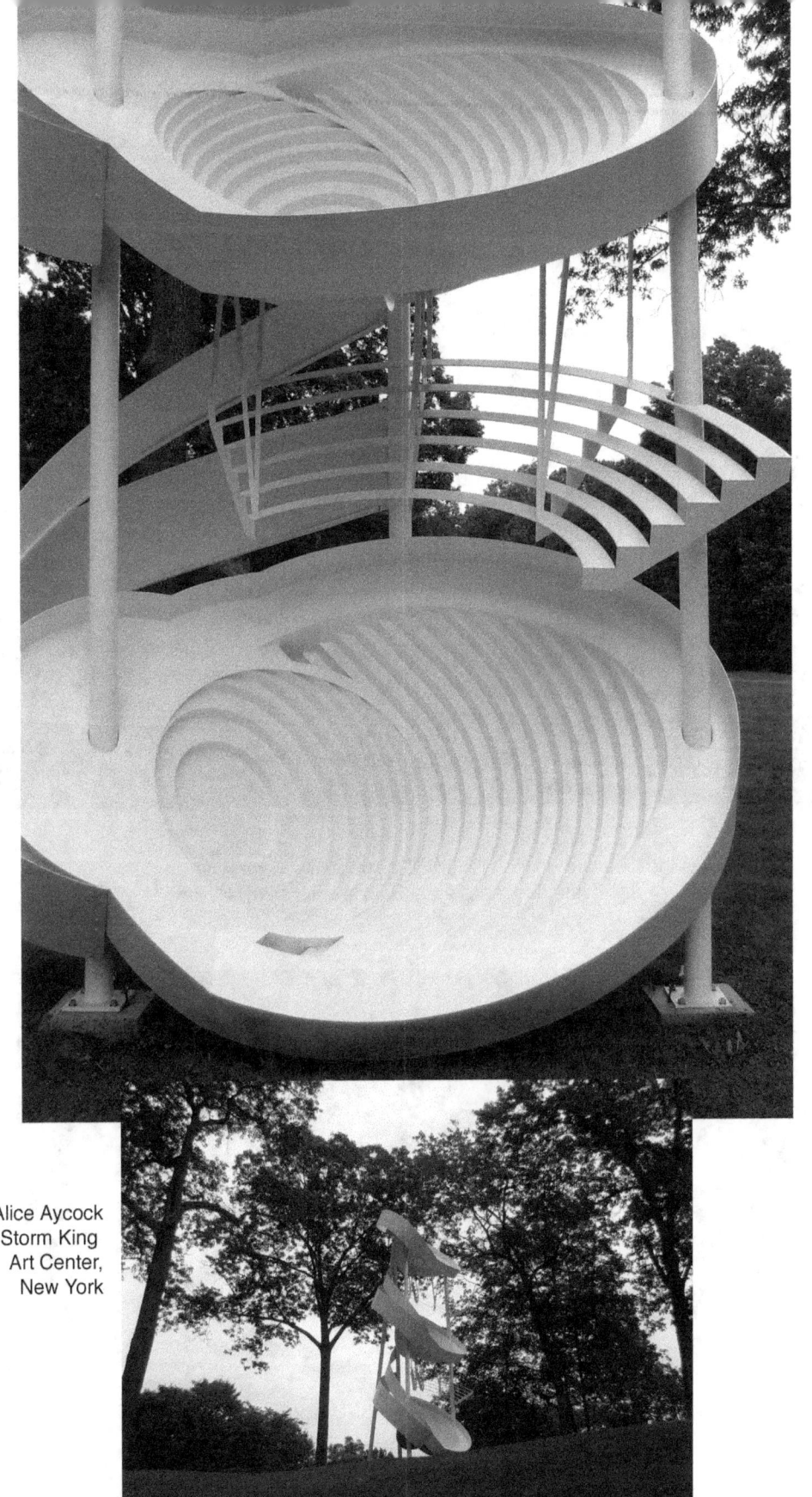

Alice Aycock
at Storm King
Art Center,
New York

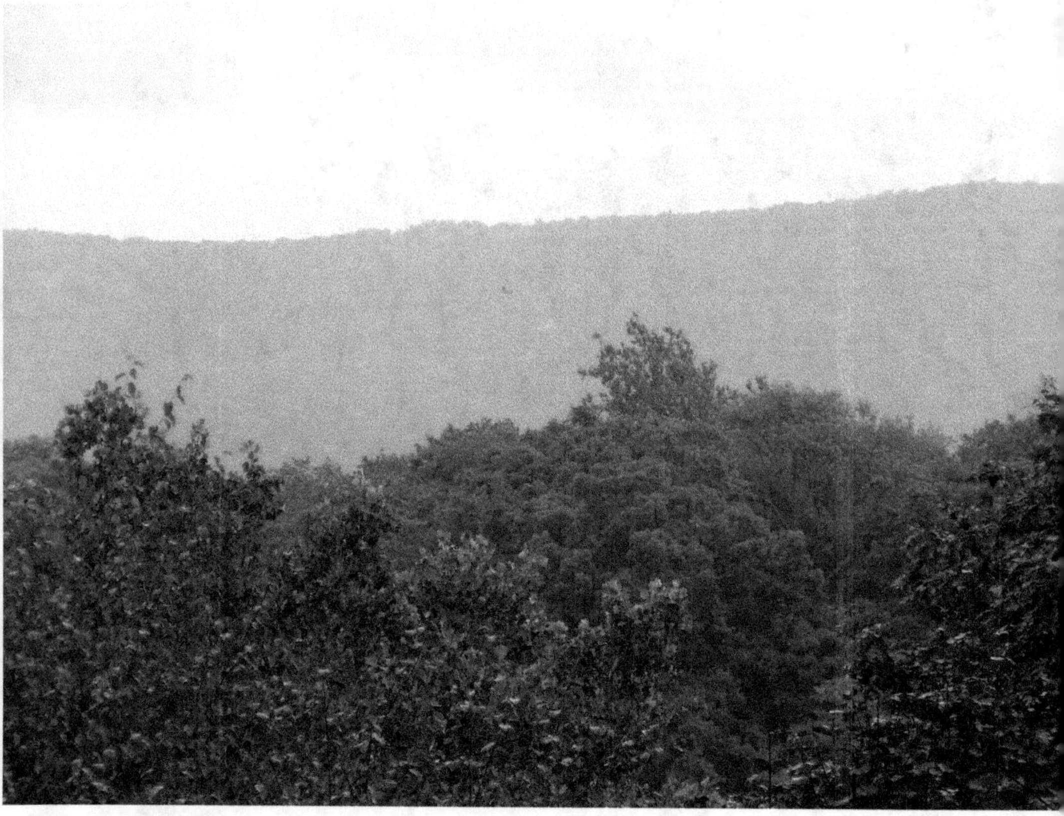

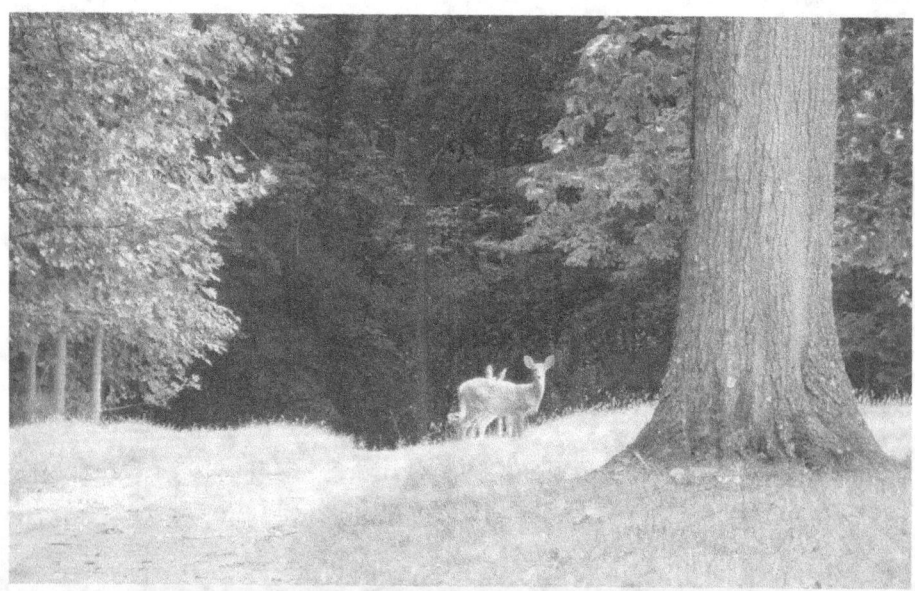

The view of the beautiful Hudson River Valley, from the Storm King Art Center (above), and some deer near Andy Goldsworthy's Wall (below).

List of Works

A list of some works by Andy Goldsworthy cited in the text

Slate Stack, 1988, Scaur Water Valley, Penpont, Dumfriesshire, Scotland; *Japanese maple leaves stitched together to make a floating chain*, Nov 21, 1987, Ouchiyama-mura, Japan; *Circular stalks in a lake*, April 29, 1987, Yorkshire Sculpture Park; *Autumn Horn*, Nov, 1986, chestnut leaves, Penpont, Dumfriesshire; *Dandelion Flowers*, May 1, 1987, 'flowers pinned to willowherb stalks laid in a ring held above bluebells with forked sticks', Yorkshire Sculpture Park, West Bretton; *Line and Cairn,* May 31 & June 1, 1985, pebbles, St Abbs, the Borders; *Oak Globe*, Sept 15, 1985, branches and oak leaves, Jenny Noble's Gill, Dumfriesshire; *Slits cut into frozen snow*, Feb 12, 1988, Blencathra, Cumbria; *Snowball in Trees*, Feb, 1980, Robert Hall Wood, Lancashire; *Touching North*, April 24, 1989, North Pole; *Touching North*, Fabian Carlsson Gallery, London, 1989; *Leadgate and Lambton Earthworks,* 1989, County Durham; *Snow and Wind Damaged Pine Trees*, Spring, 1985, Grizedale forest; *Leaves torn in two*, Nov 2, 1986, Glasgow Green; *Broken Pebbles*, April 12, 1987, Scaur Water, Dumfriesshire; *Trench*, Aug 6-7, 1987, 'trench edged with clay supported by sticks', Yorkshire Sculpture Park, West Bretton; *Slate Crack Line*, Feb, 1988, Little Langdale, Cumbria; *Scaur Water Stone*, 1992, stone and iron ore and water, Grob Gallery, London; *Herd of Arches*, stone, 1994, London; *Stone*, 1994, Grob Gallery, London; *Wall*, 1998, Storm King Art Center, New York; *Sheepfolds*, 1996-, Cumbria; *Réfuges d'Art*, 1998-, Digne les Bains, France; *Arch*, 1998, Montréal; *Snowballs In Summer*, 2000, London; *Night Path*, 2002, Petworth Park, Sussex; *Garden of Stone*, 2003, Museum of Jewish Heritage, New York, NY; *Stone Houses*, 2004, Metropolitan Museum of Art, New York, NY.

Bibliography

ANDY GOLDSWORTHY

Andy Goldsworthy, Alan Rankle, Nigel Jepson, Brampton Banks, Cumbria, 1982

Rain sun snow hail mist calm: Photoworks by Andy Goldsworthy, Henry Moore Centre for the Study of Sculpture, Leeds, Yorkshire, 1985

Land Matters, Blackfriars Arts Centre, Reed Press, 1986

"Hampstead Heath", *Aspects,* 32, Spring, 1986

& J. Fowles. *Winter Harvest,* Scottish Arts Council, 1987

Mountain and Coast: Autumn Into Winter: Japan 1987, Art Data, 1988

Parkland, Yorkshire Sculpture Park, West Bretton, 1988

Touching North, Fabian Carlsson, London, 1989

Snowballs in Summer Installation, Old Museum of Transport, Glasgow, 1989

Garden Mountain, Centre d'Art Contemporain, Castres, 1989

Leaves, Common Ground, London, 1989

Singular Visions, University of Warwick, 1989

Andy Goldsworthy, Viking, London, 1990

Hand to Earth: Andy Goldsworthy, Sculpture, 1976-1990, Henry Moore Centre for Sculpture, Leeds, Yorkshire, 1990

interview, *Third Ear,* BBC Radio 3, June 30, 1989, in 1990

"Geometry and Nature", interview, *Art & Design,* in A. Papadakis, 1991

Sand Leaves, Arts Club of Chicago, IL, 1991

Ice and Snow Drawings, Fruitmarket Gallery, Edinburgh, 1992

Andy Goldsworthy: Breakdown, Rose Art Museum, 1992

Andy Goldsworthy: Futatsu no aki, Tochigi Kenritsu Bijutsukan, Tokyo, 1993

"Andy Goldsworthy: an artist's diary", *Arts Review,* 45, Sept, 1993

"Andy Goldsworthy", *Art & Design,* 9, 5/6, May/ June 1994

Stone, Viking, London, 1994

Black Stones, Red Pools, Pro Arte Foundation, 1995

Wood, Viking, London, 1996

Sheepfolds, with S. Chettle, P. Nesbitt, A. Humphries, Michael Hue-Williams Gallery, London, 1996

Végètal, Ballet Atlantique-Régine Chopinot, La Rochelle, France, 1996

Alaska Works, Anchorage Museum of History and Art, Anchorage, AK, 1996

Andy Goldsworthy: A Collaboration With Nature, Abrams, New York, NY, 1996

Andy Goldsworthy: Jack's Fold, ed. J. Glasman, University of Hertfordshire, St

Albans, Hertfordshire, 1996

Hand to Earth: Andy Goldsworthy Sculpture, T. Friedman, Thames and Hudson, London, 1997 & 2004

Cairns, Musée départemental de Digne, Reserve Geologique de haute Provence, 1997

Andy Goldsworthy, Musée d'art contemporain de Montréal, Canada, 1998

Arch, with D. Craig, Thames & Hudson, London, 1999

Andy Goldsworthy, with M. Kuipers & T. Karreman, Province Noord-Holland aan Staatsbosbeheer, 1999

Wall, intr. K. Baker, Thames & Hudson, London, 2000

Time, Thames & Hudson, London, 2000

Midsummer Snowballs, intr. J. Collins, Thames & Hudson, London, 2001

Andy Goldsworthy - Réfuges d'Art, Editions Artha, 2002

Passage, Thames & Hudson, London, 2004

Enclosure, Thames & Hudson, London, 2007

The Andy Goldsworthy Project, M. Donovan, Thames & Hudson, London, 2010

OTHERS

H. Adams. "The Woodman", *Art and Artists,* 13, Apl, 1979

–. "Fabian Carlsson Gallery: London: Exhibit", *New Art Examiner,* 15, May, 1988

C. Adcock. *James Turrell,* University of California Press, Berkeley, CA, 1990

W.C. Agee. *Don Judd,* Whitney Museum of American Art, New York, NY, 1968

–. "Unit, Series, Site: A Judd Lexicon", *Art in America,* May, 1975

–. *The Sculpture of Donald Judd,* Art Museum of South Texas, Corpus Christi, TX, 1977

D. Alberge. "Making an impression with the elements", *The Independent,* Feb 18, 1989

L. Aldrich. *Cool Art: 1967,* Museum of Contemporary Art, 1968

P. Allison *et al. Beyond the Minimal,* Architectural Association Publications, London, 1998

L. Alloway. "The American Sublime", *Living Arts*, 1, 2, June, 1963

—. *Systematic Painting*, New York, NY, 1966

—. *Christo*, Abrams, New York, NY, 1969

—. "Robert Smithson's Development", *Artforum*, Nov, 1972

—. "Residual Sign Systems in Abstract Expressionism", *Artforum*, Nov, 1973

L. Anderson. "Mary Miss", *Artforum*, Nov, 1973

W. Anderson. *American Sculpture in Process, 1930/ 1970*, New York Graphics Society, Boston, MA, 1975

C. Andre. "Frank Stella: Preface to Stripe Painting", in D. Miller, 1959

—. "An Interview with Carl Andre", P. Tuchman, *Artforum*, 8, 10, June, 1970

—. *Carl Andre, Sculpture, 1958-1974*, Kunsthalle, Bern, 1975

—. "Object v Phenomenon", *Sculpture Today*, The International Sculpture Center, Toronto, 1978

—. *Carl Andre: Sculpture*, State University of New York Press, Albany, NY, 1984

—. *Carl Andre: works on land*, Exhibitions International, 2001

C. Andreae. "Art shaped by the weather", *Christian Science Monitor,* Sept 21, 1987

—. "Fire and ice", *Art News*, 89, 7, Sept, 1990

J. Andrews. *The Sculpture of David Nash*, Lund Humphries, London, 1999

M. Andrews. *Landscape and Western Art,* Oxford Paperbacks, Oxford, 1999

E. de Antonio & Mitch Tuchman. *Painters Painting,* Abbeville Press, New York, NY, 1984

"Andy Goldsworthy", *Rambler Magazine*, 16, Summer, 2003

M. Archer. "A Walk In the Endless Summer From Duncansby Head To the Place of the Camel Droppinh", *Art Monthly*, Sept, 1991

—. *Art Since 1960*, Thames & Hudson, London, 1997

D. Archibald. "Art forms fashioned with the help of mother nature", *Dumfries and Galloway Standard*, Nov 18, 1988

—. "Andy's unique view of nature takes him round the world", *Dumfries and Galloway Standard*, Feb 3, 1988

D. Ashton. *American Art Since 1945*, Thames & Hudson, London, 1982

—. *Modern American Sculpture*, Abrams, New York, NY, 1968

M. Auping. *Common Ground,* John and Mable Ringling Museum of Art, Sarasota, 1982

—. "Hamish Fulton", *Art in America*, 71, Feb, 1983

A. Aycock. "Work", "Maze", 1975, in A. Sondheim, 1977

J. Baal-Teshuva, ed. *Christo: The Reichstag and Urban Projects,* Prestel Verlag, Munich, 1993

Y. Baginsky. "Sculptor for whom success snowballs", *Scotland on Sunday*, Jan 15, 1989

M. Bailey. "Carve a name in ice", *The Observer*, June 11, 1989

E. Baker: "Judd the Obscure", *Art News*, 67, 2, 1968

K. Baker. "Andre in Retrospect", *Art in America*, Apl, 1980a

—. "Reckoning with Notation: The Drawings of Pollock, Newman, and Louis", *Artforum*, 18, 10, Summer, 1980b

—. *Minimalism: Art of Circumstance*, Abbeville, New York, NY, 1988

—. "Andy Goldsworthy: Haines", *Art News*, 91, 8, Oct. 1992

—. "Goldsworthy's natural approach", *San Francisco Chronicle*, June 1, 1994

—. "An earthy show", *San Francisco Sunday Examiner*, Feb 19, 1995

—. "Setting the record straight on Yves Klein", *San Francisco Chronicle*, June 11, 1995

—. "Art that knocks and sculpts and rearranges wood", *San Francisco Chronicle*, Oct 20, 1996

—. "A welcome complexity in new shows", *San Francisco Examiner*, Dec 13, 1996

—. "Feat of Clay in the (Un)making: many reverberations in cracking wall at Haines", *San Francisco Chronicle*, Dec 11, 1996

—. "Searching for the window into nature's soul", *Smithsonian*, Feb, 1997

—. review, *San Francisco Chronicle*, Oct 25, 2008

S. Bann & W. Allen, eds. *Interpreting Contemporary Art*, Reaktion Books, London, 1991

—. "Shrines, Gardens, Utopias", *New Literary History*, 24, 4, Autumn, 1994a

—. "The Map As Index of the Real: Land Art and the Authentication of Travel", *Imago Mundi*, 46, British Library, London, 1994b

G. Baro. "Toward Speculation in Pure Form", *Art International*, Summer, 1967

—. "American Sculpture", *Studio International*, 172, 896, 1968

—. "Sculpture made visible: Barry Flanagan in discussion with Gene Baro", *Studio International*, 178, 915, Oct, 1969

M. Bartlett. "A tribe of one: Andy Goldsworthy at Haines Gallery", *ArtWeek*, 23, 19, July 9, 1992

G. Battock, ed. *The New Art*, Dutton, New York, NY, 1966

—. *Idea Art*, Dutton, New York, NY, 1973

—. "Art in America: Confusions", *Domus*, Mch, 1975

—. ed. *New Artists Video*, Dutton, New York, NY, 1978

—. ed. *The Art of Performance*, Dutton, New York, NY, 1984

—. ed. *Minimal Art: A Critical Anthology*, University of California Press, Berkeley, CA, 1995

G. Beal. "Richard Long: "the simplicity of walking, the simplicity of stones"", in T. Neff, 1987

—. ed. *Art In the Landscape*, Chinati Foundation, Texas, 2000

J. Beardsley. *Probing the Earth: Contemporary Land Projects*, Smithsonian

Press, Washington, DC, 1977

–. *Art in Public Spaces*, Partners For Liveable Places, Washington, DC, 1981

–. *Earthworks and Beyond: Contemporary Art in the Landscape*, Abbeville Press, New York, NY, 1984/ 1998

M.R. Beaumont. "Romantic Sculpture", in A. Papadakis, 1988

–. "Fabian Carlsson Gallery: London: Exhibit", *Arts Review,* 40, Mch 11, 1988

–. "Andy Goldsworthy", *Arts Review*, 41, July 14, 1989

M. Beeren. *Century in Sculpture*, Stedelijk Museum, Amsterdam, 1992

A. Benjamin, ed. *Installation Art, Art & Design*, 30, 1993

L. Bennett. *The Life and Work of Andy Goldsworthy*, Heinemann, London, 2005

N. Bennett, ed. *The British Art Show: Old Allegiances and New Directions, 1979-1984*, Arts Council/ Orbis, London, 1984

M. Berger. *Labyrinths: Robert Morris, Minimalism and the 1960s*, Harper & Row, New York, NY, 1989

–. *Minimal Politics*, University of Maryland, Fine Arts Gallery

S. Bérubé. "Goldsworthy et Singer: l'art de jouer avec la nature", *La Presse*, Apl 25, 1998

R. Bevan. "A snake in the British Museum", *Art Newspaper.* 5, 43, Dec 1994

L. Biggs: *Between Object and Image*, British Council, London, 1986

W. Bishop. "A corporate collection", *British Journal of Photography*, June 12, 1987

M. Bloem, ed. *Lawrence Weiner*, Stedelijk Museum, Amsterdam, 1989

K.C. Bloomert & C.W. Moore. *Body, Memory and Architecture*, New Haven, CT, 1977

M. Bochner. "Art in Process – Structures", *Arts Magazine*, 40, 9, 1966a

–. "Primary Structures", *Arts*, June, 1966b

–. "Systematic", *Arts Magazine*, 41, 1, Nov, 1966c

–. "Serial Art Systems: Solipsism", *Arts Magazine*, 41, 8, Summer, 1967

S. Boettger. *Earthworks*, University of California Press, Berkeley, CA, 2002

Y. Bois. *Donald Judd*, Galerie Lelong, Paris, 1991

D. Bonetti, David. "Facing Eden: 100 years of landscape art in the Bay Area, is a show that limns a strong tradition", *San Francisco Examiner*, June 25, 1995

A. Bonnano. "Andy Goldsworthy", *Art and Design*, 9, 5/6, May/ June 1994

C. Borland *et al. The Cauldron,* Henry Moore Institute, Leeds, Yorkshire, 1996

D. Bourdon. "Walter de Maria: The Singular Experience", *Art International*, Dec 20, 1968

–. *Christo*, Abrams, New York, NY, 1971

–"The Mini-Conceptual Age", *Village Voice*, Oct 17, 1974

–. "You Can't Tell a Painter By His Colors", *Village Voice*, Mch 24, 1975

—. *Carl Andre: Sculpture, 1959-1977*, Jaap Rietman, New York, NY, 1978

—. *et al*: *Niki de Sant-Phalle: Fantastic Vision*, Nassau County Museum of Fine Art, Rosyln, New York, NY, 1987

—. "Andy Goldsworthy at Lelong", *Art in America*. 81, 11, Nov, 1993

—. *Designing the Earth*, Abrams, New York, NY, 1995

C. Brown. "Natural arts", *The Magazine,* July, 1987

D. Brown. "New British sculpture in Normandy", *Arts Review*, Feb 10, 1989

I. Brown. "From urban nightmare to primal scream: Chopinot/ Goldsworthy at the Playhouse", *Electronic Telegraph*, 820, Aug, 23, 1997

J. Brown *et al. Michael Heizer: Sculpture in Reverse*, see M. Heizer, 1984

—. ed. *Occluding Front: James Turrell*, Lapis Press, Larkspur Landing, CA, 1985

D. Bruckner. "Earth works", *New York Times Book Review*, Jan, 1996

P. Buchanan. "The Nature of Goldsworthy", *The Architectural Review*, Feb, 1988

J. Burnham. "Hans Haacke: Wind and Water Sculpture", 1967, in A. Sonfist, 1983

—. *Beyond Modern Sculpture*, Braziller, New York, NY, 1968

—. "A Dan Flavin Retrospective in Ottawa", *Artforum*, 8, 4, Dec, 1969

—. "Robert Morris", *Artforum*, 8, 7, 1970

—. "Haacke's Cancelled Show at the Guggenheim", *Artforum*, June, 1971

—. *Great Western Salt Works*, Brazillier, New York, NY, 1974

K. Bussman & F. Matzner, eds. *Hans Haacke*, Cantz, Stuttgart, 1993

J. Butterfield. *The Art of Light and Space*, Abbeville Press, New York, NY, 1993

D. Cameron. "When is a door not a door?", *XLIII esposizione Internazionale d'Arte La Biennale di Venezia*, Edizioni La Biennale, Venice, 1988

—. "Art for the new year: who's worth catching?", *Art & Auction*, Jan, 1994

J. Campbell. *The Power of Myth*, with B. Moyers, ed. B.S. Flowers, Doubleday, New York, NY, 1988

—. *The Hero With a Thousand Faces*, Paladin, London, 1988

—. *An Open Life*, Larson Publications, New York, NY, 1988

—. *The Hero's Journey: Joseph Campbell On his Life and Work,* ed. P. Cousineau, Harper & Row, San Francisco, CA, 1990

P. Carlson. "Donald Judd's Equivocal Objects", *Art in America*, Jan, 1984

K. Carter: "*Stone*", *New Welsh Review*, 27, Winter, 1994-95

T. Castle. "Nancy Holt, Siteseer", *Art in America*, Mch, 1982

A. Causey. *Nature as Material: An Exhibition of Sculpture and Photographs Purchased For the Arts Council Collection,* Arts Council, London, 1980

—. "Environmental Sculptures", in A. Goldsworthy, 1990

—. "Space and Time in British Land Art", *Studio International*, 193, 98, Feb, 1977

G. Celant. "Introduction", *Arte Povera*, Praeger, New York, NY, 1969

–. *Conceptual Art, Arte Povera, Land Art,* Galeria Civica d'Arte Moderna, Turin, 1970

–. "Tony Cragg and Industrial Platonism", *Artforum*, 20, 3, Nov, 1981

–. *Dennis Oppenheim*, Edizioni Charta Srl, 1997

A. Chave: "Minimalism and the Rhetoric of Power", *Arts*, Jan, 1990

H.B. Chipp, ed. *Theories of Modern Art,* University Press of California, Los Angeles, CA, 1968

A. Christian. "Art of a craftsman: the sculptures of Andy Goldsworthy reflect a deep passion for the natural world", *Resurgence Magazine*, Feb, 1998

B. Christian. "Scottsdale Center present "nature oriented" shows", *Scottsdale Life*, Aug 18, 1994

M. Church. "A shower of stones, a flash in the river", *Sunday Telegraph*, Apl 10, 1994

A. Clabburn. "A sanctuary in the city", *The Age*, Oct, 22, 1997

F. Colpitt. *Minimal Art: The Critical Perspective,* University of Washington Press, Seattle, WA, 1990

B. Commoner. *The Closing Circle: Nature, Man and Technology*, Knopf, New York, NY, 1975

M. Compton & D. Sylvester. *Robert Morris*, Tate Gallery, London, 1971

–. *Some Notes on the Work of Richard Long*, British Council, London, 1976

Concept Art, Minimal Art, Land Art, Edition Cantz, Stuttgart, 1990

L. Cooke. "Richard Long replies to a critic", *Art Monthly*, 68, July, 1983

–. *Alison Wilding*, Serpentine Gallery, London, 1985

J. Coplans. "Serial Imagery", *Artforum*, 7, 2, Oct, 1968

–. *Donald Judd*, Pasadena Art Museum, CA, 1971

–. "Robert Smithson", *Artforum,* Apl, 1974

R. Cork. "Paying the price", *Listener Guide*, Dec 9, 1985

–. "Burnished in bush country", *The Times,* May 28, 1993

–. "Andy Goldsworthy", *The Times*, Apl 23, 1994

D. Cosgrove, ed. *Mappings*, London, 1999

T. Cragg. *Writings*, Editions Isy Brachot, Brussels, 1992

–. *Sculptures on the Page*, Henry Moore Institute, Leeds, Yorkshire, 1997

M. Craig-Martin. *Minimalism,* Tate Gallery, Liverpool, 1989

D. Crane. *The Transformation of the Avant Garde: The New York Art World, 1940-1985*, University of Chicago Press, Chicago, IL, 1987

M. Crichton. *Jasper Johns*, Thames & Hudson, London, 1977

P. Crowther, ed. *The Contemporary Sublime, Art & Design,* 40, 1995

P. Curtis. *Modern British Sculpture from the Collection*, Tate Gallery, Liverpool, 1988

C. Dal Canto. "As nature dictates", *Casa Vogue*, 248, Feb, 1993

—. "Stones", *Casa Vogue*, 266, 1994

G. Danto. "A clearing in the woods", *Art News*, 93, 2, Feb, 1994

P. Davey. "Delight", *Architectural Review*, 193, Apl, 1993

A. Davies. "Richard Long and Hamish Fulton", *Art Monthly*, 25, Apl, 1979

R. Davies & T. Knipe, eds. *A Sense of Place: Sculpture in Landscape*, 1984

R. Deakin. "Zen and the art of Andy Goldsworthy", *Modern Painters*, 10, 1, Spring, 1997

W. de Maria. "The Lightning Field", *Artforum*, 18, 8, Apl, 1980

P. de Monchaux, *et al*, eds. *The Sculpture Show*, Arts Council of Great Britain, London, 1983

N. de Oliveira *et al*. *Installation Art*, Thames & Hudson, London, 1994

—. *et al. Installation Art in the New Millennium*, Thames & Hudson, London, 2003

M. Derby. "Fleeting moments: Andy Goldsworthy at Karekare", *Art New Zealand*, 63, Winter 1992

R. Deutsche *et al. Hans Haacke*, MIT Press, Cambridge, MA, 1986

E. Develing. *Carl Andre*, Gemeentenmeuseum, The Hague, 1969

—. & L. Lippard. *Minimal Art*, Stadtische Kunsthalle, Dusseldorf, 1969

J. Dibbets, in L. Bear & W. Sharp: "DIBBETTS", *Avalanche*, 1, Autumn, 1970.

R. Donnell. *Double Vision: Perspectives On Gender and the Visual Arts*, Farleigh Dickinson University Press, Rutherford, NJ, 1995

M. Dobson. "Breath of fresh air", *The New Statesman*, Jan 10, 1986

—. "Shared sentiments", *BBC Wildlife*, Jan, 1987

L. Dougherty. "Art in nature: a new site for sculpture in Denmark", *Maquette*, Sept, 1994

M. Drabble. "Andy Goldsworthy", *Modern Painters*, 2, 3, Autumn, 1989

C. Drury. *Shelters and Baskets*, Orchard Gallery, 1988

—. *Vessel: Sculpture 1990-95*, Towner Art Gallery, 1995

—. *Stones and Bundles*, Rebecca Hossack Gallery, London, 1995

—. *Silent Spaces*, Thames & Hudson, London, 1998/ 2004

—. *Journeys On Paper*, Stephen Lacey Gallery, London, 2000

—. interview with W. Furlong, in M. Gooding, 2002

—. *Defying Gravity*, North Carolina Museum of Art, NC, 2003

—. *Heart of Stone*, Aberystwyth Art Gallery, Wales, 2003

A. Dumas. "Andy Goldsworthy at Fabian Carlson Gallery", *Art in America*, May, 1988

M. Duncan. "On site: straddling the great divide", *Art in America*. 83, 3, Mch, 1995

—. "Live from the Getty", *Art in America*, 86, 5, May, 1998

R. Durand. "Andy Goldsworthy", *Le printemps de Cahors: catalogue des expositions*, Marval, Paris, 1996

L. Durrell. *Justine*, Faber, London, 1963

—. *Spirit of Place*, Faber, London, 1971

A. Dyson. *Richard Long: Sao Paulo Biennial 1994,* The British Council, 1994

J.C. Eade, ed. *Projecting the Landscape*, Humanities Research Centre, Canberra, 1987

D. Ebony. "Goldsworthy's Living Memorial", *Art in America*, Nov, 2003

M. Eliade. *Patterns in Comparative Religion*, Sheed & Ward, London, 1958

—. *Shamanism: Archaic Techniques of Ecstasy*, Princeton University Press, Princeton, NJ, 1972

—. *Myths, Dreams and Mysteries*, Harper & Row, New York, NY, 1975

—. *From Primitives to Zen: A Sourcebook*, Collins, London, 1977

—. *A History of Religious Ideas*, I, Collins, London, 1979

—. *Ordeal by Labyrinth*, University of Chicago Press, Chicago, IL, 1984

—. *Symbolism, the Sacred and the Arts*, Crossroad, New York, NY, 1988

G. Evans. "Sculpture and Reality", *Studio International*, 177, 908, Feb, 1969

J. Fabricus. *Alchemy: The Medieval Alchemists and Their Royal Art*, Aquarian Press, Northamptonshire, 1989

D. Factor. "Los Angeles", *Artforum*, 4, 9, May, 1966

S. Farr. "Andy Goldsworthy: stone works in America", *Reflex*, 8, 6, Dec, 1995

R. Ferguson *et al*, eds. *Discourses: Conversations in Postmodern Art and Culture*, MIT Press, Cambridge, MA, 1990

S. Field. "Touching the Earth", *Art and Artists*, 8, Apl, 1973

J. Fineberg: "Robert Morris Looking Back", *Arts Magazine*, 55, 1, 1980

—. *Art Since 1940: Strategies of Being*, Laurence King, London, 2000

A. Fisher & J. Saward. *The British Maze Guide*, Minotaur Designs, 1991

—. & D. Kingham. *Mazes,* Shire Publications, 1991

J. Fisher. "Richard Long", *Aspects*, 14, Spring, 1981

S. Foley. *Unitary Forms: Minimal Structures by Carl Andre, Donald Judd, John McCracken, Tony Smith*, Museum of Modern Art, San Francisco, CA, 1970

N. Foote. "Long Walks", *Artforum*, 18, Summer, 1980

W. Forma. *Five British Sculptors*, New York, NY, 1965

P. Frank & M. McKenzie. *New, Used and Improved: Art For the '80s*, Abbeville Press, New York, NY, 1987

D. Frankel. "Andy Goldsworthy", *Artforum*, Oct, 2000

M. Fried. "Shape as Form: Frank Stella's New Paintings", *Artforum*, 5, 3, Nov, 1966

—. "Art and Objecthood", *Artforum*, 5, Summer, 1967

M. Friedman. "Robert Morris: Polemics and Cubes", *Art International*, 10, 10, Dec, 1966

—. *14 Sculptors*, Walker Art Center, Minneapolis, MN, 1969

E. Fry. *Alice Aycock*, University of South Florida Art Galleries, Tampa, FL, 1981

—. "The Poetic Machines of Alice Aycock", *Portfolio*, Nov, 1981

—. *et al. Robert Morris*, Museum of Contemporary Art, Chicago, IL, 1986

R.H. Fuchs. "Memories of Passing: A Note on Richard Long", *Studio International*, 187, 965, Apl, 1974

—. *Carl Andre*, Van Abenmuseum, Eindhoven, 1978

—. *Richard Long*, text, in R. Long, 1986

P. Fuller. *Peter Fuller's Modern Painters: Reflections on British Art*, ed. J. McDonald, Methuen, London, 1993

H. Fulton. *Hamish Fulton: Selected Walks, 1969-89*, Albright-Knox Art Gallery, Buffalo, New York, NY, 1990

—. *Richard Long,* Thames & Hudson, London, 1991

—. *One Hundred Walks*, Haags Gemeetemuseum, The Hague, 1991

—. "Into a Walk Into Nature", *Thirty One Horrors*, Lenbachhaus, Munich, 1995

—. *Walking Artist*, Annely Juda, London, 1998

—. *Wild Life*, Pocketbooks, Edinburgh, 2000

—. *Walking Artist*, Richter Verlag, Düsseldorf, 2001

—. "Specific Places and Particular Events", in B. Tufnell, 2002

S. Gardiner. "Their medium is nature", *Landscape Architecture*, 80, Feb, 1990

M. Garlake. "Andy Goldsworthy", *Art Monthly*, 93, Feb, 1986

J. Gear. "Andy Goldsworthy", *Review*, Dec. 1, 1996

L. Gendron. "Le sculpteur d'éphémère", *L'actualité*, 22, 12, Aug, 1997

B. Genocchio. *Art Review*, Feb 23, 2003

J. Gibson. *The Senses Considered as a Perceptual System*, Houghton Mifflin, Boston, MA, 1966

A. Gide. *The Counterfeiters*, tr. D. Bussy, Penguin, London, 1966

J. Giovannini. *Mary Miss*, Architectural Association, London, 1987

P. Giquel. "Andy Goldsworthy: Centre d'art contemporain Midi-Pyrénées", *Art Press*, 158, May, 1991

T. Godfrey. "Richard Wilson's watertable, Andy Goldsworthy", *Burlington Magazine*, 136, 1096, July, 1994

—. *Conceptual Art*, Phaidon, London, 1998

E. Goheen. *Wrapped Walk Ways*, Abrams, New York, NY, 1978

R. Goldberg. *Performance: Live Art Since the 60s*, Thames & Hudson, London, 1998

A. Goldstein, ed. *Reconsidering the Object of Art: 1965-1975*, Museum of Contemporary Art, L.A., CA, 1995

B. Goodbody. *New York Times*, May 18, 2007

M. Gooding & W. Furlong. *Song of the Earth,* Thames and Hudson, London, 2002

A. Gopnik. "Basic Stuff: Robert Smithson, Myth, Science and Primitivism", *Art*

Magazine, Mch, 1983

A. Graham-Dixon. "Turning over an old leaf", *The Independent*, Feb 3, 1988

—. "Cutting Ice", *The Independent*, June, 24, 1989

—. "An artist does the strand", *The Independent*, Aug 5, 1989

—. "Great Britain: neo, no: still faithful to the old guard", *Art News*, 88, 7, Sept, 1989

J. Grande. *Balance: art and nature*, Black Rose Books, Montréal, 1994

—. "Back to nature?", *Sculpture*, 13, 4, July/ Aug, 1994

—. *Art Nature Dialogues*, State University of New York Press, NY, 2004

N. Graydon. "Magic in the field", *Ritz*, 133, 1989

B. Graziani. "Robert Smithson's Picturable Situation", *Critical Inquiry*, 20, 3, Spring, 1994

C. Greenberg. *Art and Culture*, Beacon Press, Boston, MA, 1961

H. Gresty & D. Reason. *Landscape*, Kettle's Yard, Cambridge, 1986

—. *Bare: Alison Wilding: Sculptures, 1982-1993*, Newlyn Art Gallery, Cornwall, 1993

G. Greig. "Circular Tours In the Name of Art", *Sunday Times*, June 16, 1991

C. Grout. "Andy Goldsworthy: une esthétique pragmatique", *Art Press*, 192, May, 1994

H. Haacke. *Framing and Being Framed*, New York University Press, New York, NY, 1975

A. Haden-Guest. "The King of Wrap", *The Sunday Times Magazine*, Jan, 1994

C. Hagen. "Art in review", *New York Times*, Sept 17, 1993

J. Haldane. *A Road From the Past To the Future*, Crawford Arts Centre, St Andrews, 1997

—. "Images After the Fact", *Modern Painters*, 11, 3, Fall, 1998

—. "Back To the Land", *Art Monthly*, June, 1999

O. Hahn & P. Restany. *Christo*, Editioni Apollinaire, Milan, 1966

C. Hall. "Shared earth", *Arts Review*, 43, June 14, 1991

—. "Site lines", *Arts Review*, 46, Oct, 1994

J. Hamlin. "Andy Goldsworthy: artist lets nature take its course", *San Francisco Chronicle*, May 4, 1994

A.M. Hammacher. *The Sculpture of Barbara Hepworth*, Abrams, New York, NY, 1968

C. Harrison. "Barry Flanagan's Sculpture", *Studio International*, 175, 900, May, 1968

—. "Sculpture's Recent Past", in T. Neff, 1987

B. Haskell. *BLAM! The Explosion of Pop, Minimalism, and Performance, 1958-64*, Whitney Museum of American Art, New York, NY, 1984

—. *Donald Judd*, Whitney Museum of American Art, New York, NY, 1988

J. Hattam. "Restoration art focussing on nature's power to reclaim [Andy

Goldsworthy]", *Sierra*, May-June, 2003

M. Hayde. "Nature is his studio: Great Britain's Andy Goldsworthy, master of the ephemeral "earth sculpture", will give a free lecture at Stanford", *Palo Alto Weekly,* Jan 27, 1995

N. Hedges. "Growth, decay and the movement of change", *World Magazine*, 45, Jan, 1991

M. Heizer, D. Oppenheim & R. Smithson. "Discussion", *Avalanche*, 1, Autumn, 1970

—. *Sculpture in Reverse*, Museum of Contemporary Art, Los Angeles, CA, 1984

A. Henri. *Environments and Happenings*, Thames & Hudson, London, 1974

—. *Total Art*, Praeger, New York, NY, 1974

C. Henry. "Lumps of the Landscape", *The World of Interiors*, Oct, 1987

—. "A style with natural life", *Glasgow Herald*, Aug 21, 1987

—. "Artist in love with nature puts down roots", *Glasgow Herald*, July 19, 1988

—. "Goldsworthy at Work or Paving the Way", *Artline*, 14, 33, Nov, 1988

—. "Royal Botanic Garden: Edinburgh: Exhibit", *Arts Review*, 40, July 15, 1988

—. "Melting moments", *Glasgow Herald*, July 28, 1989

—. "Natural History Museum: London: Exhibit", *Arts Review*, 41, Oct 6, 1989

—. "Andy Goldsworthy: Stone shapes a life", *The Herald*, Apl 22, 1994

—. "Only branching out", *The Herald*, Jan, 18, 1997

A. Hess. "Technology Exposed", *Landscape Architecture*, May, 1992

T. Hess. *Barnett Newman*, Walker, New York, NY, 1969

—. & L. Nochlin. *Woman as Sex Object: Studies in Erotic Art*, Newsweek, New York, NY, 1972

—. & E. Baker. *Art and Sexual Politics*, Art New Series, Macmillan, New York, NY, 1973

Galerie Max Hetzler. *Carl Andre, Gunther Forg, Hubert Kiecol, Richard Long, Meuser, Reinhard Mucha, Bruce Nauman and Ulrich Ruckreim*, Cologne, 1985

P. Hill. "Sjoerd Buisman", *Alba*, 11, Spring 1989

R. Hill. "Ice and snow drawings", *Crafts*, 119, Nov/ Dec, 1992

E. Hilliard. "In tribute to the wild bunch", *The Independent*, June 22, 1988

G. Hilty. *Recent British Sculpture*, Arts Council, London, 1993

—. *Alison Wilding: Immersion/ Exposure*, Tate Gallery, Liverpool, 1991

A. Hindry. "Sculpture anglaise: le clavier de l'imagination", *Art Press*, 214, June, 1996

R.C. Hobbs. *Robert Smithson: Sculpture*, Cornell University Press, Ithaca, NY, 1981

—. "Earthworks", *Art Journal*, 42, Fall, 1982

N. Hodges ed. *Art and the Natural Environment, Art & Design*, 36, 1994

—. ed. *The Contemporary Sublime, Art & Design*, 40, 1995

N. Holt. "Amarillo Ramp", *Avalanche*, Fall, 1973

—. "Hydra's Head", *Arts Magazine,* Jan, 1975

—. "Sun Tunnels", *Artforum*, Apl, 1977

P. Hovdenakk. *Christo: Complete Editions*, Schellman & Klüser, Munich, 1982

S. Howell. "Kingdom of the ice man", *Observer Magazine*, June 28, 1987

—. "Goldsworthy: the ice-man cometh", *World of Interiors*, July/ Aug, 1989

S. Hubbard & R. Sandall. "Peter Gabriel's *US*: the artists' boxes project: artists' statements", *Contemporary Art*, 1, 2, Winter, 1992

—. intr. *Sculpture At Goodwood: A Vision For 21st Century British Sculpture*, Sculpture At Goodwood, Sussex, 2002

S. Huchet. "Un exercice de la terre: le travail d'Andy Goldsworthy", *Ligeia*, 11/12, Dec, 1992

G. Hughes. "Artists in parks", *Arts Review*, 40, July 15, 1988

—. ed. *Arts Review Yearbook, 1989*, Arts Review Magazine, London, 1989

—. ed. *Arts Review Yearbook, 1990*, Arts Review Magazine, London, 1990

R. Hughes. *Nothing If Not Critical: Selected Essays on Art and Artists*, Collins Harvill, London, 1990

—. *The Shock of the New*, Thames & Hudson, London, 1991

—. *American Visions: The Epic History of Art In America*, Knopf, New York, NY, 1997

T. Hughes. *Poetry in the Making*, Faber, London, 1969

—. *New Selected Poems, 1957-1994*, Faber, London, 1995

H.E. Hugo, ed. *The Portable Romantic Reader,* Viking Press, New York, NY, 1957

L. Hull. "In residence: Grizedale Forest sculpture park", *Maquette*, May/ June 1993

S. Hunter, ed. *An American Renaissance: Painting and Sculpture Since 1940*, Abbeville Press, New York, NY, 1986

M. Hutchinson. "So follow him, follow him, down to the hollow", *Hampstead and Highate Express*, Dec 13, 1985

L. Iizawa. "Earth work", *Studio Voice*, Mch, 1988

P. Inch. "Andy Goldsworthy", *Arts Review*, 42, July 13, 1990

R. Ingleby. "Visual arts: Andy Goldsworthy", *The Independent*, Nov 8, 1996

In Praise of Trees, Salisbury Festival, Wilts., 2002

D. Isaac. "When leaves turn to gold", *Echoes*, Mch 24, 1992

Y. Ishii. "Creating beauty from nature", *Chubu Yomiuri Shimbun*, 21, Feb 2, 1988

W. Januszczak. "The Heath Robinson", *The Guardian*, Jan, 5, 1986

—. "The magic of icicle works", *The Guardian*, July 7, 1987

G. Jeppson. *Richard Long*, Harvard College, Cambridge, MA, 1980

E.H. Johnson. *Modern Art and the Object*, Harper & Row, New York, NY, 1976

—. ed. *American Artist on Art*, Harper & Row, New York, NY, 1982

W. Johnson. *Riding the Ox Home: A History of Meditation from Shamanism to Science*, Rider, London, 1982

J. Johnston. "Walling into Art", *Art in America*, 75, 4, Apl, 1987

B. Jones. "A New Wave in Sculpture", *Artscribe*, 8, Sept, 1977

C. Joyce. "Walling into History", *Flash Art*, Summer, 1989

D. Judd. "Frank Stella", *Arts Magazine*, 36, Sept, 1962

—. "In the Galleries", *Arts Magazine*, 37, 10, Sept, 1963

—. "Local History", *Arts Yearbook 7*, 1964

—. "Black, White and Gray", *Arts Magazine*, 38, 6, Mch, 1964

—. "Specific Objects", *Arts Yearbook*, 8, Art Digest, New York, NY, 1965

—. "Barnett Newman", *Studio International*, 179, 919, Feb, 1970

—. *Complete Writings, 1959-1975*, Nova Scotia College of Art and Design, Halifax, Canada, 1975

—. *Complete Writings, 1975-1986*, Van Abbemuseum, Netherlands, 1987

E. Juncosa. "Landscape as experience", *Lapiz*, 61 Oct, 1989

D. Karshan. *Conceptual Art and Conceptual Aspects,* Farleigh Dickinson University, 1970

J. Kastner, ed. *Land and Environmental Art*, Phaidon, London, 1998

R. Katz. *Naked By the Window: The Fatal Marriage of Carl Andre and Ana Mendieta*, Atlantic Monthly Press, New York, NY, 1990

B. Kedar & R. Werblowsky, eds. *Sacred Space: Shrine, City, Land*, New York University Press, Albany, NY, 1998

S. Kemal & I. Gaskell, eds. *Landscape, natural beauty and the arts*, Cambridge University Press, Cambridge, 1993

M. Kemp. "Doing what comes naturally: morphogenesis and the limits of the genetic code", *Art Journal*, 55, 1, Spring 1996

G. Kepes, ed. *Arts of the Environment*, Brazillier, New York, NY, 1972

N. Khan. "Beating nature", *Art Express*, 25, Mch, 1986

P. King *et al.* "Colour in Sculpture", *Studio International*, 177, 907, 1969

C. Kino. "Andy Goldsworthy: Galerie Lelong", *Art News*, 95, 10, Nov, 1996

M. Kirby. *Happenings*, Dutton, New York, NY, 1966

C. Knight: *Art of the Sixties and Seventies: The Panza Collection*, Rizzoli, New York, NY, 1987

N. Konstam: *Sculpture: The Art and the Practice*, Collins, London, 1984

D. Kozinska. "Stones in motion: show of Andy Goldsworthy's work gives a preview of colossal rock arch coming here soon across the Atlantic", *The Gazette*, Apl 18, 1998

R. Kostelanetz. *The Theatre of Mixed Means*, Dial, New York, NY, 1968

—. *On Innovative Performance(s)*, McFarland, Jefferson, NC, 1994

R.E. Krauss. "Richard Serra: Sculpture Redrawn", *Artforum*, May, 1972

—. "Sense and Sensibility: Reflection on Post '60s Sculpture", *Artforum*, 12, Nov, 1973

—. *Passages in Modern Sculpture,* Thames & Hudson, London, 1977

—. "Sculpture in the Expanded Field", *October*, 8, Spring, 1979

—. *Eva Hesse*, Whitechapel Art Gallery, London, 1979

—. *et al. Robert Morris*, Abrams, New York, NY, 1994

Z. Kraus, ed. *From Nature to Art, From Art to Nature*, Venice Biennale, Milan, 1978

D. Krug. "Ecological Design: Andy Goldsworthy, Ballet Atlantique", ArtsEdNet, Getty Education Institute for the Arts, 1997

D. Kuspitt. "Sol LeWitt", *Art in America*, 63, 5, 1975

—. "Authoritarian Abstraction", *Journal of Aesthetics and Art Criticism*, 36, 1, Autumn, 1977

—. "Robert Smithson's Drunken Boat", *Arts Magazine*, Oct, 1981

—. "Aycock's Dream Houses", *Art in America*, Sept, 1985

—. "Donald Judd", *Artforum*, 23, 5, Feb, 1985

J. Kutner. "Brice Marden, David Novros, Mark Rothko: The Urge to Communicate through Non-Imagistic Painting", *Arts Magazine*, 50, 1, Sept, 1975

S. Lacey. "Putting yin and yang into the landscape", *Electronic Telegraph*, 549, Nov 23, 1996

I. Lamaitre. "Interview with Tony Cragg", *Artefactum*, 2, Dec, 1985

T. Lang. "News from the imagination", *Issues in Architecture, Art & Design*, 3, 1, 1993

Land Marks, Edith C. Blum Art Institute, Bard College, Annadale-on-Hudson, 1984

D. Laporte. *Christo*, Pantheon Books, New York, NY, 1985

F. Laughlin. "Andy Goldsworthy, the geometrician", *Landscape Architecture,* Dec, 1997

B. Laws. "Where Art and Nature Meet", *The Telegraph Weekly*, Nov 12, 1988

C. Lebowitz. "Andy Goldsworthy", *Art in America*, Oct, 2000

D. Lee. "Serial Rights", *Art News*, 66, 8, Dec, 1967

—. "London Ecology Centre, Exhibit", *Arts Review*, 38, Jan 17, 1986

—. "Great art of the outdoors: bio-degrading sculptures", *Country Life*, 181, 35, Aug 27, 1987

—. "Pure, ephemeral spires", *The Times*, June 26, 1989

—. "Opinion: Richard Long and Hamish Fulton", *Arts Review*, July 26, 1991

—. "In profile: Goldsworthy", *Arts Review*, 47, Feb 1995

A. Legg, ed. *Sol LeWitt*, Museum of Modern Art, New York, NY, 1978

P. Leider. "For Robert Smithson", *Art in America*, Nov, 1973

B. Le Messurier. *Dartmoor Artists*, Halsgrove, Tiverton, Devon, 2002

K. Levin. "Robert Smithson", *Art News*, Sept, 1982

—. "Reflections on Robert Smithson's *Spiral Jetty*", *Arts Magazine*, May, 1978

G. Lewis. "No sculpture like snow sculpture", *This is London*, 1709, July 7, 1989

F. Licht. *Sculpture, 19th and 20th Centuries*, Michael Joseph, London, 1967

—. "Dan Flavin", *Artscanada*, Dec, 1968

D. Lillington. "Andy Goldsworthy: organic chemistry", *Time Out*, Apl 13, 1994

L. Lippard. "New York Letter: Apl-June, 1965", *Art International*, 9, 6, 1965

—. "New York Letter: Recent Sculpture as Escape", *Art International*, Feb, 1966a

—. "An Impure Situation", *Art International*, May 20, 1966b

—. *Ad Reinhardt*, Jewish Museum, New York, NY, 1966c

—. *Pop Art*, Oxford University Press, New York, NY, 1966d

—. "The Silent Art", *Art in America*, 55, 1, Jan-Feb, 1967a

—. "Sol LeWitt: Non-Visual Structures", *Artforum*, Apl, 1967b

—. "Tony Smith", *Art International*, Summer, 1967c

—. "Rebelliously Romantic?", *New York Times*, June 4, 1967d

—. "Escalataion in Washington", *Art International*, 12, 1, Jan, 1968

—. ed. *Surrealists on Art*, Prentice-Hall, Englewood Cliffs, NJ, 1970

—. *Tony Smith*, Thames & Hudson, London, 1972a

—. *Grids*, Philadelphia Institute of Contemporary Art, PA, 1972b

—. *Six Years: The Dematerialization of the Art Object from 1966 to 1972*, Praeger, New York, NY, 1973

—. *From the Center: feminist essays on women's art*, Dutton, New York, NY, 1976

—. *Eva Hesse*, New York University Press, New York, NY, 1976

—. *et al. Sol LeWitt*, Museum of Modern Art, New York, NY, 1978

—. "Complexities: Architectural Sculpture in Nature", *Art in America*, Feb, 1979

—. "Dinner Party", *Art in America*, Apl, 1980

—. *Ad Reinhardt*, Abrams, New York, NY, 1981

—. *Overlay*, Pantheon, New York, NY, 1983

C. Loeffier, ed. *Performance Anthology*, Contemporary Art Press, San Francisco, CA, 1979

R. Long. *Richard Long: In Conversation*, Parts 1 & 2, MW Press, Noordwijk, Holland, 1985-86

—. *Richard Long*, text by R.H. Fuchs, Thames & Hudson, London, 1986

—. *Old World New World*, Anthony d'Offay, London, 1988

—. *Richard Long: Walking in Circles*, Hayward Gallery/ Thames & Hudson, London, 1992

—. *Kicking Stones*, Anthony d'Offay Gallery, London, 1990

—. *Mountains and Water*, Anthony d'Offay, London, 1992

—. *From Time to Time*, DAP, 1997

—. *Richard Long*, Hatje Cantz, Stuttgart, 1997

—. *A Walk Across England*, Thames & Hudson, London, 1997

—. *Mirage*, Phaidon, London, 1998

—. *Selected Walks, 1979-1996*, Morning Star Press, 1999

—. *Richard Long: a Moving World*, Tate Publishing, London, 2002

—. *Richard Long - Walking the Line*, Thames and Hudson, London, 2002

M. Lothian. "Distant thunder", *Arts Review*, 40, Sept 9, 1988

O. Lowenstein. "Natural Time and Human Experience", *Sculpture*, 22, 5, June, 2003

E. Lucie-Smith. *Sculpture Since 1945*, Phaidon, London, 1987

A. Lund. "Landskab og skultur", *Landskab*, Dec, 1989

R. Lund. "Why Isn't Minimal Art Boring?", *Journal of Aesthetics and Art Criticism*, 45, 2, Winter, 1986

N. Lynton. introduction to *Tony Cragg*, Fifth Triennale India, British Council, 1982

—. *David Nash: Sculpture, 1971-90*, Serpentine Gallery, London, 1990

R. Mabey. "Art and ecology", *Modern Painters*, 3, 4, Winter, 1990

C. Maclay. "Grounds for exploration", *San Jose Mercury News*, Feb 5, 1995

D. Macmillan. "David Nash: Brancusi Joins the Garden Gang", *Art Monthly*, 65, Apl, 1983

L. MacRitchie. "Ancient Egypt", *Financial Times*, Dec 12, 1994

—. "Residency on earth", *Art in America*, 83, 4, Apl, 1995

S. Madoff. "Andy Goldsworthy", *Garden Design*, 13, June, 1994

W. Malpas. *Richard Long: The Art of Walking*, Crescent Moon, 1995/ 1998

—. *Land Art, Earthworks, Installations, Environments, Sculpture*, Crescent Moon, 1996/ 1998/ 2004

A.T. Mann. *Sacred Architecture*, Element Books, Shaftesbury, Dorset, 1993

J. van der Marck. *Wrapped Museum*, Museum of Contemporary Art, Chicago, IL, 1969

—. *Herbert Bayer*, Dartmouth College Museum, Hanover, NH, 1977

M. Marmer. "James Turrell", *Art in America*, 69, May, 1981

R. Martin. "Andy Goldsworthy: Fabian Carlsson, London", *Flash Art*, 140, May/ June, 1988

—. *The Sculpted Forest: Sculpture in the Forest of Dean*, Redcliff, Bristol, 1990

B. Matilsky. *Fragile Economies*, Rizzoli, New York, NY, 1992

D. Matless & G. Revill. "A solo ecology: the erratic art of Andy Goldsworthy", *Ecumene*, 2, 4, 1995

K. Matsui. "Column people", *Asahi Shimbun*, Feb 2, 1988

J. May. "Landscape Fired by Ice", *Landscape*, Dec, 1987

D. Mayhall. *The Minimal Tradition*, The Aldrich Museum of Contemporary Art, Ridgefield, CT, 1979

D. Marzona & E. Carlini. *Minimal Art*, Taschen, Cologne, 2004

B. McAvera. "Public art: site sensitivities", *Art Monthly*, 215, Apl, 1998

A. McGill. "Portrait of the artist as a bent twig", *London Standard*, Jan 22, 1984

D. McKinney. *Yves Klein, Brice Marden, Sigmar Polke*, Hirschl & Alder Modern, New York, NY, 1989

A. McPherson. "David Nash: interviewed by Allan McPherson", *Artscribe*, 12, June, 1978

K. McShine. *Primary Structures*, Jewish Museum, New York, NY, 1966

—. *Information*, Museum of Modern Art, New York, NY, 1970

—. *An International Survey of Recent Painting and Sculpture*, MOMA, New York, NY, 1984

W. Messer. "A tale of two festivals: Printemps de Cahors: Les rencontres d'Arles", *Art World*, 12, Winter, 1997

L. Metrick. "Disjunctions In Nature and Culture: Andy Goldsworthy", *Sculpture*, 22, 5, June, 2003

J. Meyer, ed. *Minimalism*, Phaidon, London, 2000

U. Meyer. *Conceptual Art*, Dutton, New York, NY, 1972

R. Millard. "The sculptor Andy Goldsworthy is turning part of Cumbria into a sculpture park", *The Independent*, Mch 25, 1996

D.C. Miller, ed. *Sixteen Americans*, Museum of Modern Art, New York, NY, 1959

M. Miller. *The Garden as an Art*, State University of New York Press, Albany, NY, 1993

M. Miss. *Mary Miss: Interior Works*, Bell Gallery, University of Rhode Island, Autumn, 1981

T. Mizutani. "Conversation with nature", *Bijutsu Techo,* Mch, 1988

—. "Close relation with nature", *Mainichi Shimbun*, Jan 29, 1988

R.C. Morgan. "Richard Long's Poststructural Encounters", *Arts*, 61, 6, Feb, 1987

—. *Art Into Ideas*, Cambridge, 1996

J. Morland. *New Milestones: Sculpture, Community and the Land*, Common Ground, London, 1988

H. Morphy & M. Boles, eds. *Art from the Land*, University of Washington Press, 2000

R. Morris. "Notes on Sculpture", *Artforum,* Feb, 1966, Oct, 1966, June, 1967, Apl, 1969

—. "Aligned with Nazca", *Artforum*, Oct, 1975

—. *Robert Morris: Mirror Works, 1961-1978*, Leo Castelli Gallery, New York,

NY, 1979

–. *et al. Earthworks*, Seattle Art Museum, Seattle, WA, 1979

–. *Selected Works*, Contemporary Arts Museum, Houston, TX, 1981

–. *Continuous Project Altered Daily*, MIT Press, Cambridge, MA, 1993

S. Morris. "A Rhetoric of Silence: Redefinitions of Sculpture in the 1960s and 1970s", in S. Nairne, 1981

J. Morrison. "Landmatters", *British Journal of Photography*, 133, June 6, 1986

A. Morgan. "Maze and labyrinth", *Sculpture*, 14, 4, July/ Aug, 1995

D. Morse. "At Runnymede Farm, the crop is sculptures", *San Francisco Examiner*, May 2, 1997

G. Müller. "Michael Heizer", *Arts Magazine*, Dec, 1969

–. "The Earth, Subjected To Cataclysms, Is a Cruel Master", *Arts Magazine*, Nov, 1971

A. Murphey. "White magic", *The Observer*, Dec, 1996

S. Nairne & N. Serota. *British Sculpture in the Twentieth Century*, White-chapel Art Gallery, London, 1981

H. Nakamura. "Andy Goldsworthy and Anthony Green", *Ikebana Ryusei*, 38, Apl, 1988

D. Nash. *Fletched Over Ash*, AIR Gallery, 1978

–. "David Nash", *Aspects*, 10, Spring, 1980

–. *Stoves and Hearths*, Duke Street Gallery, London, 1982

T.A. Neff, ed. *A Quiet Revolution: British Sculpture Since 1965*, Thames & Hudson, London, 1987

B. Nemitz. *Trans Plant: Living Vegetation in Contemporary Art*, Hatje Cantz, Stuttgart, 2000

C. Nemser. "An interview with Eva Hesse", *Artforum*, May, 1970

–. "My Memories of Eva Hesse", *Feminist Art Journal*, Winter, 1973

P. Nesbitt. "At Home with Nature: Andy Goldsworthy in Scotland", *Alba*, Spring, 1989

–. "A Landscape Touched by Gold", in G. Hughes, 1990

E. Newhall. "Andy Goldsworthy", *New York Magazine*, Sept 13, 1993

M. Newman. "New Sculpture in Britain", *Art in America*, Sept, 1982

R. Nilsen. "Show only a nibble of Goldsworthy art", *Arizona Republic*, Sept 25, 1994

M. Nixon. *Eva Hesse*, MIT Press, Cambridge, MA, 2002

P. Noever. *Donald Judd: Architecture*, Hatje Cantz, Stuttgart, 2003

I. Noguchi. *A Sculptor's World,* Harper & Row, New York, NY, 1968

J. Norrie. "Andy Goldsworthy", *Arts Review*, July 3, 1987

B. Oakes, ed. *Sculpting the Environment*, Van Nostrand Reinhold, New York, NY, 1995

P. Oakes. "The Incomparable Andy Goldsworthy", *Country Living*, 48, Dec, 1989

S. Oksenhorn. "Art, naturally", *The Aspen Times*, 116, 50, Dec 9, 1995

W. Oliver. "A natural at work", *Yorkshire Post*, Feb 24, 1986

R. Onoratio. "Illusive Spaces: The Art of Mary Miss", *Artforum*, Dec, 1978

—. *Mary Miss – Perimeters/ Pavilions/ Decoys*, Nassau County Museum, 1979

D. Oppenheim. *Dennis Oppenheim*, Musée d'Art Contemporain, Montréal, 1978

—. *Selected Works, 1967-1990*, Abrams, New York, NY, 1992

E. Osaka. *Andy Goldsworthy: Mountain and Coast: Autumn Into Winter*, Gallery Takagi, Nagoya, 1987

P. Osborne, ed. *Conceptual Art*, Phaidon, London, 2002

W. Packer. "Andy Goldsworthy's Transient Touch", *Sculpture*, July, 1989

—. "Sculpture from the countryside", *Financial Times*, July 7, 1987

T. Padon. "New York, New York", *Sculpture*, 13, 1, Jan/ Feb, 1994

A.C. Papadakis, ed. *British and American Art: The Uneasy Dialectic, Art & Design*, 3, 9/1, Academy Group, London, 1987

—. ed. *Abstract Art and the Rediscovery of the Spiritual, Art & Design*, 3, 5/6, Academy Group, London, 1987

—. ed. *The New Romantics, Art & Design*, 4, 11/12, Academy Group, London, 1988

—. *et al*, eds. *New Art*, Academy Group, London, 1991

R. Parker & G. Pollock. *Old Mistresses: Women, Art an Ideology*, Routledge & Kegan Paul, London, 1981

—. *Framing Feminism*, Pandora Press, London, 1987

D. Parr. "City focus: St. Louis: 'a different kind of energy'", *Art News*, 95, 3, Mch, 1996

J. Partridge. "Forest work", *Craft*, 81, July/ Aug, 1986

T. Passes. "Rain sun snow hail mist calm", *Venue Magazine*, Sept 11, 1986

A. Patrizio. "Cube garden: sculpture at the Edinburgh Festival 1990", *Arts Review*, 42, July 27, 1990

P. Patton. "Robert Morris and the Fire Next Time", *Art News*, 82, 10, Dec, 1983

E. Pavese, ed. *Christo: Surrounded Islands*, Abrams, New York, NY, 1986

N. Pennick. *Mazes and Labyrinths*, Hale, London, 1990

C. Peres. "Arte: collaborare con la natura, *Casa Vogue*, 228, Mch, 1991

J. Perreault. "A Minimal Future? Union-Made: Report on a Phenomenon", *Arts Magazine*, 41, Mch, 1967

J. Perrone. "Seeing Through Boxes", *Artforum*, 15, Nov, 1976

K. Petersen & J.J. Wilson: *Women Artists: Recognition and Reappraisal from the Early Middle Ages to the Twentieth Century*, Women's Press, London, 1978

C. Peterson. "Inside the Goldsworthy installation", *Aspen Times*, Dec 16, 1995

P. Piguet. "Vassivière: une île pour la sculpture: an island for the sculpture", *Cimaise*, 41, 228, Jan, 1994

R. Pincus-Witten. *Postminimalism*, Out of London Press, New York, NY, 1977

—. *Entries: Maximalism*, Out of London Press, London, 1983

—. *Post-Minimalism into Maximalism*, UMI Research Press, Ann Arbor, MI, 1987

J. Poetter. *Donald Judd*, Cantz, Stuttgart, 1989

G. Pollock. *Vision and Difference: femininity, feminism and histories of art*, Routledge, London, 1988

L. Ponti. "Tony Cragg", *Domus*, 611, Nov, 1980

F. Popper. *Art, Action and Participation*, New York University Press, New York, NY, 1975

J.C. Powys. *Maiden Castle*, Cassell, London, 1937

—. *A Glastonbury Romance*, Macdonald, London, 1955

—. *Wolf Solent*, Penguin, London, 1964

—. *Autobiography*, Macdonald, London, 1967

A. Price. "A Conversation With Alice Aycock", *Architectural Design*, Apl, 1980

G. Prince. "With mud on their hands, growth, decay and the movement of change", *World Magazine*, Jan, 1991

J. Prinz. *Art Discourse*, Rutgers University Press, New Brunswick, NJ, 1991

S. Prokopoff: *A Romantic Minimalism*, Institute of Contemporary Art, Philadelphia, PA, 1967

J. Prown *et al. Discovered Lands, Invented Pasts*, Yale University Press, New Haven, CT, 1992

E. Rankin. "Popularising public sculpture in Britain: from landscape gardens to forest trails", *de Arte*, 53, Apl, 1996

C. Ratcliff. *In the Realm of the Monochrome*, Renaissance Society, University of Chicago, Chicago, IL, 1979

—. "The Compleat Smithson", *Art in America*, Jan, 1980

—. *Out of the Box*, Allworth Press, London, 2001

B. Redhead. *The Inspiration of Landscape: Artists in National Parks*, Phaidon, London, 1989

M. Regimbald. "L'homme qui plantait des arches [The man who planted arches]", *Espace*, 45, Autumn, 1998

W. Reh & C. Steenbergen. *Architecture and Landscape*, Prestel Publishing, 1996

K.J. Reiger, ed. *The Spiritual Image in Modern Art*, Theosophical Publishing House, Wheaton, IL, 1987

B. Reise. "'Untitled 1969': A Footnote on Art and Minimal Stylehood", *Studio International*, 179, 910, Apl, 1969

T. Rettig. "Contextualizing the work of Reinhard Reitzenstein", *Espace*, 25, Sept, 1993

N. Reynolds. "Lottery aid elevates sheep pens to fine art", *Electronic Telegraph*,

436, July 26, 1996

T. Richardson. *Apollo*, June, 2007

H. Risatti. "The Sculpture of Alice Aycock", *Woman's Art Journal*, Summer, 1985

A.C. Ritchie: *Sculpture in the Twentieth Century*, MOMA, New York, NY, 1952

J. Roberts. *Postmodernism, Politics and Art*, Manchester University Press, Manchester, 1990

C. Robins. "Object, Structure or Sculpture: Where Are We?", *Arts Magazine*, 40, 9, 1966

—. "Empty Paintings", *SoHo Weekly News*, Apl 22, 1976

—. *The Pluralist Era: American Art, 1968-1981*, Harper & Row, New York, NY, 1984

P. Rodaway. *Sensuous Geographies*, Routledge, London, 1994

B. Rose. "New York Letter", *Art International*, Feb 15, 1964

—. "Looking at American Sculpture", *Artforum*, 3, Feb, 1965a

—. "ABC Art", *Art in America*, 53, 5, Nov, 1965b

—. *A New Aesthetic*, Washington Gallery of Modern Art, Washington, DC, 1967

—. *American Art Since 1900*, Thames & Hudson, London, 1967

—. *American Painting*, Skira/ Rizzoli International, New York, NY, 1986

—. *Robert Morris*, Corcoran Gallery, Washington, DC, 1990

H. Rosenberg. *The De-Definition of Art*, Horizon Press, New York, NY, 1972

R. Rosenblum. "Notes on Sol LeWitt", in A. Legg, 1978

—. *Modern Painting and the Northern Romantic Tradition*, Thames & Hudson, London, 1978

—. "Romanticism and Retrospective: An Interview with Robert Rosenblum", in A. Papadakis, 1988

—. "A postscript: some recent neo-romantic mutations", *Art Journal*, 52, 2, Summer, 1993

C. Ross. *Star Axis*, University of New Mexico Press, Albuqerque, NM, 1992

S. Ross. "Gardens, earthworks, and environmental art", in S. Kemal, 1993

—. *What Gardens Mean*, University of Chicago Press, Chicago, IL, 1998

M. Roth. "Robert Smithson on Duchamp", *Artforum*, Oct, 1969

—. ed. *The Amazing Decade: Women and Performance Art in America 1970-80*, Astro Artz, Los Angeles, CA, 1983

M. Rothko. *Mark Rothko in New York*, Guggenheim Museum, New York, NY, 1994

R. Rubinstein. "Andy Goldsworthy: Galerie Lelong", *Art News*, 92, 10, Dec, 1993

M. Ryan, ed. *Gravity and Grace: The Changing Condition of Sculpture, 1965-1975*, Hayward Gallery, London, 1993

A. Saalfield. *Mary Miss*, Fogg Art Museum, Cambridge, MA, 1980

T. Sakurai. "Here comes the gold light'. *Ikebana Ryusei*, 10, Jan, 1988

—. "Goldsworthy with snow", *Ikebana Ryusei*, 10, Feb, 1988

I. Sandler. *American Art of the 1960s,* Harper & Row, New York, NY, 1988

—. *Art of the Postmodern Era: From the 1960s to the Early 1990s*, Harper-Collins, London, 1997

P. Schjeldahl. *Art in Our Time: The Saatchi Collection*, Lund Humphries, London, 1984

P. Schuck. "Interview: Earth, Water, Wind", *Contemporanea*, Apl, 1990

W. Scott. "In the gallery", *New York Post,* Dec 21, 1996

P. Selz. *Directions in Kinetic Sculpture*, University of California Press, Berkeley, CA, 1966

—. *Art in Our Times: A Pictorial History 1890-1980*, Thames & Hudson, London, 1982

A. Seymour. *The New Art*, Hayward Gallery, London, 1972

—. "Walking in Circles", in R. Long, *Walking in Circles*

—. "Old World New World", in R. Long, *Old World New World*

E. Shanes: *Constantin Brancusi*, Abbeville, New York, NY, 1989

G. Shapiro. *Earthworks: Robert Smithson and After Babel*, University of California Press, Berkeley, CA, 1995

W. Sharp *et al. Earth Art*, Andrew Dickson White Museum of Art, Cornell University, Ithaca, NY, 1969

A. Sherman. "Bound to earth", *Metro*, Feb 23, 1995

N. Shulman. "Monday at the North Pole", *Arts Review*, June 2, 1989

N. Sinden. "Interview: Art in Nature: Andy Goldsworthy", *Resurgence*, 129, Aug, 1988

H.J. Smagula. *Currents: Contemporary Directions in the Visual Arts*, Prentice-Hall, Englewood Cliffs, NJ, 1983

B. Smith. *Fluorescent Light, etc, from Dan Flavin*, National Gallery of Canada, Ottawa, 1969

—. *Donald Judd*, National Gallery of Canada, Ottawa, 1975

D. Smith. *Sculpture and Drawings*, ed. J. Merkert, Prestel-Verlag, Munich, 1986

R. Smith. "Sol LeWitt", *Artforum*, Jan, 1975

—. "Review", *Artforum*, Dec, 1975

—. "De Maria: Elements", *Art in America*, May, 1978

—. review, *New York Times*, Sept, 2004

—. review, *New York Times*, Sept 3, 2004

R. Smithson. "Entropy and the New Monuments", *Artforum*, 4, 10, June, 1966

—. "Incidents of Mirror-Travel in the Yucatan", *Artforum*, Sept, 1967

—. "The Monuments of Passaic", *Artforum*, Dec, 1967

—. "Toward the Development of an Air Terminal Site", *Artforum*, Summer, 1967

–. "A Museum of Language in the Vicinity of Art", *Art International*, 12, 3, Mch, 1968

–. *The Writings of Robert Smithson*, ed. N. Holt, New York University Press, New York, NY, 1979

–. *Robert Smithson*, ed. J. Flam, University of California Press, Berkeley, CA, 1996

–. *Robert Smithson: A Collection of Writings*, Pierogi Galery New York, NY, 1997

T. Sokolowski *et al. Robert Morris*, New York University Press, New York, NY, 1989

D. Solomon, *New York Times*, May 16, 2004

A. Sondheim, ed. *Post-Movement Art in America*, Dutton, New York, NY, 1977

A. Sonfist. *Alan Sonfist*, Neuberger Museum, New York, NY, 1978

–. ed. *Art in the Land: A Critical Anthology of Environmental Art*, Dutton, New York, NY, 1983

W. Spies. *The Running Fence Project, Christo*, Abrams, New York, NY, 1977

N. Stapen. "Bringing nature inside the museum", *Boston Sunday Globe*, Mch 29, 1992

J. Stathatos. "Andy Goldsworthy's Evidences", *Creative Camera*, 255, Mch, 1986

J. Steele. "In a natural mould", *Farmers Weekly*, May 13, 1988

F. Stella. *Working Space*, Harvard University Press, Cambridge, MA, 1986

N. Stewart. "Richard Long, Lines of Thought: A Conversation with Nick Stewart", *Circa*, Nov, 1984

K. Stiles & P. Selz, eds. *Theories & Documents of Contemporary Art: A Sourcebook of Artists' Writings*, University of California Press, Berkeley, CA, 1996

S.L. Stoops. *Andy Goldsworthy: Breakdown*, Rose Art Museum, 1992

W.J. Strachan. *Open Air Sculpture in Britain*, Zwemmer, London, 1984

E. Suderburg, ed. *Space, Site, Intervention*, University of Minnesota Press, Minneapolis, MN, 2000

T. Sultan. *Inability To Endure or Deny the World: Representation and Text In the Work of Robert Morris*, Corcoran Gallery, Washington, DC, 1990

G. Sutton. "Land art", *Landskab*, Dec, 1989

D. Sylvester. *About Modern Art*, Chatto & Windus, London, 1996

L. Talbot. "Fleeting beauty from the elements forger", *Hampstead and Highgate Express*, Feb 12, 1988

H. Teague. "Good as Goldsworthy", *Aspen Magazine*, 1996

M. Thomas. "Monkeys and guerrillas", *Photofile*, 35, May, 1992

J. Thym. "An artist by nature" *Oakland Tribune*, Feb 8, 1995

G. Tiberghien. *Land Art*, Art Data, London, 1995

S. Tillim. "Earthworks and the New Picturesque", *Artforum*, Dec, 1968

C. Tomkins. *Post- to Neo-: The Art World of the 1980s*, Penguin, London, 1989

M. Treib. "Frame, moment and sequence: the photographic book and the designed landscape", *Journal of Garden History*, 15, 2, Summer, 1995

M. Tromble. "A conversation with Andy Goldsworthy", *ArtWeek*, 23, 19, July 9, 1992

—. "A conversation with Robin Lasser", *ArtWeek*, 24, 20, Oct 21, 1993

E. Tsai. *Robert Smithson Unearthed*, Columbia University Press, New York, NY, 1991

M. Tuchman. *American Sculpture of the Sixties*, Los Angeles County Museum of Art, 1967

P. Tuchman. "Minimalism and Critical Response", *Artforum*, 15, 9, May, 1977

—. "Background of a Minimalist: Carl Andre", *Artforum*, Mch, 1978

—. "Minimalism", *Three Decades: The Oliver-Hoffmann Collection*, Museum of Contemporary Art, Chicago, IL, 1988

M. Tucker. *Robert Morris*, New York, NY, 1970

W. Tucker. *The Language of Sculpture*, Thames & Hudson, London, 1974

B. Tufnell & A. Wilson. *Hamish Fulton: Walking Journey*, Tate Publishing, London, 2002

C. Turnbull. "Beautiful Behaviour: The Photoworks of Andy Goldsworthy", *The Green Book*, 2, 6, 1987

J. Turrell. *Mapping Spaces*, Peter Blum, New York, NY, 1987.

—. interview, in B. Oakes, 1995

G. de Vries, ed. *On Art: Artists' Writings on the Changed Notion of Art After 1965*, Cologne, 1974

A.M. Wagner. *Three Artists (Three Women): Modernism and the Art of Hesse, Krasner and O'Keeffe*, University of California Press, Berkeley, CA, 1996

D. Waldman. *Carl Andre*, Guggenheim Museum, New York, NY, 1970a

—. "Holding the Floor", *Art News*, Oct, 1970b

—. *Robert Ryman*, Guggenheim Museum, New York, NY, 1972

J. Watkins. "In the artist's studio: Andy Goldsworthy: Touching North", *Art International*, 9 Winter, 1989

M. Webster. "Andy Goldsworthy at San Jose Museum of Art", *ArtWeek*, 26, 4, Apl, 1995

S. Webster. "Art in the Woods [Andy Goldsworthy]", *Arts & Activities*, Sept, 2000

U. Weilacher *et al. Between Landscape Architecture and Land Art*, Birkhauser Verlag AG, 1999

L. Weiner. *Lawrence Weiner, Works*, Anatol AV und Filmproduktion Hamburg,

1977

Welsh Sculpture Trust. *Sculpture in a Country Park*, Welsh Sculpture Trust, 1983

C. West. "From genesis to box", *Modern Painters*, 5, 4, Winter, 1992

D. Wheeler. *Art Since Mid-Century: 1945 to the Present*, Thames & Hudson, London, 1991

P. Whitaker. "Andy Goldsworthy", *London Magazine*, 34, 10, Jan, 1995

J. White. *The Birth and Rebirth of Pictorial Space*, Faber, London, 1981

O. Wick *et al. James Turrell*, Turske & Turske Gallery, Zurich, 1990

G. Widdicombe. "Andy Goldsworthy: between a rock and a hard place", *The Independent*, Apl 13, 1994

A. Wildermuth. *Richard Long*, Galerie Buchmann, Basel, 1985

A. Wilding: *Alison Wilding*, with M. Tooby, Tate Gallery, St Ives, Cornwall, 1994

R. Williams. *After Modern Sculpture: Art in the United States and Europe 1965-70*, Manchester University Press, Manchester, 2000

A. Windsor, ed. *British Sculptors of the 20th Century*, Ashgate, Aldershot, Hants., 2003

C. van Winkel. "The Crooked Path, Patterns of Kinetic Energy", *Parkett*, 33, 1992

R. Wishart. "Andy Goldsworthy: art without additives", *Scotsman*, Apl 16, 1994

K. Withers. "Is it art?", *Venue Magazine*, Dec, 1989

G. Woods *et al*, eds. *Art Without Boundaries*, Thames & Hudson, London, 1972

M. Wortz. *Light and Space*, Whitney Museum of American Art, New York, NY, 1980

S. Wrede & W. Adams. *Denatured Visions: Landscape and Culture in the 20th Century*, Abrams, New York, NY, 1991

S. Yard. *Christo: Oceanfront*, Princeton University Press, Princeton, NJ, 1975

—. *Sitings*, La Jolla Museum of Contemporary Art, La Jolla, CA, 1986

M. Yule. "Andy Goldsworthy, a Lake District photowork", *National Art-Collections Fund Review*, 88, 1992

WEBSITES

Andy Goldsworthy, Sheepfolds site: <www.sheepfolds.org>
Andy Goldsworthy, *Rivers and Tides* DVD:
  <www.skyline.uk.com/riversandtides>
Earthworks: <www.earthworks.org>
The Artists: <www.the-artists.org>
Sculpture at Goodwood, CASS: <www.sculpture.org.uk>
Crescent Moon Publishing: <www.crescentmoon.org.uk>

CRESCENT MOON PUBLISHING

ARTS, PAINTING, SCULPTURE

The Art of Andy Goldsworthy: Complete Works
Andy Goldsworthy: Touching Nature
Andy Goldsworthy in Close-Up
Andy Goldsworthy: Pocket Guide
Andy Goldsworthy In America
Land Art: A Complete Guide
Richard Long: The Art of Walking
The Art of Richard Long: Complete Works
Richard Long in Close-Up
Richard Long: Pocket Guide
Land Art In the UK
Land Art in Close-Up
Land Art In the U.S.A.
Land Art: Pocket Guide
Installation Art in Close-Up
Minimal Art and Artists In the 1960s and After
Colourfield Painting
Land Art DVD, TV documentary
Andy Goldsworthy DVD, TV documentary
The Erotic Object: Sexuality in Sculpture From Prehistory to the Present Day
Sex in Art: Pornography and Pleasure in Painting and Sculpture
Postwar Art
Sacred Gardens: The Garden in Myth, Religion and Art
Glorification: Religious Abstraction in Renaissance and 20th Century Art
Early Netherlandish Painting
Leonardo da Vinci
Piero della Francesca
Giovanni Bellini
Fra Angelico: Art and Religion in the Renaissance
Mark Rothko: The Art of Transcendence
Frank Stella: American Abstract Artist
Jasper Johns: Painting By Numbers
Brice Marden
Alison Wilding: The Embrace of Sculpture
Vincent van Gogh: Visionary Landscapes
Eric Gill: Nuptials of God
Constantin Brancusi: Sculpting the Essence of Things
Max Beckmann
Caravaggio
Gustave Moreau
Egon Schiele: Sex and Death In Purple Stockings
Delizioso Fotografico Fervore: Works In Process 1
Sacro Cuore: Works In Process 2
The Light Eternal: J.M.W. Turner
The Madonna Glorified: Karen Arthurs

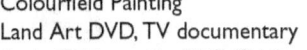
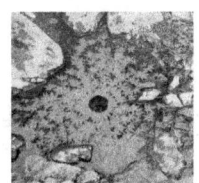
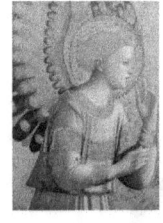

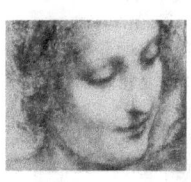
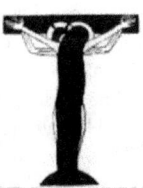
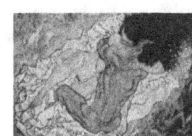

LITERATURE

J.R.R. Tolkien: The Books, The Films, The Whole Cultural Phenomenon
J.R.R. Tolkien: Pocket Guide
Tolkien's Heroic Quest
The *Earthsea* Books of Ursula Le Guin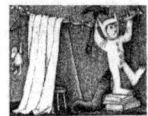
Beauties, Beasts and Enchantment: Classic French Fairy Tales
Sexing Hardy: Thomas Hardy and Feminism
Thomas Hardy's *Tess of the d'Urbervilles*
Thomas Hardy's *Jude the Obscure*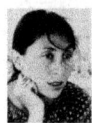
Thomas Hardy: The Tragic Novels
Love and Tragedy: Thomas Hardy
The Poetry of Landscape in Hardy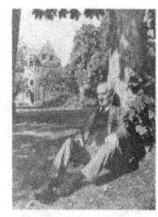
Wessex Revisited: Thomas Hardy and John Cowper Powys
Wolfgang Iser: Essays and Interviews
Petrarch, Dante and the Troubadours
Maurice Sendak and the Art of Children's Book Illustration
Andrea Dworkin
Cixous, Irigaray, Kristeva: The *Jouissance* of French Feminism
Julia Kristeva: Art, Love, Melancholy, Philosophy, Semiotics and Psychoanalysis
Hélène Cixous I Love You: The *Jouissance* of Writing
Luce Irigaray: Lips, Kissing, and the Politics of Sexual Difference
Peter Redgrove: Here Comes the Flood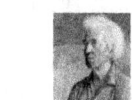
Peter Redgrove: Sex-Magic-Poetry-Cornwall
Lawrence Durrell: Between Love and Death, East and West
Love, Culture & Poetry: Lawrence Durrell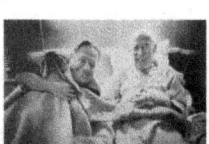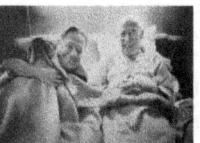
Cavafy: Anatomy of a Soul
German Romantic Poetry: Goethe, Novalis, Heine, Hölderlin
Feminism and Shakespeare
Shakespeare: Love, Poetry & Magic
The Passion of D.H. Lawrence
D.H. Lawrence: Symbolic Landscapes
D.H. Lawrence: Infinite Sensual Violence
Rimbaud: Arthur Rimbaud and the Magic of Poetry
The Ecstasies of John Cowper Powys
Sensualism and Mythology: The Wessex Novels of John Cowper Powys
Amorous Life: John Cowper Powys and the Manifestation of Affectivity (H.W. Fawkner)
Postmodern Powys: New Essays on John Cowper Powys (Joe Boulter)
Rethinking Powys: Critical Essays on John Cowper Powys
Paul Bowles & Bernardo Bertolucci
Rainer Maria Rilke
Joseph Conrad: *Heart of Darkness*
In the Dim Void: Samuel Beckett
Samuel Beckett Goes into the Silence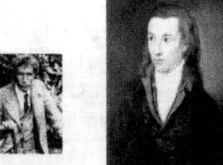
André Gide: Fiction and Fervour
Jackie Collins and the Blockbuster Novel
Blinded By Her Light: The Love-Poetry of Robert Graves
The Passion of Colours: Travels In Mediterranean Lands
Poetic Forms

POETRY

Ursula Le Guin: Walking In Cornwall
Peter Redgrove: Here Comes The Flood
Peter Redgrove: Sex-Magic-Poetry-Cornwall
Dante: Selections From the *Vita Nuova*
Petrarch, Dante and the Troubadours
William Shakespeare: *The Sonnets*
William Shakespeare: Complete Poems
Blinded By Her Light: The Love-Poetry of Robert Graves
Emily Dickinson: Selected Poems
Emily Brontë: Poems
Thomas Hardy: Selected Poems
Percy Bysshe Shelley: Poems
John Keats: Selected Poems
D.H. Lawrence: Selected Poems
Edmund Spenser: Poems
Edmund Spenser: *Amoretti*
John Donne: Poems
Henry Vaughan: Poems
Sir Thomas Wyatt: Poems
Robert Herrick: Selected Poems
Rilke: Space, Essence and Angels in the Poetry of Rainer Maria Rilke
Rainer Maria Rilke: Selected Poems
Friedrich Hölderlin: Selected Poems
Arseny Tarkovsky: Selected Poems
Novalis: *Hymns To the Night*
Paul Verlaine: Selected Poems
Arthur Rimbaud: Selected Poems
Arthur Rimbaud: *A Season in Hell*
Arthur Rimbaud and the Magic of Poetry
D.J. Enright: By-Blows
Jeremy Reed: Brigitte's Blue Heart
Jeremy Reed: Claudia Schiffer's Red Shoes
Gorgeous Little Orpheus
Radiance: New Poems
Crescent Moon Book of Nature Poetry
Crescent Moon Book of Love Poetry
Crescent Moon Book of Mystical Poetry
Crescent Moon Book of Elizabethan Love Poetry
Crescent Moon Book of Metaphysical Poetry
Crescent Moon Book of Romantic Poetry
Pagan America: New American Poetry

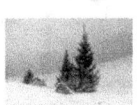
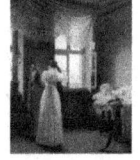
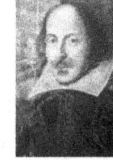
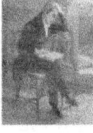
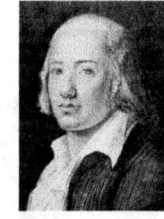
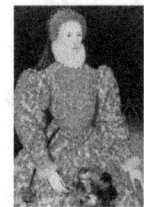

MEDIA, CINEMA, FEMINISM and CULTURAL STUDIES

J.R.R. Tolkien: The Books, The Films, The Whole Cultural Phenomenon
J.R.R. Tolkien: Pocket Guide
The *Lord of the Rings* Movies: Pocket Guide
The Ghost Dance: The Origins of Religion
Cixous, Irigaray, Kristeva: The *Jouissance* of French Feminism
Julia Kristeva: Art, Love, Melancholy, Philosophy, Semiotics and Psychoanalysis
Luce Irigaray: Lips, Kissing, and the Politics of Sexual Difference
Hélene Cixous I Love You: The *Jouissance* of Writing
Andrea Dworkin
'Cosmo Woman': The World of Women's Magazines
Women in Pop Music
Discovering the Goddess (Geoffrey Ashe)
The Poetry of Cinema
The Sacred Cinema of Andrei Tarkovsky
Andrei Tarkovsky: Pocket Guide
Andrei Tarkovsky: *Mirror*: Pocket Movie Guide
Andrei Tarkovsky: *The Sacrifice*: Pocket Movie Guide
Walerian Borowczyk: Cinema of Erotic Dreams
Jean-Luc Godard: The Passion of Cinema
John Hughes and Eighties Cinema
Ferris Bueller's Day Off: Pocket Movie Guide
Jean-Luc Godard: Pocket Guide
The Cinema of Richard Linklater
Liv Tyler: Star In Ascendance
Blade Runner and the Films of Philip K. Dick
Paul Bowles and Bernardo Bertolucci
Media Hell: Radio, TV and the Press
An Open Letter to the BBC
Detonation Britain: Nuclear War in the UK
Feminism and Shakespeare
Wild Zones: Pornography, Art and Feminism
Sex in Art: Pornography and Pleasure in Painting and Sculpture
Sexing Hardy: Thomas Hardy and Feminism

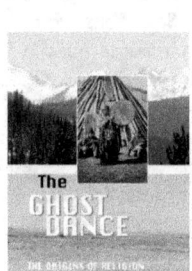

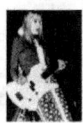

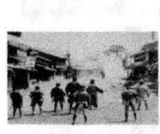
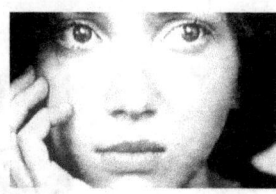
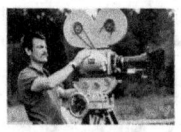

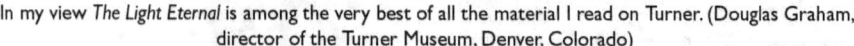

In my view *The Light Eternal* is among the very best of all the material I read on Turner. (Douglas Graham, director of the Turner Museum, Denver, Colorado)

The Light Eternal is a model monograph, an exemplary job. The subject matter of the book is beautifully organised and dead on beam. (Lawrence Durrell)

It is amazing for me to see my work treated with such passion and respect. (Andrea Dworkin)

Sex-Magic-Poetry-Cornwall is a very rich essay... It is like a brightly-lighted box. (Peter Redgrove)

CRESCENT MOON PUBLISHING

www.ingramcontent.com/pod-product-compliance
Lightning Source LLC
Chambersburg PA
CBHW071249220526

45468CB00001B/56